*The Indwelling
of the Trinity*

The
INDWELLING
of the
TRINITY

*A Historico-Doctrinal Study
of the Theory of St. Thomas Aquinas*

by

FRANCIS L. B. CUNNINGHAM, O. P.,
S.T.Lr., S.T.D.

WIPF & STOCK · Eugene, Oregon

Revisores Ordinis:

    Mannes Matthijs, O.P., S.T.M.
    Paulus Philippe, O.P., S.T.M., S.T.D.
    Ricardus T. A. Murphy, O.P., S.T.Bacc., S.T.D., SS.D.

Imprimi Potest:

    Eduardus L. Hughes, O.P., S.T.M.
    Prior Provincialis

Nihil obstat:

    Thomas C. Donlan, O.P., S.T.Lr., S.T.D.
    Censor Librorum

Imprimatur:

    ✠Leo Binz,
Die 7 Martii, 1955   *Archiepiscopus Dubuquensis*

Wipf and Stock Publishers
199 W 8th Ave, Suite 3
Eugene, OR 97401

The Indwelling of the Trinity
A Historico-Doctrinal Study of the Theory of St. Thomas Aquinas
By Cunningham, Francis L. B., O. P.
ISBN 13: 978-1-60608-254-6
Publication date 11/17/2008
Previously published by The Priory Press, 1955

To

GERALD and **AGNES CUNNINGHAM**

from their son

PREFACE

Caveat lector might reasonably be placed at the head of this book: not a work of popularization nor even of *haute vulgarisation*, this is a technical study, employing means proper to its field of inquiry, of a difficult theological problem. Yet such is the subject-matter treated, so vital and 'actual' the problem, that a larger audience than the professional theologians and trained students of the sacred sciences (for whom the work is primarily intended) may be anticipated. And whatever else may be said by critics of this work, it will have to be admitted that serious consideration of the problems it raises and the answers it proposes cannot but produce a firmer, deeper personal grasp of a central Christian mystery, and of St. Thomas' brilliant explanation of it. That result alone — even though much more may reasonably be hoped for — shall be reward enough for my labors, and justification for the publication of a book that, despite its price, cannot be expected to pay for itself.

A technical work must use technical means, and I have conceded nothing to popular taste in this respect. The style no doubt leaves much to be desired from the standpoint of literary excellence. The language used is unashamedly technical, in many cases a literal rendition of classical scholastic terminology; but every science has a right to its own vocabulary (only thus can the concepts proper to it be precisely expressed), and an accurate diction, even though Latinized, seems preferable to English circumlocutions and ambiguities. Similar reasoning has dictated my translations, which have been kept as literal as intelligibility allows; clumsiness of expression does, of course, result, but it is the cost that must be paid for permitting the original author to speak his own thoughts in a foreign tongue. All in all, clarity and precision have constituted the aim of the exposition; if that has been attained, the sacrifice of elegance will have been well made.

In accordance with modern American scientific practice, the greater number of the innumerable footnotes has been placed at the end of each chapter; Chapters Eight and Nine are exceptions to this rule, since they merely summarize the investigations of previous chapters and the references should be well known by the time these chapters are read. This procedure, it is believed, will permit, on the one hand, an unencumbered reading of the text, and will, on the other, keep the original sources close to hand for easy reference. Where the reference is of immediate import, or brief enough to permit simple citation, it will frequently appear at the bottom of the page. Cross references have been kept at a minimum, important texts being repeated wherever necessary.

The abbreviations which are used throughout are sufficiently obvious to obviate the need for a separate listing. Here again I have tried to avoid ambiguity, and where doubt might arise have attempted to indicate clearly the exact source referred to. An Appendix containing transcriptions of relevant material from medieval manuscripts will be found at the end of the book, together with a series of Tables designed to aid the reader's comprehension of the points made in the text. The bibliography which follows is neither critical nor complete; it is a simple list of works which have actually been consulted in preparing this study and which have contributed, positively or negatively, to its composition. An Index of Subjects and an Index of Names completes the work.

As a general rule no scientific study springs full grown from the mind of the author alone, and this book is far from being an exception. There have been numerous collaborators in all the numerous fields I have touched upon, and I can only hope that the appearance of the work itself will testify to my gratitude for their invaluable assistance, for it would be impossible to list my indebtedness in each instance.

In particular, however, I must publicly thank the following, whose contributions have been most notable: the Very Reverend E. L. Hughes, O.P., S.T.M., and the Very Reverend E. S. Carlson, O.P., S.T.M., for the time and opportunity to undertake the original research on which the book is based, and for the encouragement and cooperation which have made its publication possible; the Very Reverend Mannes Matthijs, O.P., S.T.M., professor of the Faculty of Theology of the Pontifical Athenaeum Angelicum, who directed the work in its early stages; the Very Reverend L.-B. Gillon, O.P., S.T.M., S.T.D., Vice-Rector of the aforementioned institution and professor of its Faculty of Theology, for his erudite advice on historical research and his generous loan of certain manuscript transcriptions; the Reverend W. B. Mahoney, O.P., S.T.Lr., Ph.D., and the Reverend T. C. Donlan, O.P., S.T.Lr., S.T.D, for the critical reading of the manuscript and for pertinent suggestions; the Very Reverend J. A. Driscoll, O.P., S.T.M., Ph.D., and THE PRIORY PRESS of which he is head, for sponsoring the work and for patiently supervising its publication.

To these, and to many others, I am deeply indebted, for their knowledge, their wisdom and, above all, their charity.

THE AUTHOR

CONTENTS

	PAGE
PREFACE	vii

CHAPTER ONE

The Mystery: The Problem

ARTICLE 1:	INTRODUCTION	1
ARTICLE 2:	THE TEACHING OF THE MAGISTERIUM	5
ARTICLE 3:	THE PROBLEM OF THE INHABITATION	8
	1. The Problem in General	8
	2. The Problem in St. Thomas	11
ARTICLE 4:	THE PURPOSE AND PLAN OF THIS STUDY	17
	1. The Ends in View	17
	2. The Means	20
	3. The Procedure	22
NOTES		25

CHAPTER TWO

The Sources of the Scholastic Teaching on the Divine Indwelling

		PAGE
INTRODUCTION	. . . .	34
ARTICLE 1:	REMOTE SOURCES OF THE SCHOLASTIC TRADITION	36
	1. The Teaching of Sacred Scripture	37
	2. The Doctrine of the Greek Fathers	40
ARTICLE 2:	IMMEDIATE SOURCES OF THE SCHOLASTIC TEACHING	46
	1. The Teaching of the Latin Fathers in General	46
	2. The Teaching of St. Augustine	48
ARTICLE 3:	CONCLUSION	55
NOTES	. . . .	57

CHAPTER THREE

The Common Teaching of the Schoolmen

INTRODUCTION	. . . .	70
ARTICLE 1:	THE CHRONOLOGY OF THE SCHOLASTIC WORKS	73
	1. The *Book of the Sentences* and the *Summa Aurea*	73
	2. *Alexandri de Hales Summa Theologica* . . .	74
	3. The Works of St. Albert	77
	4. St. Bonaventure	78
	5. Conclusion	79
ARTICLE 2:	THE COMMON TEACHING OF THE SCHOOLMEN	79
ARTICLE 3:	CONCLUSION	87
NOTES	. . . .	89

CHAPTER FOUR

Early Scholastic Solutions

		PAGE
INTRODUCTION	. . . .	103
ARTICLE 1:	THE MASTER OF THE SENTENCES	105
ARTICLE 2:	WILLIAM OF AUXERRE	107
ARTICLE 3:	THE SUMMA FRATRIS ALEXANDRI	109
	1. Analysis of the Theory of the *Summa* . .	111
	2. An Interpretation of the Theory . . .	113
	3. A Second Interpretation of the Theory . .	115
	4. The Theory of the *Summa Alexandri* and the Theory of Alexander	124
	5. Criticism of the Solution of the *Summa Fratris Alexandri*	128
NOTES	. . . .	133

CHAPTER FIVE

The Solutions of St. Albert and St. Bonaventure

INTRODUCTION	. . . .	140
ARTICLE 1:	THE SOLUTION OF ST. ALBERT THE GREAT . .	142
	1. Exposition of St. Albert's Theory . . .	142
	2. Interpretation of St. Albert's Theory . .	146
	3. Criticism of the Theory of St. Albert . .	148
	4. Conclusion	154
ARTICLE 2:	THE SOLUTION OF ST. BONAVENTURE . . .	156
	1. Exposition of St. Bonaventure's Doctrine .	156

		PAGE
	2. Conclusions	158
	3. Criticism of the Solution of St. Bonaventure .	162
ARTICLE 3:	CONCLUSION	162
NOTES	. . . .	166

CHAPTER SIX

The Solution of St. Thomas

INTRODUCTION	. . . .	178
ARTICLE 1:	THE FACTS OF THE INDWELLING	181
ARTICLE 2:	THE PRINCIPLES OF SOLUTION	185
ARTICLE 3:	THE SOLUTION OF ST. THOMAS	191
	1. Considered as an effect of God, sanctifying grace does not constitute the formal reason of the inhabitation	192
	2. A quasi-experimental knowledge, springing from the love and knowledge rooted in grace, is the proximate formal reason for the divine indwelling	196
	3. This experimental knowledge presupposes God's presence of immensity	202
	4. The experimental knowledge of Wisdom and love, presupposing the presence of immensity, is necessary as a habit, not as act .	208
ARTICLE 4:	RECAPITULATION	211
NOTES	. . . .	212

CHAPTER SEVEN

A Comparative Study of St. Thomas' Solution in the Scriptum super Sententiis

		PAGE
INTRODUCTION	. . . .	230
ARTICLE 1:	ST. THOMAS' FAMILIARITY WITH THE WORKS TO BE COMPARED	233
ARTICLE 2:	TEXTUAL DETERMINATION OF THE INFLUENCE OF THESE WORKS ON ST. THOMAS' THEORY OF THE DIVINE INDWELLING	240
	1. The Rejection of the Theory of the Inhabitation Proposed by St. Albert . . .	242
	2. The Choice of the Theory of the Inhabitation Proposed by the *Summa Alexandri* . .	253
	1) *First example*	253
	2) *Second example*	262
	3. Conclusions	269
ARTICLE 3:	TEXTUAL-DOCTRINAL COMPARISONS . . .	270
	1. The Divine Missions: A Scholastic Analysis .	271
	2. The Divine Missions: The Theory of the Inhabitation	273
	3. Conclusion	284
NOTES	. . . .	285

CHAPTER EIGHT

A Comparative Study of St. Thomas' Solution in the Summa Theologiae

INTRODUCTION	291

xv

		PAGE
ARTICLE 1:	THE SUMMA THEOLOGIAE AND THE SCRIPTUM SUPER SENTENTIIS	292
	1. Logical Differences	293
	2. Stylistic Differences	295
	3. Doctrinal Differences	300
	4. Conclusion	301
ARTICLE 2:	THE SUMMA THEOLOGIAE AND THE SUMMA THEOLOGICA OF ALEXANDER OF HALES	302
ARTICLE 3:	THE SUMMA THEOLOGIAE AND ST. ALBERT'S COMMENTARIUM	304
ARTICLE 4:	THE SUMMA THEOLOGIAE AND THE COMMENTARIUS OF ST. BONAVENTURE	305
	1. General Influence	305
	2. Influence on the Statement of the Theory of the Divine Indwelling	307
	3. St. Bonaventure's Influence: An Appraisal	316

CHAPTER NINE

Conclusion

INTRODUCTION	319
FIRST CONCLUSION: St. Thomas Teaches an Identical Doctrine on the Inhabitation in the *Scriptum super Sententiis* and the *Summa Theologiae*	322
1) Doctrinal basis for this judgment	322
2) Historical basis for this judgment	328
3) Conclusion	335

	PAGE
SECOND CONCLUSION: All theories of the indwelling which explain the triune presence from the formal point of view of God as cause, principle or 'operating' are irreconcilable with the theory of St. Thomas. None of the proponents of these proposals is justified, therefore, in quoting passages from St. Thomas in authoritative support of his peculiar ideas	337
THIRD CONCLUSION: The presentation of the solution of the problem of the inhabitation given in the *Scriptum super Sententiis* is an invaluable commentary on the solution presented in the *Summa Theologiae*	339
L'ENVOI	349
APPENDIX: Transcriptions of Pertinent Manuscripts	356
TABLE I: Comparison of the *Scriptum super Sententiis* with Possible Sources	362
TABLE II: Comparison of the *Summa Theologiae* (Part I, Question 43) with the *Scriptum super Sententiis* (Book I)	372
TABLE III: Outlines	374
TABLE IV: The Economy of the *Summa Theologiae*	377
BIBLIOGRAPHY	378
INDEX OF SUBJECTS	395
INDEX OF NAMES	411

The Indwelling of the Trinity

CHAPTER ONE

The Mystery: The Problem

ARTICLE 1

Introduction

"We are well aware that many a veil shrouds this professed truth of our union with the Divine Redeemer and in particular of the Holy Spirit's dwelling within our souls and impedes our power to understand and explain it. This mystery is enveloped in a darkness rising out of the mental limitations of those who seek to grasp it. But We know, too, that well directed and earnest study of this doctrine and the clash of diverse opinions and their discussion, provided love of truth and due submission to the Church be the arbiter, will soon open rich and bright vistas, whose light will help to progress in kindred sciences. Hence we do not censure those who in various ways and with diverse reasonings strain every effort to understand

and to clarify the mystery of this our marvelous union with Christ."*

There is something of audacity involved in attempting to explain so sublime a mystery as the presence of the triune God in the souls of the just — even when the task is limited, as in the present work, to an attempt to place in its proper light one aspect of the profound theory proposed by the Angelic Doctor. For here we have, on the one hand, God Himself under His highest aspect, the mystery of mysteries, *omnium fons et caput*:[1] God in His ineffable fecundity communicating His own infinite nature to the Son, in that loving utterance of the knowledge He has of Himself which issues in an interior Word and a consubstantial Image; God communicating, Father and Son, His own infinite nature to a Third Person, in an outpouring, a breathing forth of the love He has of Himself (and of the mutual love of Father and Son for one another) which issues in an interior sigh of love: the Spirit, the Gift of gifts, Love divine, substantial, personal. God, One and Three, "who dwells in light inaccessible, whom no man hath seen nor can see."[2]

"No one knoweth the Son but the Father; neither doth anyone know the Father but the Son, and he to whom it shall please the Son to reveal Him."[3] The divine Persons alone, Father and Son and Spirit who "searcheth all things, yea, the deep things of God"[4] — They alone know one another in Themselves. They alone can declare Themselves[5] in the gracious condescension of a self-revelation which alone enables the created intellect to speak, howsoever haltingly, of the incomprehensible Godhead.

---

* *The Mystical Body of Christ.* An Encyclical Letter Issued June 29, 1943, by Pope Pius XII under the title *Mystici Corporis*. Prepared by Joseph J. Bluett, S.J. Pp. 34-35. Cf. *Mystici Corporis*, n. 79 (*A.A.S.*, 1943, p. 231).

The Most Holy Trinity is one term of the present problem. And what is the other? It is a creature, "having nothingness,"[6] which in infinite and unintelligible love They have called to existence out of nothingness — a creature, moreover, in sullen, inexplicable revolt against its source and its very life. The light of the triune God dazzles our finite intellects into blindness, but this being They raise to Themselves, on the other hand, hovers in the darkness near the abyss. And in the darkness we understand not.

The cautions, then, of the Vicar of Christ must be borne well in mind when seeking for light to clarify, in any way, the inscrutable union we call the indwelling of the Trinity. In a certain sense, this mystery remains even more impenetrable to us than the greater mystery of God's personal union with our human nature. Because of our experienced wretchedness, the possibility of our union with God seems more incredible than the Incarnation itself; so that, as Augustine points out, the greater mystery serves to illustrate the lesser.[7] And it is this mystery we propose to study and probe in the doctrine of the Common Doctor.

The divine mysteries, the Vatican Council tells us, by their very nature so exceed the created intellect that even after revelation and the gift of Faith they remain hidden, shrouded in shadow behind the veil of Faith. Nevertheless, the same authority assures us, human reason illumined by Faith — if it but search "piously, diligently and prudently" — can attain with God's help some understanding of these supernatural realities, and that a most fruitful one.[8] And St. Thomas affirms the value of human reason even in respect to the mystery of the Trinity, not to prove the mystery but to manifest it by fitting reasons once its reality is revealed to us;[9] and he insists on the necessity of the knowledge of the divine Persons, despite the inaccessibility of such knowledge to human reason, "chiefly for right thinking concerning the salvation of the human race, which is accomplished by the Son incarnate and by the gifts of the Holy Spirit."[10]

Cognizant both of the loftiness of the mystery and the inadequacies of human instruments to mine its profundity, St. Augustine offers from his own experience and the experience of the Church the thoughtful conclusion: "Nowhere is error more dangerous, nor is anything more fruitfully discovered."[11] And Dominic Bañez, the great Spanish commentator, referring directly to the mystery of the indwelling Godhead, echoes Augustine's considered sentiment: the presence of the triune God in His creature, says Bañez, "without doubt is hard to explain and hard to understand — which in no way lessens the truth of it."[12]

Both admonition and encouragement, therefore, must be ever before the eyes of one who studies so sublime a mystery. Because of the subject matter concerned, that caution and humility which the Angelic Doctor states is so necessary when speaking of the Trinity[13] necessarily animates a sincere investigation of this truth. Yet it is, of course, the other aspect of the matter—the fruitfulness of the labor involved, the sublime truth to be contemplated—which encourages the human mind, strengthened by Faith, to attempt so intrinsically difficult a work. If the Philosopher could state unequivocally that "man should be drawn to immortal and divine things, insofar as in him lies,"[14] surely the Christian, whose wisdom is that of the Holy Spirit, must likewise seek to search the deep things of God *quantum potest*. "The contemplation of divine things which is had in this life, even though it is imperfect," says St. Thomas, "is yet more delightful than every other contemplation, no matter how perfect, because of the excellence of the thing contemplated."[15]

To shed, in various ways and with diverse reasonings, some light on a subject much controverted in our days; to attempt "to clarify the mystery of this our marvelous union with Christ" by exposing the true notion which the profound concept of similitude holds in St. Thomas' theory of the union of the triune God with the souls of the just — such is the high purpose of the present work. Derivative by definition, the task is still not an inconsiderable one: it can but be hoped that a restatement of fundamental Thomistic principles in the newly focused light of a fundamental Thomistic doctrine will dispel some of the darkness to reveal the blinding glory of man's point of contact with the Three-in-One.

ARTICLE 2

The Teaching of the Magisterium

Throughout the ages which flow from the revelation of Jesus Christ, certain features of the tremendous mystery of the divine indwelling that He has revealed to us have been so clear that, in spite of certain singular exceptions, they have been commonly and universally incorporated into the body of Christian tradition. One will seek in vain among ecclesiastical documents for formal and precise definition of these facts, since as the common teaching of the Church at all times they need no extraordinary witness. Scattered references, nevertheless, occur at various periods: to point up the continuance of that tradition and emphasize its universality; and — the point which is now of concern — to indicate the basic teaching on this mystery and the problem to which it gives rise. As a doctrinal prelude to the analysis of the problem of the inhabitation in the souls of the just which will later be made, a brief glance at these witnesses will be useful.

The doctrine is first directly affirmed in the Creed of St. Epiphanius (d. 403), an exposition of the Nicene Creed for oriental catechumens contained in his *Ancoratus* (c. 374): it is a simple confession of belief in the Holy Ghost "who dwells in the saints."[16] In the eleventh Council of Toledo, approximately three hundred years later, the same truth is indirectly taught in declaring that the Holy Spirit is sent by both Father and Son, without detriment to His divine character and dignity.[17]

The centuries of faith which carry us through the Middle Ages produce no ecclesiastical formulation of the doctrine: a silent but eloquent testimony of the lack of controversy concerning the common teaching, all the more impressive because these years encompass the Trinitarian discussion between the Latins and the Greeks. Only with the rise of Protestantism does affirmation again appear necessary, and even then the Council of Trent contents itself with a simple statement of the reality of the Holy Spirit within us.[18]

In the decline which followed the Counter-reformation, in the stress necessitated by the apologetic battle for its life, the Church all but lost sight of the dogma. For all practical purposes it appears only as the property of theologians. And so, at the end of the nineteenth century, a great pope saw fit to write a great encyclical on the Holy Ghost. In *Divinum Illud Munus*,[19] Pope Leo XIII recalls the profound truths and mysteries which Faith teaches us about the Third Person of the Trinity, among which is the mystery of man's union with God. This great document, the most explicit and complete statement from ecclesiastical authority on the subject, in all but the very words of St. Thomas exposes the teaching of the *magisterium* on the divine missions, the indwelling of the Trinity and the gifts of the Holy Ghost.[20]

"By grace God dwells in the just soul as in a temple," declares Pope Leo, "in a way entirely intimate and singular.... This marvelous conjunction, which is called by the name of inhabitation ... although effected most truly by the present power of the whole Trinity — 'We shall come to him and take up Our abode with him' (John 14:23) — is predicated, however, as peculiarly the Holy Ghost's."[21]

Fifty years later, the present Pontiff in his encyclical on the Mystical Body of Christ once more affirms the great mystery. Urging caution but encouraging study of the truths involved, this letter culminates the official pronouncements on the divine indwelling by quoting — albeit with reservation — St. Thomas' explanation of the 'how' of the mystery. "The Divine Persons are said to be indwelling inasmuch as They are present to intellectual creatures in a way that lies beyond human comprehension, and are known and loved by them in a purely supernatural manner alone within the deepest sanctuary of the soul."[22]

From these brief utterances of the ordinary voice of the Church the basic facts of the mystery clearly appear. The three divine Persons, Father, Son and Holy Spirit, are present in the souls of those in the state of sanctifying grace; this presence is a real presence, not merely a moral union, and it differs entirely from the common presence of God in all the creatures He has made. But on being confronted with facts so astonishing as these, the human mind is immediately aswirl with questions: how is so marvelous a union accomplished? what are the relations between the grace-state and the special presence of the Trinity within us? in what precise manner does this new mode of God's presence differ from His contact with other creatures? what is the significance of the mystery in the practical order? These, and innumerable related and subsidiary questions, are the natural fruit of the believing created intellect when faced with so precious and so profound a mystery.

ARTICLE 3

The Problem of the Inhabitation

1. The Problem in General

These various questions inevitably occasioned by so profound a mystery are not of equal importance, and their solutions are attendant on the solution of the central and most difficult problem of all: how is this new presence of God in the soul to which the Church bears unfailing witness effected? what brings it about? This is the pivotal question, and the one which has occupied the attention of the theologians from the Middle Ages to the present day.

What an eager faith searches to know, then, is the 'how' of the mystery — how the indwelling is realized — not what brings it into being but what explains it; not why it occurs, but what it is. The believing mind is looking for the *formal reason* of the inhabitation, not its efficient nor its final cause — although these may well have their role to play in any satisfactory explanation — but its formal cause: that which alone explains the effects testified to by the *magisterium*, that without which these effects remain unaccounted for.

To clarify this problem and illustrate its difficulty, a fundamental theological fact should be here recalled: this unique presence of the three divine Persons involves a new relationship between God and His rational creature. For "nothing can be said of God in time except what involves a relation to a creature,"[23] and the indwelling is not so singular a fact as to escape this principle. As has been shown, the *magisterium* teaches that the presence of the Trinity is a new fact, a reality distinct from all others. But since God Himself is immutable, self-complete, perfect, such a reality can not exist in Him, it must be found in something outside of Him. And if He does not change, and yet a new reality involving Him comes into being, some relation to Him is necessarily implied.

As with creation itself, what takes place in this change implicates God — here, in truth, God as subsisting in three Persons; and as with creation, no activity can be predicated on the part of divinity (although there is, from the creature's side, obediential possibility — and in this the analogy with creation fails), so that all that remains on God's part is a different relation to His creature.[24] And for Him, as in all His references to creatures, this can only be a relation of reason: insofar as man, limited in his grasp of things, can only understand God as the term of his real relation to Him by *considering* Him as related to himself.[25]

Undoubtedly, then, the new presence of the Trinity in the souls of the just involves a problem of relationship between God and the rational creature. It was so regarded by the Schoolmen — hardly surprising in the face of their careful treatment of the fact of God's presence — as Albert,[26] Bonaventure,[27] and Thomas testify.[28] From this aspect, since predicamental relations are specified by their fundament considered in relation to their terms (as John of St. Thomas has explained), [29] the problem would consist first of all in the proper determination of the *term* implied by this new presence (God as newly operative? God as object? God as object really present? etc.) and only after this in the specification of the fundament — even though in this fundament the formal reason of the new relation would be found.[30] And in fact, as will later appear, the localization of this term is the stumbling block on which more than one attempt to solve the question — from the time of the Schoolmen to our own day — has bruised itself, and lethally. Once the term is specified, however, the true formal explanation remains to be found; and here other theologians have become hopelessly lost through the misdirection given them by principles extrinsic to the problem itself.

To be able to explain how the Trinity comes to abide in the just, in what way the new relationship is constituted, where the precise newness of the presence is found, what are the respective roles played by created and uncreated grace — this is to give the *formal reason* of the divine indwelling. And it is in the profound solution of the Angelic Doctor that the most complete, precise, consistent and satisfactory answer will be found. Not that man can ever hope to understand perfectly the fact of God's presence in the just, because this ineffable presence is a mystery in the fullest sense of the word. But if absolute intellectual satisfaction be necessarily denied to man here on earth, yet he can discover with St. Thomas a grasp of the problem and a resolution of it on as deep and penetrating a level as is permitted to that participated divine science which is theology.

2   The Problem in St. Thomas

When one goes to Thomas, however, in search of his answers to the important questions which constitute the problem of the inhabitation, another difficulty arises. For despite the remarkable *material* identity of his treatment of the subject in his early work, the *Scriptum super Sententiis Petri Lombardi*, and the later and more mature *Summa Theologiae*,* even a superficial reading uncovers notable differences. These divergences, as von Rudloff points out,[31] are epitomized in the characteristic formulas of the respective works: the triune presence in the *Sentences* is described as like that of a thing in its similitude;[32]

---

* The material similarities may be schematized as follows:

a. 1 (conveniat mitti?)	= d. 15, q. 1, a. 1
a. 2 (aeterna vel temporalis?)	= d. 14, q. 1, a. 2; d. 15, q. 1, a. 1; q. 4, a. 3
a. 3 (solum sec. gratiam?)	= d. 14, q. 2, a. 1; a. 2; d. 15, q. 4, a. 1
a. 4 (Pater mittitur?)	= d. 15, q. 1, a. 2; q. 2, a. 1
a. 5 (Filius invisibiliter?)	= d. 15, q. 2; q. 4, a. 1, a. 2
a. 6 (terminus missionis?	= d. 16
a. 7 (Sp. S. visibiliter?)	— d. 15, q. 5, a. 1
a. 8 (quis mittit?)	= d. 15, q. 3
Without parallel:	= d. 14, q. 1, a. 1; q. 3; d. 15, q. 5, aa. 2 and 3

It will be noticed that this schema differs slightly from that given by Father de Guibert, S.J. (*Les doublets de Saint Thomas d'Aquin*, Paris, 1926, p. 45), as well as with the revision of de Guibert's parallelism by Father Fitzgerald (*De Inhabitatione Epiritus Sancti Doctrina S. Thomae Aquinatis*. Apud Aedes Seminarii Sanctae Mariae ad Lacum, Mundelein, Illinois, U.S.A., 1949, p. 41). For a more detailed examination of the parallels, consult the latter work, Chapter III, De Missionibus et Inhabitatione (pp. 40-53), although one cannot agree with Father Fitzgerald in all particulars.

but in the *Summa* God is said to be present like the object known is in the one knowing and the object loved in the one loving.[33] On the face of it, then — since clearly a thing is not present in its image in the same way as an object known and loved is in the subject knowing and loving — there is a diversity between Thomas' solution in one and in the other work. A diversity of language, obviously; what is more important, such a variance of expression as strongly to suggest a divergence of theory.

The following significant differences (there are others not now remarked on) further substantiate this opinion:

1) A clear-cut change of doctrine respecting a not unimportant point, the designation of the divine missions. In the *Sentences* St. Thomas holds that a mission chiefly signifies an essential notion, since it principally implies a relation to an effect of which the entire Trinity is the cause;[34] in the *Summa*, however, he maintains the exact opposite: the very notion of a mission primarily implies the eternal procession;[35] only out of reverence for his distinguished predecessors does he tolerate a secondary consideration by which the mission directly implies the effect rather than the divine procession.[36]

2) The prevalence — indeed, the insistence — on the notion of similitude (sign, appropriation, assimilation) in the earlier work,[37] and the all but total exclusion (at least in a material sense) of this idea in the *Summa*.[38] This is emphasized above all in the first article of Distinction 15, Question 4, in the solution of this article and in the answers to the first and third objection.* The solution here and

* I *Sent.*, d. 15, q. 4, a. 1, sol. and ad 1 and ad 3: ". . . sicut in exitu rerum a principio dicitur bonitas divina in creaturas procedere, inquantum repraesentatur in creatura per similitudinem bonitatis divinae in ipsa receptam; ita in reductione rationalis creaturae in Deum intelligitur processio divinae personae quae et missio dicitur, inquantum propria relatio ipsius personae divinae repraesentatur in anima per

the answer to the first objection find no parallel whatsoever in the *Summa Theologiae,* neither textually nor (ap-

similitudinem aliquam receptam, quae est exemplata et originata ab ipsa proprietate relationis aeternae; sicut proprius modus quo Spiritus sanctus refertur ad Patrem, est amor, et proprius modus referendi Filium in Patrem est, quia est verbum ipsius manifestans ipsum. Unde sicut Spiritus sanctus invisibiliter procedit in mentem per donum amoris, ita Filius per donum sapientiae; in quo est manifestatio ipsius Patris, qui est ultimum ad quod recurrimus. Et quia secundum receptionem horum donorum efficitur in nobis similitudo ad propria personarum; ideo secundum novum modum essendi, prout res est in sua similitudine, dicuntur personae divinae in nobis esse, secundum quod novo modo eis assimilamur; et secundum hoc utraque processio dicitur missio.

Ulterius, sicuti praedicta originantur ex propriis personarum, ita etiam effectum suum non consequuntur ut conjungantur fini, nisi virtute divinarum personarum; quia in forma impressa ab aliquo agente est virtus imprimentis. Unde in receptione hujusmodi donorum habenter personae divinae novo modo, quasi ductrices in finem vel conjungentes. Et ideo utraque processio dicitur datio, inquantum est ibi novus modus habendi.

Ad primum ergo dicendum, quod ad rationem missionis non requiritur quod sit ibi cognitio actualis personae ipsius, sed tantum habitualis, inquantum scilicet in dono collato, quod est habitus, repraesentatur proprium divinae personae sicut in similtudine; et ita dicitur quod mitti est cognosci quod ab alio sit per modum repraesentationis, sicut aliquid dicitur se manifestare vel facere cognitionem de se, inquantum se repraesentat in sui similitudine . . . .

Ad tertium dicendum, quod quando aliquid participatur non secundum suum actum perfectum, sed secundum aliquem modum, non dicitur proprie haberi; sicut animalia habent aliquem modum prudentiae, non tamen dicuntur prudentiam habere, quia non habent actum rationis, qui proprie est actus prudentiae, scilicet ipsa electio; unde magis habent aliquid simile prudentiae quam prudentiam. Videmus autem in cognitione duos gradus: primum, secundum quod cognitio intellectiva tendit in unum; secundum, prout verum accipit ut conveniens et bonum. Et nisi sit aliqua resistentia ex tali cognitione sequitur amor et delectatio; quia, secundum Philosophum, VII *Ethic.,* cap. xiii et xiv, delectatio consequiter operationem perfectam non impeditam. Unde felicitas contemplativa est quando aliquis pervenit ad ultimam operationem intellectus et ipsam sine impedimento exercet. Constat autem quod in processione Verbi aeterni est cognitio perfecta

parently) doctrinally, even though there is a certain similarity in the *Summa* (I, q. 43, a. 5 ad 2) to the third response.† The same may be said of the comparison in the second article of the second question of Distinction 14,* on which von Rudloff constructs practically the whole of his peculiar theory.³⁹

secundum omne modum, et ideo ex tali notitia procedit amor. Unde dicit Augustinus, III *De Trin.*, cap. x: 'Verbum quod insinuare intendimus cum amore notitia est.' Quandocumque igitur habetur cognitio ex quo non sequitur amor gratuitus, non habetur similitudo Verbi, sed aliquid illius. Sed solum tunc habetur similitudo Verbi, quando habetur cognitio talis ex qua procedit amor, qui conjungit ipsi cognito secundum rationem convenientis. Et ideo non habet Filium in se inhabitantem, nisi qui recipit talem cognitionem. Hoc autem non potest esse sine gratia gratum faciente. Unde constat quod, simpliciter et proprie loquendo, Filius nec datur nec mittitur, nisi in dono gratiae gratum facientis; sed in aliis donis quae pertinent ad cognitionem, participatur aliquid de similitudine Verbi."

† *Sum. Theol.*, I, q. 43, a. 5 ad 2: ". . . anima per gratiam conformatur Deo. Unde ad hoc quod aliqua Persona divina mittatur ad aliquem per gratiam, oportet quod fiat assimilatio illius ad divinam Personam quae mittitur per aliquod gratiae donum. Et quia Spiritus Sanctus est Amor, per donum caritatis anima Spiritui Sancto assimilatur: unde secundum donum caritatis attenditur missio Spiritus Sancti. Filius autem est Verbum, non qualecumque, sed spirans Amorem: unde Augustinus dicit, in IX libro *de Trin.*: 'Verbum quod insinuare intendimus, cum amore notitia est.' Non igitur secundum quamlibet perfectionem intellectus mittitur Filius: sed secundum talem instructionem intellectus, qua prorumpat in affectum amoris, ut dicitur Ioan. 6, 'Omnis qui audivit a Patre, et didicit, venit ad me'; et in Psalmo: 'In meditatione mea exardescet ignis.' Et ideo signanter dicit Augustinus quod Filius mittitur, 'cum a quoquam cognoscitur atque percipitur': Perceptio enim experimentalem quandam notitiam significat. Et haec proprie dicitur *sapientia*, quasi *sapida scientia*, secundum illud *Eccl.* 6: 'Sapientia doctrinae secundum nomen eius est.'

* I *Sent.*, d. 14, q. 2, a. 2: "Sicut enim in generatione naturali generatum non conjungitur generanti in similitudine speciei nisi in ultimo generationis, ita etiam in participantibus divinae bonitatis non est immediata conjunctio ad Deum per primos effectus quibus in esse naturae subsistimus, sed per ultimos quibus fini adhaeremus; et ideo concedimus Spiritum sanctum non dari nisi secundum dona gratum facientia."

3) The frequent repetition of the ideas of effect (as effect) and gift (as effect)[40]— which, as Gardeil remarks with respect to Terrien, is the characteristic term of the opinion of Vasquez.[41] In the *Summa*, on the other hand, the word is (comparatively) hardly mentioned.[42]

4) Similarly, the use in the commentary of the phrases, 'contribution of the gifts' and its correlative, 'reception of the gifts,' phrases which do not appear in the *Summa*, even where the doctrine is strictly identical.*

5) The special description in the *Sentences* of the divine Persons as present in the inhabitation in placing their seal on the soul,† imprinting their power and consequently present 'as leading to, or conjoining with the end'**— again without equivalent expression in the *Summa*.

From these facts, certainly a *prima facie* case is established for some doctrinal difference between St. Thomas' earlier and later solutions. Clearly enough, indeed, the *Sentences* seems to insist on the presence of the Trinity from the aspect of cause of the effects of grace, effects on which a likeness of the divine Persons is imprinted. This

* This identity of doctrine but dissimilarity of phraseology may be thus schematized:

d. 14, q. 1, a. 1, ad 2	=	q. 43, a. 2, ad 2
q. 2, a. 2, ad 4	=	a. 3, ad 4
d. 15, q. 5, a. 1, sol. 1	=	a. 6
sol. 3	=	a. 6, ad 3
sol. 4	=	a. 6, ad 3

For further use of these and similar phrases in the *Sentences* cf. also d. 14, q. 2, a. 1, sol. 2, ad 2; d. 15, q. 2, ad 2; q. 4, a. 1; etc.

† I *Sent.*, d. 14, q. 2, a: 2, ad 2: ". . . ipsae dininae personae quadam sui sigillatione in animabus nostris relinquunt quaedam dona quibus formaliter fruimur, scilicet amore et sapientia. . . ."

** *Ibid.*, d. 15, q. 4, a. 1: ". . . sicuti praedicta originantur ex propriis personarum, ita etiam effectum suum non consequuntur ut conjungantur fini, nisi virtute divinarum personarum; quia in forma impressa ab aliquo agente est virtus imprimentis. Unde in receptione hujusmodi donorum habentur personae divinae novo modo quasi ductrices in finem vel conjungentes."

aspect is notably lacking, even insofar as terminology is concerned, in the *Summa;* here the formulas utilized suggest that St. Thomas considers the triune presence principally or exclusively from the aspect of end or term. Apparently, then, the earlier work stresses an 'ontological' element as the reason for the inhabitation, and the later an 'intentional' element. Herein lies the subsidiary problem: how to explain the divergence between the theory expressed in the *Sentences* and that enunciated in the *Summa*.

The following possibilities are open to us:

1) St. Thomas essentially changed his doctrine, so that the theories are in open contradiction and irreconcilable. This was the opinion of the Spanish Dominican, Didacus de Deza (c. 1443-1523).[43] While the explanation cannot be rejected *a priori* on a doctrinal basis (since, in fact, the *Summa* evidences notable theological progress over Thomas' teachings as a Bachelor, and on many points a radical departure), still not a single major commentator makes the same observation,[44] and none of the modern writers on the subject recognizes such a change.

2) The *Sentences* stresses one of two complementary and almost equally important elements of St. Thomas' complete theory, the 'ontological' element; the *Summa* emphasizes the second, the 'intentional' element: neither factor is self-sufficient; both together constitute the formal reason of the indwelling. This is a popular modern theory, admitting of variation in explanation and sometimes only indirectly concerned with the actual textual difficulties. It is maintained by von Rudloff,[45] Retailleau,[46] Fitzgerald,[47] Trütsch[48] and Sagüés.[49]

3) The earlier work presents the true formal reason of the inhabitation, the presence of the Trinity from the aspect of principle, in some way (difficult to specify) as efficient and/or formal extrinsic cause; the presence of

the Persons as objects known and loved (the theory of the *Summa*) is a consequence and effect of the effective triune presence, but not a contributing factor nor part of its formal explanation. The defenders of this theory do not directly interest themselves precisely in explaining the divergencies between St. Thomas' works, but rather in presenting their own conclusions with selective authoritative citations from his teaching. This theory does provide such an explanation, nevertheless, as an obvious corollary. By far the most common of the modern attempts to resolve the problem of the inhabitation, it is coming more and more into favor.[50]

4) No substantial difference exists between the doctrine of the *Summa* and the *Sentences* respecting the formal reason of the indwelling, although there is accidental doctrinal progress in the later work and a clearer and more precise presentation of the same theory. This is the opinion commonly maintained by modern Thomists, among whom Gardeil,[51] Garrigou-Lagrange,[52] Cuervo[53] and Ciappi[54] may be mentioned.

ARTICLE 4

The Purpose and Plan of This Study

1. The Ends in View

The reasons for choosing the present topic will be obvious to anyone familiar with the modern literature on the subject of the presence of the Trinity. Intrinsically, of course, the problem of the inhabitation is a fascinating, vital and practical subject for theological consideration; it is timely now because of the awakened interest in the life of the spirit, and because many modern theologians have attempted to offer either new solutions or new interpretations of traditional answers. And this last fact indicates why any investigation of the mystery of the divine indwelling must be interested in the two statements of St. Thomas on the subject: because many of these modern attempts seek to justify themselves, as indeed they must, in the doctrine of the Common Doctor; and this process of justification finds its greatest support in an explicit or implicit hypothesis of a doctrinal difference between the presentations in the *Summa* and the *Sentences,* or in the fact that the doctrine of the *Summa* must be complemented and interpreted by the 'ontological element' clearly taught in the *Sentences.* The variations on this theme are numberless, but they all reject a solution based on final causality alone, and insist on the necessity of considering God's efficient role as a major or contributing element in the ultimate explanation of the mystery. And for this, the statement of St. Thomas' theory in the *Sentences* is their authority.

To expose the true nature of St. Thomas' treatment in the *Sentences* — to show that, in fact, it is merely a different formula stating precisely the same truth as enunciated in the *Summa* — here is a particular goal of this study. In accomplishing this it will be shown that St. Thomas' explanation involves a single element, and that this alone can satisfactorily explain — so far as it possible for man to understand the mystery — the formal reason of the presence of the Trinity. Such a procedure will necessarily involve the disproving and rejection of those modern theories which have gained much current support in holding that God (the Trinity) considered as principle accounts for His presence in the just.

Yet another subsidiary end will be served by this inquiry, one which should prove to be the most important of all. From a consideration of the *Sentences* in the light of scholastic tradition there should come a far deeper understanding of the mystery than is usually obtained by a simple explanation of the *Summa* formula alone, *sicut cognitum in cognoscente et amatum in amante*. All too often, indeed, modern theologians have considered that expression on its most superficial level, failing to appreciate its philosophical depth, and failing even worse in grasping its sublime theological implications. For such a deeper penetration of St. Thomas' mind the explanation of the *Sentences* is invaluable, if it be properly understood. For it connects the mysteries of the indwelling of the Trinity in man and of the image of the Trinity in man, and from this conjunction each mystery illumines the other, and is itself enriched by such a role. On this level the task is intrinsically difficult because of the theological profundities involved, and the difficulty is increased by the phraseology of the *Sentences* which has led so many astray. But the results to be hoped for justify so ambitious an attempt.

To demonstrate the doctrinal identity of the *Summa* and the *Sentences* on the explanation of the divine indwelling — this is the avowed immediate purpose of this work. Three ends will be served in such an effort: proof of the validity of St. Thomas' theory; rejection of false opinions and interpretations of St. Thomas; deeper penetration of the thought of the Angelic Doctor on the subject. Of these ends the second will only be indirectly touched upon, since the chief intent is to present a positive statement of the theory of the Common Doctor, analyzing and illustrating in the fullest manner possible his rich and fecund solution of the problem.

2. The Means

To solve the problem that comes from the different presentations St. Thomas has given us of his thought on the divine missions and inhabitation, and to implement the further ends such a solution subserves, an historico-doctrinal approach will be adopted. By studying the scholastic tradition from which St. Thomas so generously drew, one can determine in many cases how the problem was understood in his time, what solutions had been proposed, wherein he is debtor and where he has made original contribution. Such an approach guarantees that personal preconceptions of a latter-day point of view will not be allowed to determine the interpretation of difficult texts. It will teach the investigator how the problem was understood in St. Thomas' day, and from the similarity and dissimilarity of approaches, aspects and even phraseology reveal in a positive manner the significance these matters had in the intellectual atmosphere in which he lived.

But a simple historical approach is never self-sufficient in theology, so far as solving a problem is concerned. Valuable for the suggestions it offers as to the correct manner of interpretation, an understanding of a theological point can be obtained only if there is joined to the historical approach a profound appreciation of the doctrine in question in the larger context of the intellectual teachings of the man. This is true as a general statement, but it is most especially true in the case at hand, where a simple historical resolution of the difficulty would afford hardly any theological penetration of the depths of St. Thomas' thought. And since that insight is one of the ends in view, the necessity for a doctrinal study of his explanations is apparent.

By a combination of the two approaches, however, one may hope to enjoy the advantages of each method, at the same time eliminating the dangers or defects each is subject to. A study of history will situate the problem in the theological currents of the time, avoiding possible subjective misinterpretations; its chief, but not its only, value, will lie in showing the identity of the two diverse statements from the standpoint of medieval theories: proof, as shall be seen, of the validity of St. Thomas' solution. Less immediately it will also cast light on the deeper aspects of that solution. The doctrinal study, on the other hand, while it, too, will prove the identity of those statements and the validity of that solution, will more directly explore the more rarefied levels of the theory for a fuller understanding of St. Thomas and of the mystery of the divine indwelling.

Neither approach will be exclusive, or entered upon without regard for the other; they will frequently interlock. From both, a more complete view of the answer of the Angelic Doctor will be obtained than has, perhaps, heretofore been possible; certainly a fuller resolution of the immediate problem, the discrepancies between the presentation in the *Sentences* and that in the *Summa*, should result. But the reader need anticipate no original contribution, in the sense of new theories or unique discoveries; the solution, like the problem itself, is latent in the texts of St. Thomas. It is the high hope of this endeavor, in explaining those texts by one another in the light of tradition and in the light of St. Thomas' other doctrines and of the interpretations of his genuine commentators, to bring into focus under the combined light of these means the 'old' theory, and the true one.

3. The Procedure

The particular ends that have been proposed for this work, and the means proportioned to those ends, dictate, of course, the outline to be followed. After this introductory chapter, whose considerations have been general and preliminary, Chapter Two will trace the sources of the teaching of the Schoolmen on the presence of the Trinity in the souls of the just. Brief sections will indicate the scriptural basis for the doctrine, its elucidation with the Fathers of the East, its conservation in the works of the Latin Fathers, its interpretation by St. Augustine. The following chapter (Chapter Three) delineates the intellectual atmosphere in which St. Thomas labored—that is, the tradition recognized by the Scholastics as the inviolable substratum of their attempts at explanation. A short historical study situates the works of the authors to be studied in their proper chronological relationships; then a longer investigation reproduces in some detail the common elements of the scholastic tradition concerning this mystery, as those accepted facts appear in the teaching of various medieval theologians. By this means it is hoped that the reader will be able to grasp the problem as it was understood by St. Thomas and his predecessors and contemporaries.

Chapter Four presents the solutions to the central problem of the divine indwelling that were obtained through the theological labors of the earlier Schoolmen. A special chapter, Chapter Five, considers the attempts at a theological explanation of the mystery as they were worked out by the most renowned of the contemporaries of the Angelic Doctor, St. Albert, his teacher, and St. Bonaventure, his friend.

In the sixth chapter a synthetic presentation of the theory of St. Thomas himself on the formal reason of the indwelling of the Trinity is given. Drawing indiscriminately from both the *Sentences* and the *Summa* on all points (in a deliberate, if not always explicit, attempt to indicate the doctrinal identity of the two works), this chapter considers the facts about the mystery which St. Thomas received from scholastic tradition and the principles on which he relies for his examination of the problem, and then sets down the solution which his theological genius had determined on the basis of those facts and principles. On certain points where modern theologians have created difficulties, a more thorough analysis is given to show the validity, the profoundity and the consistency of the thought of the Angelic Doctor on this subject.

Explicit comparison between the *Scriptum super Sententiis Petri Lombardi* and the works of the other Schoolmen which have been examined comprises the subject matter of Chapter Seven. The same task of comparison with the *Summa Theologiae* as a term of reference is absolved in Chapter Eight. In both cases attention is paid not only to the actual doctrine in question but to the manner of presentation, the language employed, the obvious presuppositions involved. As a result of these comparative studies, a set of conclusions is obtained representing the accomplishment of the purposes for which this work was begun. These conclusions concern both the special problem of the apparent diversity of St. Thomas' presentations of his theory and the general and more important problem of the divine indwelling itself.

Chapter Nine is a summary of the work which has been completed in the previous chapters and a collation and critical evaluation of the conclusions which have been attained as a result of those labors. For in the end it should be clear that St. Thomas teaches identical doctrines in the *Summa* and in the *Sentences,* but that a fuller and deeper understanding of his profound solution is obtained by a correlation of the two presentations, a task greatly abetted by the historical approach to the difficulties that has been utilized.

It is the ultimate hope and the ultimate reason of this particular study that such a deeper understanding will be the end result of its efforts.

NOTES

[1] *Divinum Illud Munus.* A.S.S., XXIX (1896-1897), p. 645.

[2] I Tim. 6:16.

[3] Matt. 11:27.

[4] I Cor. 2:10.

[5] Cf. John 1:18.

[6] Cf. St. Bonaventure, I *Sent.*, Dist. XXXVII, P. I, a. 1, q. 1 (*Opera Omnia*, ed. ad Aquas Claras, I, pp. 638-639): ". . . creatura habet in se possibilitatem et vanitatem, et utriusque causa est, quia producta est de nihilo . . . quia creatura de nihilo producta est, ideo habet vanitatem; et quia nihil vanum in se ipso fulcitur, necesse est, quod omnis creatura sustentetur per praesentiam Veritatis. Et est simile: si quis poneret corpus ponderosum in aere, quod est quasi vanum, non sustentaretur."

[7] Cf. XIII *De Trinitate*, Chap. 9, n. 12 (PL 42:1023-1024): "Cum dictum esset in Evangelio quod Jesus dederit potestatem filios Dei fieri iis qui eum receperunt (Joan. 1:12) . . . ne ista hominum, quam videmus et gestamus infirmitas, tantam excellentiam desperaret, illico annexum est: et Verbum caro factum est et habitavit in nobis (Joan. 1:14), ut a contrario suaderetur quod incredible videbatur. Si enim natura Dei Filius, propter filios hominum, misericordia factus est hominis filius—hoc est enim: Verbum caro factum est et habitavit in nobis, hominibus—quanto est credibilius natura filios hominum, gratia Dei filios Dei fieri et habitare in Deo, in quo solo et de quo solo esse possunt beati, participes immortalitatis effecti eius; propter quod persuadendum Dei Filius nostrae mortalitatis effectus est?" St. Thomas teaches the same doctrine relative to the Beatific Vision. So in *De Rationibus Fidei*, Chap. 5 (ed. Vivès, XXVII, p. 133), he says: "Per hoc quod Deus factus est homo, spem nobis dedit ut etiam homo posset pervenire ad hoc quod uniretur Deo per beatam fruitionem." Cf. also IV *Contra Gentiles*, Chap. 41; Chap. 54, arg. 1; Chap. 55, ad 1; *Sum. Theol.*, II, q. 1, a. 2; *Comp. Theol.*, I, Chap. 201.

[8] Concilium Vaticanum, Sess. III, Constitutio de fide catholica, Chap. 4, De fide et ratione. *Denz.* 1796.

[9] *Sum. Theol.*, I, q. 32, a. 1 ad 2.

[10] *Ibid.*, ad 3: ". . . principalius ad recte sentiendum de salute generis humanae quae perficitur per Filium incarnatum, et per dona Spiritus Sancti."

[11] I *De Trint.*, Chap. 3 (PL 42: 822): "nec periculosius alicubi erratur, nec laboriosius aliquid quaeritur, nec fructuosius aliquid invenitur."

[12] *Scholastica Commentaria in I Partem*, q. 43, a. 3 (ed. Salmanticae, 1585): "Dico igitur, quod ipsa Persona Spiritus Sancti quando mittitur ad hominem, est in illo secundum substantiam modo quidem ineffabili quod sine dubio difficile est explicare et intelligere. Sed haec difficultas nihil detrahit veritati."

[13] *Sum. Theol.*, I, q. 31, a. 2: ". . . cum de Trinitate loquimur, cum cautela et modestia est agendum. . . ."

[14] X *Ethicorum*, Chap. VII, n. 8 (ed. Bekker, n. 1177b): "Homo debet se ad immortalia et divinia trahere quantum potest." Cf. I *Contra Gent.*, Chap. 5.

[15] *Sum. Theol.*, II-II, q. 180, a. 7 ad 3: ". . . contemplatio divinorum quae habetur in via, etsi sit imperfecta, est tamen delectabilior omni alia contemplatione quantumcumque perfecta, propter excellentiam rei contemplatae.

[16] *Denz.* 13: "Credimus et in Spiritum Sanctum qui locutus est in lege, et per prophetas praedicavit, et ad Jordanum descendit, in apostolis locutus est, et in sanctis habitat." Cf. PG 43: 234 ff.

[17] *Denz.* 277: "Hic igitur Spiritus Sanctus missus ab utrique sicut Filius a Patre creditur; sed minor Patre et Filio non habetur, sicut Filius propter assumptam carnem minorem se Patre et Spiritu Sancto esse testatur."

Although this text does not explicitly affirm the invisible mission of the Holy Spirit — the reference is to His visible mission in the context — nevertheless according to the common teaching of the Fathers and of theologians, the visible mission testifies to His invisible presence in the soul, and so in fact the two are inseparable, and to affirm the visible mission is to certify the invisible mission (although, obviously, not vice versa).

[18] Sess. VI, Doctrina de iustificatione, Chap. 7: Quid sit iustificatio impii, et quae eius causae. *Denz.* 791: "Huius justificationis [causa est] efficiens vero misericors Deus, qui gratuito abluit et sanctificat signans et ungens 'Spiritu promissionis Sancto, qui est pignus

hereditatis nostrae.' " The Council likewise speaks of those who "accepto Spiritus Sancti dono, scientes 'templum Dei violare' et 'Spiritum Sanctum contristare' non formidaverunt." (Sess. XIV, Chap. 8, *Denz.* 904.)

From this same period also dates the condemnation by Pius V of Michael du Bay, two of whose propositions deny the efficacy of the 'indwelling Holy Spirit.' (Numbers 13 and 15, *Denz.* 1013 and 1015).

[19] *A.S.S.*, XXIX (1896-1897), pp. 644-658.

[20] If, as Pope Pius XII explicitly teaches (*Humani Generis*, A.A.S., XLII [1950], p. 562: "Neque putandum est, ea quae in Encyclicis Litteris proponuntur, assensum per se non postulare, cum in iis Pontifices supremam sui Magisterii potestatem non exerceant. Magisterio enim ordinario haec docentur, de quo illud etiam valet: 'Qui vos audit, me audit.' (Luc. 10: 16.)"), the words of the Supreme Pontiffs in dogmatic matters carry the authority of the ordinary magisterium, this document summing up the traditional doctrine of the triune inhabitation should certainly be cited in the *Enchiridion Symbolorum*, as Father Garrigou-Lagrange with justice demands (*De Deo Trino et Creatore*, Taurini, 1943, p. 208).

[21] *Divinum Illud Munus*, A.S.S., XXIX (1896-1897), p. 653: ". . . ex gratia Deus insidet animae justae tamquam in templo, modo penitus intimo et singulari. . . . Haec autem mira conjunctio, quae suo nomine inhabitatio dicitur . . . tametsi verissime efficitur praesenti totius Trinitatis numine, 'ad eum veniemus et mansionem apud eum faciemus' (Joan. 14: 23), attamen de Spiritu Sancto tamquam peculiaris praedicatur."

[22] *The Mystical Body of Christ*, ed. cit., p. 23. Cf. *A.A.S.*, XXV (1943), p. 231, n. 80.

In view of the reserve of the Pope, one cannot share the view of Father Cuervo, O.P. ("La inhabitación de la Trinidad en toda alma en gracia según Juan de santo Tomás," from *La Ciencia Tomista*, 69 [1945], reprinted at Salamanca, 1946) that this "equivale implicitamente a una aprobación de su [Santo Tomás] doctrina," *reenforced* by the "modo impersonal . . . sin elogio alguna, ni adjetivo que indique su aprobación" (p. 49) of the Pope's citation. Nor, therefore, can one believe that the doctrine of St. Thomas has "triumphed with this encyclical, and with it that of his best expositor, John of St. Thomas," as Father Cuervo later claims (p. 107).

In fact, Father Urdánoz, O.P., will claim the same authority for *his* interpretation of St. Thomas, which is diametrically opposed to the exposition of Father Cuervo and of John of St. Thomas (' La inhabitación del Espiritu Santo en el Alma," *Rev. Española de Teología,* VI [1946], p. 516). Father Tromp, S.J., is clearly justified in listing the mode of the inhabitation as one of the theological questions left by the Pope to open discussion. Cf. Sebastian Tromp, S.J., *Mystici Corporis Christi,* 29 iun. 1943, edidit uberrimisque documentis illustravit. "Textus et Documenta," Ser. theol. XXVI, Pont. Univ. Greg. Romae, 1943.

[23] St. Thomas, I *Sent.,* d. 30, q. 1, a. 1: ". . . nihil ex tempore de Deo dicitur nisi quod importat habitudinem ad creaturam."

[24] Cf. St. Thomas, *Sum. Theol.,* I, q. 45, a. 3; a. 2 ad 2.

[25] Cf. St. Thomas, *De Pot.,* q. 7, a. 11: "Et similiter aliqua nomina relativa Deo attribuit intellectus noster, in quantum accipit Deum ut terminum relationum creaturam ad ipsum; unde huiusmodi relationes sunt rationis tantum." Cf. *Sum. Theol.,* I, q. 13, a. 7. Capreolus (*Defensiones Theologicae Divi Thomae,* I *Sent.,* d. 30, q. 1, a. 3; ed. Paban-Pègues, II, p. 319) says excellently: "Secundum theologos et philosophos, communiter verum est quod relationes quibus Deus ad creaturam refertur, non sunt in Deo secundum rem, sed tantum secundum rationem; quia intellectus noster non potest accipere aliquid dici relative ad alterum, nisi aliud sub opposita habitudine intelligat. . . . Invenit in [Deo] virtutem et essentiam et operationem, qua creatura producitur, in ipsum relationem habens; et ideo essentiae illi vel operationi habitudinem attribuit. Et sic, secundum quod intelligit, nomina relativa imponit."

[26] I *Sent.,* d. 14, a. 7, sol. (*Opera Omnia,* ed. Borgnet, XXV, p. 396): ". . . in veritate aeterna substantialiter et accidentaliter [Deo] nihil addi potest: sed tamen aliquid se ad ipsum aliter habere potest, quam ante habuit: et ita dico hoc, quod processio temporalis claudit in se intellectum aeternae processionis, et addit respectum qui causatur ex hoc quod creatura rationalis ex dono Dei aliter se habet ad ipsum in gratia quam ante habuit."

Cf. *Sum. Theol.,* I, Tract. VII, p. 32, memb. 3, sol. 1 (ed. cit., XXXI, p. 347): ". . . dantis ad datum non est relatio originis, quae aliquam ponat distinctionem inter dantem et datum, sed tantum secundum Augustinum relatio habitudinis secundum rationem, quae fundatur in hoc, quod per effectum in creatura rationali causatum, aliter se habet nunc creatura rationalis ad Deum quam prius quando illum effectum non habuit in se causatum: et ideo aliter est in ea Deus nunc, quam prius. Et illa alterietas non ponitur in Deo, sed in creatura. Deus enim in quantum est de se, uno modo se habet ad omnia: quamvis non omnia uno modo se habeant ad ipsum."

[27] *Op. cit.*, d. 37, p. 1, a. 3, q. 2 (ed. cit., I, p. 648): "Diversitas autem modorum essendi accipitur penes diversitatem effectuum, et non qualemcumque, sed solum trimembrum. . . . Quoniam igitur tres sunt modi effectuum, secundum quos creatura diversimode comparatur ad Deum: ideo tantum tribus modis dicitur esse in rebus." (The three effects are those of nature, grace and union, following the comparison of Pseudo-Dionysius, *de Div. Nom.*, Chap. 4.)

[28] *Sum. Theol.*, I, q. 43, a. 2 ad 2: ". . . divinam Personam esse novo modo in aliquo, vel ab aliquo haberi temporaliter, non est propter mutationem divinae Personae, sed propter mutationem creaturae: sicut et Deus temporaliter dicitur Dominus, propter mutationem creaturae.

I *Sent.*, d. 14, q. 2, a. 1, sol. 1 ad 1: ". . . cum dicitur Deus esse ubique, importatur quaedam relatio Dei ad creaturam, quae quidem realiter non est in ipso, sed in creatura. Contingit autem ex parte creaturae istas relationes multipliciter etiam diversificari secundum diversos effectus quibus Deo assimilatur; et inde est quod significatur ut aliter se habens ad creaturam quam prius. Et propter hoc Spiritus sanctus, qui ubique est, secundum relationem aliquam creaturae ad ipsum, potest dici de novo esse in aliquo, secundum novam relationem ipsius creaturae ad ipsum.

Cf. also *ibid.*, q. 1, a. 1: ". . . sic dicetur processio temporalis ex eo quod ex novitate effectus consurgit nova relatio creaturae ad Deum, ratione cujus oportet Deum sub nova habitudine ad creaturam significari, ut patet in omnibus quae de Deo ex tempore dicuntur." Also *ibid.*, d. 15, q. 3, a. 1 and ad 3; d. 37, q. 1, a. 2, sol. and ad 1.

[29] *Cursus Philosophicus Thomisticus*, Logica, II, q. 17, a. 6 (ed. Reiser, I, pp. 602-603): ". . . terminus vel sumitur formalissime in ratione termini oppositi, vel fundamentaliter ex parte absoluti fundantis istam rationem terminandi. Primo modo terminus concurrit pure terminative ad specificationem, non autem causando illam, quia sic est purus terminus et est simul natura et cognitione cum relatione; ergo ut sic non est causa specificans, quia causa non est simul natura, sed prior effectu. Si secundo modo consideratur, habet se ut causa formalis extrinseca, et specificat ad modum obiecti, et sic ex fundamento et termino consurgit unica ratio specificandi relationem, quatenus fundamentum continet in se terminum in proportione et virtute; non enim est ad talem terminum, nisi sit tale fundamentum, et e converso. Et sic quatenus inter se proportionantur, conficiunt unam rationem specificandi relationem quae et tale fundamentum postulat et talem terminum ei correspondentem."

[30] Capreolus, *op. cit.*, a. 1 (II, p. 299): "Dico igitur quod causa efficiens similitudinis prima, est illud quod causat utram albedinem,

vel unam illarum; nam eadem actio terminatur, per se, ad absolutum, et ex consequenti, ad relationem. Sed causa efficiens proxima, est suum fundamentum et terminus; et haec causatio non est per transmutationem, sed per simplicem emanationem; non solum autem fundamentum est causa effectiva relationis, immo et formalis quodammodo, cum relatio ab extremis speciem recipiet, ut patet 5. *Metaphysicae*."

[31] Leo von Rudloff, O.S.B., "Des heiligen Thomas Lehre von der Formalursache der Einwohnung Gottes in der Seele der Gerechten," *Divus Thomas* (Fr.), 1930, pp. 181-182: "Eine auf den ersten Blick durchaus andere Sprache reder der Aquinate im Sentenzenkommentar (1254-1256). Die Lehre dieses Werkes ist—so scheint uns—bisher noch nicht genügend zur Erklärung herangezogen worden. Sie lässt sich kurz auf die Formel bringen: Deus secundum modum novum essendi, *prout res est in sua similitudine,* dicitur esse in nobis."

[32] I *Sent.*, d 15, q. 4, a. 1.

[33] *Sum. Theol.*, I, q. 8, a. 3; q. 43, a. 3. Although in the *Sentences* God is described as present *per modum objecti* (d. 37, Expositio Primae Partis Textus) the formula does not definitively appear until Question 8 of the First Part of the *Summa*. There is no doubt, of course, that St. Thomas regards it as the happiest expression of the solution of the problem.

[34] I *Sent.*, d. 15, q. 1, a. 2. Cf. Expositio Primae Partis Textus.

[35] *Sum. Theol.*, I, q. 43, a. 1.

[36] *Ibid.*, a. 8. Cf. Cajetan on this article: "In 1° articulo huius quaestionis Auctor dixit quod de ratione missionis est processio missi a mittente: loquebatur enim de primaria intentione missionis. Hic autem non oblitus, distinguit, ut secundam intentionem ejusdem adjiceret, praesertim ob reverentiam Augustini, Sanctorum, et Magistri."

[37] I *Sent.*, d. 14, q. 1, a. 2 ad 2; q. 2, a. 1, sol. and ad 1 and 4; a. 2, sol. and ad 3; d. 15, q. 2 ad 2 and ad 5; q. 4, a. 1, sol. and ad 1 and ad 3; d. 16, q. 1, a. 2 ad 3.

[38] *Sum. Theol.*, I, q. 43, a. 5 ad 1 and ad 2.

[39] *Op. cit.*, pp. 183-184: "Diese Stelle ist schwer verständlich und, kann man sagen, auf den ersten Blick verblüffend. Sieht man doch nicht gleich ein, was der Vergleich zwischen der wirklichen Verbindung mit Gott und der ideellen des Erzeugen mit dem Erzeuger bedeutet. Und doch ist die Stelle *von höchstar Bedeutung und erschliesst das Verständnis fur die Lehre des Sentenzenkommentars.* Aller-

dings stellt Thomas hier hohe Anforderungen an die Abstraktionsfähigkeit und das spekulative Vermögen seiner Jünger. Der tiefe Sinn kann nur der folgende sein: Wie das Gezeugte im Endstadium des Zeugungsprozesses mit seinen Wesen, *seiner Idee* verbunden ist, jener Idee, die sich auch im generans verwirklicht findet, so ist das mit der heiligmachenden Gnade gezeirte Geschöpf mit der Idee Gottes verbunden, ist mit ihr eins, da es an diesm Wesen teil hat. Nun ist aber Gott nich ein Ding, das nur an einer Idee (einem Wesen) teil hat, *Gott ist Idee*, seine Idee, *die subsistierende Gottesidee*. Demzufolge ist die Kreatur, die mit der Gottesidee verbunden, eins ist (wie der gezeugte Mensch eins ist mit der Idee des Menschen, sie in sich realisiert), mit dem lebendigen Gott selber verbunden, eins. Man vergliech hierzu die Lehre des hl. Thomás von der Individuation subsistierender Formen: In jeder gestigen Natur kann es nur ein einziges Individuum geben. Wenn auf übernatürliche Weise ein niederes Wesen an einem höheren teil hat, so folgt daraus eine zugleich ideelle und reele, wirkliche und wahrhafte Verbundenheit.

Was heisst nämlich bei geistigen Dingen einander gegenwärtig sein? Von *örtlichem Beieinanderweilen* kann doch nicht die Rede sein. Also bloss von geistigem Zusammengehören, Wenn also ein Geistwesen 'zu Gott gehort,' weil es ihm ähnlich ist, dann ist es *bei* Gott und Gott bei ihm.

Somit haben wir—da die anderen Dinge, wenn man sie als zu Gott zurückkehrend betrachtet, veilmehr unendlich von Gott entfernt, als ihm gegenwärtig sind—zwei *wesentlich verschiedene* Arten göttlicher Gegenwart in den Dingen: In allen Dingen ist Gott wie die Ursache in den Wirkungen (und insofern ist diese Art für alle anderen Arten Voraussetzung). In der mit der heiligmachenden Gnade geschmückkten vernunftbegabten Kreatur wohnt Goot 'wie in seinem Ebenbild.' "

[40] I *Sent.*, d. 14, q. 1, a. 2, ad 2; q. 2, a. 1, ad 1; q. 3 (cf. d. 16, a. 4, sol. and ad 5); d. 15, q. 1, a. 1 ad 4; q. 2 ad 5 and ad 6; q. 4, a. 2 ad 5; etc.

[41] *La structure de l'âme* (Paris, 1927), II, p. 22 and note 2: "Je souligne portant ce mot [effet]. C'est le terme charactéristique de l'opinion de Vasquez."

[42] The word occurs only three times: *Sum. Theol.*, I, q. 43, a. 3, and ad 3; a. 4, ad 2.

[43] *Novarum Defensionum Doctoris Angelici S. Thomae super quatuor Libros Sententiarum* (Hispali, 1517), I. d. 14: "Propter hoc S. Thomas, licet in primo opere, in hac scilicet distinctione illud idem sentire videatur quod isti [nominalisti], in secundo tamen opere,

subtiliter considerans, non assignavit processionem temporalem Dei ad creaturas in aliqua eius operatione, primo et per se, aut secundum effectus quibus Deus circa creaturam rationalem operatur, sed magis secundum operationes creaturae rationalis in Deum, quibus scilicet Deum cognoscit et amat, secundum quas Deus dicitur esse in creatura rationali sicut cognitum in cognoscente at amatum in amante." (Cited by Manuel Cuervo, O.P., *La inhabitación de la Trinidad en toda alma en gracia, según Juan de Santo Thomás* (reprinted from *La Ciencia Tomista*), Salamanca, 1946, p. 52.

[44] The following have been consulted: Capreolus, Cajetan, Ferrariensis, Bañez, Porrecta, Nazarius, Sylvius, Vasquez, Suarez, John of St. Thomas, Salmanticenses, Gonet, Billuart.

[45] In the article previously cited; cf. *supra* page 30, note 39.

[46] Marcel Retailleau, *La Sainte Trinité dans les âmes justes* (Université Catholique d'Angers, 1932).

[47] In the doctorate thesis cited in the note on p. 11.

[48] Joseph Trütsch, SS. *Trinitatis Inhabitatio apud Theologos Recentiores* (Trento, 1949).

[49] J. F. Sagüés, S.J., "El modo de inhabitación del Espiritu Santo según Santo Tomás de Aquino," *Miscelánea Comillas*, II, 1944, pp. 160-201.

[50] The proponents of this view of most immediate interest for this work are Father Paul Galtier, S.J. in his *L'habitation en nous des trois Personnes* (Roma, 1949) and *De SS. Trinitate in Se et in Nobis* (Paris, 1933) and Father Teófilo Urdánoz, O.P., in two articles published in the *Revista Española de Teología*, "La inhabitación del Espiritu Santo en el Alma del Justo" (6 [1946], pp. 466-533) and "Influjo causal de las Divinas Personas en la inhabitación en las almas justas" (8 [1948], pp. 141-202).

With these modern theologians the following may also be listed (their works will be found in the bibliography)—although it should be noted that the interpretations of the central and common fact (that the Trinity is present as cause, as principle, and that this is the formal reason of the inhabitation) are at wide variance: J. Alonso, C.M.F.; L. Chambat, O.S.B.; M. de la Taille, S.J.; P. de Letter, S.J.; E. Delaye, S.J.; M. Donnelly, S.J.; Enrico di S. Teresa, O.C.D.; P. Gachter; P. J. J. de la Immaculada, O.C.D.; F. Joret, O.P.; S. M. Lozano, O.P.; C. Martinez-Gomez; I. G. Menendez-Reigada, O.P.; K. Rahner; X. Zubiri.

⁵¹ *Op. cit.* (cf. note 41). See the bibliography for his numerous articles on the subject.

⁵² E.g., *L'amour de Dieu et la Croix de Jésus* (Paris, n.d., *imprimatur*, 1929). A full listing of works pertinent to the subject will be found in the bibliography.

⁵³ In the fine article cited in note 22. Cf. also, *Summa Theologica de Santo Tomás* (Spanish trans., Madrid, 1948), II, pp. 598-640.

⁵⁴ "The Presence, Mission, and Indwelling of the Divine Persons in the Just," *The Thomist*, XVII (1954), pp. 131-145.

CHAPTER TWO

The Sources of the Scholastic Teaching on the Divine Indwelling

To understand the problem with which St. Thomas was faced in dealing with the divine missions and the indwelling of the Trinity, it is important to understand how these mysteries were accepted by theologians of his own time, what features were generally admitted, on what points disagreement was common or tolerated, what was the common ground on which theological speculation was based: in other words, what was the 'tradition'* concerning the presence of the Trinity to which the medieval theologians gave their adherence. If the un-

---

* It should be noted that the word 'tradition' is used throughout this work in no defined sense, but rather as a vague description of the common store of theological knowledge, more or less widely accepted. On the doctrinal relations of St. Thomas to 'tradition' (in the stricter meaning of Patristic teaching and in the most proper sense of the teaching of the Church), see the articles by G. Geenen, O.P., "Saint Thomas et les Pères," *Dict. théol. cath.*, XV, 1, coll. 738-761; "L'usage des "auctoritates" dans la doctrine du baptême chez S. Thomas d'Aquin," *Ephem. theol. Lovan.*, 15 (1938), pp. 279-329; "The Place of Tradition in the Theology of St. Thomas," *The Thomist*, 15 (1952), pp. 110-135.

disputed facts of this tradition can be established, the problems which then remained for the Schoolmen to solve will be brought into proper perspective, and the reasons which lie behind some of the proffered solutions will become more evident.

But the scholastic tradition on this subject can only be grasped if, in turn, one knows where the medieval teaching represents a mere acceptance of received tradition and where it incorporates new elements of thought and where it introduces its own explanations. Thus it is first of all necessary to consider briefly the sources of medieval tradition: the teaching of Sacred Scripture on the mystery and the doctrine of the Fathers which attempts to explain the revelation contained in Scripture. No intention or pretense of attempting an exhaustive or critical exegesis of these sources dictates this survey: for such there is nether necessity nor time.[1] Merely to recall the incontestable facts of the doctrine of the triune presence as they are revealed in their theological bases will be sufficient for the ends of this study.[2]

The consideration of the sources of scholastic tradition will be divided into two sections. The first will comprise an examination of the remote sources of the common teaching relative to the divine indwelling as they appear in Sacred Scripture and the eastern Fathers; necessarily brief, this survey will rely for confirmation of its facts on the literal significance of the texts quoted and, on controverted questions, on the authority of recognized specialists in the several fields. In the second section, a more specialized study of the immediate sources of St. Thomas' doctrine will be attempted, with particular emphasis on those Latin Fathers — above all, St. Augustine — from whom scholastic tradition receives its inspiration and the authority for its traditional facts.

ARTICLE 1

Remote Sources of the Scholastic Tradition

One of the reasons for the paucity of official teachings of the *magisterium* on the mystery of the union of the just with the Holy Trinity is the very clarity of Sacred Scripture and tradition in affirming the principal features of the mystery. From this teaching the following points can be abstracted:

1) The three divine Persons really, personally and substantially dwell in man.[3]

2) This special presence of the Trinity is entirely distinct from the common presence of God in all things.

3) It is realized only in the just, and therefore in some way by means of grace.

4) It is not exclusive to the Holy Ghost, but because of His personal property it is appropriated to Him.[4]

In this section the reader can see in a cursory manner how these truths are founded in Holy Scripture and how they are brought out by the Fathers, chiefly by those of the eastern branch of the Church, since the Latin Fathers will have little to offer on the subject until the fourth century, at which time they will accept the Tradition affirmed by the eastern Church. The purpose here is not to criticize this evidence but merely to present it, as the necessary preliminary for a comprehension of the tradition the Scholastics will receive and as an aid in the appreciation of that tradition as a vital force for medieval theologians in their grappling with supernatural reality.[5]

1. The Teaching of Sacred Scripture

Adumbrated in the Old Testament ("For the Holy Spirit of discipline will flee from the deceitful, and will withdraw himself from thoughts that are without understanding: and he shall not abide when iniquity cometh in"),[6] it is Christ Himself who most clearly announces the fact of the coming of the divine Persons to the just soul and their abiding in it. "If any one love me, he will keep my word. And my Father will love him: and we will come to him and will make our abode with him."[7] All three Persons, then, will dwell in the just, for the Holy Spirit "is given to us,"[8] and "he that abideth in charity abideth in God, and God in him."[9]

This presence of the Trinity cannot but differ from God's ordinary presence in all things. We must glorify and bear God in our bodies because our members are the "temple of the Holy Ghost."[10] The Spirit of God "dwells" in us, so that we become "temples of God."[11] Therefore, if we contemn or dishonor this temple where God wishes to be honored and adored, it is God Himself whom we dishonor and contemn.[12]

Since the Holy Spirit is not only "in" us but is given to us,[13] we "possess" Him.[14] In Christ we are "signed with the Holy Spirit of promise," so anointed by God and signed by God that He even gives us the Holy Spirit as an earnest (*arrha*) of our eternal glory: an imperfect possession of what we shall have perfectly in the Beatific Vision.[15] Directed by Him we shall be sons of God, and in this spirit of adoption we can cry: Abba,[16] as the Spirit Himself cries in our hearts: Abba.[17] For we are one with Him, and the Father, and the Son in this union: as Christ Himself besought in the prayer to His Father before His passion and death: "that they all may be one, as thou,

Father, in me, and I in thee; that they also may be one in us. . . . I in them and thou in me: that they may be perfect in one."[18]

So unique and distinctive a presence of the Godhead, as is obvious, could not be realized in sinners: "The Lord is far from the wicked."[19] For it is only to those "who are born not of blood, nor of the will of the flesh, nor of the will of man, but of God" that is given the power to be made sons of God, to receive the Son of God and to believe in His name.[20] It is only by what theologians call sanctifying grace, then, that the divine Persons dwell in the soul. To those who love God, Father and Son and Holy Ghost will come;[21] They will remain so long as man remains in Their love.[22] "But you are not in the flesh," writes Paul to the Romans, "but in the spirit, if so be it that the Spirit of God dwell in you. Now if any man have not the Spirit of Christ, he is none of his. And if Christ be in you, the body indeed is dead, because of sin: but the spirit liveth, because of justification."[23]

The connection between the triune presence, realized in the grace-state, and the divine missions is clearly evident in respect to the Holy Ghost. "Because you are sons," observes St. Paul, "God hath sent the Spirit of his Son into your hearts."[24] Christ promises to send the Paraclete (whom the Father also sends in Christ's name, to teach all things)[25] when he departs this earth.[26]

The mission of the Son is usually described in terms which can only refer to the 'mission of missions,' His Incarnation.[27] The text from St. Mark — "whosoever shall receive me receiveth not me but him that sent me"[28] — which at first glance seems to affirm the invisible mission, on closer inspection does not even refer to the visible mission of the Son of God, but rather to Christ's mission as man. Nevertheless, that the Second Person not only comes to us in the indwelling but is sent to us is indirectly implied in the fact of the conjunction of His visible mission with His presence as cause of sanctification in the souls of the just. And St. Augustine[29] sees a direct affirmation of it in the words of Wisdom: "Send him [Wisdom, i.e., the Son] out of thy holy heaven, and from the throne of thy majesty, that he may be with me, and may labour with me."[30]

The fact that this sublime mystery is peculiarly attributed by Sacred Scripture to the Third Person is abundantly evident, as the texts already quoted sufficiently show. He is Love itself, and this His proper name;[31] and it is by love that the Trinity comes to man. But that this attribution is not His by personal warrant but only in virtue of appropriation,[32] can only be shown indirectly, although no less clearly and certainly than direct testimony would give us.

The central point in this respect in the teaching of Sacred Scripture is not that the relations between the Holy Spirit and the supernatural life are affirmed, but that they are in no way exclusively reserved to Him. If He dwells within us, so also do the Son and the Father.[33] We live by the Spirit, but Christ is also our life.[34] "Holy" is not a name proper to Him but applied to Jesus as well.[35] And St. John clearly attributes the role of sanctifier to Christ, by no means restricting it to the Third Person.[36] Even the title of Charity is not exclusively His.[37]

So one can only conclude from these facts that in Sacred Scripture the indwelling pertains to the Holy Spirit in no more exclusive and personal way than the inspiration of the sacred books, the revelations of the prophets, the virginal conception of Christ, the assistance promised to the Apostles or any other of the external works usually attributed to Him.

From this scriptural testimony it is clear that the substance of the mystery is revealed. But the explanation of its causes is only hinted at, and it will be left to the theological labors of the Fathers and of later ages to develop the basic facts that have been revealed into an orderly doctrinal exposition.

2. The Doctrine of the Greek Fathers

Since the Church is the rule of faith — a condition *sine qua non* of its formal object, in technical terminology — it is necessary to know how these utterances of Sacred Scripture are understood by the *magisterium* before they can be accepted as positively as they have been summarized in the four points mentioned above. As a matter of fact, however, tradition has unswervingly affirmed the literal significance of the texts that have been quoted. One has only to turn to the Fathers to see the truth of this statement, chiefly to the Fathers of the Greek Church, since they first teach these facts received from the sacred books in such written accounts as have come down to us. In this examination of sources the reader will notice how this tradition leads to the doctrine of the Latin Fathers, from whom the Scholastics directly inherit it.

Presentation of the doctrine of the Greek Fathers will be chronological rather than systematic, to indicate the growth of the understanding of the doctrine of the inhabitation and to bring into clear light the chronological contributions of the great eastern writers. But again it should be noted that the attempt will be only to give some significant texts illustrating this tradition; critical examination and justification of the interpretations given will be presupposed on the basis of the scientific studies previously referred to.*

A direct echo of the teachings of St. Paul and St. John is found in the letters of St. Ignatius of Antioch, martyred under Trajan (97-118). "Guard your flesh as the temple of God," he exhorts the Philadelphians;[38] and to the Ephesians he writes: "Members of His Son, enjoy your constant participation of God."[39] His language is that of St. Paul when he calls his flock "Christ-bearers"[40] and "God-bearers."[41] So that here is as clear an attestation to the fact of the indwelling of the Trinity as the words of Scripture understood literally; and indirectly he teaches that it is not the prerogative of the Holy Ghost, since he prefers *theophoros* and *christophoros* to the *pneumaticos* of later Fathers.

"The first, the most ancient of the doctors and fathers of the Church,"[42] St. Irenaeus, Bishop of Lyons, continues this tradition in the second century (c.140-c.202). "Those who are baptized receive the Spirit of God," he teaches in the *Demonstration of Apostolic Teaching*;[43] and they shall not remain just "unless the Holy Spirit abide with them in strict conjunction. But the Spirit from God given in baptism abides in him who receives Him, so long as he lives in truth and sanctity."[44] The same doctrine — the indwelling of the Trinity a condition of man's perfection, dependent on the preservation of grace — is found in his magnificent apologetic, *Against Heresies*.[45]

Clement of Alexandria (c. 150-211/15) and Origen (185/6-254/5) represent the early tradition of the great Egyptian school of theology. And that tradition is an outright acceptance of the facts provided by Sacred Scripture: the Trinity, the three divine Persons, dwell in the just soul, and so long as They remain the soul re-

* Cf. *supra*, p. 35, note 1.

mains holy.[46] "I know what is an inhabited soul," Origen writes:

> and I know what is a deserted soul. If it does not have God, if it does not have Christ who has said: 'my Father and I shall come to him and We shall take up our abode in him,' if it does not have the spirit, the soul is deserted. It is inhabited when it is filled with God, when it has Christ, when the Holy Spirit is in it.[47]

The great combatant against the first heresies concerning the Third Person of the Holy Trinity, St. Athanasius, continues the tradition of Alexandria in teaching the same truths:

> If we love one another, God dwells in us. We recognize that we remain in Him and He in us in that He has given us his Spirit . . . God being in us, the Son, He also, is in us, for He has said so Himself: 'My Father and I shall come and We shall there take up our abode.'[48]

So we come to St. Basil, who, with St. Cyril of Alexandria, is claimed by the sponsors of the special role of the Holy Ghost as their chief support.[49] But the great fourth century theologian (c. 330-379), the theologian of the Holy Spirit, shows only that the divine qualities of sanctification, divinization, inhabitation are *properly* predicated of the Third Person *as compared with creatures;* anxious to vindicate the divinity of the Spirit against the attacks of the heretics, he still does not claim that these qualities are proper to the Holy Ghost in comparison with the other divine Persons — indeed, he could not, for the force of his argument rests on the fact that these notes are characteristic of the divinity as such, of the Father and of the Son, and hence since they are predicated of the Third Person prove His divinity as well.[50]

The same observation is valid — for the same procedure is followed and the same essential teaching is proclaimed — for St. Gregory of Nyssa,[51] St. Epiphanius,[52] Didymus the Blind.[53] And it is no less true of St. Cyril of Alexandria, the last and chief of the Greek Fathers with respect to Trinitarian theology.[54]

Gross can remark with reason, then, in a phrase that summarizes the proper interpretation of these great doctors, that they have this in common: they interest themselves in the notion of divinization less for itself than for the fact that it offers them arguments to prove the divinity of the Word and of the Holy Spirit.[55] If this fact is borne in mind, the interpretation of certain passages in their works which suggest a personal intervention in the work of sanctification, unique to the Third Person, becomes clear: they certify this work as His not in denial of the common workings of the Trinity *ad extra* but in affirmation of the Holy Spirit's participation in that work and therefore proof of His divinity. It is the law of appropriation which is operative in the Fathers of this epoch; and if this is recalled as a basic fact in understanding them, as they remembered it as a basic theological principle, one can listen to their utterances on the subject with great theological profit.

St. Basil has this beautiful passage on the indwelling of the Spirit in the souls of the just:

> He fashions them spiritual, those who are cleansed from all soiling, growing lightsome in the communion they have with him. And as bright and glittering bodies touched by a ray become themselves beyond measure brilliant, so the souls who bear the Spirit and are illumined by the Spirit become themselves spiritual and send forth grace to others. From this source is perseverance in God, from this source similitude with God, and — than

which nothing more sublime can be sought — from this source you become godlike.'[56]

Didymus (c. 313-398), blind heir of Basil and the Gregorys, was content to repeat their doctrine. The Three are one in Their relation with men, and it is the grace-state which necessarily comes for Their coming and is a condition of Their sojourn in us: "The Holy Spirit glorifies the Son," he writes in his short and magnificent treatise on the Third Person:

> in showing and manifesting Him to those whose pure heart is worthy to see and to understand that the Son is the splendor of the substance and the image of the invisible God. In His turn, this image showing Itself to chaste souls glorifies the Father, in making Him appear to those who know Him not, for He has said: 'who sees Me, sees also my Father.' But the Father, revealing the Son to those who have merited to come to the summit of knowledge, glorifies His only Son, in showing His magnificence and His power. And finally, the Son Himself, in according the Holy Spirit to those who by their preparation have been made worthy of this gift, glorifies the Spirit, in manifesting the subblimity of His glorification and the virtue of His grandeur.[57]

Noteworthy in this pasasge is the insistence of the blind bishop on the *manifestation* of the Persons. He connects this notion only incidentally with the coming of the Holy Spirit, to be sure; and with His coming alone. Yet here is a suggestion which will bear rich fruit in St. Augustine's explanation of the divine missions; and it will have its full development with the medieval theologians.

Another notion the Fathers add to their affirmation of the common truths concerning the mystery which they receive from Scripture is its intimate connection with their beloved doctrine of the image of God in man. Although this idea is the common property of them all (it has, after all, obvious roots in revelation itself), it is perhaps best expressed by St. Cyril of Alexandria.

> 'You are signed by the Holy Spirit of promise.' If, signed by the Holy Spirit, we are made conformable to God, how can that by which the image of the divine essence and the signs of uncreated nature are imprinted on us — how can that be created? Neither does the Holy Spirit — the very likeness of a painter — depict the divine essence in us while He is something other than it; nor in this way does He lead us to the similitude of God. But being God and proceeding from God, so in the hearts of those who receive him he is imprinted after the manner of a seal, and He depicts His nature both by communication of Himself and by His likeness to the beauty of the archetype, and He restores to man the image of God.[58]

Conclusions: The examples that have been cited from the eastern Fathers, partial and *à parti pris* though they be, illustrate the continuous tradition of the Church in respect to the central facts of the inhabitation of the Trinity. They clearly affirm the special nature of this presence, its substantial reality, the fact that it is common to the three Persons as such, the necessity of grace —a state of righteousness—for its realization. Properly interpreted, they will be understood to attribute this mystery to the Holy Spirit only on the grounds of appropriation.[59]

The connection between the divine missions and the indwelling is less explicitly advanced, but it is latent and indirect in all they say, if not precisely phrased.[60]

Two "new" ideas spring into prominence in the thinking of the eastern Fathers on the subject: the notion of manifestation of the Persons coming (or sent) to us, and the relation between the image of the Trinity and Its indwelling. In the chapter to follow, in tracing and delineating the scholastic tradition in which St. Thomas worked, the development of these notions and their integration in the received doctrine of the mystery will stand out as the most prominent contributions added by the Schoolmen toward the attempt to explain the common teaching.

ARTICLE 2

Immediate Sources of the Scholastic Teaching

The investigation of the primary sources of scholastic tradition (in the specific form in which St. Thomas received it) comprises two sections. The first section is an exposition of the doctrine of the Latin Fathers in general. A special study of the thought of St. Augustine follows this general exposé, since in all matters he is the Scholastics' primary patristic authority but most especially is he their source in the elucidation of the mysteries of the divine missions and the divine inhabitation.

1. The Teaching of the Latin Fathers in General

Although doctrinal works by the Fathers of the Latin Church are less rich than those of the Greek Fathers, despite the paucity of written evidence on the mystery no one can doubt the existence of the same tradition. It is indicated in the famous treatise of Novatian, *On the Trinity*, composed by him when he was yet a Catholic, the first Latin work ever composed at Rome on a theological subject (250). An explanation of the Christian faith as formulated in the Creed, it owes much to Tertullian and perhaps Hippolytus; what is of interest is the fact that he explicitly predicates the divine attributes of the Holy Ghost, and among them the fact of the indwelling.[61]

Only in the fourth century, however, do the great lights of the western tradition appear; and with them is found firm affirmation of the common teaching that was evident among the Greeks.

Thus St. Hilary in his *De Trinitate* (written between 356-359) will merely echo the tradition that the Church has accepted. He writes:

> We are all spiritual, if the Spirit of God is in us. But this Spirit of God is also the Spirit of Christ. And when the Spirit of Christ is in us, there is yet in us the Spirit of Him who raised Christ from the dead, and He who raised Christ from the dead shall also vivify our mortal bodies because of His Spirit dwelling within us. We are vivified, therefore, by Him who raised Christ from the dead because of the Spirit of Christ dwelling within us.[62]

In the *De Spiritu Sancto* of the great Bishop of Milan the traditional doctrine again finds a restatement. This work, and the fact of Jerome's translation on papal orders of the treatise of Didymus, forcibly demonstrate the acceptance which the theology of the Greeks obtained in the West and the influence it wielded. St. Ambrose, as a matter of fact, studied both Origen and St. Basil; St. Jerome, it is known, spent a month with Didymus at the latter's school for catechists in Alexandria. So one can hardly be surprised to find in St. Ambrose's teaching on the Holy Ghost, which he wrote in 381/2, not only the doctrine taught by the Greek Fathers but their very expressions.[63] So, for example, he takes over and makes his own their characteristic explanation of the inhabitation in terms of the image of God in man.

"We are signed, therefore," he writes:

> in the Spirit from God. For as in Christ we die that we may be reborn, so also in the Spirit we are signed in order that we may possess His splendor and image and grace; which is indeed a spiritual seal. For even though we are signed in the body in semblance, yet we are signed in truth in the heart, since the Holy Spirit expresses in us the likeness of a heavenly image.[64]

In a yet more explicit passage he enunciates the following facts: the indwelling of the Holy Ghost; the connection of His being given to us and His invisible mission; the necessity of grace for the inhabitation; the reality of the presence of the divine Persons—the whole Tradition, in other words, which the eastern Fathers hold on the ground of scriptural revelation.[65]

But it is in St. Augustine, as might be expected, that are found the most complete and profound writings on the subject. His doctrine must be considered in some detail before taking up the theologians of the Middle Ages: he is their authority *par excellence*.[66]

2. The Teaching of St. Augustine

The two principal sources of St. Augustine's doctrine for the Scholastics are his *De Trinitate* and his 187th letter, *ad Dardanum, De Praesentia Dei,* the work from which their doctrine on the presence of God is drawn.* From this last a passage admirably sums up Augustine's restatement of the common notions on the inhabitation:

> It is much more marvelous that, while God is everywhere entire, He nevertheless does not dwell in all things. But who dares to think—unless someone is completely ignorant of the inseparability of the Trinity — that the Father or Son can dwell in someone in whom the Holy Ghost does not dwell, or the Holy Ghost in someone in whom the Father and Son [do not dwell]? Hence it must be acknowledged that God is everywhere by the presence of divinity, but He is not everywhere by the grace of inhabitation. For because of this inhabitation, where beyond doubt the grace of His love is perceived, we do not say 'Our Father who is everywhere'—even though this be true—but 'Our Father who is in heaven,' so that in the prayer we rather recall His temple to mind, which we ourselves should be, and in so far as we are, just so far do we belong to His fellowship and His adopted family.[67]

From this summation the following truths can be extracted: 1) the entire Trinity, and each member thereof, really and substantially and personally dwells in man; 2) this is a unique presence, utterly distinct from God's common presence in all things; 3) it is realized only in

---

* It should be noted that even though only one quotation is given in support of each of these points, and that either from the *De Trinitate* or *Epistula* 187, there is an abundance of texts which we might possibly cite in confirmation of the particular aspects of the inhabitation to be illustrated. But since the primary purpose is not to elucidate the doctrine of St. Augustine but merely to indicate his influence, the citation of further evidence, from these or other works (of which evidence there is more than a sufficiency), seems superfluous and pedantic.

those in a state of grace; 4) it is in no way proper to any one Person.

Great as these affirmations are, the profound and fecund mind of the greatest Latin Father is not content merely to repeat the teaching of the tradition he received. His own deep and intimate study and contemplation of the mysteries of the Trinity and of the presence of God leads him to a new conclusion respecting the indwelling which constitutes a genuine theological contribution to our grasp of the mystery. Taking an idea previously noted in Didymus* — that of a manifestation of the Persons—he first connects it with Their visible missions and then applies it to Their invisible missions as an explanation of the indwelling.

To answer the objections of the heretics that the missions of the Son and the Holy Spirit imply inferiority, he proposes in his treatise on the Trinity the solution that a mission is nothing else than a manifestation in time of a divine Person: "The invisible Father, one with the Son invisible with Him, by making the same Son visible is said to have sent Him."[68] The purpose of this manifestation is obvious: to dispose the souls of men to recognize the truth.[69]

The true notion of a mission, then, Augustine points out, has to be determined not from the eternal point of view but from the temporal, and the difference of equality implied by the missions comes not from the eternal processions themselves but from the fact of those proces-

---

* Cf. *supra*, pp. 44. It is not suggested that Augustine notes this idea in Didymus, and develops derivatively a notion barely hinted at in the Greek Doctor (although the possibility cannot be entirely eliminated). In fact, quite the opposite is suggested: that Augustine's careful and logical elaboration of the idea from its foreshadowing in Scripture to its function as explanation indicates a completely original contribution, even so far as inspiration is concerned.

sions being recognized in time. Such a notion has a wider application than its explanation of the visible missions; it must be extended to the invisible missions as well, if the equality of the divine Persons is to be preserved. So he extends the concept, which takes its origin in the fact of the visible missions of the Son and Holy Spirit, to explain Their invisible missions as well.[76] In both cases, a proceeding Person is known in time as coming forth from another Person or Persons, i.e., *known precisely in His divine relations,* in the one case through sensible means, in the other through insensible means.

"He is sent to someone," he writes of the Second Person:

> at the very time when He is known and perceived by some one, insofar as He can be known and perceived by the grasp of a rational soul progressing toward God or perfected in God. It is not, therefore, by the fact that He is born of the Father that the Son is said to be sent; but either by the fact that the Word made flesh appears in this world ... or that He is perceived in time by the mind of someone, as it is said: 'Send him [Wisdom] that he may be with me and may labor with me.'[71]

The same facts apply to the mission of the Holy Spirit. "Just as 'to be born' is for the Son 'to be from the Father,' so 'to be sent' is for the Son 'to be known that He is from another.' And as 'to be the gift of God' is for the Holy Spirit 'to proceed from the Father,' so 'to be sent' is 'to be known that He proceeds from Him.' "[72] The divine missions, visible and invisible, may be summed up in the phrase: *mitti est cognosci.*

For Augustine, therefore, a mission necessarily implies some sort of manifestation of a proceeding Person. But because of this very fact, one must carefully distinguish between the processions themselves and the knowledge of them acquired in time: hence there is no basis for the heretical contention that the missions are incompatible with divinity. To send does not involve authority but rather the intention of making evident the proceeding Persons or Their processions; *to be sent* is to be known or knowable in time. The authority of God is entailed not in respect to the Persons, then, but in respect to something created, by means of which the Persons become recognizable by the rational creature on whose behalf the Persons are sent.

Two new notions evolve from this profound theorizing. The first proclaims the practical identification of the indwelling of the divine Persons with the missions of the Son and the Holy Ghost, and Their sending by the Father; it is new in the sense that Augustine explicitly unites two scriptural teachings which are theologically separable and in no way necessarily united. The other involves a definition of the missions—and therefore of the inhabitation — in terms of temporal and created knowledge of the proceeding and indwelling Persons, or at least of a unique and direct connection between the two.

This last is truly an original idea with the great Doctor of the Church, a real testimony to the theological fertility of his saintly mind. But how is it to be understood? Although the knowledge involved in the visible missions of Son and Holy Ghost is evident enough, in what sense can They (and the Father who sends them) be known in their invisible indwelling? And what is the precise connection between this manifestation and the stupendous fact manifested? Does it precede, or follow, or accompany? Is the knowledge in some way a determining factor of the missions or does it presuppose something? And if so what is presupposed?

St. Augustine neither asks nor answers these questions directly, because they were not to his purpose; he remains content to have solved the objections of the heretics. But he does suggest in what direction the answers may lie when he resolves another difficulty, the question whether the manifestation required for the divine missions is necessarily actual.

In the epistle previously quoted, the saint responds negatively to this further question—an obvious response since the missions certainly come to those who cannot have actual knowledge of them:

> God is the inhabitor of some not yet knowing God, and not [the inhabitor] of some knowing God. For those who knowing God do not glorify Him as God do not belong to the temple of God. To the temple of God belong children sanctified by the sacrament of Christ and born by the Holy Spirit, who are not yet capable of knowing God. The first, Him whom they could know they could not have; these could have Him before they could know Him. But most blessed are those who have this possession of God because they know Him.[73]

Father Galtier, S.J., comments on this passage that it "formally excludes the knowledge of God as necessary to His inhabitation in just souls,"[74] but in his exposition of Augustine's doctrine he carefully refrains from quoting the last sentence of the passage. What Augustine actually seems to say, if one considers the whole passage, is that *actual* knowledge of God need not be present for the indwelling, that *any* knowledge of God does not suffice, but that *some sort* of knowledge of God, founded on the grace-state, at least a *habitual* knowledge, is intimately connected with the presence of God in the soul, and that those in whom this knowledge is realized actually are most blessed. Hence an objective reader cannot but prefer the commentary of Peter Lombard on this text to that of the learned Jesuit. The Master of the Sentences says: "Here Augustine declares to a certain extent how God dwells in someone, that is, is possessed, when namely He is so in someone that He can be known and loved by him."[75]

The Bishop of Hippo in this refinement of his theory at least suggests an explanation of how the inhabitation takes place. Do his words indicate any more than the hint of a solution? If taken in their strictest and most formal sense, it would seem not. The connection has been made, but its determination and explanation still must be considerably clarified before anything approaching a 'theory' of the inhabitation can be recognized.[76] It will remain for the great Scholastics to attempt to formulate a theological construction from the truths bequeathed them by tradition; but this suggestive instrument—the notion of manifestation—that Augustine has discovered and placed at their disposal will be the most important single means employed by the medieval doctors to explain the divine indwelling and missions. In this respect, the contribution of the Bishop of Hippo can hardly be overvalued.

One more point needs to be noted before we pass to the immediate tradition of St. Thomas. Does the great theologian utilize the fertile notion of the image of God to explain the triune presence? In view of the prevalence of this notion among the eastern Fathers (to say nothing of its adumbrations in Holy Scripture) and its acceptance by his immediate predecessors, St. Ambrose and St. Jerome; in view of his own predilection for the idea and his complicated explanation of it in the last part, from the eighth to the fifteenth books, of his *De Trinitate*

—in view of these facts one anticipates before the fact what the saint affirms in the *De Praesentia Dei*: that by living piously we receive the similitude of God, and in that similitude we draw closer to Him; and though He always is present to us, as light is to a blind man, this similitude brings us in contact with Him, as the power of sight gives a new contact with light to the blind man.[77]

Here again, however, the notion is rather suggested by St. Augustine than developed; it is certainly not an essential, nor even perhaps an integral, part of his explanation. The reasons for this should become clearer when among the Scholastics the difficulties which the combination of these two mysteries produces in the intellectual order will come to the fore. Whether Augustine foresaw the confusion likely to result or not, the fact remains that the mystery of man as an image of the Trinity cannot be considered as an elucidation used by Augustine to explain the mystery of the indwelling. At most it is accorded casual mention in this function, an illustration rather than an explanation, a confirmation from a different aspect rather than an instrument of analysis.

ARTICLE 3

Conclusion

In their writings on the Holy Trinity—most especially in the works in which they prove the divinity of the Third Person against the heretics—the Fathers of the

Oriental Church unhesitantly and unanimously affirm the literal reality of the astonishing facts revealed in Sacred Scripture: that the three divine Persons are really present in a special manner in the soul in the state of grace. This tradition is accepted wholeheartedly by the Latin Fathers, without any break or change in the interpretation. St. Augustine will examine the notion of the inhabitation most profoundly of all, and from his scientific analysis two major steps will be taken toward a theological explanation of the mystery: the connection of the indwelling with the divine missions, and the description of these in terms of a manifestation.

NOTES

[1] For the exegesis of pertinent texts of Sacred Scripture, cf. Bardy, *Le Saint-Esprit en nous et dans l'Eglise d'après le Nouveau Testament* (Albi, 1950); Lebreton, *Histoire du dogme de la Trinité* (8th ed.), I, Bk. III, Chap. 3 and 6; Prat, *La théologie du saint Paul* (7th ed.), II, Bk. V, Chap. 3, par. 2; Galtier, *Le Saint Esprit en nous d'après les Pères Grecs,* Part I, Chap. 1, pp. 21-30. See the same works for the evidence from the Fathers; also Galtier, *L'habitation en nous des trois personnes,* Part I, Chap. 2, Art. 2 and 3; Froget, *De l'habitation du Saint-Esprit dans les âmes justes,* Part I, Chap 2, nn. II, III and IV; de Régnon, *Etudes de théologie positive sur la S. Trinité* (Paris, 1898), IV.

Briefer and more synthetic accounts of the positive sources will be found in Galtier, *De SS. Trinitate in Se et in Nobis* (2nd ed. Paris, 1933), pp. 274 ff.; Garrigou-Lagrange, *De Deo Trino et Creatore* (Taurini, 1943), pp. 205 ff.; Retailleau, *La Sainte Trinité dans les âmes justes* (Université catholique d'Angers, 1932), pp. 195-219, 242-258; Trütsch, SS. *Trinitatis Inhabitatio apud Theologos Recentiores* (Trento, 1947), pp. 27 ff.

Abundant Patristic texts will be found, of course, in the works of Petau, Thomassin, Scheeben, Waeffelert and other supporters of the theory of some sort of union proper to the Holy Ghost. But these will obviously cite only the selected texts which advance their peculiar theories.

[2] To call the facts to be cited 'incontestable' does not mean that they have not been, in fact, called into question by this or that theologian at this or that time, as will appear when they are treated singly. It does mean that they have sufficient authority to merit unassailability, considering the weight of the tradition behind them.

[3] This is not to be undertsood in the sense in which de Régnon and others hold that the divine Persons, in virtue of their "proper and special character," have a proper mode of indwelling peculiar to each, and that each exercises a special role and a "distinct personal influence" relative to man's justification (cf. *op. cit.,* pp. 542, 552-553). A more modern version of the same theory founded on de la Taille's "Actuation créée par l'Acte incréé (*Recherches de science religieuse,* 18 [1928], pp. 253-268) is proposed by the American Jesuit, Father Malachi Donnelly, in the Catholic Theological

Society of America's *Proceedings of the Fourth Annual Meeting,* 1949, n.p., pp. 39-77. See also his article "The Inhabitation of the Holy Spirit: A Solution according to de la Taille," *Theological Studies,* 8 (1947), pp. 445-470. P. de Letter proposes a modification of this presentation in "Sanctifying Grace and Our Union with the Holy Trinity," *Theological Studies,* 13 (1952), pp. 33-58, which criticizes Donnelly on minor points but leaves the theory substantially intact; Fr. Donnelly replied to this criticism in the same magazine, *ibid.,* pp. 190-204. The same fundamental position is espoused and promulgated by François Bourassa, S.J. See his articles: "Les missions divines et le surnaturel chez Saint Thomas d'Aquin," *Sciénces ecclésiastiques,* 1 (1948), pp. 41-94; "Dom Chambat et l'habitation des personnes divines," *ibid.,* 3 (1950), pp. 194-198; "Adoptive Sonship: Our Union with the Divine Persons," *Theological Studies,* 13 (1952), pp. 309-335. Father de la Taille's explanations of his theory have been collected, and the French articles translated, by Cyril Vollert, S.J. in the brochure, *The Hypostatic Union and Created Actuation by Uncreated Act* (published by West Baden College, West Baden Springs, Indiana).

Since de la Taille's theory is itself fundamentally opposed to basic Thomistic principles (cf. T. U. Mullaney, O.P., "The Incarnation: de la Taille and Thomistic Tradition," *The Thomist,* 17 [1954], pp. 1-42), an explanation of the divine indwelling based upon it will necessarily deviate from St. Thomas' solution.

Certainly the Persons are present as distinct and as They are in Themselves: but this does not mean and cannot mean that They intervene in the created order and communicate Themselves to us each (or one of them) *in a proper and unique manner.* There is a capital distinction here, the ignorance or ignoring of which has caused great confusion in interpreting the Fathers. See Galtier, *Le Saint Esprit en nous d'après les Pères Grecs* (Analecta Gregoriana XXIV. Rome. 1946), Introduction, "La question posée et à poser," pp. 1-20.

[4] One does not forget the modern theories which, following Petau, 'the father of patristic studies,' directly contest this last conclusion: so Thomassin, Scheeben, de Régnon, Waefflert, de la Taille, Dockx, *et al.* These teach a special proper influence of the Holy Ghost in the work of sanctification in general and the inhabitation in particular. The question does not directly concern this thesis, and shall not be discussed, although in fact it appears to be a theological impossibility. So far as the evidence of positive theology is concerned, Father Galtier, S.J., shows (in his critical study of these sources cited in the previous note) that if the Fathers be read in their his-

torical context, with regard to their polemical purpose and stylistic peculiarities, and with reference to their other teachings — according, that is to say, to recognized principles of critical exegesis — then the texts which seem to favor a distinct influence of the Holy Ghost appear no stronger than their attribution of the conception of Christ and the inspiration of Scripture to the same Third Person: a case of simple appropriation. The conclusion of Father Urdánoz, O.P. ("Influjo causal de las Divinas Personas en la inhabitación en las almas justas," *Revista Española de Teología,* 8 [1948], p. 159) that in these Petavian theories we are dealing with "interpretaciones arbitrarias y subjectivas de teólogos positivos que no pueden presentarse como base de una theología constructiva" is only too justified by the history of the question.

This is not to overlook the fact, on the other hand, that Galtier's position has been seriously criticized (especially by G. Philips, "Le Saint Esprit en nous, à propos d'un livre récent," *Ephem. theol. Lovan.,* 24 [1948], pp. 127-135) as being too theological and polemical, and insufficiently historical and objective; that criticism, however, and others similar to it, seem dictated more by the individual polemics of their authors and their own personal theories on the point than by an objective analysis of Galtier's work. The approbation that work has received by men such as Glorieux (*Mélanges de science religieuse,* 4 [1947], p. 382) and Lebon (*Revue d'histoire ecclésiastique,* 43 [1948], pp. 761 f.) more than offsets the adverse opinion of Galtier's critics.

[5] For the later history of the problem of the presence of the Trinity in the just soul, the following works can be consulted. Retailleau, *op cit.,* pp. 49-91, for a brief summary; for the Nominalists, Father Cuervo's article, already cited, pp. 50-86, an excellent survey of the period between St. Thomas and John of St. Thomas which well explains the necessity for, and the value of, John of St. Thomas' revival of the theory of the Angelic Doctor; for the German Nominalists, especially the school of Cologne, see M. Rivière, "Justification," *Dict. théo. cath.,* coll. 2158 ff.; the best historical study of the 19th century, with reference to the historical tradition from Lessius on which prompted the attitude of the 19th century theologians, is to be found in H. Schauf, *Die Einwohnung des Hl. Geistes.* Die Lehre von der nichtapproprierten. Einwohnung des Hl. Geistes als Beiträg zur Theologiegeschichte des 19. Jahrhunderts unter besonderer Berücksichtigung der beiden Theologen C. Passaglia and Cl. Schrader. "Freiburger Theol. Studien," Frieburg (im B.), 1941 (his interpretations, however, must be understood as advanced by one who himself main-

tains a *proprium* theory, *op. cit.*, pp. 224-254); on the same subject, A. Eröss, "Die Lehre über die Einwohnung des Hl. Geistes bei M. Jos. Scheeben," *Scholastik*, 11 (1936), pp. 370-395. For a list of modern opinions, see J. Bittremieux, "Utrum unio cum Spiritu Sancto sit causa formalis filiationis adoptivae iusti," *Ephem. theol. Lovan.*, 10 (1933), pp. 427-440; Trütsch, *op. cit.*; P. de Letter, S.J., "Sanctifying Grace and the Divine Indwelling," *Theological Studies*, 14 (1953), pp. 242-272.

[6] Wisdom 1:5.

[7] John 14:23.

[8] Rom. 5:5.

[9] I John 4:16.

[10] *Ibid.* 3:16.

[11] Cf. I Cor. 3:17; Eph. 4:30.

[12] I Thess. 4:8.

[13] I Cor. 6:19.

[14] Eph. 1:13; cf. 4:30.

[15] II Cor. 1:21-22. The Vulgate translates the Greek weakly as *pignus* (*pledge*). A Semitic borrowing, the word originally signified the money given by a purchaser to seal a bargain and as a guarantee of future payment in full. See Zorell, *Novi Testamenti Lexicon Graecum*, p. 74.

[16] Rom. 8:11-16.

[17] Gal. 4:6.

[18] John 17: 21-23. On this passage see M. J. Lagrange, O.P., *Evangile selon S. Jean* (Paris, 1925), pp. 450-451.

[19] Prov. 15:29; cf. Psalm 118:155.

[20] John 1:11-13.

[21] John 14:23 and Rom. 5:5.

[22] I John 4:16.

[23] Rom. 8:9-10.

[24] Gal. 4:6.

25 John 14:26.

26 *Ibid.*, 16:7.

27 E.g. John 3:17, 5:37; Gal. 4:4; Rom. 8:3.

28 Mark 9:36.

29 IV *De Trinitate*, Chap. 20, n. 28 (PL 42:907). St. Thomas quotes the same passage as his argument from authority in the Sed Contra of the article which shows the fittingness of the invisible mission of the Son (*Sum. Theol.*, I, q. 43, a. 5).

30 Wisdom 9:10.

31 *Sum. Theol.*, I, q. 37, a. 1.

32 Father Lebreton, S.J., observes that in St. Paul "l'Esprit et le Christ sont representés comme l'élément vital du Chrétien" (*op. cit.*, I, p. 434). Even more explicitly, Father Prat, S.J., states: "Les trois personnes contribuent ensemble, chacune dans sa sphère d'appropriation, à l'oeuvre commune de notre salut" (*op. cit.*, II, p. 159). For a fuller working of this argument see Galtier, *Le Saint Esprit en nous d'après les Pères Grecs*, pp. 21-30.

33 John 14:23; Rom. 8:9-10; I John 3:24.

34 Compare Gal. 4:25 with Col. 3:4 and Philip. 1:22.

35 Acts 2:27, 3:14, 4:27 and 30.

36 Cf. John 15:4-5; I John 2:24 and 29; 3:24.

37 Cf. Galtier, *op. cit.*, pp. 27-29.

38 *Philad.*, 7:2 (SS. *Patrum Apostolicorum Opera*, ed. Sixtus Colombo, S.S. S.E.I., Torino, 1949; p. 375).

39 *Ephes.*, 4:2 (p. 303); 15:3 (p. 315).

40 *Ibid.*, 9:2 (p. 309).

41 *Ibid.*, 20:2 (p. 321).

42 Galtier, *op. cit.*, p. 37. From St. Irenaeus on the Fathers will commonly attribute the inhabitation to the Holy Spirit, as they do the work of sanctification. But, as has been stated (cf. *supra*, p. 39, and note 32), this attribution must be understood as appropriation and the texts must be read with that fact in mind.

43 *Patrologia Orientalis* (Griffin-Nau), XII, n. 7, p. 760.

⁴⁴ *Ibid.*, n. 42, p. 777.

⁴⁵ *Adv. Haer.*, V, 6:1, 2 (PG 7:1137-1139). Cf. 8 (*ibid.*, 1141-1142).

⁴⁶ For St. Clement cf. *Strom.* IV, 26 (PG 8:1373).

⁴⁷ *In Jerem. hom.* 8:1 (PG 13:336). Cf. *In Cant.*, 1, II (PG 13:139), where he also cites John 14:23.

⁴⁸ *Ad Serap.*, I, 19 (PG 26:576).

⁴⁹ Petavius, *Dogmata Theologica, De Trinitate*, Bk. VII, Chap. 13, n. 21; Bk. VIII, Chap. 6, n. 7 (ed. nova, Parisiis, 1865). De Régnon, *op. cit.*, IV, pp. 314-316, 570-571, etc.

⁵⁰ Cf. Galtier, *op. cit.*, pp. 136 ff., who cites abundant testimony from St. Basil's own works to substantiate this view.

⁵¹ Cf. Isaye, "L'unité de l'operation divine dans les écrits trinitaires de saint Gregoire de Nysse," *Recherches de science religieuse*, 27 (1937), pp. 421-439. In the letters of St. Basil (189:7) we read this statement by St. Gregory: "The Holy Spirit sanctifies, vivifies, illumines, consoles. But all that, the Father and the Son and the Holy Spirit do equally." (PG 32: 693).

⁵² In his *Ancoratus* 10 (PG 43:36), the saint writes: "There is only one God, the Father in the Son and the Son in the Father with the Holy Spirit. That is why in the saints there dwells the Holy One, the Father true and subsistent, and the Son true and subsistent, and the Holy Spirit true and subsistent, three subsistences, one only divinity, one only substance, one only doxology, one only God."

Father de Régnon observes (*op. cit.*, IV, p. 544) that Petau "ne l'a point rapporté, parce qu'il cadrait mal avec sa thèse." One would think that the Bishop of Cyprus' emphasis on the single Godhead of the Three Persons indwelling in the saints would have recommended a similar cautiousness to de Régnon himself, since the obvious meaning of the words is a literal contradiction of his theory.

⁵³ He faithfully echoes the Cappadocians, his doctrine being, as Galtier observes (*op. cit.*, p. 206) "exactement le même que la leur"—a point to be returned to. Respecting the inhabitation, he teaches explicitly that the Trinity and the Trinity alone can be participated according to its essence, and so can fill the temple They have created. Cf. *De Spiritu Sancto*, I, 20 (PG 39:369).

⁵⁴ Petau finds in St. Cyril his principal authority, but his interpretation of Cyril's doctrine has been substantially modified even by his

own followers (cf. de Régnon, *op. cit., passim;* Mahé, "La sanctification d'après saint Cyrille d'Alexandre," *Revue d'histoire ecclésiastique,* 9 [1909], pp. 476-480). More critical studies of the great Doctor of the Incarnation seriously discredit Petau's theory. Cf. Weigl, *Die Heilslehre des hl. Cyrillus von Alexandrin* (1905), pp. 184-200 (who holds, however, that St. Cyril teaches—*De Trinitate,* III; PG 75:837 —that *each* Person dwells in us in His proper manner, imprinting thereby His personal property. Cf. *op. cit.,* pp. 192-193); Manoir de Juaye, *Dogme et Spiritualité chez s. Cyrille;* Galtier, *op. cit.,* pp. 217-272. See especially B. Monsegú, "Unidad y trinidad, propriedad y apropriación en las manifestaciones trinitarias según la doctrina de Cirilo Alejandrino," *Revista española de teología,* 8 (1948), pp. 1-57, 275-328.

[55] *La divinisation des chrétiens d'après les Pères grecs,* p. 252: "Les Pères qui incarnent, au IVe siecle, le mouvement doctrinale appelé école d'Alexandrie . . . ont ceci de commun qu'ils s'interessent à l'idée [de divinisation] moins pour elle-même qu'en tant qu'elle fournit des arguments en faveur de la divinité du Logos et du Saint Esprit."

[56] *Adv. Eun.* 9:22 (PG 32: 109).

[57] *De Spiritu Sancto,* 38 (PG 39: 1066). In another section he explicitly affirms the reality, personal and substantial, of the indwelling Persons: "Since, therefore, it is taught that the Holy Spirit, like the Father and Son, dwells in the soul and the interior man, I will call it not foolish but impious to call Him a creature. It is possible, I say, for sciences, virtues, arts . . . and affections to dwell in souls: but not as substances, rather as accidents. In this sense it is impossible for a created nature to inhabit." (*Ibid.* 25; PG 39:1058).

[58] *Thesaurus,* assertia 34 (PG 75: 609). St. Cyril devotes an entire dialogue of his *De Trinitate* (VII; PG 75:1089 ff.) to proving that the Holy Ghost dwells in us and by His union with our soul makes us participaters of the divine nature; the main purpose of argument, of course, is to prove the divinity of the Third Person.

[59] St. Cyril of Alexandria formulates the law of appropriation with precision: "Where the nature is absolutely the same, the activity could not be diverse, howsoever diverse and varied the works appear. Since, then, the essence—that is to say the divinity considered in its nature—is one in the three hypostases, in the Father, in the Son, and in the Holy Spirit, it is beyond doubt that any work attributed to one of Them is the work of the entire and one divinity considered as a physical principle of action." (*Comm. in Joan.,* Bk. X, Chap. 2, [on Joan. 15:1]. PG 74:337).

⁶⁰ Scheeben has summarized the evidence from these positive sources as follows: "Durch zahlreiche Stellen der Hl. Schrift und die gesante Tradition ist es zweifellos festgestellt, dass mit der Erhebung in den Gnadenstand eine Einwhohnung Gottes, speziell des Hl. Geistes, in den Begnadeten verbunden ist, d.h. eine bleibende substantielle Gegenwart Gottes in der Kreatur, in welcher er sich selbst schenkt ober zueigen gibt und folglich als eine substanielle und ungeschaffene Gnade-Gabe sich ihr mitteilt. Ebenso sicher ist es, dass diese Einwohnung Gottes etwas dem Gnadenstande Eigentümliches, also von derjenigen Gegenwart, welche Gott gegenüber den blossen Kreaturen zukommen muss oder kann, wesentlich Verschiedenes ist. Es kann sich nur fragen, wie das Wesen dieser Schenkung und ihre Bedeutung für den Gnadenstand näher zu bestimmen ist, und namentlich ob und wie sie sich zur Konstitution des Gnadenstandes selbst verhält." (*Handbuch der katholische Dogmatik*, II, par. 832, p. 359. Freiburg im B., 1941).

It is obvious that for Scheeben the indwelling of God, "especially of the Holy Spirit" (speziell des Hl. Geistes) has a different meaning than for us, for whom the special presence of the Third Person is explained by appropriation. Abstracting from his theory, however, and taking the words as written, they sum up the positive evidence on the question very well.

⁶¹ Cf. *De Trinitate*, n. 29 (PL 3:944): "[Spiritus Sanctus est] qui nos Dei faciat templum et nos efficiat domum . . . inhabitator corporibus nostris et sanctitatis effector." This passage alone would show the injustice of the Pneumatochi's interpretation of Novatian.

⁶² VIII *De Trinitate*, Chap. 21 (PL 10:252): "Spiritales omnes sumus, si in nobis est Spiritus Dei. Sed hic Spiritus Dei, et Spiritus Christi est. Et cum Christi Spiritus in nobis sit, eius tamen Spiritus in nobis est, qui Christum suscitavit a mortuis, et qui suscitavit Christum a mortuis, corpora quoque nostra mortalia vivficabit propter habitantem Spiritum eius in nobis. Vivificamur ergo propter habitantem in nobis Spiritum Christi per eum qui Christum suscitavit a mortuis."

⁶³ That this work is hardly more than a paraphrase of Didymus the Blind's work of the same title is well known, but it matters little so far as its patristic authority is concerned. As Father de Régnon, S.J., has written, Didymus became for the West a "ray of light" (*op. cit.*, IV, p. 469). Disturbed by the powerful eastern heresies which denied the divinity of the Third Person, Pope Damasus (who also introduced the Doxology at the end of the recitation of the psalms) ordered St. Jerome to translate Didymus' masterpiece. But

SOURCES OF SCHOLASTIC TEACHING 65

St. Ambrose was dissatisfied with this rendition; desirous of reaching a wider public, he composed his own treatise, borrowing unreservedly from the Greek author. Cf. de Régnon, *op. cit.*, pp. 469, 479, 481.

Since Didymus faithfully reproduces the doctrine of St. Basil and St. Gregory of Nyssa (cf. *supra*, p. 44), the Greek tradition enters directly as a written tradition into the main current of western thought. St. Augustine will imbibe it from St. Ambrose; Cassian, St. Gregory and St. Bernard will pass it along in its spiritual form to the Middle Ages. Its theological content will be taken chiefly from St. Augustine by the Victorines, and through them and especially through Peter Lombard the great centuries of scholastic theology will participate in a current of thought which is both Oriental and Latin. The medieval scholastics, of course, knew Hilary, Jerome and Ambrose very well, as well as Augustine; they will, in fact, cite all four in the specific tract on the inhabitation.

[64] I *De Spiritu Sancto*, 6:79 (PL 16:723): "Signati ergo Spiritu a Deo sumus. Sicut enim in Christo morimur ut renascamur, ita etiam Spiritu signamur ut splendorem atque imaginem eius et gratiam tenere possimus: quod est utique spiritale signaculum. Nam etsi specie signemur in corpore, veritate tamen in corde signamur, ut Spiritus Sanctus exprimat in nobis imaginis caelestis effigiem." Cf. St. Jerome, *In Esp. ad Ephes. Comm.*, I, Bk. I, Chap. 3, v. 30 (PL 26:514): 'Signati sumus Spiritu Dei Sancto, ut et spiritus et imprimantur signaculo Dei . . . . Hoc signaculum Sancti Spiritus, Deo imprimente signatur."

The markedly Greek character of these images and phrases is worth noting, since it clearly indicates the acceptability both of Greek thought and of Greek modes of expression. This, in turn, argues for the fact that the Latin Fathers saw nothing opposed in the Greeks to the so-called Latin tradition of the inhabitation and the sanctification of man (as a work common to the three Persons). Living in the era of the great Trinitarian controversies, conversant with the tradition of the Oriental branch of the Church and the nuances of Greek expression—who can doubt that the Latin Fathers are far better intepreters of the Greeks than theologians some fifteen centuries later, no matter how learned they be? The silence of the western Church on a point which surely would have occasioned at least comment, were there the divergence on these doctrines too commonly supposed (or presupposed), is impressive—admitted that the argument from silence is a weak one.

[65] *Op.cit.*, 5:64-66; 7:81-82 (PL 16: 749-753); "Omnis mutabilis est creatura; sed non mutabilis Spiritus sanctus. Quid autem dubitum

dicere, quia datus est Spiritus Sanctus, cum scriptum sit, 'Charitas Dei diffusa est in cordibus nostris per Spiritum sanctum qui datus est nobis'? Qui cum sit inaccessibilis natura, receptibilis tamen propter suam bonitatem nobis est, complens virtute omnia; sed qui solis participetur justis, simplex substantia, opulentes virtutibus, unicuique praesens, dividendo de suo singulis, et ubique totus. Incircumscriptus ergo est et infinitus Spiritus sanctus, qui discipulorum sensus separatorum infundit; quem nihil potest fallere. Angeli ad paucos mittebantur; Spiritus autem sanctus populis infundebatur. Quis ergo dubitet, quin divinum sit quod infunditur simul pluribus, nec videtur? Unus est Spiritus sanctus, qui datus est omnibus, licet separatis, apostolis."

The argument proving His divinity from the Holy Spirit's power to be infused, as contrasted with the inability of the creature so to be present, is a common one with the Greek Fathers, as has been seen. It will be repeated by St. Thomas in IV *Con. Gen.*, Chap. 17.

[66] Peter Lombard, for example, in the 14th, 15th, 16th and 37th distinctions of the *Sentences*, quotes Augustine forty-two times, Ambrose six times, Bede and Hilary twice, Gregory and Chrysostom once apiece. As Bonaventure has written, of all the Fathers known to the Scholastics, Augustine has most fully spoken on the subject of the inhabitation. (I *Sent.*, d. 15, p. 1, a. un., q. 4; ed. Ad Claras Aquas, I, p. 265: ". . . Augustinus, qui plus super hac materia locutus est. . . .")

For an exposition of Augustine's general doctrine on the presence of God, a useful background for the present considerations, see S.V. Grabowski, "St. Augustine and the Presence of God," *Theological Studies*, 13 (1952), pp. 336-358. The saint's perception of, and insistence on, the *realness* of the divine presence clearly illustrates the validity and depth of the Schoolmen's specification of this presence as a necessary prerequisite for the indwelling, a doctrine which so obviously depends on him that the indebtedness need not be stressed.

[67] *Epistula* 187 (*ad Dardanum. De Praesentia Dei*), 5:16 (PL 33: 837-838): "Illud est multo mirabilius quod, cum Deus ubique sit totus, non tamen in omnibus habitat . . . . Quis porro audeat opinari, nisi quisquis inseparabilitatem Trinitatis penitus ignorat, quod in aliquo habitare possit Pater aut Filius, in quo non habitet Spiritus Sanctus, aut in aliquo Spiritus Sanctus, in quo non et Pater et Filius? Unde fatendum est ubique esse Deum per divinitatis praesentiam, sed non ubique per habitationis gratiam. Propter hanc enim habitationem, ubi procul dubio gratia dilectionis ejus agnoscitur, non dicimus: Pater noster, qui es ubique, cum et hoc verum sit, sed: Pater noster, qui es in caelis, ut templum ejus potius in oratione commemoremus, quod

et nos ipsi esse debemus, et in quantum sumus, in tantum ad ejus societatem et adoptionis familiam pertinemus."

The phrase, 'gratia dilectione ejus agnoscitur,' might be better and more significantly translated: 'the grace of his love is *recognized as our own*,' in accord with the primary meaning of 'agnosco.'

[68] IV *De Trinitate*, Chap. 5, n. 9 (PL 42:850): "Quapropter Pater invisibilis, unus cum Filio secum invisibili, eumden Filium visibilem faciendo, mississe eum dictus est." The same applies to the Holy Spirit, who is made visible in a manifestation by a corporeal creature (dove or tongues of fire) produced for this purpose (*ibid.*, n. 10; PL 42:851).

[69] *Ibid.*, Chap. 19, n. 25 (PL 42:905): "Quaecumque propter faciendam fidem, qua munderemur ad contemplandam veritatem . . . temporaliter grata sunt, aut testimonia missionis hujus fuerunt, aut ipsa missio Filii Dei."

[70] *Ibid.*, Chap. 20, n. 27 (PL 42:907).

[71] *Ibid.*, n. 28 (PL 42:908): "Tunc unicuique mittitur, cum a quoquam cognoscitur, atque percipitur, quantum cognosci et percipi potest pro captu vel proficientis in Deum, vel perfectae in Deo animae rationalis. Non ergo eo ipso quod de Patre natus est missus dicitur Filius; sed vel eo quod apparuit huic mundo Verbum caro factum . . . vel eo quod ex tempore cujusquam mente percipitur, sicut dictum est: 'Mitte illam ut mecum sit et mecum laboret.' "

The word 'mens' (here weakly rendered as 'mind') signifies for Augustine the higher, spiritual part of the soul, embracing both intellective and appetitive powers, as the word 'percipitur' (and 'percipi') suggests—a point the Scholastics will not be slow to recognize. The quotation is from Wisdom, 9:10.

[72] *Ibid.*, n. 29 (PL 42:908): "Sicut enim natum esse est Filio a Patre esse, ita mitti est Filio cognosci quod ab alio sit. Et sicut Spiritui Sancto donum Dei esse est a Patre procedere, ita mitti est cognosci quia ab illo procedat."

[73] *Epistula* 187, 6:21 (PL 33:840): ". . . Deus est inhabitator quorumdam nondum cognoscentium Deum, et non quorumdam cognoscentium Deum. Illi enim ad templum Dei non pertinent qui cognoscentes Deum, non sicut Deum glorificant. Ad templum Dei pertinent parvuli sanctificati sacramento Christi, et generati Spiritu sancto, qui nondum valent cognoscere Deum. Ergo quem potuerunt illi nosse nec habere, isti potuerunt habere antequam nosse. Beatissimi autem sunt illi quibus hoc est Deum habere quod nosse."

Concerning the fact that actual knowledge is not required for the invisible missions, even for those who are "children not by age but by spirit," see *ibid.*, 8:26 (PL 33:841-842). St. Augustine, however, does not deny that God must be *knowable*, even by children (whether they be children by age or spirit), even when He is not *actually* known.

[74] Galtier, *L'habitation en nous des trois Personnes* (éd. revue et augmentée. Roma, 1949), p. 189: "Elle [la lettre 187] exclut formellement que la conaissance de Dieu soit nécessaire a son habitation dans les âmes justes." In this whole section of his work the learned Jesuit is battling against a windmill: the notion that the indwelling is contingent on an actual experience of God—an indefensible position maintained by no serious student of the question, whatever be Father Galtier's understanding of John of St. Thomas and Gardeil.

[75] I *Sent.*, d. 37 (ed. Mandonnet, *Scriptum Super Libros Sententiarum S. Thomae Aquinatis*, Parisiis, 1929), p. 849: "Hic aliquatenus aperit Augustinus quomodo Deus habitet in aliquo, id est habeatur, cum videlicet ita est in aliquo ut ab eo cognoscatur et diligatur." Alexander of Hales (*Summa Theologica*, III, q. 63, memb. 1; ed. Ad Claras Aquas, I, p. 495) likewise understands this text of St. Augustine as distinguishing between actual and habitual knowledge, actual knowledge not being required: "et hac ratione dicit Augustinus quod quosdam inhabitat non cognoscentes per gratiam sanctificantem."

Quotations are given from the Mandonnet edition of St. Thomas commentary, which contains the 'vulgar text' of Peter Lombard (*op. cit.*, p. viii), rather than from the critical edition of the Quaracchi editors, because there is no serious discrepancy between the two, so far as the inhabitation is concerned, and Mandonnet's edition is more easily available. The last two volumes of this unfinished edition (edited by M. F. Moos, O.P.) utilizes the critical Quaracchi text, at least in footnote emendations.

[76] The notion of manifestation comes easily to St. Augustine, because he considers the divine missions primarily from the point of view of 'evidence' for the Trinity, as one among several instances of the *theophanias*, an examination of which comprises the first part of his *De Trinitate*. (On this point cf. Father Lebreton, S.J., "Saint Augustin théologien de la Trinité. Son exégèse des théophanies," in *Miscellanea Agostiniana* (Roma, 1930), II, *Testi e Studii*, pp. 821-836. From this point of view, however, the *inhabitation* is not a principal concern; so that the lack of an explicit connection of the two notions is readily intelligible.

[77] *Epistula* 187, 5: 17 (PL 33:838): "Ii ab eo longe esse dicuntur, qui peccando dissimillimi facti sunt; et rei propinquare, qui eius similitudinem vivendo recipiunt. Sicut recte dicuntur oculi ab hac luce tanto longius esse quanto fuerint caeciores, quamvis lux praesto sit atque oculos perfundat extinctos; propinquare autem luci oculi merito perhibentur qui sanitatis accesse aciem recipiendo proficiunt." By itself, of course, such a text is hardly adequate to inculcate a conviction that the image of God in man is a form of explanation of the inhabitation; taken in conjunction with St. Augustine's numerous writings on the image, however, the application is logical and natural.

CHAPTER THREE

The Common Teaching of the Schoolmen

Within the limited scope that has been proposed, this study cannot trace historically and in detail the preservation and handing down of the doctrine of the inhabitation. Nor is the task necessary, for so unanimous is this tradition that any deviation from common teaching is immediately attacked by a score of theologians.*

Actually the early Scholastics have little or nothing to offer on the subject: not even a trace of the doctrine appears in the works of St. Anselm (c. 1003-1109) nor

---

* As has previously been noted (cf. *supra*, p. 64, note 63) tradition will perpetuate the doctrine of the inhabitation through the dark years by such spiritual writers as Cassian, St. Gregory, St. Bede and St. Peter Damian, to climax in St. Bernard. But there will be little properly theological activity from the seventh to the eleventh century; what intellectual work is accomplished will be largely restricted to the collection of texts from the Fathers as commentaries on the Bible, the *florilegia* on which scholastic theologians will by force of necessity so largely depend for their patristic sources. So the intellectual movement inaugurated by St. Anselm and by Abelard will be a true revival; and theological tradition will find its primary source in St. Augustine.

in the *Theologia Christiana* of Abelard (c. 1079-1142), the two acknowledged inaugurators of one of the most brilliant intellectual eras the Church has ever known. The School of St. Victor, unrivaled in the Middle Ages for its doctrinal authority on the theory of the spiritual life, exercises no direct influence on the scholastic explanations of this mystery so intimately linked with the mystical life of the soul. Hugh of St. Victor (c. 1096-1141) accepts the reality of the special presence of the Trinity in the soul,[1] as does his disciple and heir, Richard (?-1173), whose treatise *De Trinitate* was well known to the 13th century doctors;[2] but perhaps just because their interests were so largely mystical they fail to give a scientific theological treatment of the subject. Only with the work of Peter Lombard (c. 1110-1160) does the doctrine become a corporate part of Trinitarian theology handled in a systematic and scientific manner, although even in this case the teaching of the Master of the Sentences is rather of extrinsic than intrinsic interest.

By quoting from the Master of the Sentences, from William of Auxerre (?-1231; called Altissiodorensis by the Scholastics) and Alexander of Hales (c. 1170/80-1245) — who link Peter with the flower of Scholasticism — and from St. Albert the Great (c. 1193-1280) and St. Bonaventure (1221-1274), the contemporaries of the Angelic Doctor, a summary of the theological tradition which St. Thomas inherited, in the atmosphere of which he worked, can be satisfactorily obtained.

The reasons for choosing these particular men as representatives of the tradition of the Schoolmen should be obvious: there is a direct genealogical connection and a strong family resemblance among them. Like St. Thomas, Alexander (who probably introduced the *Sentences* as a textbook at the University of Paris), Albert and Bonaventure all comment on the text of Peter Lombard. Altissiodorensis is an immediate source of the teaching of Alexander of Hales,[3] and he, in turn, the master of St. Bonaventure, so outstanding a teacher and theologian that even Albert and Thomas are profoundly affected by him.[4] The mutual relations between Albert and Thomas, and between these Dominicans and St. Bonaventure, complicated though they may be to detail historically, nevertheless are too well known to call for any justification in citing the Universal Doctor and the Seraphic Doctor as illustrating the tradition of St. Thomas.

To present the common teaching on the divine indwelling given by these representative Schoolmen is, then, the purpose of this chapter. But in order to achieve that end it is first imperative to consider explicitly the historical dating of these early theological considerations of the mystery, inasmuch as the question of influence and counter-influence is necessarily implied by the historical approach of this study. To specify the precise origins of these several expositions, to trace in detail their evolution, is not of primary importance, for they are of immediate interest solely for the light they may throw on St. Thomas' theory and on the difficulties occasioned by its apparently diverse presentations. But to see the relations among his various predecessors and among their efforts at theological elucidation of the indwelling of the Most Blessed Trinity is, obviously, a necessary preliminary of a comparative investigation such as this.

So the first part of this chapter assumes this preliminary duty, presenting (so far as they have been determined) the historical facts regarding the time and order of composition of the different works to be considered. In the second part of the chapter the common teaching of the masters and doctors of the twelfth and thirteenth century on the indwelling will be unfolded — that is to say, the *facts* concerning the mystery universally agreed upon by the Schoolmen, not their solutions of the problems to which these facts give rise, which is the concern of the following chapters.

The importance of this common scholastic tradition should not be overlooked. For it is precisely from these facts that St. Thomas' thought on the subject takes its rise. And it is his interpretation of these facts, of this tradition, which leads to his solution of the central problem of the inhabitation and which provides, moreover, for the presumedly disparate resolutions of that problem in the *Sentences* and in the *Summa*.

ARTICLE 1

The Chronology of the Scholastic Works

1. The *Book of the Sentences* and the *Summa Aurea*

The exact date of the composition of Peter Lombard's *Sentences* little influences our study: de Ghellinck concludes to the year 1148,[5] but a difference of a few years would not affect the fact of his influence on the Schoolmen who are concerned here (although that influence is perhaps less determinate with William of Auxerre than with the others). Similarly, the suggested date for the composition of the *Summa Aurea* of Altissiodorensis, 1220,[6] may be accepted as at least pragmatically true, insofar as it indicates his precedence of, and influence on, Alexander of Hales and the *Summa* bearing his name.

2. *Alexandri de Hales Summa Theologica**

It is with the work of the first and great Franciscan Master and Regent, the *Summa* traditionally subtitled *fratris Alexandri*, that historical difficulties arise. For it is quite clear that the tract on the divine missions is not his — not only the question on the visible missions, which is certainly of much later date,[7] but even the questions on the invisible missions.[8] Just who is responsible for this theological compilation which will be of such interest cannot certainly be determined on the basis of present knowledge; but the Quaracchi editors of the *Summa* suggest, with good reason, that Alexander's disciple (or at least co-worker and co-regent), Jean de la Rochelle (Joannes de Rupella), Master together with him at Paris,[9] is the one responsible for the collecting of material and the composition of this particular tract.[10]

In the questions on the divine missions, to be sure, the influence of Alexander can be found on a few points — but remote and indirect, through the works of Eudes Rigaud (Odo Rigaldus) and the anonymous author of Codex Vaticanus latinus 691.[11] But these last two works are more clearly indicated as sources: it would seem that many specific points of the tract can be attributed to them, even though the Franciscan editors rather doubt the direct influence of the Vatican manuscript and (without conclusive proof) offer the suggestion that there is, instead, an unknown common source for this tract of the *Summa Alexandri*, the Vatican *Commentary* and the

* Cited hereinafter as *Summa Alex(andri)*.

Commentary of Eudes.¹² At the same time, there are a few places, a very few, where St. Albert's commentary on the *Sentences* seems indicated as the source;¹³ but in general these two works bear little resemblance in their handling of the subject of the divine missions, curious enough considering Albert's use of the *Summa Alexandri* on other points.*

Since the authorship of this work cannot be attributed to Alexander, a special section of this study will be devoted to a comparison between the teaching of the *Summa Alexandri* and the brief commentary to be found in Alexander's indisputably authentic work, the *Glossa in Quatuor Libros Sententiarum Petri Lombardi* (1223-1227). For the same reason selections from his *Quaestiones Disputatae de Missionibus* (from Codex Vaticanus latinus 782) are included in an Appendix; this is an authentic work dating from before his entrance into the Franciscans,¹⁴ probably from the years 1226-1236,¹⁵ and certainly later than the *Glossa*. To these excerpts references from time to time will be made.

Because of the relations (whatever they may finally be determined to be) between Eudes Rigaud (d. 1275) and the *Summa Alexandri*, likewise included in the Appendix are pertinent passages from his *Commentary on the Sentences* (Codex Vaticanus latinus 5981, a work dating from 1243-1245).¹⁶ This great Franciscan scholar, later Archbishop of Rouen, was a Bachelor of the *Sentences* at the

---

* Surprise is occasioned by the fact that Albert later revises his *Commentary* with reference to the *Summa Alex.* on other points. Cf. O. Lottin, "*Commentaire des Sentences et Somme Théologique* d'Albert le Grand," *Recherches de théologie ancienne et médiévale*, 8 (1936), pp. 117, 153; "Notes sur les premiers ouvrages théologiques d'Albert le Grand," *ibid.*, 4 (1932), pp. 77-82; P. Mignes, "Abhängigkeitsverhältnis zwischen Alexander von Hales und Albert dem Grossen," *Franziskanische Studien*, 2 (1915), pp. 208-229.

University of Paris about 1240-1245.[17] He is of interest not only for the tremendous and well-known influence he exercised on his greatest student, St. Bonaventure, but also because of his amicable fraternal and intellectual relations with the Dominicans of St. Jacques.[18]

In the same Appendix, too, (and for the same reasons), will be found a brief excerpt from Codex Vaticanus latinus 691. This perplexing work, a marginal commentary on the text of Peter Lombard, is, it would seem, a compilation in varying degrees from the commentaries of Alexander, Hugh de Saint Cher, Jean de la Rochelle,[19] John Pagus, perhaps Guerric de Saint-Quentin, and other authors not yet determined.[20] Yet if the authorship of this abbreviated compilation remains uncertain, the sources it uses plus the fact that it does not cite either the commentary of Eudes (1243-1245, at the latest) nor that of St. Albert (1244-1245) argues for the certainty of its early composition, at least some time before 1245.

If the tract on the divine missions of the *Summa fratris Alexandri* is not that of Alexander of Hales, its composition must still be placed before the end of 1245. Such is the final conclusion of the Quaracchi editors, and their arguments both from intrinsic and extrinsic criticism are entirely convincing, and definitively replace the suggestions of earlier scholars.[21]

Since the examination of the doctrine of St. Albert is synthetic, drawing indifferently from his *Commentary on the Sentences* and the *Summa Theologica,* the presentation of the doctrine of the Franciscan *Summa* has been considered before that of St. Albert — even though the Dominican's commentary on the missions may slightly antedate and is clearly contemporaneous with this part of the Halesian compilation. Justification for this order of treatment will be also found in the fact that the compilator uses sources — Eudes Rigaud and perhaps Codex Vaticanus latinus — certainly prior to Albert's work. If that compilator is assumed to be Jean de la Rochelle, which seems reasonable, further weight is given to the order, since he is considerably older than Albert, having held the chair of Master of Theology in 1238.[22]

3. The Works of St. Albert

Whether one accepts the dates of Albert's term as Bachelor of the *Sentences* as 1240-1242 (Glorieux[23] and Chenu[24]) or 1245-1246 (Franciscan editors of the *Summa Alexandri*[25]) does not affect the date of the composition of his *Commentary* in the form in which it has come down to posterity, for this is certainly a redaction or a revision of his previous public lectures. The order of composition does not follow the order of the *Sentences,* an order necessarily imposed on the Bachelor actually teaching. In this work, as Lottin has shown,[26] Distinctions 1 to 8-15 of the first book are immediately followed by Distinctions 1 to 10-11 of the third; then comes the rest of the first book, and the rest of Book III; only after these does Book II appear, followed at a later date by Book IV. The fact that the extant work is a private revision rather than the original public lectures is strengthened by the date 1249 read in Book IV: on the earlier dating of his term as Bachelor he would certainly have been by this time a Master of Theology (no one passed ten years as Bachelor!); and even on the later dating it is probable that he would have taken his advanced degree by 1249.

It is certain that the first book of the *Commentary on the Sentences* was composed before 1246. For one reads in Book II: "Iam elapsi sunt mille ducenti quadraginta sex anni,"[27] and Book I is quoted by St. Albert in this part of his commentary. Since this written work represents a redaction, it is probable that the actual lectures were given some time previous, a fact which argues for the acceptance of the earlier dating for Albert's bachelorship given by Mandonnet, Glorieux and Chenu.[28] The possibility exists, therefore, that Albert's work exercised some influence, at least oral, on the *Summa Alexandri*, to an extent considerably greater than that admitted by its editors. Yet since one can but guess on this point, one must concede what the written works portray: that the *Summa Alexandri* is a source for Albert's *Commentary* rather than vice versa (with the few exceptions in the tract on the divine missions previously noted).[29]

For the date of the composition of Albert's *Summa Theologica*, all medieval historians are in general agreement on the years about 1270-1274. The question of the nature of this composition, however, is another matter. But that question need not be of concern at the moment.

4. St. Bonaventure

Saint Bonaventure appears on the intellectual scene as a student at the propitious moment, just at the great times of Alexander, Jean de la Rochelle, Guerric de Saint-Quentin, Eudes Rigaud and St. Albert. With St. Thomas he will reap the intellectual harvest sown by these mighty medieval minds, whose originality, intellectual courage and integrity and gigantic genius today escape us.

Born in central Italy, near Viterbo, in 1221, Bonaventure enters the Order of Friars Minor at Paris in 1243.[30] Both Alexander of Hales (as Bonaventure himself testifies) and Eudes Rigaud (whose *Commentary* he so frequently uses) were his masters. Biblical Bachelor by 1248,[31] he began to read the *Sentences* in 1249-50 or 1250-51, receiving his doctorate in 1252 or 1253. It is from his lectures as a Bachelor of the *Sentences* that his *Commentary* dates, and hence from the years 1250-1252, or 1249-1251.[32]

5. Conclusion

These are the Scholastics whose common teaching on the divine indwelling shall now be considered. Their chronological order relative to the tract on the missions is approximately as follows: Peter Lombard; William of Auxerre; the *Glossa* of Alexander of Hales; his *Quaestiones Disputatae de Missionibus*; Jean de la Rochelle; Codex Vaticanus latinus 691; Eudes Rigaud; St. Albert's *Commentary on the Sentences*; the *Summa fratris Alexandri* (except the last question on the visible missions); St. Bonaventure; and the *Summa Theologica* of St. Albert the Great.

ARTICLE 2

The Common Teaching of the Schoolmen

The limited purpose of this section is to delineate, in a summary manner, the immediate ambient intellectual atmosphere respecting the inhabitation which was the theological element of the Angelic Doctor; to examine the complete theories of each of these Schoolmen in detail will be the task of the following chapters. In the present summary the permanence and vitality of the Church's tradition on the mystery will clearly appear, and its unity will be strikingly manifested. But no less evident will be the theological approach of these medieval thinkers to the problem and their deep understanding of the mystery; and their debt to St. Augustine will appear so strongly as to need no commentary.

To facilitate the presentation of this summary and restrain its possible magnitude, a series of conclusions representing the principal elements of scholastic tradition will be given; these will be individually illustrated by appropriate quotations from the theologians mentioned above.

1) *The indwelling of God in the soul is a real presence, i.e., physical and substantial, not merely moral.*[33]

This basic fact, the very existence of the mystery revealed in Sacred Scripture and accepted so unanimously by all the Fathers, is vigorously affirmed by Peter Lombard against "some one say that the Holy Spirit, God Himself, is not given, but His gifts, which are not the Holy Ghost himself."[34] To combat this error, he cites three passages from St. Augustine and two from St. Ambrose attesting to the common and universal tradition.[35]

Altissiodorensis answers the same fundamental objection concerning the Holy Spirit and His gifts in this way: "grace is given properly that it may be in the soul and that it make the soul enjoy God. And the Holy Spirit is given properly as spiritual food, and so both are given, each in his own way."[36]

The great Scholastics unanimously affirm the same doctrine: both the Holy Spirit and His gifts are given. The Persons are so truly given, insists the *Summa* attributed to Alexander of Hales, that they actually dwell in the soul, and are therefore present in a more special way than before.³⁷ St. Albert argues that if the Persons were not really present, man could not be sanctified (which is the purpose of the divine missions), because the divine gifts can only dispose to such sanctification, they cannot effect it.³⁸ For St. Bonaventure, the real presence of the Holy Spirit is a fact "determined by faith and by Scripture; and therefore he who would think contrary to this would be heretical."³⁹

2) *This presence is a new presence, completely different from God's common presence in all things.*

"But in the saints," writes the Master of the *Sentences*, "in whom He is by grace, He even dwells: for not everywhere He is, does He there dwell, but where He dwells, there He is. In the good alone, who are His temple and His seat, does He dwell."⁴⁰ William of Auxerre describes the new presence of the Holy Spirit as after the manner of "spiritual food."⁴¹ So it is that this "more familiar and more special" manner of God's existence,⁴² by which the Holy Spirit actually belongs to us,⁴³ is described and analyzed by the Scholastics in the terms given them by Scripture and tradition: 'temple,' 'to dwell in' and the like. In its simplest and most abstract formulation, it is affirmed as a "new *way*"⁴⁴ of God being present, *presupposing* His general existence in all things.⁴⁵

From the terms traditionally employed and from this abstract notion, the precise newness of the triune presence is delineated by the great medieval doctors in virtue of an analysis of the notion of 'giving.' The correlative of giving is 'having'; the saints have, possess the divine Persons in some way. Although St. Albert uses this expression, it is not an operative idea with him nor part of his theory.⁴⁶ For the *Summa Alexandri*⁴⁷ and St. Bonaventure,[48] however, it will be the key by which they will open up their similar solutions. For them all, regardless of the use they make of the concept, it points up the vast difference between God's general presence and the special presence He takes in the just.

3) *This divine inhabitation is realized only by grace.*
"But in the saints, in whom He is by grace, He even dwells." This basic affirmation of Peter Lombard testifies to the universal recognition by the Schoolmen of the indissoluble link between the indwelling and grace. So closely are they united that Altissiodorensis will even state that the Holy Ghost "in grace is had and is given . . . in some way as a contained thing is in its container. For the Holy Spirit is the proper and inseparable matter with which grace deals. Hence He is, in some way, contained in grace. Therefore, as when a vessel full of wine is given the wine is properly given, so when grace is given the Holy Spirit is given in it."[49]

But this simple affirmation, true as it is, will not be sufficient for the great theologians, because they recognize various kinds of supernatural assistance which can be called 'grace.' They will equate the inhabitation only with that grace-state which results from what modern theologians call sanctifying grace, but which in their terminology is named 'gratia gratum faciens.' They will insist, as an inevitable conclusion, that the triune presence is not realized by charismata or actual graces or unformed faith or hope; all these special supernatural aids which, without the *gratia gratum faciens,* are powerless to save and sanctify man (albeit they may serve as remote dispositions), they frequently term *gratiae gratis datae.* Graces of this kind, because of the connection between the divine missions and the divine indwelling, cannot effect even the divine missions (except in a very secondary manner which is not a mission in the proper sense of the word). What is required is that special gift of God which makes man pleasing to Him, His sons and heirs, His saints: a permanent quality, inhering intrinsically in the soul after the manner of a form (and not, therefore, a substance), the principle of supernatural life. Such is the *gratia gratum faciens*: habitual and sanctifying grace.

This is the common teaching of the *Summa Alexandri*,[50] St. Albert the Great,[51] St. Bonaventure.[52] It is a classic example of how the clarification of one mystery will illumine our perception of another.

4) *This divine inhabitation, realized by grace, is common to the three Persons, Father and Son and Holy Ghost.*

Despite his identification of Charity with the Third Person of the Blessed Trinity,[53] even Peter Lombard explicitly teaches that the indwelling is common to all of the Persons. Not only does he devote the entire fifteenth distinction to the invisible mission and consequent inhabitation of the Second Person, he states without equivocation: "The Holy Spirit dwells in us, who not without the Father and Son dwells in us."[54]

The author of the Alexandrian *Summa* is quite as explicit. "Not only do the Son and the Holy Spirit come to dwell in the creature," he says, "but even the Father; hence John 14.23: 'We shall come to Him and make our abode with Him.'"[55] His frequent considerations of the inhabitation of the Second Person lead to the same conclusion.[56]

St. Albert is no less certain on the point: the three Persons inseparably dwell in the souls of the just:

> For in the contributing of dilection, by reason of appropriation only the Spirit is sent, but not

only the Spirit inhabits; rather, the inhabitation is simultaneously of the three.[57]

"The whole Trinity comes anew," teaches the Seraphic Doctor similarly, "to dwell within the sinner, when grace is given to him."[58]

The point does not need to be labored. For the great Scholastics as for their predecessors an inhabitation which would be proper to the Holy Spirit alone or peculiar to each person in some proper manner — such an idea is unthinkable.*

5) *This inhabitation of the triune God, realized by grace, is, for the Son and Holy Spirit, the result of Their invisible missions.*

The evident connection between the indwelling and the divine mission, latent in Sacred Scripture, so well brought out by St. Augustine, was not lost on the theologians of the Middle Ages, who eagerly subscribed to this interpretation. For Peter Lombard, the special triune presence pertains to the very essence of the invisible missions.[59] The *Summa Alexandri* teaches that the inhabitation is the proper effect of the missions,[60] and its author includes it in his definition.[61]

The definitions of St. Albert and St. Bonaventure will not essentially differ from these concepts. "The procession of the Holy Spirit," declares Albert, "by the immediate effect in which the Holy Spirit Himself necessarily exists, the temporal procession, I say, manifests the eternal

---

* No doubt the fragments quoted *could* be misunderstood by the partisans of a *proprium* theory as inculcating no more than the obvious *perichoresis* of the divine Persons. That more than this is taught can only be seen in context, or if the formulas be taken as formally as they should be; if the Scholastics do not explicitly refute such theories, it is obviously because they have not considered them, imbued as they were in the common tradition.

procession."[62] St. Bonaventure writes that the visible mission "bespeaks a manifestation with an apparition, or an apparition manifesting the indwelling of an emanating Person or the emanation of an indwelling Person."[63] *A fortiori,* then, "in the invisible mission there is a contributing of gifts, in which there is manifestation and inhabitation";[64] and if knowledge is of the very nature of the missions, it can only be knowledge of some indwelling in a soul.[65]

6) *The notion of manifestation.*

The solution which the Bishop of Hippo found to explain the concept of the divine missions was also taken up by the Schoolmen, although not without some reservations and considerable refinement. Peter quotes the famous phrase from the fourth book of the *De Trinitate* as an explanation of the invisible missions: "et tunc unicuique mittitur cum a quoquam cognoscitur atque percipitur. . . ."[66] But good as the notion may be for the divine missions, it is ultimately abandoned in favor of Charity when it is necessary to explain the inhabitation.[67]

Yet the thirteenth century masters examine the concept more closely. They accept Augustine's formula, 'mitti est cognosci,'[68] and, despite some important divergencies,[69] they agree on several revealing conclusions.

First of all, the manifestation of the eternal processions must take place by means of some created effect. "When something is effected in the soul," the *Summa Alexandri* teaches, "in which the procession of the Son or Holy Ghost has to be known, then the Son or Holy Ghost is said to be sent."[70] Albert says: "In truth Augustine excellently determines a mission when he says that 'to be sent is to be known,' and I quite concede that this takes place by an effect."[71] "From its very understanding," Bonaventure agrees, "a mission, as is evident from Augustine's reason and will later appear more evident, always has two things, that is emanation and manifestation by an effect."[72]

But their precisions concerning the nature and different kinds of grace force them to the immediate conclusion that not just any effect can manifest a divine mission. So it must be an effect of sanctifying grace — only by such grace does God dwell in the soul. And therefore the manifestation must be not only of a proceeding Person but of an indwelling Person. So reason the three scholastic sources, the *Summa Alexandri*,[73] Albert[74] and Bonaventure.[75]

It is obvious what important theological progress has here been made. The notion of the divine missions has been clarified to the point where an analysis of one of its elements will open the way to a deeper understanding of the mystery involved. And, what is for this study more important, this new perspective lights up the shadows in which the mystery of the inhabitation lies hidden. To be sure, the chief advantage of these clarifications lies in placing the problem clearly in view. But in theology, as in every other science, the perception of a problem is the first and absolutely necessary step to any progress in the science; and correct understanding of the problem itself must precede any attempt to solve it.

7) *The notion of image.*

Another of Augustine's insights — the notion of explaining the inhabitation in terms of the image of the Trinity in the soul — is all but disregarded by the Schoolmen, although it is hardly fair to say they disregard an explanation on which St. Augustine himself so little relied. Despite the universal agreement on manifestation, with which it seems closely allied, only the author of the tract on the divine missions in the Franciscan *Summa* employs the concept of image as a functional part of his explanation of the triune presence.[76] Peter Lombard does not even quote the passage from the *De Praesentia Dei* which connects the two doctrines; following his lead rather than that of the *Summa Alexandri,* neither Albert nor Bonaventure uses the suggestion as a formal part of their theories, large though the notion of image will loom in their general theology.

This may at first sight seem strange, in view of the obvious connection of the doctrines, the use the Greek Fathers made of the notion and St. Augustine's profound analysis of the image of God in the *De Trinitate;* but certain suggestions occur almost immediately to explain the omission. Could it be that they feared to confuse the matter by combining two such profound and difficult mysteries? More specifically, did they experience such confusion themselves in the explanation of the *Summa* attributed to Alexander of Hales? However this may be, the fact still remains. St. Albert and St. Bonaventure, like St. Thomas in his *Summa,* use a simpler, more scientific approach to the problem of the inhabitation than that afforded by the notion of image. This suggestion of St. Augustine's does not receive the logical development one might have anticipated for it.

ARTICLE 3

Conclusion

From the preceding summary it is clear that the traditional teaching of the indwelling of the Most Blessed Trinity which has its roots in Sacred Scripture and the writings of the Fathers is perfectly preserved by the medieval theologians as it was received, without alteration in any one of its essential elements. All are in perfect agreement, as were the Greek Fathers and the Latin Fathers before them, that each of the three divine Persons is really (i.e., substantially, properly) present in a special manner in the soul living in the state of grace, in a way entirely distinct from God's common presence in all things. It would be difficult to explain this unanimity of teaching on such important points except on the basis of a received tradition which is, at the same time, a vital and energizing one.

More than this, the Schoolmen appreciate keenly Augustine's contribution — the notion of manifestation — seize on it, analyze it more closely, refine it and apply it to the fact of the special presence of the Trinity. From their common labors new elements will be added to the tradition — that is to say, a better understanding and explanation of that tradition will be made. It becomes clear that the divine indwelling is dependent on a state of sanctifying grace, that some created effect which must be an effect of this same supernatural nature is involved in the manifestation which determines the divine missions, that eternal procession and inhabitation and manifestation are all combined in so intimate a way that an analysis of one concerns them all.

These are the facts: the revealed facts attested to by tradition, the theological facts explaining that revelation and tradition. This is the tradition which St. Thomas imbibed and the base on which he must construct his own theological explanation of the mystery. But his labors are preceded by the efforts of these same theologians to explain the same facts and to offer a solution of the problems to which they give rise; and his explanation and solution are seriously influenced by these preliminary attempts. Hence in the next chapter a detailed examination will be made of the work of these early Schoolmen.

NOTES

¹ *De Sacramentis*, Bk. I, Part VI, Chap. 14 (PL 167:27 ff.).

² VI *De Trinitate*, Chap. 14 (PL 186:979 ff.).

³ According to Glorieux (*Répertoire*, I, n. 129), the *Summa Aurea* is dated around 1220, a conclusion with which Lottin agrees. The Franciscan editors of Alexander's Gloss on the Sentences (*Glossa in Quattuor Libros Sententiarum Petri Lombardi*, Quaracchi, 1951) place its composition between 1223-1227 (p. 116) and admit William of Auxerre as one of the principal sources of Alexander's doctrine (*loc. cit.*).

The same predominance is represented in the *Summa Alexandri*, where Altissiodorensis, although cited only twice explicitly, receives 695 implicit citations (ed. Quaracchi, IV, Prolegomena, p. LXXXIII; cf. p. CXXXII), far more than any of the scholastic 'ancients' except Peter Lombard (321 explicit, 549 implicit citations; *ibid.*, p. LXXXV). On this influence see P. Mignes, "Die theologischen Summen Wilhelms von Auxerre und Alexanders von Hales," *Theologische Quartalschrift*, 97 (1915), pp. 508-529.

⁴ Or at least by the *Summa* bearing his name. As will shortly be determined, the tract on the divine missions is almost certainly not that of Alexander, but perhaps of his disciple, Jean de la Rochelle (Joannes de Rupella).

⁵ J. de Ghellinck, "Pierre Lombard" (*Dict. théol. cath.*, XII, 2, coll. 1941-2019), col. 1963.

⁶ Cf. note 3, this page.

⁷ A fact recognized by the Quaracchi editors on manuscript basis from the first (cf. *op. cit.*, I, Prol., p. XXIV); it seems clear that this is extracted from St. Bonaventure's *Commentary* (*ibid.*, IV, Prol., p. CCLXVI).

⁸ *Ibid.*, pp. CCLXIII-CCLXVI.

⁹ Cf. V. Doucet, "Maîtres Franciscaines de Paris," *Archivum Franciscanum Historicum*, 27 (1934), pp. 539-541; Glorieux, *Répertoire*, II, n. 302.

¹⁰ *Op. cit.*, p. CCLXVI. They base their argument on the following grounds: the tract is left unfinished, although internally it shows

the work of one hand, which argues for an interruption of the labor; this can hardly be explained if we assign an author yet living (e.g., Eudes Rigaud) when the incomplete work was given to the libraries. Both Jean and Alexander died in 1245: the death of the author would sufficiently explain the incompleteness of the work. On internal grounds, the style and form are similar to that of Jean de la Rochelle, and on the other hand there are no traces of Alexander's *Gloss on the Sentences* nor his *Disputed Questions,* nor does the literary form correspond to his. Hence Jean de la Rochelle seems to be the compilator.

[11] *Ibid.,* pp. CCLXIII-CCLXIV.

[12] *Ibid.,* p. CCLXIV.

[13] *Summa Alex.,* I, p. 708, first opinion and solution=I *Sent.,* d 15, a. 5
     p. 709, last part of ad 1 = d. 15 a. 5
     p. 710, first opinion   = d. 15 a. 9
But no other correspondences are noted (*op. cit.,* IV, p. CCLXV).

[14] *Summa Alex.,* ed cit., IV, Prol., p. CLVI.

[15] *Ibid.,* p. CLII.

[16] According to the dating of the Franciscan editors, *ibid.,* p. CCXXIX, a conclusion by no means beyond dispute (cf. *infra,* p. 91, note 28).

[17] M. D. Chenu, "Maîtres et bacheliers de l'Université de Paris vers 1240," *Etudes d'histoire littéraire et doctrinale du XIIIe siècle* (Paris-Ottawa, 1943), I, pp. 33 ff.

[18] Cf. F. Henquinet, ' Les manuscrits et l'influence des écrits théologiques d'Eudes Rigaud," *Recherches de théologie ancienne et médiévale,* 11 (1939), pp. 349-350. The Chronicle of Salimbène de Adam, O.M., specifically records the love of the Franciscan Regent for the Order of Preachers (*loc. cit.*).

[19] I.e., from the anonymous Codex Tuderti 121, perhaps to be ascribed to him (cf. *Summa Alex., ibid.,* pp. CCIV ff.).

[20] Cf. A. Landgraf, "Bemerkungen zum Sentenzenkommentar des Cod. Vat. lat. 691," *Franziskanische Studien,* 26 (1939), pp. 183-190; O. Lottin, *Bulletin de théologie ancienne et médiévale,* 3 (1939), n. 1186. This considerably modifies the opinion of A Fries, "De Commentario Guerrici de S. Quintino in libros Sententiarum," *Archivum*

Fratum Praedicatorum, 5 (1935), pp. 326-340, which ascribes the entire commentary to the early Dominican Master.

[21] *Summa Alex., ibid.*, pp CCCXXXIX-CCCLV. They reach the following conclusion: "Quamvis igitur unum alterumve testimonium adhuc in dubium forte verti possit, talis est tamen summa testimoniorum internorum simul ac externorum et talis eorum concordia, ut velut factum historicum certe probatum iam haberi possit, quod *Summa* I-III, incepta post annum 1236, iam existebat anno 1245, qualis fere nunc asservatur, mutila scilicet et incompleta." (*ibid.*, p. CCCLV).

[22] Cf. H. Denifle, *Chartularium Univ. Paris* (Paris, 1889), I, p. 158, n. 108.

[23] *Répertoire des Maîtres en théologie de Paris au XIIIe siècle* (Paris 1933-1934), I, p. 62.

[24] *Op. cit.*, p. 34.

[25] *Summa Alex., ibid.*, pp. CCXXIX, CCXXXIV, CCXXXVI.

[26] O. Lottin, "*Commentaire des Sentences* et *Somme Théologique* d'Albert le Grand," *Recherches de théologie ancienne et médiévale*, 8 (1936), pp. 117-153.

[27] I *Sent.*, d. 6, a. 9 (ed. Borgnet, XXVII, p. 139).

[28] The earlier dates should clearly be preferred—although it matters not at all so far as this monograph is concerned—because, first, they better correspond to the facts of St. Albert's life and work, as they are now known; and, second, the later dates suggested by the Franciscan editors are not offered on intrinsic grounds but instead as a conclusion *and* a confirmation of the dates they give to the Bachelor's term of Eudes Rigaud, 1243-1245. Thus on the one hand they will insist on the validity of Lottin's argument for a revision of Albert's commentary (*op. cit.*, p. CCXXXVI), and then flatly contradict themselves in asserting that the 1246 date mentioned in Book II shows that Albert was *teaching* the *Sentences* at that time, and that this confirms the dates assigned to Eudes (since Albert, according to the Paris manuscripts 15652 and 15702 began his lectures after Eudes had completed his term) *ibid.*, pp. CCL and CCXXIX. In this last place they will have the intellectual effontery to say: "Supponi quidem posset illum esse annum ultimae redactionis et non ipsius lecturae [Alberti baccalaurei]; at in rebus historicis quidquid *naturaliter* explicari potest et suppositionibus dimissis, praeferendum est."

The dates given—for Eudes, and as a necessary consequence for Albert—seem dictated rather by a desire for the confirmation of external criticism for their attempt to render nugatory the possible influence of Eudes on the *Summa Alexandri* than by an honest consideration of the facts—a superfluous gesture, since this thesis appears soundly based on internal grounds alone. One cannot be convinced that they have definitively accounted for the circumstances which would (and do) argue against this later dating. The fact that he speaks of the "errors of 1241" in the first book of the commentary in a way different from that of the second, is hardly sufficient warrant for presupposing *two* condemnations, one less severe in 1241 (censure), one definitive in 1244 (condemnation), after which date (according to their theory) the second book would have been composed as Eudes' public lectures: Denifle, in fact, assigns both the prior and later lists of these acts in the manuscripts to 1241 (*Chart. Univ. Paris*, I, pp. 170 ff., n. 128); and, even if the double condemnation were admitted, this would not exclude the possibility that Book Two is a later recension of the public lectures—a common enough practice among these medieval theologians when they attained the eminence of Master. Similarly, the explanation of Eudes' presence among the four authors of the *Expositio Regulae Quatuor* (so-called) *Magistrorum* of 1242 (cf. Gratien, *Histoire de la fondation et de l'évolution de l'Ordre des Fr. Mineurs au XIIIe siècle*, Paris, 1928, pp. 228 ff.) as a 'biblical Bachelor' seems far from adequate. Would such pedagogical callowness lead to a ranking as an authority on the level with the great Masters of the province, Alexander of Hales and Jean de la Rochelle? It does not appear likely. On the other hand, if Eudes had already earned a reputation as a 'biblical Bachelor' and confirmed that by his teaching as a Bachelor of the *Sentences*, his presence in this distinguished company is more reasonably explained.

A last point is that the Chronicle of Salimbène de Adam mentions that Eudes taught for "many years" (quoted in F. Henquinet, "Les manuscrits et l'influence des écrits théologiques d'Eudes Rigaud," *Recherches de théologie ancienne et médiévale*, 11 [1939], pp. 349-350). Since he was made Archbishop of Rouen in 1248, that would give him on the Quaracchi editors' basis only four years of teaching; eight years seems a more fitting space of time to justify the designation "many years."

The dates assigned in the Prolegomena (p. CCXXIX) for Eudes Rigaud's terms as Bachelor of the *Sentences* appear to be grounded on a desire, a contradiction and two suppositions. Their effort remains unconvincing, to say the least.

²⁹ Cf. P. Minges, "Abhängigkeitsverhältnis zwischen Alexander von Hales und Albert dem Grossen," *Franziskanische Studien*, 2 (1915), pp. 222 ff.; *Summa Alex.*, ed. cit., IV, Prol., pp. CCXXXVIII-CCXL.

³⁰ A. Callabuet, "L'entrée de S. Bonaventure dans l'ordre des Frères mineurs," *La France Franciscaine*, 4 (1921), pp. 41-51. Since one could become a biblical Bachelor only after eight years of studies according to the statutes of the University, and Bonaventure was made a Bachelor in 1248, it is presumed that he came to Paris some three years before his entrance into the order.

³¹ *Cronica fr. Salimbène de Adam.*, O.M., ed. Holder-Egger, in *Mon. Germ. Hist. Scriptores*, XXXII, p. 299.

³² The earlier date is given, without evidence, by the Quaracchi editors of the *Summa Alex.*, IV, Prol., p. CCXLVI. In any case, Bonaventure's *Commentary* would definitely seem to antedate St. Thomas' work.

³³ That this is *in effect* denied by some of the Scholastics in virtue of their inadequacies in explaining the mode of the inhabitation does not concern the point; they admit the fact, however ill they account for it. For the total history of the question it is far otherwise. Under the influence of the Nominalists, Alarcón will deny the necessity of a real presence and even that it is taught by St. Thomas (*I Pars Theol. Scholast.*, tract, V, disp. 9, c. 9. [Lugduni, 1633]: "Prima conclusio: Missio qua perfecte mittitur Persona divina ut sit in anima . . . non requirit praesentiam aliquam realem . . . . S. Thomas non agnoscit alium modum quo Deus existat in anima iusti praeter comunem."); Arriaga holds that only a moral union is involved (*Disp. Theol. in I. P. D. Thomae*, tract. de Trinitate, disp. 55, sect. 4 et 5 [Pragac, 1624]: "Respondendum est eam Dei in nobis existentiam per dona gratiae non esse ullo modo physicam sed solum moralem et affectivam . . . ."); Godoy will astonishingly conclude: "Ergo praesentia ista physica ad mentem D. Thomae non est, immo contra illius mentem defenditur." (*In I P.*, q. 43, tract. 14, disp. 10, par. 1, n. 27 [Brugis Oxomensis, 1671]. Cf. nn. 39, 40, 51, 58-78). For a survey of the opinions of the Nominalists and their followers, see the excellent study of Father Cuervo already referred to, from which these quotations are drawn.

According to John of St. Thomas, Vasquez (I, Iae Part., disp. 30, c. 3) likewise denies a real presence of the divine substance in the soul beyond the presence of immensity (*Cursus Theologicus*, I, q. 43, disp.

37, a. 3, n. 4; ed. Solesmnes, IV, fasc. II, p. 365). This interpretation directly contradicts most modern writers on the subject, who hold that Vasquez teaches that the inhabitation is constituted by God's production of the supernatural gifts. (Cf. Froget, *De l'habitation du Saint-Esprit dans les âmes justes*, p. 8; Galtier, *De SS. Trinitate*, p. 209; Gardeil, *La structure de l'âme*, II, pp. 12 ff.; Garrigou-Lagrange, "L'habitation de la Sainte Trinité," *Revue Thomiste*, 11 [1928], p. 452; Retailleau, *La Sainte Trinité dans les âmes justes*, p. 142; von Rudloff, "Des heiligen Thomas Lehre von der Einwohnung Gott in der Seele der Gerechten," *Divus Thomas* [Fribourg], 8 [1928], pp. 175-176.). Suarez likewise holds this opinion, *De Trinitate*, Bk. XII, Chap. 5, n. 11. In a recent study of the question, however, *Justification and the Inhabitation of the Holy Ghost, the Doctrine of Father Gabriel Vasquez, S.J.*, (Pont. Univ. Greg. Rome, 1940), Father Leo D. Sullivan, S.J., vindicates the interpretation of John of St. Thomas. He says (p. 31): "we must conclude, then, that for Vasquez the inhabitation of God in the soul is not formally a substantial inhabitation. God is present substantially only through His immensity, and the union which grace establishes between the soul and God is one which postulates, not a substantially present term, but one present intentionally as the object of cognition and love." Cf. *ibid.*, pp. 19-25, 29-32.

[34] I *Sent.*, d. 14 (ed. cit., p. 313).

[35] *Ibid.*, pp. 313-314.

[36] *Summa Aurea*, c. 7, 3a quaestio principalis, q. 3 (Parisiis, fol. 21b-22a): "Ad hoc enim videtur dicendum quod gratia proprie datur ut insit et ut faciat animam frui Deo. Et Spiritus Sanctus proprie datur ut cibum espiritualis, et ita utrumque datur suo modo." (Quoted in Cuervo, *op. cit.*, p. 6).

[37] *Summa Alex.*, Pars II, Inq. II, Tract. III, Sect. II, q. 2, tit. 2, memb. 1, c. 4, a. 2, [solutio] I, II (ed. cit., I, p. 732): ". . . in missionibus eorum [Filii et Spiritus Sancti] non solum dantur dona eorum, sed etiam ipsi, et inhabitant animam et sunt ibi specialiori modo quam prius." Cf. p. 729, resp.; p. 728; II, p. 743, where the fact is proved by citing I Cor. 3:16 and Eph. 3:16. (Hereinafter, citations from this work will be by tome and page, with such other indications as are necessary, because of the impossibly complicated schematization.)

[38] *Sum. Theol.*, Tract. VII, q. 32, membr. 2, a. 1, sol. ad q. 3 (*Opera Omnia*, ed. Bourgnet, XXXI, p. 345): "Si enim in dono

non daretur persona divina ut operans, caderet a fine datio et missio: finis enim dationis et missionis est manifestatio et reductio creaturae rationalis, quam solum donum facere non potest, nisi dispositive: sed oportet, quod persona divina in dono operatur." Cf. *ibid.*, sol. ad obj. 6 and 7 (p. 340); sol. ad q. 1 (p. 341); q. 33, sol. ad q. 3. Always the same argument is used: an infinite effect is produced, for which the created gift can be only a disposition; therefore the divine Person must be really present. This argument *is* S. Albert's solution of the problem of the inhabitation: the Trinity is present as efficient exemplary cause of the sanctification of men.

[39] I *Sent.*, d. 14, div. text. (*Opera Omnia*, ed. Ad Claras Aquas, I, p. 244): "Hoc a fide et a Scriptura determinatur; et ideo, qui contrarius hujus sentiret, esset haereticus." Cf. d. 14, a. 2, q. 1 (p. 249) for his interesting theological argument based on the notion of giving. Other arguments against these "heretics" will be found in the same question.

The strength of the Seraphic Doctor's condemnation is noteworthy; St. Thomas merely calls the opinion erroneous (I *Sent.*, d. 14, div. textus: 'Hic excludit errorem dicentium in processione temporali Spiritum sanctum non dari sed tantum dona ejus . . . .") However, it would be a mistake to distinguish between the two words on the basis of the technical theological meanings they later were to acquire.

[40] I *Sent.*, d. 37, p. 847: "In sanctis vero etiam habitat in quibus est per gratiam: non enim ubicumque est, ibi habitat; ubi vero habitat, ibi est. In solis bonis habitat, qui sunt templum ejus et sedes ejus."

[41] *Loc. cit.* Cf. *supra* p. 94, note 36.

[42] *Summa Alex.*, ed. cit., I, p. 723, ad 3.

[43] *Ibid.*, p. 733, ad 2.

[44] *Ibid.*, p. 732, [solution] I, II: ". . . esse ibi secundum aliud quam prius . . . ."; S. Albert, I *Sent.*, d. 16, a. 1, ad 1: ". . . per seipsum adesse aliter vel ad aliud quam sit ubique . . . ."; S. Bonaventure, *op. cit.*, d. 15, p. 2, a. un., q. 1 (I, p. 270): ". . . novus modus essendi, addens super esse per naturam."

[45] The *Summa* of Alexander teaches that there is a double 'esse' of the soul, the first that of nature, the second (presupposing the first) that of grace: "Gratia creata duplicem habet comparationem, scilicet ad primum esse animae, quod est natura; et ad esse secundum ipsius quod est bene esse vel esse ordinis . . . ." (*op. cit.*, IV, p. 962, sol.) Similarly there is a double presence of God according to this double

'esse,' and the second presupposes the first: ". . . Spiritus sanctus dicitur mitti, non quia modo sit ubi non erat prius, sed quia est ibi alio modo quam prius." (*ibid.*, I, p. 725, Contra, b). Cf. p. 723, ad 3.

St. Albert says quite simply: ". . . inesse per gratiam supponit inesse communiter . . . ." (*op. cit.*, d. 37, a. 9, ad 1; XXVI, p. 241. Cf. a. 5, sol., p. 235). St. Bonaventure says the same: "Esse per gratiam inhabitantem praesupponit esse per essentiam . . . ." (IV *Sent.*, d. 1., p. 1, a. un., q. 3, ad 5; IV, p. 17). As previously noted (*supra*, p. 81), Peter Lombard states that God is where He dwells, but He does not dwell everywhere He is: an equivalent affirmation of the same truth.

⁴⁶ *Op. cit.*, d. 16, a. 1, q. 1 (XXV, p. 445): ". . . mitti non dicitur persona respectu cujuscumque doni, sed tantum in dono in quo ipse est, et habetur . . . ."

⁴⁷ Ed. cit., I, p. 737, ad 5: "[missio visibilis] addit manifestationem personae in quantum existentis ab alio et existentia in alio tamquam inhabitantis vel possessae ab alio, quia in missione efficitur ut persona missa ad nos habeatur a nobis et inhabitet in nobis; et hoc est alio modo esse quam in aliis creaturis." P. 738, ad 2: "Quando autem aliquid mittitur in ratione doni, donum illud non habet completam rationem missionis donec habeatur et possideatur ab eo cui mittitur." Cf. *ibid.*, p. 737, ad 6. In another place the *Summa* distinguishes between two different ways of 'having' the Holy Spirit, one resulting from His common presence, the other from His indwelling: ". . . prius habebatur in quantum Spiritus, sed non in quantum Sanctus nec per modum fructus" (*ibid.*, I, p. 732, sol.). But it is clear that for this author the Holy Spirit is possessed *simpliciter* only by the inhabitation.

⁴⁸ That St. Bonaventure teaches the same is apparent in a text already cited (*supra*, p. 95, note 39). In his 'definition' of the inhabitation in the *Breviloquium* (p. 5, c. 1; ed. cit., V, p. 253), he includes the notion as an essential part of his explanation: "Habitare . . . dicit effectum spiritualem cum acceptatione, sicut est gratiae gratum facientis quae . . . Deum facit nos habere, et haberi a nobis, ac per hoc et inhabitare in nobis." See also I *Sent.*, d. 14, a. 2, q. 1, ad 2 (I, p. 250). He will, however, analyze the idea more precisely and profoundly than his master: "Aliquid datur alicui ut finiens, sicut praemium merenti; aliquid ut perficiens, ut gratia consentienti; aliquid ut subserviens, ut equus militi. Quod autem dicitur, quod datum est in potestate accipientis, verum est de datione tertio modo dicto,

non primo et secundo, quia illi sunt duo modi habendi, in quibus habens habetur. Unde homo habetur a gratia et habetur a Dono, quo fruitur." (*Ibid.*, ad 3; I, p. 250).

[49] *Op. cit.*, ad 1 (fol. 21b-22a): "Per gratiam et in gratia habetur et datur Spiritus sanctus . . . ut contentum in continente quodam modo. Est enim Spiritus Sanctus propria et inseparabilis materia gratiae circa quam negotiatur gratia. Unde, quodammodo in gratia continetur. Unde, sicut cum datur vas plenum vino datur vinum proprie, sic cum datur gratia datur Spiritus Sanctus in ea." (Quoted in Curvo, *loc. cit.*)

[50] I, p. 732, ad 1: "Licet ergo per effectum gratiae gratis datae possit cognosci Filius a Patre procedere et similiter Spiritus Sanctus ab utroque, tamen per solum effectum gratiae gratum facientis potest cognosci Filium et Spiritum Sanctum procedere in animam ad inhabitandam ipsam, cum per illam solam sit inhabitatio. Unde si illa definitio integre complectatur rationem missionis, oportet quod in illo effectu habeat cognosci processio Filii et Spiritus Sancti et quantum ad terminum a quo et quantum ad terminium ad quem: et tunc illud cognosci non habet esse nisi in effectu gratiae gratum facientis." Cf. the solutions in this second article and the answer to the third objection.

[51] *Op. cit.*, d. 14, a. 3, sol. (XXV, p. 392): "Dicendum, quod in veritate optime determinat Augustinus missionem quando dicit, quod 'mitti est cognosci quod ab alio sit': et bene concedo, quod hoc fit per effectum, sed non quemlibet; sed duo exiguntur, scilicet appropriabilitas ad proprium, et quod sit effectus gratiae gratum facientis, cui conjuncta semper sit processio personae, et persona ipsa: oportet enim ipsam personam cum effectu suo praesentem novo modo monstrari, si debeat dici temporaliter procedere . . . ." More clearly still in his *Sum. Theol.*, I, Tract. VII, q. 32, memb. 1, sol. ad q. 1 (XXXI, p. 341): ". . . processio Spiritus Sancti dupliciter dicitur: scilicet simplex manifestatio processionis per signum, et sic procedit Spiritus sanctus in donis gratuitis gratis datis. Et est etiam manifestatio processionis aeternae, simul et procedentis Spiritus per proprium ejus actum, quem non operatur nisi in illis in quibus habitat per inhabitantem gratiam. Et hoc modo non procedit nisi in donis gratum facientibus." Cf. also *ibid.*, q. 3, sol. ad q. 1 and q. 2 (XXXI, pp. 349-350).

[52] *Op. cit.*, d. 15, p. 2, a. un., q. 1 (I, p. 270): ". . . dari vel mitti est dupliciter: vel simpliciter, vel ad hoc. Tunc datur simpliciter, quando simpliciter habetur, videlicet non tantum ad usum, sed ad fructum; hoc autem est solum per dona gratiae gratum facientis, et

ideo solum in illa datur simpliciter vel Filius vel Spiritus sanctus. Alio modo dicitur dari ad hoc, quando non ad fructum, sed ad auxilium sive aliquem usum aliqua dona donantur; et hoc quidem, cum dantur aliqua dona gratiae gratis datae, in quibus manifestatur Filius vel Spiritus Sanctus . . . ." Cf. *ibid.*, d. 14, a. 2, q. 1 (I, p. 249); d. 16, a. un., q. 1 (I, p. 279); d. 37, p. 2, a. 1, q. 2 ad 4 (I, p. 655); II *Sent.*, d. 9, a. un., q. 2 (II, p. 244).

[53] *Op. cit.*, d. 17, (p. 382): ". . . ipse idem Spiritus sanctus est amor, sive caritas, qua nos diligimus Deum et proximum: quae caritas cum ita est in nobis ut nos faciat diligere Deum ac proximum, tunc Spiritus sanctus dicitur mitti ac dari nobis; et qui diligit ipsam dilectionem qua diligit proximum, in eo ipso Deum diliget: quia ipsa dilectio Deus est, idest Spiritus Sanctus." He explains, however, how this is to be understood (*ibid.*, p. 389): "Ad quod dicimus, hoc ita esse dictum, sicut dicitur, psalm. LXX: Deus est spes nostra et patientia nostra; quia facit nos sperare et pati. Ita caritas dicitur esse motus sive affectio animi, quia per eam movetur et afficitur animus ad diligendum Deum."

Many modern theologians, (e.g., Galtier, *de Ss. Trin.*, p. 286; Teófilo Urdánoz, O.P., "La inhabitación del Espiritu Santo en el Alma del Justo," *Rev. Española de Teología*, 6 (1946), p. 477; van der Meersch, "Grace," *Dict. théol. cath.*, col. 1609; etc.), despite this later clarification that the Master of the Sentences himself gives, understand him as teaching that the Third Person is the sole and unique *formal* cause of our sanctification. This is rather, according to St. Bonaventure (I *Sent.*, d. 17, p. 1, a. 1, q. 1), the conclusion taught by his disciples: "Spiritus sanctus potest considerari *in se*, et sic est amor Patris et Filii; potest rursus considerari *ut in anima humana habitans*, et sic Spiritus sanctus dicitur gratia; potest etiam considerari *ut unitus voluntati*, et sic est charitas qua nos diligimus Deum. Unde dicunt quod Spiritus sanctus est nostra charitas, non per appropriationem, sed per unionem. Quemadmodum enim solus Filius est homo vel incarnatus, et tamen tota Trinitas est incarnationem operata, sed tamen solus Filius unitus; sic, quamvis tota Trinitas faciat unionem Spiritus sanctis cum voluntate, solus tamen Spiritus sanctus unitur voluntati, et ideo solus est charitas . . . ."

And St. Thomas says (I *Sent.*, d. 17, q. 1, a. 1): "Magister tamen vult quod charitas non sit aliquis habitus creatus in anima; sed quod sit tantum actus qui est ex libero arbitrio moto per Spiritum sanctum, quem charitatem dicit." And he offers the opinion S. Bonaventure calls that of Peter's disciples, not as the Master's own, but as that of "quidam."

Peter Lombard, in short, does not teach that there is any such personal union between the soul and the Holy Spirit as the notion of formal cause implies; he is not being inconsistent in affirming that all three Persons dwell in the soul, nor does he explain this purely on the grounds of concomitance or circuminsession.

⁵⁴ *Op. cit.*, d. 37, p. 848: ". . . ex parte enim cognoscimus et ex parte prophetamus, quomodo Spiritus sanctus habitet in nobis qui non sine Patre et Filio inhabitat." Cf. also p. 385, where Peter quotes St. Augustine, XV *De Trin.*, Chap. 18: "Dilectio ergo quae Deus est et proprie ex Deo est, Spiritus Sanctus est, per quem diffunditur in cordibus nostris Deus, charitas, per quem nos tota inhabitat Trinitas."

⁵⁵ *Op. cit.*, p. 741, e: "Item, non solum Filius vel Spiritus Sanctus veniunt ad inhabitandam creaturam, sed etiam Pater: unde Joan. 14, 23: Ad eum veniemus et mansionem faciemus . . . ." Cf. *ibid.*, p. 737 ad 2: "Ad aliud solvendum per interemptionem, quod non semper dicuntur Filius et Spiritus Sanctus mitti, quia temporaliter veniunt ad nos, quia etiam Pater cum Filio et Spiritu Sancto dicitur venire ad inhabitandam creaturam, Joan. 14, 23: Ad eum veniemus et mansionem apud eum faciemus. Sed cum significatur ad significandam praecedentem inhabitationem, tunc dicitur mitti."

⁵⁶ See *ibid.*, p. 732, ad 1, 2, 3; p. 733, ad 1. Cf. also the whole of articles 1, 2 and 3, pp. 727 ff.

⁵⁷ I *Sent.*, d. 14, a. 13, q. 2, ad obj. (XXV, p. 403): ". . . cum missio vel datio non fiat nisi in illa [dona] quae sanctificant, non sequitur quod in illis donis Pater det se: tamen de Patre dicit Filius: 'Ad eum veniemus, et apud eum mansionem faciemus.' Sed hoc contingit, eo quod inhabitant inseparabiliter sanctas animas tres personae: unde in illa mansione solus Spiritus mittitur, sicut patet per id quod praecedit: 'Si quis diligit me, sermonem meum servabit: et Pater meus diliget eum, et ad eum veniemus,' etc. In collatione enim dilectionis solus Spiritus mittitur ratione appropriationis, non tamen solus Spiritus inhabitat, imo inhabitatio est trium simul."

⁵⁸ I *Sent.*, d. 15, a. un., q. 3, arg. ad opp. 2 (I, p. 262): "Tota Trinitas de novo venit ad habitandum in peccatore, cum gratia datur ei."

⁵⁹ *Op. cit.*, p. 384: "Tunc enim mitti vel dari dicitur, cum ita in nobis est ut faciat nos diligere Deum et proximum: per quod manemus in Deo, et Deus in nobis." Cf. p. 333: ". . . dicitur mitti . . . cum se in animas pias sic transfert ut ab eis percipiatur ac cognoscatur."

⁶⁰ *Op. cit.*, p. 731: "Est Filium mitti, et effectus huius missionis est inhabitatio." P. 729, a: ". . . non terminatur ad Spiritum Sanctum sed ad hoc quod est habere Spiritum Sanctum inhabitantem animam tamquam templum suum." Cf. p. 732, ad 3.

⁶¹ *Ibid.*, p. 714, [solutio]: ". . . non semper datur definitio per priora simpliciter, sed per priora quoad nos; unde non semper datur definitio per genus et differentiam, sed aliquando per causam, aliquando per effectum consequentem. Unde concedo quod haec definitio 'mitti est cognosci' etc. datur per effectum; unde cum efficitur aliquid in mente in quo habet cognosci processio Filii vel Spiritus Sancti, tunc dicitur mitti Filius vel Spiritus Sanctus, et intelligo non de quocumque effectu, sed de effectu pertinente ad gratiam gratum facientem." P. 736, sol., I: ". . . ratio missionis est inhabitatio creaturae rationalis per aliquem effectum gratiae gratum facientis; est enim missio ad inhabitandum." Cf. p. 732, ad 3.

⁶² *Sum. Theol.*, I, Tract. VII, q. 32, memb. 1, sol. (XXXIII, p. 339): ". . . processio Spiritus sancti per effectum immediatum in quo ipsum Spiritum sanctum necesse est esse, processio (dico) temporalis, manifestativa est processionis aeternae." Cf. *ibid.*, ad 6 and 7 (p. 340) and sol. ad q. 1 (p. 341); also I *Sent.*, d. 14, a. 3, sol. (XXV, p. 392).

⁶³ *Op. cit.*, d. 16, a. un., q. 1 (I, p. 272): ". . . dicit manifestationem cum apparitione, sive apparitionem manifestantem personae emanantis inhabitationem vel personae inhabitantis emanationem."

⁶⁴ *Ibid.*, q. 2 (I, p. 279): ". . . in missione invisibili est donorum collatio, in quibus est manifestatio et inhabitatio."

⁶⁵ *Ibid.*, ad 4 (I, p. 282): ". . . etsi cognitio sit de ratione missionis, non tamen quaecumque vel cuiuslibet, sed inhabitantis . . . ."

⁶⁶ IV *De Trin.*, Chap. 20 (PL 42: 908), quoted in d. 15 (p. 333). Peter also cites the similar definition: "Cum ex tempore cujusquam mente percipitur, mitti quidem dicitur, sed non in hunc mundum" (p. 334).

⁶⁷ *Op. cit.*, d. 17 (p. 384): "Tunc enim mitti vel dari dicitur, cum ita in nobis est ut faciat nos diligere Deum et proximum: per quod manemus in Deo, et Deus in nobis."

⁶⁸ *Summa Alex.*, p. 714 [Solutio]; St. Albert the Great, I *Sent.*, d. 14, a. 3, sol. (XXV, p. 392); St. Bonaventure, *op. cit.*, d. 15, p. 1, a. un., q. 4 (I, p. 265).

⁶⁹ Where the *Summa Alexandri* considers Augustine's definition as given by the effect, and therefore "per priora quoad nos" but not "per priora simpliciter" (*loc. cit.*), a fact S. Albert concedes (*loc. cit.*), S. Bonaventure insists that the mission "principaliter de ratione suae significationis importat manifestationem" (*loc. cit.*). The point is not pressed, but there is room here for essential disagreement between the disciple and his master.

⁷⁰ *Loc. cit.*: ". . . cum efficitur aliquid in mente in quo habet cognosci processio Filii vel Spiritus Sancti, tunc dicitur mitti Filius vel Spiritus Sancti . . . ."

⁷¹ *Loc. cit.*: ". . . in veritate optime determinat Augustinus missionem quando dicit, quod 'mitti est cognosci quod ab alio sit': et bene concedo, quod hoc fit per effectum . . . ."

⁷² *Op. cit.*, q. 3 (I, p. 263): ". . . missio, sicut patet ex ratione Augustini et melius infra patebit, semper duo habet ex suo intellectu, scilicet emanationem et manifestationem per effectum."

⁷³ *Op. cit.*, p. 732, ad 1: "Licet ergo per effectum gratiae gratis datae possit cognosci Filius a Patre procedere et similiter Spiritus Sanctus ab utroque, tamen per solum effectum gratiae gratum facientis potest cognosci Filium et Spiritum Sanctum procedere in animam ad inhabitandam ipsam, cum per illam solam sit inhabitatio. Unde si illa definitio integre complectatur rationem missionis, oportet quod in illo effectu habeat cognosci processio Filii et Spiritus Sancti et quantum ad terminum a quo et quantum ad terminum ad quem: et tunc illud cognosci non habet esse nisi in effectu gratiae gratum facientis."

⁷⁴ *Sum. Theol.*, I, Tract. VII, q. 32, memb. 1, sol. ad q. 1 (XXXI p. 341): ". . . processio Spiritus Sancti dupliciter dicitur: scilicet simplex manifestatio processionis per signum, et sic procedit Spiritus sanctus in donis gratuitis datis. Et est etiam manifestatio processionis aeternae, simul et procedentis Spiritus per proprium ejus actum, quem non operatur nisi in illis in quibus habitat per inhabitantem gratiam. Et hoc modo non procedit nisi in donis gratum facientibus."

⁷⁵ *Op. cit.*, d. 16, a. un., q. 1 (I, p. 279): "Missio autem communiter dicta, ut dictum fuit supra in praecedenti distinctione, praesupponit circam missum emanationem et superaddit manifestationem. Et quoniam manifestatio emanationis, secundum quam attenditur missio, non fit nisi super eum, quem Spiritus Sanctus inhabitat per effectum gratiae inhabitantis, hinc est, quod missio de ratione generali dicit manifestationem emanantionis et inhabitationis."

[76] *Op. cit.*, p. 77, sol.: ". . . [Deum esse per gratiam] ponit necessario gratiam creatam in creatura, quae quidem gratia est similitudo, qua anima est imago actu, id est in imitatione actuali; et cum se habet anima per conformitatem ad Deum in similitudine expressa, dicitur Deus inhabitare in ipsa per gratium." He then quotes Augustine, *De praesentia Dei, Epist.* 187, Chap. 5, n. 17 (PL 33: 838); cf. *supra*, p. 69. Cf. *ibid.*, p. 723, ad 3: ". . . non propter quemcumque effectum appropriatum Filio vel Spiritui Sancto dicitur mitti Filius vel Spiritus Sanctus, sed propter illos in quibus expresse habet cognosci Filius vel Spiritus Sanctus, non solum per modum vestigii, sed per modum imaginis; et tales effectus sunt cognitio et amor vel dona pertinentia ad cognitionem et amorem, in quibus relucet processio Filii et Spiritus Sancti per modum imaginis; et quia talium effectuum est capax sola rationalis creatura, ideo ratione alicuius effectus appropriati non dicitur mitti ad aliam creaturam, quia in aliis creaturis non dicitur cognosci effectus nisi per modum vestigii." It should be noted, however, that this explanation is given to solve an objection, not in virtue of its inherent value as a solution of the problem.

CHAPTER FOUR

Early Scholastic Solutions

From the preceding chapters it is clear that there is a definite, well-established and universal theological tradition in the Middle Ages respecting the mystery of the presence of the Trinity in the souls of the just. The scriptural facts, literally understood by the Church as the Fathers testify, have become the subject of scientific analysis by human intelligence elevated and illumined by Faith. This investigation has proceeded to the point where the major problem set by the mystery comes clearly to light: how are the Persons present? What formal reason distinguishes this special presence from God's common presence in all things? In what manner is God now in man?

In many ways the isolating of this aspect of the ineffable mystery testifies to the vitality and validity of the Christian renaissance now shortly to burst into the full flower of the thirteenth century. To be sure, this is only one among many similar instances — and not the most important, at this stage — where the believing, seeking mind of the Middle Ages would reap a rich intellectual harvest and thereby render all subsequent Christian ages its debtor. Yet historical imagination would be dulled, indeed, and appreciation of the history of ideas (of that subjective growth of the knowledge of God which constitutes a true evolution of dogma) would truly be stifled, were one to fail to recognize the theological progress that has been attained by scholastic tradition.

To pose the right question, to pose it in the right order and manner, is, in fact, to isolate the heart of the matter: to prepare the essential foundation on which a true construction may be securely and triumphantly erected. Had the Schoolmen done no more than this, their contribution to our understanding of the inhabitation of the Trinity would still, on any formal scale of values, have been enormous — as anyone familiar with modern confusions on the point would unhappily testify. Still their efforts do not subside with this accomplishment. Having seen clearly where the difficulties lay, they seek, "in various ways and with diverse reasonings," to understand and to clarify the mystery of this marvelous union with God.

The answers first given will naturally be tentative, experimental, exploratory: avenues of approach far more than attempts at definitive solution. But it will be well to consider those Scholastics whose works have previously been expounded, in order that the cross currents and interplay, the action and reaction, of a truly vital intellectual culture (it hardly seems too much to say that this vitality is providential — and supernatural) may reveal the main stream of the medieval theological tradition on this subject, this tradition of which St. Thomas is both heir and father, at once debtor and creditor. Of its influence on him as well as of his contribution to it there can be no doubt. What remains to be determined is the extent of both influence and contribution, their mutual relations. And in this determination one can hope truly to delineate his solution of the problem, to illustrate it through comparative studies, its originality and profundity, and thus to attain some knowledge of the height and the depth and the richness of one of the most inaccessible of the mysteries of God.

In this chapter, then, the solutions of the early Schoolmen will be first examined, leaving the more refined and mature answers of the great scholastic doctors, St. Albert and St. Bonaventure, for the chapter to follow. For the reasons advanced in Article 1 of Chapter Three, these early scholastic works will be studied in the following order: the *Book of Sentences* of Peter Lombard; the *Summa Aurea* of Altissiodorensis; the *Summa fratris Alexandri*. The other works and theologians previously mentioned will be considered within these various sections, as one or other serves to confirm or illuminate the exposition. Besides the exposition, an attempt will also be made to judge the theological value and the practical influence of the works considered, in this way anticipating, on the one hand, the response to modern objections, and, on the other, the important question of the manner in which these solutions will filter to the schoolroom and cell of the Angel of the Schools.

ARTICLE 1

The Master of the Sentences

"How God dwells in the good," says Peter Lombard in Distinction 37, "you will be able to understand in some measure from the things which have been said above, when the temporal procession of the Holy Spirit was treated. . . ." And he continues with well-merited reserve: "where, although only partially, for in part we know and in part we prophesy, is exposed how the Holy Spirit dwells in us, who inhabits not without the Father and the Son."[1]

If one turns to Distinction 14, where the temporal procession of the Holy Spirit is discussed, he will find Peter's reservation optimistic. The only explanation he has here to offer is that the Holy Spirit is given to us, is infused in us and 'sinks down' (*illabitur*) in our minds — a simple repetition of St. Ambrose's cited text which adds nothing to our understanding of the mystery.[2]

His real solution, however, is found in the famous Distinction 17, when he identifies Charity with the Holy Spirit. "Then He is said to be sent or to be given," he declares of the Third Person, "when He is so in us that He makes us love God and neighbor: by which we abide in God, and God in us."[3] How is this gift, the personal Gift who is the Spirit, given to us? "When He is so communicated to someone — that is, so has being in someone — that He makes him a lover of God and neighbor; when He does which, then He is said to be given or sent to someone, and then that person is said properly to have the Holy Spirit."[4]

The solution is a sound one on two conditions: that this direct and immediate union with God is not peculiar to the Holy Spirit but appropriated to Him (the inhabitation would then parallel the manner in which God is present to man in the Beatific Vision); and that his premise, the identification of Charity and the Holy Spirit, is a valid one. But the first condition is very doubtful — all the medieval theologians understand him as speaking properly and not by appropriation. And the second condition is impossible, whether the Third Person be understood as moving cause of the free will (as with Peter himself) or as formal cause united to man's will (as with his disciples).* There must be, in the clear teaching of St. Thomas and the other Scholastics, a created habit of Charity in the will.[5]

Hence Peter Lombard's solution is no solution at all. It presupposes a new relation in the creature, yet places the fundament for such a relation not in the creature but in God alone. So it can hardly be surprising that later theologians search elsewhere for a solution; nor can it be surprising, on the other hand, in view of Peter's position as an *auctoritas*, that his insistence on love as the answer to the problem will find sympathetic interpreters. If he has not given a solution he has indicated an approach.

ARTICLE 2

William of Auxerre

For Altissiodorensis the solution appears to be so tentative and tenuous that his only contribution might be said to be the fact that he sees there is a difficulty and a mystery involved. The Holy Spirit is given "as spiritual food," He is possessed and given in grace, in some way as a contained thing is in the container. If we press him for further elucidation, his answer is that "the Holy Ghost is the proper and inseparable matter about which grace is concerned."[6]

* Cf. *supra*, p. 98, note 53.

No doubt the operative word here is 'inseparable.' But William does not explain why God is inseparable from His grace, why He is really present in grace — which is the point under discussion. To be present as the matter about which grace is concerned leads to no more than an intentional, objective presence: so, too, the matter with which the intellect is concerned is the essence of material things, which does not necessitate their real presence; and the matter of Charity is the divine goodness, without God (on that score alone) being necessarily really present, since love abstracts from presence or absence.

But if one considers William's solution in the general context of scholastic tradition rather than in the abstract, then a different light is thrown on his contribution. For the medieval theologians of the mystical life, the notion of 'tasting' God is a fundamental one, and universally accepted. So that when Altissiodorensis maintains that the Holy Spirit is given as spiritual food he is stating equivalently that the Holy Ghost is present as object of our experiencing, as fruit to be enjoyed. The same metaphor will be employed as late as the time of Odo Rigaldus and in precisely the same sense.* Considering these facts, it would seem that there is a direct influence on later solutions attributable to William of Auxerre, insofar as he has determined the *term* of the relation involved. Yet his solution, as is obvious, suffers from the general failure that will be noted in the Franciscan theologians: explaining a real union through the efficacy of love, when love, *formally* considered, can account only for a moral union.

Once again a relation is predicated without a fundament sufficient to explain it. The Archdeacon of Beauvais gives no answer to the question.

* Cf. Codex Vaticanus latinus 5982 in the Appendix, p. 359.

ARTICLE 3

The Summa Fratris Alexandri

Of the general importance of this theological compilation there can be little doubt, despite some modern aspersions prejudicially cast upon it. This general interest, however, becomes intensified when one turns to its teaching on the presence of the Trinity in the souls of the just, for only then does one realize the tremendous debt St. Bonaventure and St. Thomas owe to this Franciscan effort for their own solutions of the problem.

The answer here contained is, accordingly, of paramount value, and it will be worth while to consider its doctrine in some detail, not out of an abstract historical interest for a theological curiosity but for the significant similarities and the revealing differences it will exhibit, on subsequent comparison, with the doctrine of St. Thomas. And yet the task implicates intrinsic difficulties, for the Halesian *Summa* is not a consistent or coherent work from the doctrinal point of view, at one point or another involving contradictions and inconsequences. Can an analysis of this one tract be given without misinterpretation and prejudice, without regard for extrinsic opinions and the inevitable differences?

It would seem that a satisfactory exposition can be accomplished along these lines. Where interpretation is necessary beyond the tract on the divine missions itself, one may be justified in presuming that the general principles to which the Franciscan school of theology adheres can be followed—else this part of the *Summa fratris Alexandri* would in no manner have been accepted, transmitted and defended by the heirs of that tradition, to say nothing of the fact that it is unquestionably the product of the early years which gave it birth, truly representative of its early formative forces. In consequence, the procedure which can reasonably be followed is this: to quote from other parts of the work not in defense of a peculiar interpretation but in confirmation of a general point of view accepted by this school, or to illuminate for non-Franciscan eyes the manner in which a subject would be understood by those theologians. Such an exegesis demands, not that this specific author of this particular tract be regarded as teaching some *peculiar* point taken from another section of the Franciscan *Summa,* but, on the contrary, that this other text indicates what all (or the generality) of the theologians and Masters of this school hold on this point.

A practical point: with this defined and limited use of other material from the Halesian *Summa,* one may legitimately cite references even from the fourth part of the work, despite the fact that this was composed some years or even two decades after the tract which is of immediate interest. For it is certain that this represents — on the points to be cited — the accepted Franciscan tradition.* By the necessity of circumstance the uncritical Cologne edition must be used for these citations, yet even here, since only obvious interpretations given by the Franciscan school are quoted, one can be confident that no exegetical injustice results. So much for method.

For the present it will be sufficient simply to expose the teaching of the *Summa fratris Alexandri,* leaving to a later chapter the comparative study of the literary and

* The Quaracchi editors of the Halesian *Summa* attribute Book IV to William of Miltona (student at Paris in the time of Alexander and Jean de la Rochelle) and his associates, Franciscans to whom Pope Alexander IV entrusted the completion of the work. Cf. ed. cit., IV, Prol., p. CCCXXXVII.

doctrinal correspondences and differences between this compilation and the solution of the Angelic Doctor. The doctrine will first be studied as found in the *Summa Theologica* which bears Alexander's name, rather than in the *Glossa*, which bears his teaching. For this last a special section at the end of this exposition is reserved. The presentation of the doctrine of the Halesian *Summa* is divided into four sections: an analysis of the theory; an interpretation of it as based on appropriation; a contrary interpretation, which considers the solution as offered from the point of view of final causality; and a criticism of the theory.

1. Analysis of the Theory of the *Summa*

The special presence of God in the souls of the just is distinguished precisely from His common presence in all things (which it nevertheless presupposes),[7] insofar as by the inhabitation man *possesses* God,[8] albeit in a passive, i.e., receptive, sense.[9] God is possessed, moreover, not in any manner whatsoever, but under the precise aspect of 'fruit,' as the object of our enjoyment: for the author of the Franciscan *Summa*, this is the characteristic note of the inhabitation, as his innumerable uses of the phrase clearly indicate.[10] Such a designation may even serve as a sort of definition, specifying, like the inhabitation itself, the very purpose of the divine missions.[11]

But if the divine Persons are present as fruits to be enjoyed by the just, two facts immediately follow. First, the inhabitation is an effect of the missions, and their end;[12] secondly, the inhabitation cannot be explained on the grounds of efficient causality, since God is there present as principle but not as gift or fruit.[13]

And so one element of the special relation which the presence of the Trinity implies is clearly delineated: its term is the Holy Spirit (i.e., as has been noted,* the Trinity) precisely as an object of enjoyment. But what is the fundament for this relation?

The Gordian knot of the problem is here. Much as the specification of the terms has advanced us toward a solution, the central, capital question still remains: *how* do the just possess the divine Persons as objects of enjoyment? Since the inhabitation and the invisible missions are so indissolubly linked, in the author's analysis of the latter an answer perhaps may be found.

Although he points out that Augustine's definition 'to be sent is to be known' does not include the principal element of the missions (the eternal processions), he admits its value *quoad nos*.[14] Hence he states that the Son or the Holy Spirit is sent and inhabits "by reason of some effect which can be appropriated to the Son or Holy Spirit, in which the Son or Holy Spirit can be known to be from another."[15]

What is the function of this knowing of the divine processions? Is it the reason for the missions and the consequent inhabitation? No, the reason lies in the effect itself, insofar as the processions are *represented* in that effect and hence *can* be known.[16] Moreover, it must be such an effect as to be known not by any kind of knowledge but specifically by the knowledge which springs from love.[17] In the knowledge and love which come from grace (more accurately, in the gifts pertaining to knowledge and love), insofar as they are *images* of the divine processions, the Persons are represented. As such They are knowable as proceeding from another; as capable of be-

---

* Cf. *supra*, pp. 83-84.

ing known, They are said to be sent and They dwell in the soul.

The Trinity abides within us, then, not in virtue of our knowing Them but by reason of a representative effect pertaining to sanctifying grace in which They can be known.

2. An Interpretation of the Theory

How is this conclusion to be understood? Does it mean, as at first sight it seems to mean, that the Persons are there by representation, is representation the *formal reason* of the indwelling? Such is the way Father Cuervo interprets "Alexander,"[18] and certain phrases substantially support this exegesis. According to "Alexander," a Person is sent (and consequently inhabits) "by reason of the representation in an effect appropriated to Him."[19] "Even if that effect should never be known, or by that effect the procession of the Son or Holy Ghost, nevertheless by that effect that by which it can be known is represented, that is, in some spiritual sign it is represented in a knowable way."[20]

Despite such apparently clear declarations, serious doubts prohibit the acceptance of this interpretation. In the first place, it could in no way explain the real presence of the Persons in the soul, as Father Cuervo rightly observes;[21] and although the Franciscan author could err in believing that it did (many good theologians after him have fallen into similar error), still if this fact be taken in conjunction with other elements of his theory to be exposed shortly, the presupposition exists that he recognized the inadequacies of such an explanation. Secondly, and more importantly for this argument, this solution would ultimately have to fall back on God's causal operation, His efficient and exemplary causality; and this is explicitly rejected as an answer, not only in general,* but directly so far as appropriation is concerned:

> Even though as often as the Father works through the Son He also works the same effect through the Holy Spirit, nevertheless not so often as He sends the Son does He send the Holy Spirit, and this because that effect is not appropriated to both but to one Person: therefore only that Person is said to be sent to whom the effect is appropriated. Nor is a Person said to be sent by reason of operation, but by reason of the representation in the effect appropriated to Him.[22]

The reasoning is clear. Different Persons are sent, and distinctly; but God's activity is common to all three and so cannot account for the difference of the missions. There is, then, some real distinction between various effects, and because of this difference which is intrinsic in the effects one can be appropriated to the Son, another to the Holy Ghost. But if no difference can be accounted for on the basis of efficient causality, the quality which justifies this appropriation cannot be explained on such a basis either. Neither efficient nor exemplary causality can explain why one Person rather than another is sent, because they cannot explain why this effect pertains to the Son, this to the Holy Ghost: as effects they are caused indistinctly by all three Persons.

Nor would placing the formal reason of the indwelling in representation explain the unquestionable insistence of the *Summa Alexandri* on the presence of the Persons as the object of the soul's enjoyment. To be *represented* as being present is not *to be* really present as something to be enjoyed. Yet precisely this presence of the Persons —

---

* Cf. *supra*, p. 111.

as the object of man's beatitude — constitutes in the author's mind the very essence of the inhabitation.* If They are there as fruits to be enjoyed, They are really present in some way and not merely by reason of representation.

3. A Second Interpretation of the Theory

By reason of some effect of sanctifying grace (the gifts pertaining to knowledge or love) in which the procession of the Son or Holy Ghost is represented and in which, therefore, the Son or Holy Ghost can be known as proceeding from another, the Son or Holy Ghost is said to be sent and to inhabit. This is indisputably the conclusion of the analysis formulated by the Franciscan *Summa* of the divine missions and inhabitation.

Are the Persons present, then, *because They are represented?* Such was the interpretation proposed in the preceding section, an interpretation which cannot square with the author's own teaching. Another question suggests itself: *can* the Persons be represented *because They are somehow in the effect?* Does representation depend on presence, rather than vice versa? A deeper study of this doctrine obliges one to ask and answer the second question; to ask, in other words, not only why They are capable of being known (the answer: because They are represented) but why and in what manner They are represented.

The justification for this further question rests not only in the fact that the first answer given is wholly inadequate to explain the solution of the Halesian *Summa;* it is even founded, *usque ad verba,* in the very phrases quoted in support of Father Cuervo's interpretation. As has been pointed out, the author appropriates an effect

---

* Cf. *supra,* p. 111.

of grace to the Holy Spirit not precisely as an effect (as produced by Him), but because by this effect the soul is given the faculty or power to love Him.[23] Such an effect, therefore, can represent the procession of the Third Person, who proceeds as love; and this makes Him knowable, and in consequence He is said to be sent and to inhabit. But does not such an explanation justify the inquiry: which is the real basis for the mission and the inhabitation, the representation? or the power (the gift of grace: Charity) whose very nature makes such representation possible? And the answer must be — for in line with the author's principles it can only be — that it is the gift, not the representation. For it is the gift alone which makes the Holy Spirit present *as an object* (speaking formally, not causally), something which mere representation could never do by itself.

Similarly when he states that the procession is capable of being known (hence the Person is sent and inhabits) in a spiritual sign which represents Him, the context of the phrase invites a closer scrutiny. For he says the effect represents *"that by which* the procession (or the Person) can be known."[24] Is the effect, then, in virtue of its function as a sign the basic reason for the presence of the Persons? No more than it can account by itself for the fact that it *is* such a sign.

The effect *can* be a sign, it can represent the processions and the Persons in so perfect a way that They can be known in it and therefore can be said to be sent and to dwell in the just. But to be a sign of so exalted a nature depends on this: that the particular effect in question (the gift pertaining to supernatural knowledge and love) is *a power whose object is the Persons Themselves*. Otherwise one would be forced to argue that natural knowledge and its faculty, natural love and its power — which are true signs and representations of the Trinity, for this author as for all the Scholastics who follow Augustine's doctrine — would likewise reveal the Persons. And in this natural knowledge They would also be sent and would inhabit.

The sign the Halesian *Summa* has in mind, however, is a practical sign, which effects what it signifies; the representation is an effective one which produces what it represents; the appropriation is dynamic, giving the just person the Person who is represented by the appropriation. The sign, the representation, the appropriation produce these results not in virtue of their representative formality but in virtue of their material aspect, the gift of knowledge or love which at one and the same time makes them truly signs *because* this gift makes the Trinity present as an object of knowledge or love.*

---

* This is the vital point of the author's doctrine. He states explicitly: ". . . gratia habitus est per quam efficitur anima deiformis; quod autem est deiforme dicitur habere divinam formam et sic per consequens Deum" (*op. cit.*, p. 76, ad 1). But grace is to be understood in the dynamic sense, as issuing in acts of knowledge and love of which the Trinity is the object; only in this sense is there an image of God "in act," "in actual imitation," (cf. *ibid.*, p. 77, sol.); only *in* the operations are the Persons represented (therefore capable of being known; therefore sent and indwelling), only *by* the operations, then, can They be had, possessed, enjoyed: which is to inhabit. This is clearly taught by his notion of appropriation, *ibid.*, p. 732, ad 3: ". . . licet sit una gratia gratum faciens, tamen plures sunt effectus gratiae gratum facientis. Dicendum ergo quod non distinguuntur missiones Filii et Spiritus Sancti penes ipsam gratiam, sed penes eius effectus; sed sicut in missione sua conveniunt in fine, scilicet in hoc quod est inhabitare animam vel esse in anima secundum hanc rationem; differunt tamen penes diversos actus gratiae gratum facientis, secundum quod illi actus appropriantur Filio vel Spiritu Sancto. Unde si datur gratia gratum faciens ad sanctificandam animam vel gratificandam vel accendendam ad amorem, cum huiusmodi actus sint appropriati Spiritu Sancto et in illis habeat cognosci, dicitur mitti Spiritus Sanctus. Si vero detur gratia ad illuminandam

What is, then, the answer of the *Summa fratris Alexandri* to the 'how' of the inhabitation? As previously noted, it is not placed in our actual knowledge of the Persons but in Their ability to be known insofar as They are present as objects. Is it therefore by the supernatural *faculty* of knowing them that They will become present? As such, no. For the knowledge implied by the mission is not its formal *reason* but its formal *effect*, as the passages already seen abundantly testify.

Not in knowledge but in love the author sees the formal reason of the inhabitation. For the Persons are

<small>animam vel instruendam vel ad aliquos actus pertinentes ad sapientiam, quae appropriatur Filio, cum in huiusmodi effectibus habeat cognosci Filius, dicitur mitti Filius; et sicut unus effectus potest esse sine alio, ita una misso potest esse sine alia, sicut supra dictum est. Et licet non possit dari aliquis effectus gratum faciens sive aliquod donum quin gratificetur et sanctificetur anima, non tamen datur principaliter ad hoc, sed solum gratia in se datur principaliter ad hoc, non in hoc effectu vel illo: et ideo non dicitur mitti nisi Filius, cum datur actus pertinens ad cognitionem, licet sit actus gratiae gratum facientis. Et si daretur aliquod donum aeque principaliter ad utrumque actum appropriatum Filio et Spiritu Sanctio, diceretur mitti sive dari Filius et Spiritus Sanctus, et ideo donum sapientiae et donum intellectus dicuntur dona Spiritus Sancti, non ratione actus proprii, sed communis, sive ratione finis, qui est unire animam Deo; et similiter alia dona, ut fides, prophetia et huiusmodi, quia per haec unitur et communicat anima Christo et corpori ejus mystico, quod est Ecclesia. . . ."</small>

It should be noted that the teaching that the missions of the Son and the Holy Ghost are not only distinct but separable and separated is unique with him; neither St. Thomas (*Sum. Theol.*, I, q. 43, a. 5 ad 3) nor St. Bonaventure concur (*op. cit.*, d. 15, p. 2, a. un., q. 2; ed. cit., I, p. 272). The editors of St. Bonaventure cite Richard of Middleton as a follower of Alexander; Peter of Tarantasia, Giles of Rome and most others, however, follow the opposite opinion (*loc. cit.*, scholion).

But it should likewise be noted that it is the placing of the formal reason of the missions and the inhabitation in the *effects* of grace (rather than in the *cause* of grace) which fosters such a conception, since the effects are distinct and separable, whereas the cause is one: the divine essence, not the individual Persons.

present as fruits to be enjoyed, and enjoyment postulates a supernatural habit capable of such an act. To possess the Persons as fruits is the very definition of the indwelling; and although possession of an end and enjoyment of it are not the same thing, in Franciscan psychology and theology they involve the same faculty.²⁵ In love, then, the mystery becomes formally resolved.

He does not state this conclusion in so many words, but his thinking is clear. Where there is simply knowledge of the processions, as in unformed faith, the Persons are not sent, do not abide with the soul; it must be knowledge "conjoined to the affection of love, which, when it is in man, God is said to inhabit, and when it comes anew, He is said to be sent."²⁶ Love is the note which characterizes the missions and the indwelling, because the Persons are present as objects to be enjoyed by the just. And fruition is the ultimate act of love.*

---

* This doctrine, common to the Irrefragable Doctor and his foremost disciples, is based on Augustine's teaching in I *De Doctrina Christiana*, Chap. 3, which was assumed verbatim in large part by Peter Lombard in his first distinction (*op. cit.*, pp. 25-26). It is summed up in the famous definition, "Frui est amore inhaerere alicui rei propter seipsam." Alexander explains this, in effect, as a definition *per priora simpliciter* (cf. *Glossa in Quatuor Libros Sententiarum Petri Lombardi*, I, d. I, nn. 6, 7, 9, 10; ed. Quaracchi, I, pp. 9-12, *passim*.) Although he says that dilection follows knowledge, which is its cause, the formal cause of union is love, knowledge being only dispositively necessary (*Glossa*, n. 23; pp. 17-18).

The vast difference between St. Thomas and the Franciscan masters on this point is no better exemplified than by their respective commentaries on the same passage of the *Sentences*. In the first article of the first question of the first distinction, St. Thomas proposes the question, "Utrum frui sit actus intellectus"—a question Alexander or his disciples could not even conceive of asking. But St. Thomas asks and affirmatively answers the question: from the point of principle by which the union with God is formally effected, fruition is an act of knowledge, the best act of the highest potency respecting its noblest object, i.e., the vision of God. From this union, as a con-

But actual love is not required. The Trinity abides with children, incapable of such acts.²⁷ The inhabitation is the necessary concomitant of grace, and vice versa, so that one is never had without the other.²⁸ And yet actual fruition is the lot in this life only of a few, of those in a state of 'consummate justice,' i.e., the perfect.²⁹ So one may legitimately conclude that for the *Summa* of Alexander of Hales the grace-given habitual ability of enjoying the Trinity is the formal reason which explains Their presence in the just.*

What part does knowledge have to play in this theory? It has been shown that the knowledge of the divine pro-

sequence of it, comes love, delectation, fruition as an appetitive act. *Ex parte sui complementi,* enjoyment signifies an act of the will according to the habit of Charity; but the union is made by knowledge.

* Father Cuervo, *op. cit.*, p. 7, implicitly admits this interpretation (or at least recognizes its possibility) when to his criticism of "Alexander's" theory considered as a theory of appropriation he adds: "Ni vale añadir que la gracia nos une a Dios y nos hace gozar de las divinas Personas." And he considers it sufficiently grounded in the teaching of the Doctor Irrefragabilis to merit criticism: ". . . esto [theory based on the unitive power of grace and on the Persons as objects of fruition] puede verificarse en el orden moral sin que por eso las divinas Personas existan realmente en nosotros, tanto más cuanto que los actos de nuestro conocimiento y amor se distinguen realmente de ellas. Bastaría por lo tanto una presencia objectiva e intencional, lo que es muy distinto de la presencia real y sustancial de las divinas Personas."

The same interpretation as here given is maintained by Father Primeau in his special study of the subject (*Doctrina Summae Theologicae Alexandri Halensis de Spiritus Sancti apud Justos Inhabitatione.* Apud Aedes Sanctae Mariae ad Lacum, Mundelein, Illinois, U.S.A., 1936), who sums up the teaching of the *Summa* thus: "Specialiter praesens est Spiritus Sanctus 'in ratione fructus,' in quantum est objectum fruitionis animae. Haec autem inhabitatio Dei, uti objectum fruitionis, non necessario importat ex parte animae fruitionem actualem; sufficit, ut anima per gratiam sanctificantem facultate seu capacitate ad Deo fruendum gaudeat" (p. 74).

cessions represented in the effects of grace is the formal effect, not the formal reason, of the missions and the inhabitation. Relative to the power and act of fruition, however, knowledge is merely presupposed, a *sine qua non* or disposition for the complete act of fruition which is found in the will. This relationship appears when the Franciscan *Summa* talks of delectation,[30] for fruition is nothing else than an act of delectation.[31] As with prayer, so in the indwelling, knowledge is necessary for the apprehension of the object (the divine Persons), but it is the act of the appetitive faculty or habit to unite us with the Persons and terminate the union, and therefore by this act (or the power to elicit such an act) the inhabitation is formally constituted.

To sum up: in the gifts of grace of Faith and Charity the Son and Holy Ghost are sent to us and the Trinity abides in us. By Faith we can know the divine Persons, but this must be a loving-knowledge, if They are to dwell in us, since They must be more than apprehended, They must be possessed, had: for in the indwelling They become capable of being enjoyed by us. The state of grace in general, Charity in particular, is absolutely necessary. In virtue of making the Persons present to us as objects of enjoyment (Faith or Wisdom as disposing, Charity as formally effecting), these gifts from this very fact naturally represent the Son and the Holy Ghost: as God in knowing Himself by Himself utters the Word of love, so we knowing God by God image that procession: Faith and Wisdom represent the procession of the Son; as God in loving Himself by Himself produces personal Love, so we in loving God by God represent the procession of the Holy Spirit: Charity images the Holy Ghost. And this ability of the Persons to be known in these effects by our loving-knowledge enables us to say that the Son and the Holy Ghost are sent to us and consequently dwell within us.

Such is a complete presentation of the doctrine of the *Summa Alexandri* on the presence of the Trinity in the souls of the just. Its central, pivotal point is that God comes to us and takes up His abode in us in virtue of the fact that we possess a God-given supernatural power of possessing the Persons in order to enjoy them. This power follows knowledge, a prerequisite disposition; but formally the power is an appetitive one of the supernatural order: Charity.

Confirmation for this interpretation is by no means lacking. The Halesian *Summa* insists that God can dwell only in those who are capable of grasping Him by knowledge and love.[32] This suggests what it actually affirms: that since the inhabitation is a union with God, it cannot be realized by God's efficient causality nor by His exemplary causality but only in virtue of a supernatural operation (reductively a habit or power) on the part of the creature: "the ultimate effect of grace is more perfect, to unite us to God; but in others besides Christ only by knowledge and love is there union with God."[33] And so the formal reason of the inhabitation — which is inchoatively what the ultimate union of the Beatific Vision is consummately — must be found in knowledge or love or some subordinated or coordinated action or relation between the two.

The author's teaching on the image of God in man similarly corroborates this conclusion.* The image of re-creation, which is only in the just, is simply the re-

---

* According to the editors of the critical edition (IV, Prol., p. CCLXXIII), the doctrine on the image found in the *Summa* is taken (most often only so far as the sense is concerned) chiefly from Jean de la Rochelle. Alexander does not seem to be a source.

formation of the image of nature, which is found in the Augustinian trinity of memory, intelligence and will.[34] By grace the soul is an image in act, in actual imitation of the Trinity:[35] and it is as such that it represents the processions of the Persons and makes Them capable of being known.[36] If we have the power of knowing God as He knows Himself and loving Him as He loves Himself we image the Most Holy Trinity: the Father as principle, the Son proceeding as Word, the Holy Spirit proceeding as love. But to know and love God in this way — what is this but to have the Trinity present as an object of our loving-knowledge, whose ultimate explanation is found formally in Charity as it informs Faith?[37]

Corroboration is found again in the fact that for the Franciscan school in general, love, not knowledge, is the unitive power, that which effects a physical oneness with its object. Fruition is described as an adherence, a certain contact, a union.[38] Where knowledge only apprehends a thing, Alexander of Hales explicitly teaches, love joins us to that thing; and in its ultimate act of fruition or delectation it consummates, terminates and perfects.* So it is not surprising to find him praising one of Peter Lombard's formulas and making it his own: "In the *Book of the Sentences* the Master assigns the end of the rational creature, saying that it has been created 'in order that it might know the ultimate good, and knowing it might love it, and loving it possess it, and possessing it enjoy it.' "[39] On the basis of such principles as these the author of the tract on the invisible missions in the *Summa Alexandri* could well believe that he had found a real solution to the problem, one which explains the real and physical presence of the Trinity in the souls of the just.

---

* Cf. *supra*, p. 119, note.

Finally, the interpretation here sponsored is indirectly confirmed by the testimony of Codex Vaticanus latinus 691. Whether this be considered as a source of the *Summa Alexandri* or a work stemming with it from a common root,* its importance for the understanding of that compilation cannot be gainsaid, since it is at least a contemporaneous document and probably somewhat earlier. And on this important point the manuscript offers perfect confirmation for the exegesis which has been given:

> Spiritus Sanctus utroque modo datur, in se et in suis donis et potest dici quod in iustis est Spiritus S. sicut fructus: omnis enim fruuntur eo. Dona autem sive gratie sunt sicut dispositiones mentis nostre ad fruendum. Quod obiicitur quod Spiritus S. sufficienter facit nos Deo gratos *effective,* gratie et virtus *formaliter,* quia informant mentem ad hoc quod sit templum Dei. Dicimus etiam quod licet sine suis donis possit agere, tamen nos *sine suis donis* aliquid meritorium non possumus agere. Et licet ab eo habeamus quod operemur, tamen non est forma mentis nostre.[40]

4. The Theory of the *Summa Alexandri* and the Theory of Alexander

But the most telling confirmation of the exposition that has been advanced is the fact that the solution of Alexander in his earliest work, the *Gloss* on the *Sentences* of Peter Lombard, is so completely different from the solution that has been offered as that of the Franciscan *Summa.* The apparent contradiction of these words demands explanation.

Alexander's commentary on Peter's texts in the tract on the divine missions is justly titled a gloss, since it ex-

---

* Cf. *supra,* p. 76.

pands the text very little; yet there is sufficient interpretation by the secular Master of Theology to obtain a notion of his mind at the time. He accepts the common scholastic tradition: the indwelling is a special presence of the whole Trinity, dependent on grace; Augustine's definition of the missions is adequate in terms of the effect connoted, which is produced by the entire Trinity.[41] But when forced to explain the way in which this special presence is realized, he finds no other answer than the fact of appropriation: it cannot be by reason of God's efficient causality, since that is common to the three Persons; so he explains that the "mission, by reason of the effect, is in us by appropriation either to the Son or to the Holy Spirit."[42] Ultimately, then, exemplary causality must account for the fact of the missions and the inhabitation.*

* *Ibid.*, d. 17, n. 3 (I, p. 168). Against an objection that uncreated Charity is in us only as efficient cause, but since no mission can be designated from the point of view of this causality it is not right to say that the Holy Spirit is the Charity which dwells in us, Alexander answers: "in caritate respectu nostri tria notantur, scilicet quod sit causa effectiva, quod causa exemplaris, quod ens in nobis sicut motivum essentialiter in suo moto ab alio; et tunc dicitur recte mitti. Unde, licet primum conveniat Patri, non tamen secundum et tertium per appropriationem, quia Pater non est causa exemplaris per appropriationem vel motivum ab alio."

This same doctrine is equivalently taught, so far as its essentials are concerned, in his *Quaestiones Disputatae de Missionibus* (as they appear in Cod. Vat. lat. 782; see Appendix, pp. 356-359), which are certainly of a later date than the *Glossa*, although before he became a Franciscan, c. 1236 (cf. *supra*, p. 75). The important teaching of these questions concerns the *end* of the invisible missions: not that man might have, possess and enjoy the Persons, not that They inhabit in him as in a temple, but that man might know Them, and thereby be recalled from sensible things—and this is even true of the divine donation: "Omnia enim facta sunt propter hominem, ut homo cognoscat, quia apparitio facta est ut homo essentiam cognosceret, missio ut processionem, datio ut cognoscamus potentiam communi-

But if this fact at first glance would seem to favor the interpretation of the theory in the *Summa* attributed to Alexander as one of appropriation, another singular fact must be taken into consideration. For never, in the whole of this brief commentary, does Alexander mention even once the element which occupies so prominent a part — at the very least, in a material sense — of the later explanation: that the Persons are present 'per modum fructus,' as possessed and had by the just soul, as objects to be enjoyed. This strange omission is emphasized by the fact that his definition of 'giving' in the *Gloss* does not make a single reference to its natural correlative, the notion of having or possessing as one's own.[43]

Can one reconcile this essential omission with the possibility of a doctrinal influence of the *Gloss* on the tract on the invisible missions of the *Summa Alexandri*? Assuredly, such a reconciliation is impossible. On the contrary, the omission is a clear indication that Alexander

candi." (f⁰ 7vb, circa 2m). "Est ergo missio spiritualis ad ostendendum spiritualiter processionem eternam et utilitas est ad revocandam creaturam a sensibilibus ad eterna" (f⁰ 8va.).

This significant specification of the end of the missions—so essentially different from that of the Halesian *Summa* and so similar to the doctrine of the *Glossa*—seems to stem from two facts: the insistence, following Augustine, on the notion of manifestation (f⁰ 7vb.) and the concentration on grace *as an effect* by which the 'power of communication' of the Persons is made known, which can only be explained in terms of appropriation: ". . . non omnis creatura manifestat, sed creatura que est appropriata Filio et Spiritui Sancto quia sapientia est effectus appropriabilis Filio . . . ." (*loc. cit.*); "essentia enim divina incognoscibilis est, quantum est de se et persona procedens. Sed divina persona communicat aliquid creature, quia Filius sapientiam, Spiritus Stus, amorem. Est ergo ibi essentia et processio, que eterna est, que, quantum est de se, incognoscibiles sunt, sed cognoscibiles sunt in effectibus" (f⁰ 7vb, circa 2m). Here, as in the *Glossa*, Alexander is defeated before he begins, because he regards God as the principle of the effects produced.

is not the doctrinal father of this part of the *Summa* given his name as he is not its literary father either. For the author of the *Summa* appreciates the fact that the appropriation of effects in no way explains the reality of the indwelling, that it was necessary to specify more accurately and scientifically the precise nature of the presence of the Trinity before one could attempt to explain it.*

* Would not a modification or revision of the original tract be the explanation for its late appearance and its incompleteness? This seems a legitimate conclusion, based on the following reasons: first, the tract is referred to in the beginning of Bk. III, the most ancient part of the *Summa,* with specific reference to the missing question on the visible mission ("Determinationem huius quaestionis require supra, Libro I, in inquisitione de missionibus. Q. de missione"; IV, p. 97): it would certainly seem, then, that the questions actually existed when this oldest part of the *Summa Alexandri* was composed, or at least that the author had well in mind what was there to be taught, a fact with which the late composition of the tract and its incompleteness hardly square. Second, no trace of Alexander's style or works or doctrine (as we know it) can be found, except very remotely—an odd fact, at least, except on the basis of a deliberate revision of an original tract which was, in some manner and to some degree, his.

This leads to some conjectures, the worth of which the reader may judge for himself. But two are suggestive: either Alexander changed his mind respecting the theory he proposes in his early written works, or at least is not so convinced of its certitude as to object to the changes made by his disciples and co-worker (by no means impossible, since the only evidence for his state of mind is founded on works dating 10-20 years before the composition of the tract on the missions); or, if one presumes his intransigence on the point and his autocratic control of the work, then the revision was made or inserted by Jean de la Rochelle immediately upon his death or relinquishing of control—a possibility if not very probable.

In any case, from Codex Vaticanus latinus 691 and the *Commentary* of Eudes Rigaud (cf. Appendix, pp. 359-361) it is certain that an essentially different theory, one based on the aspect of final causality, was seriously maintained and even prevalent at the time of the composition of the tract of the Franciscan *Summa*. On the other hand, as will later be seen, St. Albert holds the older theory of Alexander, based on efficient causality. This argues for two opposed views

The *Summa*, then — and the fact must be regarded as incontestable — represents a definite theological advance in the understanding of the mystery of the indwelling and the problem it raises. At the very least the comparison between the two works suggests that the later Franciscan master considerably revised Alexander's appreciation of the facts about the mystery so readily accepted by both. And the most logical explanation, in view of the insistence in the Halesian *Summa* on that triune presence as characterised by the notion of the Persons as objects of the just soul's enjoyment, is that the explanation of that work *must* be interpreted in those terms.

It would seem, in sum, that the difference of treatment argues convincingly for the exposition that has been given. For the *Summa Alexandri* the triune pesence is explained by the fact that man, in a state of grace, knows or is capable of knowing the three Persons, and consequently can love Them; and in loving Them he possesses Them, They are his as objects of his enjoyment, as fruits for his delectation: as dwelling within him.

5. Criticism of the Solution of the *Summa Fratris Alexandri*

The inadequacies of this theory — proposing the faculty of enjoying the Trinity as a formal reason for the real presence of the divine Persons — are immediately apparent. Against such an explanation, the criticism simultaneously taught in the Schools by different Masters. In these circumstances, since the two explanations are opposed and the Halesian *Summa* explicitly rejects that of appropriation, it can only be understood as sponsoring the theory of final causality.

A revision of the original tract in the light of this 'new' theory, seems, in consequence, highly probable, other factors being taken into consideration.

John of St. Thomas will later level against the proposals of Suarez is equally valid.[44] As St. Thomas himself points out,[45] real, physical union is an *efficient* effect of love, but love itself can never be the *formal* reason for this real presence, nor even a disposition by means of which the loved one becomes present.* No matter how perfect love may be, neither on the natural nor on the supernatural plane can it do more than seek and tend toward real and physical union. It must remain in the moral and intentional order, as opposed to the order of substantial presence.

Fruition is an act of an appetitive faculty, as all the Scholastics agree; on the intellectual level, it is an act of the will or a perfecting power modifying the will: for it is the enjoyment of an end possessed, ultimately of eternal life, of God Himself in His trinity of Persons. Such an enjoyment, obviously, can only be imperfect in this life, where beatitude is possessed not in the physical order but only in expectation and intention; it will be perfect in heaven, when we enjoy our final end — but an end *already* possessed.[46] But to possess the Trinity in intention and hope does not explain our real possession of the Trinity here on earth, the fact of Its real presence in those in whom the Three dwell as in a temple. If enjoyment *follows* real possession, it cannot account for it. "This end — the vision of God which is our beatitude — the intellect attains as an active power," says St. Thomas, "but the will attains it as a power moving toward the end and enjoying the end already attained."[47] The will, or a supernatural gift elevating the will, can urge us toward God, can rejoice in the presence of God once He is possessed:

---

* Such a disposition, for example, is found in the *lumen gloriae* in respect to the real union of the divine essence with the created intellect in the Beatific Vision.

neither the will nor any supernatural appetitive habit can possess God, in the proper sense of that word. The power of enjoying the Trinity is not identical with the supernatural gift of possessing Them as objects of enjoyment. And so it cannot be the formal reason of the inhabitation.

Certainly the author of the tract on the divine missions in the Franciscan *Summa* believed the presence of the Trinity was real and substantial; no less certain is the fact that he insisted, in contradistinction to Suarez, on the presence of God as cause of all things as a necessary presupposition to this enjoyment. And just as certainly, for him the union between the soul and the indwelling Persons was a real, physical union, not, as Father Primeau believes,[48] simply a moral union.

But despite these theological principles he failed to explain the triune presence. His failure, however, lies not in a misunderstanding of the problem nor in a misapplication of principles: to have well understood the problem, to have developed the intrinsic principles of solution — these are his triumph, and a tribute to his theological greatness and scientific acumen. His failure lies with his *extrinsic* principles. For he holds, with all the Franciscan school, following the tradition of Augustine and the Victorines and Peter Lombard, that love formally effects a real union with the object loved.

Despite its inadequacy, the author's contribution is immense. He has specified the term of the new relation involved — this is the infinite distance which separates the *Gloss* of Alexander from the *Summa* attributed to Alexander — and then has attempted to determine the fundament which, in relation to that term, will formally account for the relation in question being this sort of thing, a real and substantial presence of the three divine Persons in the souls of those in the state of sanctifying grace. His procedure, then, has been scientific, profound and suggestive. In his delineation of the problem and in the principles of his solution he provides a real development for our grasp of the mystery.*

On the other hand, not only is his solution false (the fault of extrinsic considerations), it must also be admitted that it is obscured rather than illumined by the way he presents it. In general, of course, there is a tendency to criticize the Schoolmen for not answering the questions *we* ask as directly as we would wish; the criticism is unjust, springing mainly from difficulties in our own understanding of the problem rather than from difficulties inherent in the matter itself. But in this case, the explanation of the divine missions, an explanation in terms of representation, confuses the issue. The author would seem here to be a victim of Augustine's ingenuity in

---

* This is not an original contribution, of course, since the same solution is to be found in Codex Vaticanus latinus 691 and Eudes Rigaud—in how many others we do not know. Its elements are certainly present in St. Augustine, and William of Auxerre gives metaphorical expression to the same specification of the term of the new relation. The fact remains, however, that this will be the classic formulation of the problem and of the principles by which a solution becomes possible. Thus John of St. Thomas will repeat the findings of the author of this tract of the *Summa Alexandri* in all but its very words. Cf. *Cursus Theologicus*, I, q. 8, Disp. 8, a. 7, n. 8 (II, p. 38): "supposita dispositione gratiae et caritatis in anima, et contactu Dei per modum operantis et producentis illam (quod pertinet ad modum communem immensitatis), resultare specialem modum praesentiae realis et physicae respectu Dei, in quantum existit in anima per modum rei possessae et fruibilis ab ipsa: consummate quidem in gloria ubi erit fruitio in actu consummata, et specialis unio divinae essentiae ratione speciei: hic autem est unio ista fruitionis inchoata et imperfecta. Vere tamen ratione illius dicitur Deus, non solum communi modo suae immensitatis et contactu operationis esse in anima, sed per modum inhabitantis et amici conviventis, et finis possessi." This expression of the problem and its principles John of St. Thomas receives, of course, from his master.

theological explanation rather than a beneficiary: for it is undoubtedly the concept of manifestation that has led him to so elaborate and confusing an elucidation.

As is evident from the corrected analysis of this theory, the basic solution (man's possession of the power of enjoying the divine Persons) is now hidden under an apparent solution (man's ability to recognize in these powers a representation of the divine Persons). Three questions must now be asked where only one should suffice: why are the Persons sent? (because They are now capable of being known); how are They capable of being known? (because They are represented in certain effects); why are They represented in such a way as to be capable of being known in these effects and not in any other? (because these effects possess the Persons as objects of knowledge and love, i.e., as fruits of the enjoyment of the just).

Such complication can hardly clarify a difficult problem. The way is open to serious misunderstanding and misinterpretation. Indeed, if it were not that in other parts of the tract he has stated more simply the principles which can be used to interpret his theory of the inhabitation, one may reasonably doubt that a true appreciation of his solution could be obtained from this statement of it alone. That the theory is nonetheless contained there substantially as it has been interpreted will, doubtless, appear more clearly and more evident as the solutions of the other scholastic Doctors are brought to light. For the present one can only assert the value of the Franciscan *Summa* as evidenced in this explanation of the inhabitation; proof of its tremendous intellectual importance will have to await the further consideration of other theories.

NOTES

[1] *Op. cit.*, d. 37 (pp. 847-848): "Quomodo autem Deus habitet in bonis, ex illis aliquatenus intelligere valebis quae supra dicta sunt, cum de Spiritus sancti processione temporali ageretur, ubi, licet ex parte, exponitur, ex parte enim cognoscimus et ex parte prophetamus, quomodo Spiritus sanctus habitet in nobis, qui non sine Patre et Filio inhabitat."

[2] *Ibid.*, d. 14 (p. 313): "Et quod ipse Spiritus sanctus, qui Deus est ac tertia in Trinitate persona, nobis detur, nostrisque infundatur atque illabitur mentibus, aperte ostendit Ambrosius in lib. I *De Spiritu sancto*. . . ."

[3] *Ibid.*, d. 17 (p. 384): "Tunc enim mitti vel dari dicitur, cum ita in nobis est ut faciat nos diligere Deum et proximum: per quod manemus in Deo, et Deus in nobis."

[4] *Loc. cit.* (p. 385): ". . . cum ita impartitur alicui, id est ita habet esse in aliquo, ut eum faciat Dei et proximi amatorem: quod cum facit, tunc dicitur dari sive mitti alicui; et tunc ille dicitur proprie habere Spiritum sanctum."

[5] St. Thomas, I *Sent.*, d. 17, q. 1, a. 1; *Sum. Theol.*, II-II, q. 23, a. 2; *De Car.*, q. un., a. 1; St. Albert, I *Sent.*, d. 17, a. 1 (XXV, pp. 464-465); St. Bonaventure, *op. cit.*, d. 17, p. 1, a. un., q. 1 (I, pp. 294-295).

[6] Op. cit.: "Per gratiam enim et in gratia habetur et datur Spiritus Sanctus. . . . Est enim Spiritus Sanctus propria et inseparabilis materia gratiae circa quam negotiatur gratia. Unde, quodammodo in gratia continetur."

[7] *Op. cit.* (ed. ad Claras Aquas), I, p. 725, contra, b: "Item, missio Spiritus Sancti ponit alium modum essendi in creatura quam prius. Unde Spiritus Sanctus dicitur mitti, non quia modo sit ubi non erat prius, sed quia est ibi alio modo quam prius." Cf. *ibid.*, p. 723, ad 3: "Si autem quaeratur quae sit ratio huius: dicendum quod hoc est quia 'mitti' de ratione sua dicit aliquid effici in creatura per quod dicitur alio modo esse in creatura quam prius, licet non sit ubi non esset prius. . . ."

[8] *Ibid.*, p. 737, ad 5: "[missio visibilis] addit manifestationem personae in quantum existentis ab alio et existentia in alio tamquam in-

habitantis vel possessae ab alio, quia in missione efficitur ut persona missa ad nos habeatur a nobis et inhabitet in nobis. . . ." Cf. *ibid.*, p. 738, ad 2: "Quando autem aliquid mittitur in ratione doni, donum illud non habet completam rationem missionis donec habeatur et possideatur ab eo cui mittitur."

[9] *Ibid.* (ed. Coloniensis), Part IV, q. 26, m. 1, a. 1: ". . . secundum Priscianum sunt quaedam verba, quae licet secundum vocem activa sunt, significatione tamen sunt passiva, ut hoc verbum, video. Videre enim non est agere sed recipere; licet igitur finitum non potest agere in infinitum, nec attingere ad illud in agendo; potest tamen illud recipere et sic potest creatura delectabiliter videre Deum, ab ipso recipiendo, non in ipsum agendo. . . . Et isto modo potest creatura frui creatore, sed quia istud non est nisi quantum dat Dominus et quatenus dat et ulterius secundum quod creatura se disponit; ideo convenienter dicitur 'ad fruendum quamdiu licet' in definitione superadicta."

[10] *Ibid.* (ed. ad Claras Aquas), I, p. 729, resp.: "Unde datur Spiritus Sancti in se et in donis suis. Et ratio huius est: quia Spiritus Sanctus est in justis in ratione fructus, quia eo fruuntur justi; dona autem Spiritus Sanctus in justis sunt, non sicut fructus, sed sicut dispositiones mentis vel liberi arbitrii ad fruendum; anima de se non habet virtutem fruendi bono increato, sed per gratiam et virtutes." Cf. *ibid.*, p. 730, c; p. 732, sol.; p. 733, II, ad I; p. 737, ad 6; etc. The same phrases are found in Codex Vaticanus latinus 691 (see Appendix, pp. 360-361) and, metaphorically, in Eudes Rigaud (Appendix, p. 359).

[11] *Ibid.*, p. 732 ad 3: "[Missiones invisibiles] conveniunt in fine, scilicet in hoc quod est inhabitare animam vel esse in anima secundum rationem fructus."

[12] *Ibid.*, p. 731: "Effectus huius missionis est inhabitatio." Cf. *ibid.*, p. 736, sol., I: "Ratio missionis . . . est inhabitatio creaturae rationalis per aliquem effectum gratiae gratum facientis; est enim missio ad inhabitandum." The same affirmation is made *ibid.*, p. 725, ad 2; 727, 3.

[13] *Ibid.*, IV, p. 101, II: "Dicendum quod Spiritus Sanctus datur et quod Spiritus Sanctus operatur. Datur enim in quantum donum, datur etiam in quantum charitas; operatur vero in quantum Spiritus: charitas enim nomen est doni, spiritus autem nomen est potestatis." Cf. I, p. 733, ad 3: "Unde in eo [Saul] erat Spiritus Sanctus in quantum Spiritus, non in quantum Sanctus, hoc est in quantum inspirans, non in quantum sanctificans sive inhabitans." Also *ibid.*, p. 730, c.

The Codex Vaticans latinus 691 makes the indentical distinction: "... S. S. in impio non est ut Sanctus, sed ut Spiritus et cum justificatur, sic est ut Sanctus." Cf. Appendix, p. 361.

[14] *Op. cit.*, p. 714, ad 1: "... praedicta definitio non datur per illud quod principaliter significatur in hoc quod dico 'mitti'; nec tamen sequitur quod propter hoc male assignetur, quia datur per illud quod prius simpliciter. Unde quia per effectum illum cognosci habet processio Filii vel Spiritus Sancti, et quia ratione illius effectus dicitur mitti Filius vel Spiritus Sanctus, ideo datur definitio missionis per effectum, licet in intellectu missionis cadat ille effectus oblique. Sed si deberet definiri per illud quod est prius simpliciter, diceretur missio processio manifestata vel manifestatio processionis alicuius personae per aliquem effectum in rationali creatura." Cf. *loc. cit.*, [solutio].

[15] *Ibid.*, ad 4: "... ratione alicuius effectus appropriabilis Filio vel Spiritui Sancto, in quo potest cognosci Filius vel Spiritus Sanctus esse ab alio."

[16] *Ibid.*, ad 2: "Ibi dicitur cognitio non actus ipsius cognitivae, sed repraesentatio ipsius processionis in effectu, ordinata ad actum cognitivae; unde illud cognosci est repraesentari in effectu sive per effectum aliquid per quod potest cognosci Filium vel Spiritum Sanctum esse ab alio." Cf. *ibid.*, p. 723, ad 3, where he specifies these effects and their representative function: "... tales effectus sunt cognitio et amor vel dona pertinentia ad cognitionem et amorem in quibus relucet processio Filii vel Spiritus Sancti per modum imaginis; et quia talium effectuum est capax sola rationalis creatura, ideo ratione alicuius effectus appropriati non dicitur mitti ad aliam creaturam, quia in aliis creaturis non dicitur cognosci in effectu nisi per modum vestigii." Cf. also *ibid.*, p. 719, ad 1.

[17] *Ibid.*, p. 714, ad 5: "... non ratione cuiuscumque effectus sive doni, in quo cognoscitur Filius vel Spiritus Sanctus ab alio esse, dicitur mitti Filius vel Spiritus Sanctus, sed exigitur quod ille effectus sive illud donum pertineat ad gratiam gratum facientem, quia solum secundum illam inhabitant animam et sunt in ea modo speciali quo Deus dicitur inhabitare in iustis, sicut postea plenius determinabitur. Unde ratione fidei informis non dicitur mitti, licet per fidem informem possit aliquo modo cognosci processio Filii vel Spiritus Sancti, quia Augustinus non intelligit de cognitione qualicumque, sed de cognitione coniuncta affectioni amoris, quae cum est in homines dicitur Deus inhabitare, et cum de novo est, dicitur mitti."

[18] *Op. cit.*, pp. 6-7: "Así Alejandro de Ales afirma que sólo la gracia santificante puede ser la causa de la existencia de las divinas

Personas en el alma, en cuanto que los effectos distintos de ésta se *aproprian* a las Personas divinas. Pero una existencia por apropriación no es una existencia real de las Personas."

[19] *Summa Alex.* (ed. ad Claras Aquas), I, p. 720, ad 2: ". . . ratione repraesentationis in effectu sibi appropriato."

[20] *Ibid.*, p. 714, ad 3: "Etsi nunquam cognosceretur ille effectus vel per illum effectum processio Filii vel Spiritus Sancti, nihilominus per illum effectum repraesentatur illud per quod potest cognosci, scilicet signo aliquo spirituali cognoscibiliter repraesentari."

[21] *Op. cit.*, p. 7: "Pero una existencia por apropiación no es una existencia real de las Personas. Esa apropriación existe también en los efectos de orden natural, y sin embargo, Dios no existe en las cosas nada más que con la presencia de immensidad, como uno en esencia, no como trino en Personas."

[22] *Op. cit.*, I, p. 720, ad 2: ". . . licet quotiescumque operatur Pater per Filium, operetur etiam illum eundem effectum per Spiritum Sanctum, non tamen quotiescumque mittit Filium, mittit Spiritum Sanctum, et hoc quia ille effectus non est appropriatus utrique, sed alteri personae; unde solum illa persona dicitur mitti, cui appropriatur ille effectus; nec ratione operationis dicitur mitti persona, sed ratione repraesentationis in effectu sibi appropriato."

So, too, Codex Vaticanus latinus 691 maintains that the gifts of the Holy Spirit are necessary, even though He *effectively* makes us pleasing to God, to make us *formally* pleasing to God, "quia informant mentem *ad hoc quod sit templum Dei.*" This capital distinction rejects both an explanation based on God's efficient causality and that based on his formal causality (followers of Peter Lombard). Cf. Appendix, p. 361.

[23] *Op. cit.*, p. 732, ad 3: ". . . si datur gratia gratum faciens ad sanctificandam animam vel gratificandam vel accendendam ad amorem, cum huiusmodi actus sint appropriati Spiritui Sancto et in illis habeat cognosci, dicitur mitti Spiritus Sanctus."

[24] *Ibid.*, p. 714, ad 3: ". . . per illum effectum repraesentatur illud per quod potest cognosci. . . ."

[25] So the *Summa Alex.* will hold that although man's beatitude (formal) consists in both an act of the will and an act of the intellect (cf. Hugh of St. Victor, *Expos. in Hierarchiam Coelestem S. Dionysii*, Bk. VII; PL 175: 1065), it will consist principally in the former and only dispositively in the latter. Cf. ed. Coloniensis, Part IV, q. 26, m. 3, a. 5.

[26] *Op. cit.* (ed. ad Claras Aquas), I, p. 714, ad 5: ". . . cognitione coniuncta affectioni amoris, quae cum est in homine, dicitur Deus inhabitare, et cum de novo est, dicitur mitti."

[27] *Ibid.*, IV, p. 1000, ad 4: ". . . in parvulis est cognitio sicut forma et amor similiter, quia informant animam ipsorum; sed non sunt in eis sicut actus; unde in eis sunt habitu et non actu, sicut vidimus in adulto dormiente, quod in eo est scientia sicut forma informans animam et non sicut actus sive in usu." Thus he explains the assertion (*loc. cit*), "ad templum autem Dei pertinent parvuli sanctificati sacramento Christi," a fact he has previously affirmed (*ibid.*), "praesens autem apud animam dicitur [Deus] inquantum praesentat sive praesentem facit beatitudinem, quae est in ipso. Quod est tripliciter: vel in habitu tantum, sicut in parvulis . . . ." Cf. also *ibid.*, IV, p. 1024, ad 1.

[28] *Ibid.* (ed. ad Claras Aquas), I, p. 729, ad b: ". . . licet gratia non sit Spiritus Sanctus, non tamen sequitur quod unum possit haberi sine alio, quia unum est dispositio ad aliud. Unde sicut non sequitur: 'forma substantialis non est dispositio, ergo potest imprimi sine sua dispositione,' sic nec in proposito. Et cum Beda dicit quod 'cum gratia hominibus datur, mittitur Spiritus Sanctus,' non vult dicere quod nihil aliud datur in missione Spiritus Sanctus quam gratia, sed quod unum concomitatur aliud nec unum habetur sine alia." The *Commentary* of Eudes Rigaud and Codex Vaticanus latinus 691 both teach that the powers of grace, not their acts, constitute the real presence of the indwelling Persons as objects. Cf. Appendix, pp. 359-361.

[29] *Ibid.* (ed. Coloniensis), Part IV, q. 26, m. 1, a. 1, resp: ". . . status justitiae consummatae in subjecto suo ponit gratiae affluentiam; affluens autem gratia reddit animam ad contemplandam expeditam et ad fruendum idoneam." 'Consummated justice' means the state of the perfect (*loc. cit.*).

[30] *Ibid.*, Part IV, q. 26, m. 4, resol.: "Si sumitur [oratio] primo modo, prout est ad gustandum dulcedinem, cum in gustu tali non fit modica delectatio, ideo necessario requiritur actus affectivus ad coniungendum et cognitivus ad apprehendendum, secundum quod philosophus dicit quod 'delectatio est conjunctio convenientis cum conveniente cum sensu eiusdem;' itaque actus orationis partim est cognitivus et partim affectivus, quia inchoatur in cognitione et in affectione terminatur et consummatur." The same subordination of knowledge to love appears in the teaching on the image; cf. *infra*, note 37.

³¹ *Ibid.*, (ed. ad Claras Aquas), II, p. 732: "Frui se est delectari in se."

³² *Ibid.*, I, p. 723, ad 2: "Mitti non dicitur [Deus] nisi ad illas creaturas in quibus dicitur inhabitare et hoc est solum in illis quae possunt ipsum capere per cognitionem et amorem." Cf. *ibid.*, p. 602, sol.; p. 722, contra a.

³³ *Ibid.*, IV, p. 161, sol.: "Ultimus effectus gratiae perfectior est nos unire Deo; sed in aliis a Christo non est unire nisi per cognitionem et amorem. . . ."

³⁴ *Ibid.*, II, p. 414, sol.: "Imago attenditur penes utrumque, scilicet penes naturalia et penes gratuita; sed differenter. Nam est imago creationis et est imago recreationis. Imago autem creationis attenditur penes potentias naturales, scilicet memoriam, intelligentiam, et voluntatem. Imago vero recreationis attenditur penes gratiam reformantem illas potentias. Prima est indifferenter in peccatoribus et justis, alia autem est tantum in justis."

³⁵ *Ibid.*, I, p. 77, sol.: ". . . [Deum esse per gratiam] ponit necessario gratiam creatam in creatura quae quidem gratia est similitudo, qua anima est imago actu, id est in imitatione actuali."

³⁶ *Ibid.*, p. 723, ad 3: ". . . non propter quemcumque effectum appropriatum Filio vel Spiritus Sancto dicitur mitti Filius vel Spiritus Sanctus, sed propter illos in quibus expresse habet cognosci Filius vel Spiritus Sanctus, non solum per modum vestigii, sed per modum imaginis; et tales effectus sunt cognitio et amor vel dona pertinentia ad cognitionem et amorem, in quibus relucet processio Filii et Spiritus Sancti per modum imaginis; et quia talium effectuum est capax sola rationalis creatura, ideo ratione alicuius effectus appropriati non dicitur mitti ad aliam creaturam, quia in aliis creaturis non dicitur cognosci nisi per modum vestigii."

³⁷ *Ibid.*, II, p. 412: "Cum ergo imgo plus adhaereat natura quam similitudo et sit prior naturaliter quam similitudo superinducta imagini, recte penes potentiam cognoscendi, determinatur imago, similitudo penes potentiam diligendi. . . ." Cf. *ibid.*, p. 408, b: "Item Hugo: 'Imago secundum rationem, similitudo secundum dilectionem.'"

³⁸ *Ibid.* (ed. Coloniensis), Part IV, q. 26, m. 1, a. 1: "Sed frui est per adhaerentiam et contactum quemdam." *Ibid.* (ed. ad Claras Aquas), II, p. 223, sol.: "Cum introductus fuerit servus bonus et fidelis in gaudium Domini sui totaliter pergit in Deum et deinceps adhaerens ei, unus spiritus erit."

³⁹ *Ibid.*, II, p. 402: "Assignat iterum Magister in libro sententiarum finem animae rationalis, dicens quod creata est 'ut intelligeret summam bonitatem, et intelligendo amaret et amando possideret et possidendo frueretur.'" The quotation is from II *Sent.*, d. 1, c. 4.

⁴⁰ Cf. Appendix, pp. 360-361. On this same point, the *Commentary* of Eudes Rigaud likewise serves as corroboration, since in metaphorical terms he affirms the presence of the Persons as objects, fruits of the just soul's enjoyment. Cf. Appendix, p. 359.

⁴¹ The whole Trinity (I, d. 37, n. 13; ed. ad Claras Aquas, I, p. 369) is present by grace (I, d. 14, n. 6; I, p. 151) habitually (I, d. 37, nn. 15 and 16; I, p. 370). 'Mitti est cognosci' (I, d. 15, nn. 9 and 14; I, pp. 155 and 157): an effect is connoted (I, d. 15, n. 2; I, p. 153) which is produced by the whole Trinity (*ibid.*, n. 3 and n. 5; I, pp. 153 and 154).

⁴² *Glossa*, I, d. 15, n. 26 (I, p. 161): ". . . missio ratione effectus est in nobis per appropriationem vel Filii vel Spiritus Sancti."

⁴³ *Ibid.*, d. 15, n. 7 (I, p. 155): "Spiritus dat se, id est, est ens a Patre et Filio dans effectum gratiae in creatura, ut personalis discretio denotetur respectu Patris et Filii."

⁴⁴ *Cursus Theologicus*, I, q. 43, Disp. 37, a. 3, n. 15 (ed. cit., IV, fasc. II, p. 368); cf. also *ibid.*, q. 8, Disp. 8, a. 6 (II, pp. 36-39).

⁴⁵ *Sum. Theol.*, I-II, q. 28, a. 1 and ad 1.

⁴⁶ St. Thomas, *Sum. Theol.*, I-II, q. 11, a. 4: "Est ergo perfecta fruitio finis iam habiti realiter. Sed imperfecta est etiam finis non habiti realiter, sed in intentione tantum."

⁴⁷ *Ibid.*, a. 1, ad 1: ". . . hunc finem intellectus consequitur tamquam potentia movens ad finem, et fruens fine iam adepto." Cf. *ibid.*, q. 3, a. 4.

⁴⁸ *Op. cit.*, p. 60: ". . . gratia gratum faciens non est vinculum immediate conjungens animam et Deum, sed, ut ait Alexander, 'est sic ut necessitas uniendi animam veritati summae et bonitati' (*op. cit.*, t. I, p. 83), seu disponit animam ut uniatur Deo. Haec autem unio formaliter habetur per cognitionem et dilectionem. Quare, secundum doctrinam Alexandri, dici debet unio moralis." A union by knowledge and love is certainly only intentional, objective, moral; but according to the doctrine of Alexander of Hales the union achieved by love is physical and real. Father Primeau has allowed his own theological views (true as they are—that is not the point) to intrude in his exposition of Alexander's doctrine.

CHAPTER FIVE

The Solutions of St. Albert and St. Bonaventure

There are special historical and doctrinal reasons for devoting a separate chapter to the theories of St. Albert and St. Bonaventure concerning the indwelling of the Trinity in the souls of the just, whatever the intrinsic value of their explanations may be found to be. For one of these great medieval doctors and masters inaugurates a new intellectual era in the history of western theological thought, and the other culminates the theological tradition which links the doctrines of the Schools to the burning mind of Augustine. One of St. Albert's claims to fame as Mandonnet points out, lies "in the sagacity and the efforts he employed to bring a summary of the human learning already garnered to the notice of the cultured society of the Middle Ages"; but of far greater and more permanent importance than this encyclopedic task were his attempts, successful in the event, "to create a new and vigorous intellectual movement in his own century, to win over to Aristotle the best minds of the Middle Ages."[1]

The genius of St. Bonaventure, on the contrary, was synthetic: reaping the harvest of two centuries of intense and fruitful Christian thought, he codifies in a complete and powerful synthesis that Augustinism which was the hallmark of Franciscan teaching and even today its proud boast.*

Historically, then, these two giants meet at a crossroads in the evolution of theology. Yet it would be a mistake to oversimplify the tendencies of either of them. Aristotelian, St. Albert may well be considered, but he retained much of the Augustinian tradition, he is profoundly influenced by the *Liber de Causis* and the works of Pseudo-Dionysius, by the neo-Platonists and the neo-Platonising Aristotelians — in many matters far more than by the historic Aristotle. And St. Bonaventure, for all his *ex professo* devotion to the masters of the Augustinian tradition, adopts not a few Aristotelian ideas — to such an extent, indeed, that Van Steenberghen characterizes his philosophy as "an eclectic and neo-Platonising Aristotelianism, put at the services of an Augustinian theology."[2]

One of these men was Thomas' colleague and friend; the other, in Copleston's phrase, "was (*mutatis mutandis*) Thomas' Socrates."[3] Which way will their divergent theological and philosophical tendencies take them with respect to the problem of the divine inhabitation: in the direct line of their dominant characteristics or, obliquely, in accord with their recessive traits? Will the efforts of the earlier Schoolmen have any influence on their thinking or will they develop new theories, discover new approaches, advance completely different solutions? Of

---

* In one sense, of course, St. Bonaventure is rather the founder than the heir of this Franciscan doctrinal tradition, and his work will not be completed until radically revised along Aristotelian lines by Duns Scotus.

the two chief avenues of approach opened up — that of final causality as definitively proposed by the *Summa Theologica* called by Alexander's name and that of exemplary causality expressed by the historic Alexander in his *Glossa* and *Quaestiones Disputatae* — which will prevail with these great lights of scholastic tradition?

These are the questions implicitly posed by this chapter. In answering them, not only will an immediate reward be obtained: an insight into the intimate thought of two of the greatest Christian doctors on one of the most inaccessible of the Christian mysteries; but the groundwork will be laid for a detailed investigation of the comparative influences of St. Albert and St. Bonaventure on the explanation which will be given by St. Thomas to the problem of the indwelling of the Trinity.

ARTICLE 1

The Solution of St. Albert the Great

1. Exposition of St. Albert's Theory

As was disclosed in Chapter Three when the general teaching of the Schoolmen on the divine indwelling was the subject of investigation, Albert begins with the same facts and works in the same intellectual milieu (so far as the inhabitation is concerned) as the author of the *Summa Halesiana*: real presence of the Trinity by means of grace; the connection of the indwelling and the divine missions; the explanation of the missions, following Augustine, as a temporal manifestation of the eternal processions of the divine Persons.⁴ But Albert's account of how the Persons abide in the just soul is completely and radically different. The three Persons are present in the production of grace and in Their cooperation with the acts of grace; They are present *in virtue of* this production and this cooperation.

Time after time he repeats the phrase "the divine Person is present in (or with) the effect."⁵ The Holy Spirit sends Himself or is sent in the conferring of the gift of sanctifying grace.⁶ Charity is so exalted a gift that God is actually present in it, and in consequence of this presence it is a finer thing than any other created good.⁷ And he describes the advent of the divine Person to the soul as an 'illapsus,' that peculiar scholastic term which well pictures the mysterious nature of God's action without thereby contributing to our understanding of it.⁸

How is God present in the just soul? He is there — personally, substantially, really, in His trinity of Persons — as operating, as producing grace and cooperating in its effects:

> As God, the Spirit is everywhere, because He is God: but nevertheless, through this effect by which He is manifested in the Saints, He does not show Himself everywhere. And therefore He is said to be sent according to this: that He is present, personally and essentially, in a special way where He so operates.⁹

If the divine Persons were not given "as operating," the divine mission and donation would fail in its end, which is to sanctify man and bring him back to God.¹⁰ And in this way divine Charity contains God within it: as operating.¹¹

Why does Albert hold such a view? His reasoning is profound:

Truly, indeed, the Spirit proceeds by an eternal procession: and His procession is manifested by the effect of the gifts, in which the Holy Spirit is present by way of essence, power and presence. And the reason of this is, that the operation of such gifts is of infinite power; but infinite power can belong to no created thing, and therefore without the Holy Spirit the gifts do not have infinite power. Yet it cannot be denied that, as Damascene says, the operator is where he operates by his proper power. Where an infinite act appears, consequently, there must be an infinite power and the operation of an infinite power. But it is an infinite act to join man to God at the good pleasure of the will, and to be able to merit an eternal reward. This cannot be, therefore, except by an infinite power, which exists itself only by a divine Person operating by way of essence, power and presence: to which, on our part, the gifts dispose; but they cannot elicit the act, neither from itself nor from us, without the Holy Spirit.[12]

The validity of the argument is incontestable: infinite effects demand an infinite power, an infinite cause. But where does this reasoning lead us? God operating as efficient cause cannot, by a necessity of His nature, work as three in Persons, because His operations *ad extra* are products of His omnipotence and intellect and will, attributes of the common essence: God's exterior action is His substance. St. Albert admits this in the passage quoted; indeed, insists upon it: the Holy Spirit is present in His gifts "by way of essence, power and presence"; the divine Person operates "by way of essence, power and presence"— the classic scholastic phrase, taken from the *Glossa ordinaria*,[13] to specify the presence of immensity by which the essence of God is in all things as their creating and conserving cause. He will firmly maintain this fundamental metaphysical and theological truth:

> For when it is said 'the Father sends,' or 'the Son sends,' or 'the Holy Ghost sends,' the word 'sends' bespeaks an act coming forth from a person as from a substance. And since this act becomes an operation (as Augustine says) in respect to a creature, and such an operation is always common to the Three, it is necessary that this operation be referred to the Person by means of the essence which is common.[14]

The divine Person is sent, then, by reason of the essence, for God as one in essence produces the gifts of grace and works in their effects. Yet Albert has also said that a specific Person comes or is sent (and therefore inhabits). To explain such a distinction on the basis of efficiency, only one solution is possible: appropriation. And that *is* Albert's answer.

He argues as follows. Something which the Trinity produces can be appropriated to one of the Persons: this is a recognized fact. But if this is so, then the productive operation itself must be proportioned both to the form (*ratio*: the exemplary idea realized ontologically, in the real order, in the effect) of the effect which is appropriated and to the personal property of one of the Persons to whom the appropriation is made. There must be, then, in the effect the participated form and thus the sign of some one Person, both from the point of view of what it is and from the fact that it is the product of such or such an action proportioned to one or other Person.[15]

Moreover, since between every cause and effect there is a relationship between the one operating and the thing produced, so a relationship exists between God and the effects of grace He causes, by means of which the relation and notion of a personal property is represented as in a sign.[16] As a consequence of this intimate correspondence, God is differently related to His creature in the indwelling, not precisely on the basis of His efficient action but rather on the grounds of exemplarity: there is only one idea of which He is the exemplar for all the things to which He is related by essence, by the presence of immensity (God as one in essence); but there is a completely different idea of which He is the exemplar (God as three in Persons) in respect to the rational creature in whom He dwells by the effects of grace He produces and with which He operates.[17] And in this difference of exemplarity is found the explanation of the presence of the Trinity in the souls of the just.[18]

2. Interpretation of the Theory of St. Albert the Great

It is not on the basis of efficient cause that St. Albert attempts to explain the presence of the Trinity. He is too good a theologian, too profound a metaphysician to postulate separate and distinct personal activities in God's causal action on creatures. He falls back on appropriation, on the predication of an essential attribute (or of a created effect which represents an essential attribute) of one or other of the Persons because of the similarity between this attribute and the personal property or notion of this particular Person.

But it seems evident that St. Albert considers the notions of exemplarity and appropriation from a special point of view. While one would hardly go so far as to class him with the modern "school" — Galtier, Urdánoz, von Rudloff, de la Taille and the rest — which conceives exemplary causality as a kind of intrinsic causality which yet remains external and really distinct from the creature, certain passages are strongly redolent of the exemplarism of St. Augustine, of which St. Bonaventure is the great medieval exponent.[19] He seems to say that there is a real intrinsic necessity involved in appropriation (of the effects of grace, in any case), in virtue of which the effect, far from being a sign *ad placitum,* is predetermined to represent one or other Person. This specification — which is bound up with the very nature of the effect rather than coming externally, from our apprehension of it — is determined by the divine idea which the effect mirrors. And the effects of grace image the divine Persons.

But Albert does not fall into the hyperplatonism of modern supporters of an exemplarist theory. Exemplarity serves to explain the divine missions, to give a higher value to the notion of appropriation, to make it more certain and less arbitrary — that is all. By reason of appropriation, he claims, the Son or the Holy Ghost is sent, the Father cannot be sent.[20] But even though only one Person is sent, all three Persons simultaneously are present in the just.[21] This would be an inconceivable result were he to profess a rigorist exemplarism: for then, since the effect signifies only the Holy Ghost (or Son), only the Holy Ghost would be present by right, and the other Persons would come only by concomitance and circuminsession. Yet he expressly teaches that the Father comes by His own right, not by reason of the missions of the Son or Holy Spirit.[22]

So for Albert the new relation implied by the presence of the Trinity is explained on the basis of exemplary causality, of appropriation. The *reality* of this new presence is guaranteed, because it presupposes the real presence of immensity.[23] Already present by reason of Their common essence in virtue of the divine creative and conservative action on all creatures, the Trinity is now present in a new way because the rational creature, through the gifts of grace, is referred specifically to the Persons as his exemplar: *non alius quam prius erat, tamen ad aliud datur quam prius habebatur . . . alia ratione exemplaris.*[24]

3. Criticism of the Theory of St. Albert the Great

The Albertinian theory cannot escape the limits he has placed on it. By itself, formal extrinsic causality cannot produce a real presence of the cause to the effect, for the very reason that it is, by definition, external to the effect and in a different order of being.* Appropriation as such

---

* To postulate an exemplary causality which by itself alone produces the effect it represents (as in the theory of which Galtier and Urdánoz are the most vocal representatives) is to make this causality efficient: for efficient causality is defined precisely by its relation to the production in the order of real existence of the effect which depends on it. Exemplary causality, on the other hand, by *its* very definition presupposes and involves efficient causality. For the exemplar is not the form *by which* something is effected but the form according to whose similitude an agent produces something (cf. De Ver., q. 3, a. 1). Remove the agent cause, then, and you eliminate the exemplar.

So there can only be an exemplar where there is an agent, and an agent who works from knowledge of what is to be imitated. "*De ratione* exemplaris," says Cajetan (I, q. 15, a. 1), "est esse formativum rei mediante agente per intellectum."

This applies strictly to the divine causality. As T. M. Sparks, O.P., points out in his study of St. Thomas' doctrine on exemplarity (*De Divisione Causae Exemplaris apud S. Thomam.* Somerset, Ohio; 1936), the proximate exemplary cause is always the exemplary idea in the mind of the agent (cf. pp. 55, 56, 60, 61). The divine essence *as such* is not the exemplar of things, but the divine essence known by God as imitable in this or that way; and as *quod intelligitur*, not as *quo*. To be the exemplary idea of existing things, moreover, it must represent them as existing; and for this, as Capreolus points out, the divine essence is not, not even as known by God, by its nature

can never explain this real presence; and, if it could, then one would have to admit the real presence of the Trinity in natural effects, the inhabitation in the image of the Trinity which Scripture and the Fathers teach us is truly found in the intellectual nature of man, in his intellectual powers and acts. And if, in rebuttal, it is argued that it must be this special effect, an effect of grace, which is alone sufficient explanation. God's free-will (His efficient causality to our way of understanding) must be invoked: ". . . divina essentia, naturaliter, et non secundum arbitrium voluntatis, repraesentat quidditates rerum creabilium; et ideo, sumendo ideam ut est ratio quidditatis praecise, ipsa praecedit actum intellectus et voluntatis. Sed essentia divina, non naturaliter, sed secundum arbitrium voluntatis, repraesentat quidditatem sub existentia. . . . Divina enim essentia nonnisi libere repraesentat lapidem esse vel non esse; et ita de aliis enuntiabilibus. Imaginandum est enim quod intellectus divinus, primo intelligit essentiam suam absolute; secundo, intelligit eam ut continet perfectiones communicabiles creaturis communes, scilicet actum, et esse, et vivere, et hujusmodi; tertio, intelligit eam ut continet quidditates cum earum proprietatibus et accidentibus, existentiis, et hujusmodi; et ad hoc facit actus voluntatis. Quod enim intelligatur quidditas lapidis sub esse, vel in tali tempore causanda, et hujusmodi, istam complexionem non repraesentat divina essentia naturaliter, sed secundum arbitrium voluntatis, ut continet tot vel tot, aut nudam quidditatem lapidis, aut quidditatem sub esse." (*Op. cit.*, d. 36, q. 1, a. 1; II, pp. 418-419).

Were one to admit an exemplary causality which effects real existence by a sort of self-effusion or self-radiation, one would be led to two absurdities. First: all possible beings would actually exist, and from all eternity (since God from all eternity knows His essence as imitable). Second: God would have to cause necessarily; a self-contradiction, since no necessary cause operates by exemplary causality but only according to the form which it itself possesses, a *quo* and not a *quod* (cf. *Sum. Theol.*, I, q. 15, a. 1).

Hence, formally understood, the divine exemplar includes a relation (of reason) to its term, and cannot be known (as exemplar) before the creature which is its term. And the exemplary idea is defined by Capreolus (*op. cit.*, p. 409): "forma quam aliquid imitatur, ex intentione agentis qui praedeterminat sibi finem"; and by Bañez (*op. cit.*, I, q. 15, a. 1; I, pp. 370-371): "forma objecta intellectui intra ipsum existens, ad quam artifex operatur."

appropriated, then no longer in virtue of appropriation does the inhabitation take place but in virtue of something else.

It would be hard to prove, also, that there is any such direct and necessary correspondence between the effect and the Person it represents as Albert seems to teach. The Angelic Doctor invariably maintains that the divine *essence* is the exemplar of all created things;[25] but the divine essence is not and cannot be the exemplary idea of the Son nor of the Holy Spirit. *Per se primo*, then, as Bañez says, a Person cannot be the exemplar of any created effect.[26] Moreover, in this manner of thinking of the divine exemplarity there is a basic fault of the imagination, as if this created thing imitates one divine attribute, this another; when, in fact, the divine essence, as containing these things supereminently and representing them most perfectly, is the proper idea of each and every thing, not the divine attributes. And each created thing represents the whole divine essence, not in all its perfection but as it is imitable in this particular way.[27] Thus St. Thomas states that the divine essence itself, just as it is wisdom and goodness, so it is also charity.[28]

Still another confusion is present in St. Albert's thought, if not explicitly at least implicitly. He teaches, with perfect truth, that since an infinite effect is wrought in the acts of grace an infinite cause must be present.[29] So the Holy Spirit is present as operating as efficient cause, i.e., the three Persons acting by their one essence, an act appropriated to the Third Person. Yet behind this thinking lurks the grave danger of confusing the formal operation of the created gift with the efficient operation of the uncreated gift, so that God would be present not merely as efficient cause but in some way as formal cause; and the appropriation attributed to the Holy Ghost would acquire a reality consonant with a personal presence.

St. Albert does not make so drastic and false a conclusion. But it is still implied by his insistence on the necessary character and the rigidity of appropriation by which he attempts to account for the divine missions and the inhabitation. It is inherent in any theory which works from the point of view of God's efficient causality, and it will become explicit with later theologians who, arguing from the divine nature of the effects of grace, either try to make more of extrinsic formal causality than this can give, or try to justify the divine presence on the basis of an efficient divine causality essentially different from God's causality in the natural order which comes from God only as He is one in essence.[30]

Cajetan analyzes and resolves the profound difficulty of the infinite nature and effects of grace in his clear and deep commentary on Charity.[31] In virtue of a double principle — the explanation of the efficacy of accidental forms by reason of the substances from which they come; and the reduction of the power of participated forms to the subject which possesses this power essentially — he explains the coordinated causality of created and uncreated grace.

Since they are accidental forms, the efficacy of grace and the gifts of grace must be reduced, like all accidents, to a substance of the same order as themselves from which they derive. But grace is connatural only to the divine substance, not to any created being. So its efficacy must be based on its proximate and connatural principle, God Himself.[32] It is, therefore, from the power of God, the true author of grace, that such infinite efficacy flows[33]—

of God, moreover, 'specially operating,' as the author of grace and not as the author of nature.*

* No one—certainly no Thomist—would deny that God operates in a special manner (according to our way of conceiving things) when He produces such divine effects. But that this "intenser and fuller" operation (to borrow the words of St. Augustine and the Master of the Sentences) is the formal foundation of a special *presence* of God does not follow: the causality involves a divine substance but in no way (*per se primo*) a divine person. There is a different and higher presence of immensity, more fully revealing God's nature and its transcendence, a special love which is love absolute and infinite; but still no essentially different kind of presence, and no ground for postulating any difference in God's contact with things because of this operation.

This is evident in the *gratiae gratis datae* (in the medieval sense of the word), in prophecy, in miracles, especially in the operations of actual grace: certainly *quoad modum* these are supernatural and of the divine order; yet no special presence can be deduced from God's special operation in these effects. It is more evident yet in that most special operation by which the Trinity as one in essence efficiently causes the union of the divine nature and the human nature in the Second Person. (For this reason, since he attempts to explain the special presence of God in the Incarnation by efficient causality, Father de la Taille, S.J., *must* postulate a special influence of the Son in the effecting of the union, a theory totally at variance with St. Thomas' explicit principles; cf. "Actuation créée par Acte incréé," *Recherches de science religieuse*, 18 [1928], pp. 253-268, and "Entretien amical d'Euxode et de Palamède sur la grâce d'union," *Revue apologétique*, 48 [1929], pp. 5-26, 129-145.)

The basic error of this kind of thinking seems to be its failure to recognize, in practice, that God is an equivocal or analogical cause. For such causality an essential diversity of effects does not imply an essential diversity on the part of the cause. But the fact of this diversity is precisely the ground on which they argue for a diversity in the causality of God which would explain the essentially different modes of His presence. St. Thomas envisages the matter quite differently: ". . . dicendum quod per unum et idem Deus in ratione diversarum causarum se habet: quia per hoc quod est actus purus, est agens, et est bonitas pura et per consequens, omnium finis" (*De Pot.*, q. 7, a. 1 ad 3).

This profound explanation is evident from another point of view. Grace produces its proper effects as a formal principle, not as an efficient principle. What, then, produces as active cause such an infinite effect? Its efficient principle cannot be the subject which uses it and in which it inheres, because it is merely participated by this subject; its activity can only be explained by something to which such power is connatural, not participated, from which the participated form and its efficacy derive, which can account by its very nature for such an effect. Grace acts as form, and man uses this form participated by him to produce infinite supernatural acts; but only God, for whom such infinite acts are connatural, for whom this form is His by essence and not by participation, can account for this divine activity.

This may become clearer by an example. Heat does not belong to an animal by essence but by participation: heat is a participation in the animal of fire. Thus although the animal may grow, there is no necessary increase because of this of the formal effect of heat (to make warm), unless the participation is intensified. The active cause of the formal effect (to warm), it is clear, is not the animal, who merely uses it, but something for which heat itself is connatural, namely, fire. So in the present case, grace and its gifts produce their formal effects in virtue of the active cause for whom such effects are connatural: and this is God.[34]

The conclusion, then, is most important. Grace is infinite *as form*, not as agent. But God is present *as agent*, not as form. Each, *in its own order of causality*, accounts for the effect produced. To confuse the two is to introduce chaos into any possible solution of the presence of the Trinity in the soul in grace. God is specially present as active cause, but this in no way proves that His action — which in this case, as in all others where He acts efficiently, is produced by His substance, by the essence common to all three Persons — is the *formal* reason of His indwelling. It does prove — and the fact is important — that in the order of efficient causality, the first and determining principle of the created gifts according to which the presence of the Trinity is established is the Uncreated Gift, the presence of God Himself.[35]

4. Conclusion

St. Albert has succeeded even less than his Franciscan colleague in explaining in what manner the divine Persons are present. The author of the tract on the invisible divine missions in the Halesian *Summa* knew at least the term of the new relationship and defined the problem concerned. But Albert's solution, historically, antedates the more profound treatment of the *Summa Alexandri* in its thinking, if not in its time of composition.

Is there any explanation for this apparent anomaly? Although the historical data is confused and one must be wary of conclusions where the evidence is so uncertain, the following hypothesis may be suggested. In the commentary on the *Sentences,* an early product, implicit and explicit citations of Alexander's *Glossa* manifest close familiarity with that immature work of the Archdeacon of Coventry.[36] The theory on the inhabitation proposed by both is identical: God present as efficient cause, but the several Persons sent and distinctly present in virtue of appropriation.

Where the Halesian *Summa,* however, indicates tremendous progress in understanding the problem and in the new solution, St. Albert's later theological work shows no such intellectual advance: as the indiscriminate citation of both works indicates, there is no essential difference between his *Summa* and his *Sentences* so far as the inhabitation is concerned. But this is hardly surprising, since his *Summa Theologica,* on many points, is little more than a re-editing of his earlier work and a re-arrangement of it in the new form which had earned popular enthusiasm in the Schools.* The lack of change argues not for a reaffirmation of a theory in the face of the new solutions proposed by the *Summa Alexandri,* Bonaventure and Thomas, but a failure to reconsider the matter at all. Otherwise the treatment in the *Summa* would have to be more complete than it is, and one might reasonably anticipate a more direct consideration of the opposed theories. In fact, however, Albert's theory here is little more than a restatement of the solution proposed by him in the *Commentary on the Sentences* and by Alexander in the *Glossa* and the *Quaestiones Disputatae.*

In this sense, then, St. Albert is twice removed (a geometrical and not an arithmetical regression) from the true formal reason of the presence of the Trinity. Where the *Summa* attributed to Alexander at least focuses the

---

* This is not, one may believe, a contradiction of Dom Lottin's conclusion, "il est surtout arbitraire de voir dans la *Somme* d'Albert une compilation de ses propres écrits antérieurs" ("Commentaire des Sentences et Somme théologique d'Albert le Grand," *Recherches de théologie ancienne et médiévale,* 8 [1936], p. 153); but the learned Benedictine far oversteps the just limits of his own limited comparisons when he delivers the universal conclusion: "il se désintéresse dans la plupart des cas de ses propres conceptions antérieurs, pour se mettre dans le sillon traditionnel de l'école franciscaine" (*loc. cit.*).

problem by defining the term of this new relation, the solution of the master of St. Thomas answers the wrong question because he is working from the fact of God's efficient causality. This "old" explanation will be abandoned by Bonaventure, as it was by others; and St. Thomas will follow these Franciscan theologians rather than his Dominican confrère. To the end, however, St. Albert will persist in giving his unsatisfactory and false solution. For appropriation can never account for a real presence of the triune God.

ARTICLE 2

The Solution of St. Bonaventure

1. Exposition of St. Bonaventure's Doctrine on the Inhabitation

"Just as in the first book I have adhered to the teachings of the Master of the Sentences and the common opinions of the masters, and above all to those of our master and father, Brother Alexander of revered memory," writes St. Bonaventure in his prologue to the second book of his commentary, "so in the following book I shall not depart from their footsteps."[37]

In fact, however, when one sees St. Bonaventure's solution of the presence of the Trinity, serious doubts concerning the validity of this claim must arise. For here he follows Eudes Rigaud and the Halesian *Summa*, in evident opposition to his acclaimed master's explications (as we know them). So close does Bonaventure adhere to this later doctrine, in fact, that one knows not how better to consider his work: as the perfect commentary and explanation of the *Summa fratris Alexandri*, or as a lucid exposition and perfecting by a master of an imperfectly realized theological construction of his predecessors. He gives the same formal reason for the inhabitation, but clearly, explicitly, without the superfluities and extraneous considerations which obscure the earlier presentation.

Bonaventure, like Alexander, carefully defines the special nature of this new way of God's being present which is called the inhabitation.[38] Recall his definition: "to inhabit bespeaks a spiritual effect with acceptance, as is the effect of sanctifying grace, which is God-like and brings us back to God and makes us have God and God to be had by us, and by this even to dwell in us."[39] No new presence of God is entailed but a new way of being present: as now possessed by us.[40] And he will specify the term of this new relation in the lapidary formula, "for us to have God is nothing else than God to dwell in us."[41]

If this is, then, the distinctive feature of the inhabitation — God present as possessed — the conclusion should logically follow that the indwelling can be explained as our power to possess God. But how this is to be understood, as well as the fact of it, is well determined by the Seraphic Doctor:

> Giving is for having or possessing something; but to have or possess something is when something is in the power of the one having or possessing. To be in the power of the one having or possessing, however, is to be present for enjoying or using. But there is perfect possession when man has that which he can use and enjoy. But only God is rightly enjoyed, and to use something rightly takes place only by sanctifying grace; therefore the possession in which God is had and His grace is the perfect one.[42]

From this clear argumentation for the real presence of both the Holy Spirit and His gifts, these facts should be singled out: God is present in the inhabitation as something to be enjoyed, grace as something to be used; He is present when we *can* enjoy Him, regardless of actual fruition. These important conclusions are explicitly confirmed in many other passages.[43]

God inhabits when He is possessed by man; He is possessed when He is enjoyed; He is enjoyed when man can enjoy him. The power of enjoying God is for St. Bonaventure, more clearly even than for the *Summa Alexandri*, the formal reason of the inhabitation. But what is this power? There can be no doubt of the answer of the Franciscan doctor: "fruition by its general notion bespeaks a union of love, that is, of the enjoyable with the one enjoying."[44] *Essentially* this act is an act of the will, for which knowledge serves merely as a disposition.[45] And since God is the object envisioned as enjoyable, fruition takes place by means of grace.[46] And so the power involved is not the naked will, but the supernatural virtue of Charity.[47] The enjoyment of God by the gift of Charity will be perfect in heaven,[48] like the inhabitation itself;[49] here on earth, whether by act or habit, it can only be imperfect. And the special presence of the Trinity in the souls of the just, like Their enjoyment by the just here on earth, will have as its formal reason the theological virtue of Charity.[50]

2. Conclusions

Since no interpretation of so clear a statement of the formal reason for the divine indwelling is necessary, the only need is to point out here some concomitant elements of St. Bonaventure's thought, the emphasis on which will illumine the problem being considered.

First of all, the mere fact that Bonaventure should so evidently and certainly advance this particular solution is strong confirmation for the interpretation that has been given of the *Summa* attributed to Alexander of Hales. A well-defined tradition is in evidence in this matter, for Richard of Middleton (whom Gilson characterises as having at times a clearer knowledge and a preciser exposition of St. Bonaventure's profound theological tendencies than the Seraphic Doctor himself)[51] teaches exactly the same doctrine: the presence of the Trinity not a new presence of God but a presence in a new way, in virtue of the just man's power to enjoy him.[52] Previous expositions have shown that this theory is adumbrated by Altissiodorensis and sponsored by Eudes Rigaud, Bonaventure's master.

Secondly, St. Bonaventure rejects absolutely any explanation of the triune presence founded on efficient causality. "No one has the Holy Spirit, *no matter how much the Holy Spirit works in him*, except him who can enjoy Him."[53]

So, too, he insists that while God is present in natural effects *per modum exeuntis*, through grace he is present *per modum redeuntis, quantum ad reditum*.[54] And he maintains that in the inhabitation the Holy Spirit is given to us "ut finiens, sicut praemium merenti."[55] The whole purpose of God's giving of Himself to us in the special presence of the inhabitation is that we may possess the Trinity in order to bring us back to God: this is an integral part of St. Bonaventure's definition.*

Besides completing the theory of the *Summa* of Alexander of Hales by making explicit what that work left

* Cf. *supra*, p. 157 and note 39.

unsaid, the Seraphic Doctor performs a notable service in clarifying the obscurities of its position and simplifying its unnecessary complexities. This is nowhere more evident than in his discussion of the notion of manifestation as characteristic of the divine missions and in his analysis of its connection with the inhabitation. Although he disagrees with the author of the *Summa* in assigning the principal element in the missions to the manifestation rather than to the divine processions,[56] he yet gives a faithful rendition of his position on all the essentials of this notion, but free of its confusions.

For Bonaventure a divine mission really involves three things: the eternal procession of a divine Person, the manifestation of this procession and consequently of the Person in a created effect of grace, and the inhabitation of the divine Person as a result of this effect.[57] This is to state simply what the *Summa Alexandri* has already said in a far more difficult way: that the manifestation of a Person by an effect in which His procession is represented by appropriation constitutes also the special presence of that Person in the souls of the just.* St. Bonaventure will likewise state that by appropriation one mission is distinguished from another;[58] but since he has made clear that the effect appropriated establishes the real presence of the Persons not in virtue of its appropriation but because it serves as a partial element (dispositive for the gift of knowledge, perfective and essential for those of love) in constituting the power of enjoying the Persons which is the formal reason of Their presence (partial, we say, because God must be present as efficient cause), there is no occasion for confusion or false interpretation. The appropriation can be made because the gifts make the

* Cf. *supra*, pp. 115-128.

Persons present; the Persons are not present because the gifts can be appropriated.

Moreover, contrary to the Halesian *Summa,* he holds that the divine missions, although distinguishable, are never really separated; and thus he more forcibly underlines the real purpose of the gifts of grace — not to manifest the Trinity but to make It present.[59] And He will offer as an explanation of a new mission by the increase of grace, the fact that this must invoke a new use of the gift or a new gift leading to a new ability to possess the Trinity.[60]

All these facts state simply, clearly, indisputably the central fact of the divine missions: the coming of the Persons to dwell in us, and this inhabitation effected formally by the gifts of grace. To be sent is to be known: to be known as proceeding in virtue of the appropriation of some gift, to be known as indwelling in virtue of the function of the same gift in obtaining the presence of the Trinity. That is the *Summa fratris Alexandri's* theory, too, but here is a far better statement and exposition than the master himself made of it.

It is hardly necessary to remark that for the Seraphic Doctor as for the author of the Halesian *Summa* this solution sufficiently accounts for the *real* presence of the Trinity. As the analysis of the problem and the specification of the terms of the new relation is the same for both, so the basic premise and principle on which they will found their theory is the same: the primacy of love and its efficacy in accomplishing a real union. The wonder is not that they failed to answer the problem successfully with such a principle, but that they succeeded so well, within the limits of the particular question, in delineating so accurately its nature and in proposing the particular principles proper to the inhabitation which make a solution possible.

3. Criticism of the Solution of St. Bonaventure

There is no need to repeat the criticism offered of the *Summa Alexandri's* theory: it will apply equally well to Bonaventure's solution. The defects are obvious enough to those who enjoy St. Thomas' profound analysis of the psychology and metaphysics of love and knowledge. Love can only achieve an intentional, affective union, not a real and physical one; as efficient cause it can tend to such a union, can even effect it, but as formal cause it can do nothing. And fruition, the ultimate act of love, can only enjoy what is possessed by some means other than itself.

It is futile to press the matter. The *Summa Alexandri* and Bonaventure fail. But in their failure, it should not be forgotten, they have nobly succeeded in advancing our comprehension of the problem and in determining what principles will be useful in solving it, what approaches must be abandoned. Theirs is a notable instance of theological progress.

ARTICLE 3

Conclusion

The point has now been reached where St. Thomas' solution of the problem can profitably be considered, preparatory to a comparison of it with those other theories the Schoolmen have proffered. From the study of these answers that has been undertaken in this and in the preceding chapter, the theological progress that has been made stands out. Beginning with the facts bequeathed them by Tradition (the teaching of the Church, as shown by her Fathers and theologians, concerning the revealed notions contained in Holy Scripture), they seize upon a fertile element of Augustine's explanation and attempt to apply it to the questions which these facts give rise to. On the one hand the avenue of final causality will be opened up: William of Auxerre suggests it by metaphor, and that notion will be developed years after his *Summa Aurea* by such men as the anonymous compiler of Codex Vaticanus latinus 691 and Eudes Rigaud and Jean de la Rochelle, to find its definitive canonization in the *Summa Theologica* attributed to Alexander of Hales. Here Bonaventure will find the source for his own more reasoned and scientific presentation of the solution, and from him it will descend to his disciples, such as Richard of Middleton.

But another, and opposed, attempt will be made to resolve the difficulties, an attempt using the same facts, seizing on the same notion of manifestation. This is the course plotted by Alexander of Hales in his *Glossa* and *Quaestiones Disputatae*: God's presence explained on the grounds of special operation, accounted for by exemplary causality. Even in face of the popular opposition of the contradictory theory, this early effort of the great Franciscan Master does not die, for it is found adopted and richly defended by Saint Albert, as well in the years of his maturity as in the days of his early teaching career.*

* It is thus a curious fact that the Aristotelian (Albert) adopts a quasi-Augustinian exemplarism to explain the indwelling, while the Augustinian abandons his exemplarist predilections (indeed, deliberately purges his model of them) to apply an Aristotelian realism to the problem. It is, nevertheless, a fact, and of considerable historic import.

What value do these diverse solutions possess? Neither can ultimately explain the special facts of the mystery. But they do not fail for the same reasons nor in the same degree. Alexander and Albert, in effect, adhere *too* closely to Augustine: like him they regard the divine missions (and the apparitions and the donations) simply as a *theophania* of the divine persons; the fact that this manifestation proceeds from the real presence of the Persons escapes them. So they fall back upon the notion of appropriation, of God's presence as efficient cause of effects exemplifying the distinct Persons. But this does not and cannot explain the real presence of the Trinity as distinct Persons; and, indeed, it might even be doubted that they considered the problem explicitly at all, so unsuccessful are they in defining the nature of this presence and specifying the term of the creature's new relation to God thereby established.

The other avenue is more hopeful, but in the end no less seriously inadequate. Here is seen the fact that the missions constitute a new manner of the presence of God, that this mode gives the Trinity to the creature as an object to be enjoyed, that the gifts by which this is accomplished can thereby manifest the Persons. Obviously, these facts represent a considerable theological progress: but they still leave unanswered the question of the formal reason of this inhabitation. And the solution they give is ultimately and radically unsatisfactory, because love, even the divine love of Charity, explains an affective union but not the real union they have so brilliantly shown to be characteristic of the divine indwelling.

The question still remains unsolved. Does that mean that each of these attempts is equally worthless? Final judgment can only be passed when a true theory is supplied: now one can only affirm that neither has succeeded. It is in this state of doubt and suspended judgment that one turns to St. Thomas, to see which of these approaches he will take, which reject; or whether he will offer a solution proper to himself.

NOTES

[1] P. Mandonnet, "Albert le Grand," *Dict. théol. cath.*, I, 1, coll. 672-673.

[2] Fernand Van Steenberghen, *Aristote en Occident* (Louvain, 1946), p. 147. This, like the opposition Gilson finds between the views of St. Bonaventure and St. Thomas in regard to the pagan philosophers, is no doubt something of an exaggeration for literary effect: but it shows that Bonaventure's Augustinism is not completely 'unsullied.'

[3] Frederick Copleston, S.J., *A History of Philosophy* (London, 1950), II, p. 303.

[4] *Sum. Theol.*, I, Tract. VII, q. 32, memb. 1, a. 1, sol. ad q. 3 (ed. cit., XXXI, p. 345): ". . . mitti est cognosci per effectum, quod ab alio est. . . ." Cf. I *Sent.*, d. 14, a. 3, sol. (XXV, p. 392): ". . . in veritate optime determinat Augustinus missionem quando dicit quod 'mitti est cognosci quod ab alio sit': et bene concedo, quod hoc fit per effectum, sed non quemlibet: sed duo exiguntur, scilicet appropriabilitas ad proprium, et quod sit effectus gratiae gratum facientis, cui conjuncta semper sit processio personae, et persona ipsa. . . ."

[5] *Ibid.*, d. 16, a. 1, q. 1 (XXV, p. 445): ". . . mitti non dicitur persona respectu cujuscumque doni, sed tantum in dono in quo ipsa est, et habetur. . . ." Cf. *ibid.*, d. 14, a. 3, sol. (p. 392); a. 4 ad obj. (p. 393); a. 6, sol. (pp. 395-396); *Sum. Theol.*, I, Tract. VII, q. 32, memb. 1, sol. (XXXI, p. 339); etc., etc.

[6] I *Sent.*, d. 15, a. 5 ad 1 (XXV, p. 416): ". . . Spiritus mittit se, id est a collatione Spiritus in qua dat se, est effectus in quo cognoscitur quod ab alio sit. . . ." Cf. *ibid.*, d. 14, a. 1 (p. 390).

[7] *Ibid.*, d. 17, a. 1 ad 1 (p. 465): "Charitas per hoc quod accidens est et genere accidentis, indignius aliquid est in genere quam substantia. Si autem attenditur ratio boni, tunc ipsa est dignior omni bono creato: quia ratio boni in ipsa est, quod est effectus simillimus bonitati Dei, ita quod etiam ipse Deus ab effectu hoc nunquam separatur, sed semper cum ipso datur ei cui datur charitas; et ideo in quantum est similitudo bonitatis Dei, et Deum habet in se ad aliud quam aliae creaturae, unde ipse inferior in naturam bonitatis ratione potest conjungere naturae superiori." Cf. *loc. cit.*, ad 2.

[8] *Ibid.*, d. 16, a. 1 ad 5 (XXV, p. 444): ". . . missus cum gratia habetur illapsus in substantiam animae ejus cui missio fit . . . :

Angelus autem non potest illabi in substantiam mentis nostrae: ergo per ipsum non potest administrari hujusmodi missio."

The imprecision of the word is no better exemplified than in the fact that the Nominalists, who follow Scotus in rejecting St. Thomas' realistic solution of the presence of God in all things on the basis of efficient causality, explain this same presence as a 'diffusion' of the divine substance, an *illapsus*. The word, nevertheless, has an honorable history among the early Scholastics, signifying the immediate contact which God, and He alone, has with all created essences; it is a descriptive word for the intimacy and immanence of God in all things which St. Thomas will specify as a property of the divine power, concomitant with His creative and conserving action. As such it is used by his commentators (e.g., John of St. Thomas, *Cursus Theologicus*, I, q. 8, disp. 8, *passim*), although St. Thomas prefers 'infusus' (e.g., IV *Con. Gen.*, c. 17). As pointed out in the Deferrari-Barry-McGuiness *Lexicon* (Catholic University of America Press, 1948-49), the Angelic Doctor uses the word only in quotations (p. 501).

[9] I *Sent.*, d. 14, a. 13 ad 1 (XXV, p. 403): ". . . Spiritus ubique est ut Deus quia Deus est: sed tamen per hunc effectum quo manifestatur in Sanctis, non ostendit se ubique: et ideo quoad hoc mitti dicitur: quia ipse personaliter et essentialiter adest speciali modo ubi sic operatur: sed in omni loco modis generalibus est, scilicet praesentialiter, potentialiter, et essentialiter."

[10] *Sum. Theol.*, Tract. VII, q. 32, memb. 2, a. 1, sol. ad q. 3 (XXXI, p. 345): "Si enim in dono non daretur persona divina ut operans, caderet a fine datio et missio: finis enim dationis et missionis est sanctificatio et reductio creaturae rationalis, quam solum donum facere non potest, nisi dispositive: sed oportet, quod persona divina in dono operetur."

[11] I *Sent.*, d. 17, a. 1 ad 2 (XXV, p. 465): ". . . charitas in se considerata est essentiae et virtutis finitae: in quantum agit per rationem boni similis bonitati Dei, Deum habens in se operantem, sic potest conjungere infinita distantia, hoc est, sine proportione."

[12] *Sum. Theol.*, I, Tract. VII, q. 32, memb. 1, sol. ad 6 (XXI, p. 340): "Quinimo, Spiritus procedit aeterna processione: et processio ejus manifestatur per effectum donorum, in quibus essentialiter, potentialiter, et praesentialiter est Spiritus sanctus. Et hujus ratio est, quia operatio talium donorum est virtutis infinitae: virtus autem infinita nulli creato convenire potest: et ideo dona sine Spiritu sancto

virtutem infinitam non habent. Negari autem non potest, ut dicit Damascenus, quin operans sit ubi per propriam virtutem operatur. Unde ubi apparet infinitus actus, ibi necesse est esse virtutem infinitam et operationem virtutis infinitae. Est autem infinitus actus conjungere hominem Deo ad beneplacitum voluntatis, et posse mereri aeternum praemium. Unde non potest esse nisi virtutis infinitae, quae non est nisi divinae personae essentialiter, potentialiter, et praesentialiter operantis: ad quod dona ex parte nostra disponunt, sed actum nec ex se, nec ex nobis elicere possunt sine Spiritu sancto." Cf. also, *loc. cit.*, ad 7.

[13] Cf. *Glossa ordinaria* super Cant. 5:17 (PL 113: 1157). Like Peter Lombard, St. Thomas cites St. Gregory as the author of the phrase (*Sum. Theol.*, I, q. 8, a. 3, Sed contra), but it is clear that the Gloss quotes Gregory's doctrine (cf. *In Ezech*, I, hom. 8, n. 16 [PL 76: 860]; *ibid.*, II, hom. 5, n. 11 [PL 76: 991]; *Moral.*, II, Chap. 12, nn. 20 and 21 [PL 75: 565-566]) rather than his words.

[14] *Sum. Theol.*, I, Tract. VII, q. 32, memb. 2, a. 1, sol. (XXXI, p. 343): "Cum enim dicitur, Pater mittit, vel Filius mittit, vel Spiritus sanctus mittit, verbum, mittit, dicit actum egredientem a persona sicut a substantia: et cum actus ille fit operatio (ut dicit Augustinus) circa creaturam, et talis operatio semper sit communis tribus, oportet quod illa operatio ad personas referatur gratia essentiae quae communis est."

[15] *Loc. cit.*: ". . . cum operatum a Trinitate, appropriabile sit uni personae, et omnis operatio secundum rationem appropriati debeat fieri, et secundum relationem ad proprium, oportet quod in operato illo sit ratio et signum alicujus unius personae."

[16] *Loc. cit.*: "Adhuc etiam, cum in omni operante et operato intelligitur habitudo operantis ad operatum, oportet quod in habitudine illa, habitudo personalis proprietatis et notio significetur sicut in signo. . . ."

[17] I *Sent.*, d. 37, a. 5 ad 1 and 2 (XXVI, pp. 235-236): ". . . quod objicitur, quod Deus uno modo se habet ad omne quod est, Dicendum quod hoc sic intelligitur, quod se habet modo non variato per essentiam, vel per aliquid additum sibi: non tamen se habet in eadem ratione exemplaris ad omne quod est, sicut de facili patet unicuique.

Ad aliud dicendum, quod cum dicitur, quod inest per inhabitantem gratiam, notatur aliud connotum quod magis elevat naturam, et notatur alia ratione exemplaris, quia scilicet voluntatis bonae, eo quod Spiritus datur cum donis suis, licet non alius quam prius erat, tamen ad aliud quam prius habebatur . . . ."

[18] A modern analysis of the Thomistic notion of exemplary causality which reveals both the inadequacies of these explanations and the confusions of innumerable recent works will be found in the brief but lucid article of David L. Greenstock, T.O.P., "Exemplar Causality and the Supernatural Order," *The Thomist*, 16 (1953), pp. 1-31.

[19] Cf. F. Anciaux, "La cause exemplaire: notion de cette cause et nature de sa causalité," *Revue Augustinienne*, 2 (1907), pp. 685-704; J. Bissen, *L'exémplarisme divin selon s. Bonaventure*. Paris, 1929.

[20] *Op. cit.*, d. 16, a. 1, q. 1 (XXV, p. 445): ". . . potentia attribuitur Patri: sed, ut dictum est, mitti non dicitur persona respectu cujuscumque doni, sed tantum in dono in quo ipsa est, et habetur: unde si Pater daretur in potentia illa, esset potentia gratum faciens. Potentia autem illa non est distincta a donis intellectus et affectus, quia per donum hujusmodi sumus potentes in actibus gratiae: ergo datio Patris non habet distinctum donum ab eo in quo datur Filius, et in quo datur Spiritus sanctus: et ideo a Sanctis expresse non invenitur, quod Pater det se, vel detur a se." Cf. *ibid.*, d. 14, a. 13, a. 2 ad obj. (XXV, p. 403); a slightly different explanation, still working from the point of view of the effect and of appropriation, is found in *Sum. Theol.*, I, Tract. VII, q. 32, memb. 1, a. 1, sol. ad q. 3 (XXXI, p. 345). But elsewhere he maintains that the Father cannot be sent because He does not proceed (cf. I *Sent.*, d. 14, *a.* 13, q. 2 [XXV, p. 403]; *Sum. Theol.*, *loc. cit.*) a solution more in keeping with his principles, since like Alexander he insists that the mission principally signifies the eternal procession, the effect only by connotation (cf. I *Sent.*, d. 14, a. 5, sol. [XXV, p. 394]; d. 15, a. 5 ad 1 [p. 416]; *Sum. Theol.*, Tract. VII, q. 32, memb. 2, a. 1, sol. ad q. 2 [XXXI, p. 345]; etc.).

[21] I *Sent.*, d. 14, a. 13, q. 2 ad obj. (XXV, p. 403): ". . . inhabitant inseparabiliter sanctas animas tres personae: unde in illa mansione solus Spiritus mittitur, sicut patet per id quod praecedit: 'Si quis diligit me, sermonum meum servabit: et Pater meus diliget eum, et ad eum veniemus, etc.' In collatione enim dilectionis solus Spiritus mittitur ratione appropriationis, non tamen solus Spiritus inhabitat, imo inhabitatio est trium simul."

[22] *Ibid.*, d. 15, a. 7 ad 3 (XXV, p. 420): ". . . missio est . . . ostendens fidem secundum distinctionem personarum, quam ostendit in effectu appropriabili uni magis quam alio: sed verum est quod superflueret, si ad nihil aliud esset nisi ut Pater (quia alias venire non posset per Filium missum, et per Spiritum sanctum) veniret ad nos. Hoc enim absurdum esset et infidele sentire. Pater enim per seipsum

venire potest, sicut et Filius, et Spiritus sanctus. Sed utilis est nobis missio, ut dictum est: quia ostendit nobis fidem distinctionis personarum."

[23] Cf. *ibid.*, d. 37, a. 5, sol. (XXVI, p. 235); a. 9 ad 1 (p. 241).

[24] *Ibid.*, ad 2 (XXVI, p. 236): ". . . cum dicitur, quod inest per inhabitantem gratiam notatur aliud connatum quod magis elevat naturam, et notatur alia ratione exemplaris, quia scilicet voluntatis bonae, eo quod Spiritus Sanctus datur cum donis suis, licet non alius quam prius erat, tamen ad aliud datur quam prius habebatur. . . ."

[25] Cf. I *Sent.*, d. 36, q. 2, a. 2; III *Sent.*, d. 14, a. 2, sol. 2; *De Ver.*, q. 3, a. 2; I *Con. Gent.*, Chap. 54; *Sum. Theol.*, I, q. 15, a. 1 ad 3, a. 2; q. 44, a. 3; q. 47, a. 1 ad 2; *De Pot.*, q. 3, a. 16 ad 12, 13; *Quod.* IV, q. 1.

On St. Thomas' understanding of, and use of, appropriation, especially with respect to the divine indwelling, see R. Morency, *L'union de grâce selon S. Thomas* (Montréal, Canada; 1950). He conclusively shows that for St. Thomas appropriation refers the just soul to the Persons only through the medium of the essential divine attributes, not in virtue of any special distinct relations to each member of the Trinity. This is the meaning of 'assimilation by grace.' Cf. especially pp. 128-135.

[26] *Op. cit.*, q. 15, a. 1, ad 3um argumentum Durandi (I, pp. 375-376): ". . . idea *per se primo* non convenit Verbo Divino, sed Divinae Essentiae. Et ratio est duplex: prima, quoniam idea habet rationem causae exemplaris. At quod Deus sit causa creaturarum, sive efficiens, sive exemplaris, sive formalis competit Deo, quatenus est unus ratione Divinae Essentiae, et non competit *per se primo* alicui Divinae Personae. . . . Secunda est, quoniam idea per se primo respicit intellectum divinum, ut intellectus divinus est, at Verbum non est forma objecta intellectui divino, sed prout est intellectus Patris. Unde ad argumentum respondetur, quod Essentia Divina est forma objecta intellectui divino *absolute*: est enim primarium et formale objectum divini intellectus, et ita *per se primo* illi competit ratio ideae."

[27] Cf. Capreolus, *op. cit.*, p. 418: "Sciendum tamen quod non intelligit sanctus Thomas quod ex distinctione attributorum et suarum perfectionum veniat distinctio idearum, ita quod intellectus divinus primo distinguat attributa et perfectiones suas secundum rationem, et postea recipit de illa multitudine perfectionum aliquas, dimittendo alias, ut inde formet ideas; sicut videntur praetendere exempla posita. . . . Sed intendit quod Deus intelligendo essentiam omnimode

perfectam, nulla praevia distinctione rationis facta de perfectione sua, intelligit omnia essentia sua eminenter continet et perfecte repraesentat. Hujusmodi autem sunt omnes perfectiones et quidditates creabiles, et omnes respectus reales seu rationis, et omnes negationes; omnia enim talia, divina essentia sufficientissime repraesentat, et distinctissime. Ipsa igitur divina essentia, sumpta prout continet supereminenter, et repraesentat, ut perfectissima similitudo, quidditatem lapidis, est ratio propria lapidis; et ita de aliis quidditatibus. Cum autem divina essentia sic sumitur, scilicet ut praecise continet et repraesentat lapidem, ipso *tota sumitur secundum rem, sed non totaliter.* Quia, licet non immo capiatur tota realitas divinae naturae, tamen ipsa capiatur ac si esset quid finitum adaequatum lapidi; quia sumitur ut repraesentat lapidem praecise, et non ut continet aut repraesentat alia, quae sunt extra rationem lapidis; hoc autem fit, quia sumitur cum respectu proportionis et imitabilitatis ad lapidem; sicut enim lapis defective non plene repraesentat essentiam divinam, ita essentia divina imperfecte repraesentatur a lapide; et ideo ipsa potest sumi cum tali respectu imitationis imperfectae a lapide; et hoc est sumere eam totam, non totaliter. Non ergo intelligit sanctus Thomas, quod una divina perfectio sit ratio lapidis, et alia sit ratio animalis; sed intendit quod essentia divina, ut continet perfectionem lapidis praecise, est propria ratio lapidis, modo praedicto. (Emphasis added.)

[28] *Sum. Theol.* II-II, q. 23, a. 2 ad 1: "... ipsa divina essentia caritas est, sicuti et sapientia est, et bonitas est. Unde sicut dicimur boni bonitate, quae est Deus, et sapientes sapientiae, quae est Deus ... ita etiam caritas qua formaliter diligimus proximum est quaedam participatio divinae caritatis. Hic enim modus loquendi consuetus est apud Platonicos, quorum doctrinis imbutus fuit Augustinus; quod quidam non advertentes, ex verbis eius sumpserunt occasionem errandi." We know who these last are: Peter Lombard and his disciples.

[29] *Sum. Theol.*, Tract. VII, q. 32, memb. 1, sol. ad 6 (XXXI, p. 340). Cf. *supra*, p. 167, note 12.

[30] As Mullaney has shown in his excellent analysis of de la Taille's novel and attractive theory ("The Incarnation: de la Taille vs. Thomistic tradition," *The Thomist*, 17 [1954], pp. 1-42), the tragic flaw of that theory lies in "an unfortunate confusion of the efficient and formal (or quasi-formal) orders" (p. 15).

[31] *Op. cit.*, II-II, q. 23, a. 2.

[32] *Loc. cit.*: "... cum formae accidentales a substantialibus proficiscantur, oportet efficaciam formarum accidentalium in substan-

tiarum virtutes resolvere, quibus sunt connaturalia accidentia secundum se, vel secundum principia. . . . Propter quod, cum charitas talis forma accidentalis sit, ut nulli creaturae factae, aut factabili connaturalis esse possit, sed soli divinae substantiae: et non secundum accidentis naturam, sed substantialiter connaturalis sit: efficacia ejus, in quocumque reperiatur, secundum divinitatis naturam pensanda est, et in Deum resolvenda, ut proximum et connaturale ejus principium."

[33] *Loc. cit.*: ". . . auctor efficaciam charitatis in Deum reducit, non ea ratione, qua omnium rerum est auctor, sed ea speciali ratione, qua charitas est divini ordinis soli Deo connaturalis. Nec intendit auctor ponere aliquam infinitatem in effectu charitatis, quam non ponere intendat in ipsa charitate, ut superficies litterae prae se ferre videtur, penes quam procedit dubium motum. Non enim minus est infinita charitas, quam in charitate esse, et dilectio Dei ex charitate; sed intendit docere unde habet charitas hujusmodi infinitatem, quae in suo effectu apparet. Et dicit quod hoc habet ex virtute Dei, qui est proprius auctor charitatis, non sicut communiter est creator, sed sicut connaturalium sibi soli commicator. Hinc enim fit quod charitas, quae divini ordinis est, et formaliter faciat hominem sic conjunctum Deo habitualiter et per actum elicitum actualiter. Sic autem esse conjunctum Deo, infinitum quid est, excedens omnem efficaciam omnis agentis creati et creabilis."

[34] Cajetan, *loc. cit.*: ". . . advertere oportet quod formae participatae in subjecto alterius naturae referuntur in duplex agens ut quod. Alterum, ut quod utitur tantum illa: alterum, ut a quo proficiscitur et cui connaturalis est. Verbi gratia, calor participatus in animali et refertur in animal quod utitur ipso et refertur in ignem unde est. Et licet utrumque horum dici possit quod agit et operatur per calorem, non solum tamen different praedicto modo, quia hoc ut utens, ille ut causa: sed etiam, quia proprius effectus caloris ut sic non attribuitur, proprie loquendo, animali utenti sed igni: nec resolvitur in illud utens sed in ignem, ut patet in exemplo allato ex II *de Anima* de augmento igneo et augmento animalis. Sic autem est in proposito. Charitas enim est forma participata in voluntate creata a Spiritu sancto. Et ipsa quidem semper operatur formaliter, id est ut quo et non ut quod: sed cum habeat duplex quod, scilicet hominem utentem ea et Deum, unde est, licet respectu aliquorum effectuum homo possit dici quod agit et charitas quo, respectu tamen proprii effectus charitatis, qui ex suae cognitionis origine se tenet, solus Deus est proprie causa agens ut quod. Talis autem effectus est infinitus quae charitate fit. Et propterea efficacia charitatis in faciendo effectum infinitum in

Deum reducitur ut causam activam, et quod vere et proprie agit, et in ipsam charitatem ut formaliter operantem."

[35] St. Thomas holds this explicitly: "Gratia enim causatur in homine ex praesentia divinitatis, sicut lumen in aere" (*Sum. Theol.*, III, q. 7, a. 113). But he explains clearly how this is to be understood: "Gratia gratum faciens disponit animam ad habendam divinam personam: et significatur hoc, cum dicitur quod Spiritus sanctus datur secundum donum gratiae. Sed tamen ipsum donum gratiae est a Spiritu sancto: et hoc significatur, cum dicitur quod 'caritas diffunditur in cordibus nostris per Spiritum sanctum.'" (*Ibid.*, I, q. 43, a. 3 ad 2). He teaches the same doctrine, significantly enough, in I *Sent.*, d. 14, q. 2, a. 1, sol. 2: ". . . ordo aliquorum secundum naturam potest dupliciter considerari. Aut ex parte recipientis vel materiae, et sic dispositio est prior quam id ad quod disponit: et sic per prius recipimus dona Spiritus sancti quam ipsum Spiritum, quia per ipsa dona recepta Spiritui sancto assimilamur. Aut ex parte agentis et finis; et sic quod propinquius erit fini et agenti, dicitur esse prius: et ita per prius recipimus Spiritum sanctum quam dona ejus, quia et Filius per amorem suum alia nobis donavit. Et hoc est simpliciter esse prius." Cf. *ibid.*, d. 15, q. 3, a. 1: "Et quia tota Trinitas facit Spiritum sanctum esse in aliquo secundum novam habitudinem, propter donum collatum totius Trinitatis; ideo tota Trinitas dicitur mittere Spiritum sanctum. . . ."

[36] The Franciscan editors of the *Glossa* find "in the first book of St. Albert's commentary" at least 75 of these references to Alexander's first book. See *op. cit.*, Index II, p. 490.

[37] *Op. cit.*, Praelocutio Proemio in Secundum Librum Sententiarum Praemissa (II, p. 1): "At quemadmodum in primo libro sententiis adhaesi Magistri Sententiarum et communibus opinionibus magistrorum, et potissime magistri et patris nostri bonae memoriae fratris Alexandri, sic in consequentibus libris ab eorum vestigiis non recedam." The authenticity of this Prologue has been contested by modern scholars, assertively by Gorce ("La Somme théologique d'Alexandre de Hales est-elle authentique?" *The New Scholasticism*, 5 [1931], p. 56), scientifically by J. Friedrichs ("Zum 'Vorwort des hl. Bonaventura' [*Op. cit.*, II, 1-3]," *Franziskanische Studien*, 29 [1942], pp. 78-89). The editors of the Quaracchi *Summa* of Alexander vigorously defend it (IV, Prol., pp. CCCXLIII-CCCXLIV), as they must—how successfully others may care to judge.

[38] *Ibid.*, I, d. 15, p. 2, a. un., q. 1 (I, p. 270): [Inhabitatio est] novus modus essendi, addens super esse per naturam." Cf. *ibid.*, d. 21, dub. 2 (p. 387): "Quamvis Deus sit in omnibus et cum omnibus,

tamen specialiter dicitur esse cum Sanctis propter effectum gratiae inhabitantis." See also *ibid.*, d. 37, p. 2, a. 1 ad 4 (I, p. 655); IV *Sent.*, d. 1, p. 1, a. un., q. 3 ad 5 (IV, p. 17).

[39] *Breviloquium*, p. 1, c. 5 (ed. cit., V, p. 214): "Habitare ... dicit effectum spiritualem cum acceptatione, sicut est effectus gratiae gratum facientis quae est deiformis et in Deum reducit et Deum facit nos habere, et haberi a nobis, ac per hoc et inhabitare in nobis." According to Stohr, the phrase 'per hoc' clearly indicates that the inhabitation is constituted by our possession of God, an interpretation apparently justified by the text and context. Cf. *Die Trinitätslehre des heiligen Bonaventure*, p. 182: "Deshalb ist sie fähig, uns zu Gott zurückzuführen, uns zum Besitz Gottes zu machen, und in den Besitz Gott zu setzen. Dies leztere ist eben die Einwohnung, die ganze Trinität in unser Herz einziehen lasst." (Quoted in H. Koenig, *De Inhabitatione Spiritus Sancti Doctrina Sancti Bonaventurae*, Apud Aedes Seminarii Sanctae Mariae ad Lacum, Mundelein, Illinois, U.S.A., 1934, p. 44, note 9).

[40] I *Sent.*, d. 14, a. 2, q. 1 ad 2 (I, p. 250): "Ad illud quod objicitur: nihil plus est in isto quam prius: dicendum, quod dari non ordinatur ad esse, sed ad habere, licet enim Spiritus Sanctus esset prius in peccatore, non tamen habebatur ab eo."

[41] II *Sent.*, d. 27, a. 1, q. 3 (II, p. 660): "Nos habere Deum non est aliud quam Deum habitare in nobis." From these phrases, if from nothing else, the great difference between St. Albert's theory and that of St. Bonaventure would be evident. For St. Albert, God is had even before the infusion of grace, even, therefore, by the sinner (cf. I *Sent.*, d. 37, a. 5 ad 2; XXVI, p. 236; quoted *supra*, p. 168, note 17); for St. Bonaventure, as for the Alexander of the *Summa*, 'to have God' is an operative phrase specifying the very nature of the inhabitation, which distinguishes the sinner from the just.

[42] I *Sent.*, d. 14, a. 2, q. 1 (I, p. 249): "... dare est ad aliquid habendum vel possidendum; habere autem aliquid vel possidere est, cum aliquid est in facultate habentis vel possidentis. Esse autem in facultate habentis vel possidentis est esse praesto ad fruendum vel utendum. Perfecta autem possessio est, cum homo habet illud, quo possit uti et quo possit frui. Sed recte frui non est nisi Deo, et recte uti non contingit nisi per gratiam gratum facientem; ergo perfecta possessio est, in qua Deus habetur et eius gratia." That this does not place God in man's power St. Bonaventure clearly teaches (*ibid.*, ad 3; I, p. 250). See *supra*, p. 96, note 48.

⁴³ *Ibid.*, d. 18, dub. 5 (I, p. 335): "Nullus habet Spiritum Sanctum, quantumcumque Spiritus Sanctus operetur in eo, nisi qui potest eo frui." II *Sent.*, d. 26, a. 1, q. 2 ad 1 (II, p. 636): "non enim ob aliud dicitur nobis dari Spiritus Sanctus nisi ex eo, quod sic est in nobis a Deo ut habeatur a nobis. Tunc autem habetur a nobis, quando habitum habemus quo possimus eo frui; et hoc est donum gratiae creatum." Cf. I *Sent.*, d. 14, a. 2, q. 1 ad 2 (I, p. 250).

⁴⁴ *Ibid.*, d. 1, dub. 12 (I, p. 44): "Fruitio de sui generali ratione dicit amoris unionem, scilicet fruibilis cum fruente."

⁴⁵ *Ibid.*, a. 2, q. un. (I, p. 36): "Quia ergo frui secundum omnem acceptationem dicit delectationem vel quietem vel utrumque, et omne tale habet rationem boni, et hoc est obiectum voluntatis: ideo loquendo essentialiter, frui est actus voluntatis. Sed quia voluntas nec delectatur nec quietatur nisi in eo, quod cognoscit vel per fidem vel per speciem, et in eo, quod habet per spem vel in re, ideo actus aliarum virium ad hunc disponunt, non tamen sunt ipsum frui, essentialiter loquendo."

⁴⁶ III *Sent.*, d. 2, a. 3, q. 2 ad 3 (III, p. 53): "Fruitio ponit aliquem actum qui fit ab anima, respectu cujus gratia infusa est causa, et ad quem habilitatur anima mediante gratia, et in quem exit, cum a gratia est adjusta et regulata."

⁴⁷ Cf. I *Sent.*, d. 1, a. 2 ad 4 (I, p. 37); II *Sent.*, d. 38, a. 1, q. 2 ad 3 (II, p. 885): III *Sent.*, d. 29, a. un., q. 2 (III, p. 642); d. 34, p. 2, a. 1, q. 1 ad 1 (p. 755). Although St. Bonaventure distinguishes really between grace and Charity (II *Sent.*, d. 27, a. 1, q. 2 [II, pp. 656-658]; III *Sent.*, d. 27, a. 1, q. 3 [III, pp. 596-598]), the basis for this real distinction is not clear, but it is certainly not that of St. Thomas; he teaches that grace and Charity do not differ "per essentiam, sed sola comparatione . . . et secundum esse" (II *Sent.*, d. 27, a. 1, q. 2, concl.; II, p. 657).

⁴⁸ Unlike most of the Scholastics and certainly unlike Alexander, formal beatitude consists for St. Bonaventure in an *active* habit, not in operation (IV *Sent.*, d. 49, p. 1, a. un., q. 1 ad 5; IV, p. 1001); from the gifts of glory which make man a perfect image of God and in which his beatitude formally consists follow acts of vision, fruition and comprehension by the memory: these acts consist *principally* in the act of fruition, secondarily in that of vision and comprehension (*ibid.*, q. 5 ad 1-3; IV, p. 1009; *Breviloquium*, p. 7, c. 7; V, p. 289). Hence the primacy of Charity (I *Sent.*, d. 1, a. 2, q. un. ad 2; I, p. 37).

⁴⁹ II *Sent.*, d. 27, a. 1, q. 3 (II, p. 660): "Habere . . . contingit dupliciter; vel perfecte, et sic habet homo Deum in actione quiescentis; vel semiplene, et sic habet homo Deum in ratione tendentis. Primum, scilicet quies, competit statui patriae; secundum est gratiae. . . . Et quoniam nos habere Deum non est aliud, quam Deum inhabitare in nobis; ideo gratia et gloria non solummodo distinguuntur secundum modum habendi Deum, sed etiam secundum rationem habitandi Deum in nobis."

⁵⁰ *Ibid.*, d. 38, a. 1, q. 2 (II, p. 884): "Caritas vero creata et consummata, utpote caritas patriae, est finis, quo quiescitur simpliciter in Deo. Caritas vero inchoata, utpote charitas viae, est finis, quo quiescitur in Deo ut nunc."

⁵¹ *La Philosophie au moyen âge* (Paris, 1930), p. 158: "Chez [Richard] les tendances authentiques et profondes de la pensée de saint Bonaventure arrivent parfois a une conscience plus claire et trouvent une expression plus précise que chez la maître lui-mème."

⁵² *Commentum Richardi a Mediavilla*, I, d. 14, a. 2, q. 1: "Si homo pauper haberet alicujus divitis pecuniam in sua domo, non propter hoc diceremus quod haberet illam pecuniam sicut rem suam. Unde non obstante, quod illa pecunia praesens erat in domo pauperis, posset sibi dari de novo a divite; quo facto non tantummodo haberet eam per solam pecuniae praesentiam in domo, sed haberet eam sicut rem suam. A simili aliqualiter dico, quod quamvis Spiritus sanctus sit per essentiam praesens omni rei, quia tamen peccator non habet facultatem ad fruendum eo, ideo, non obstante illa praesentia, potest a Deo vere dari persona Spiritus Sancti." (Quoted by the Quaracchi editors, *Opera Omnia Sancti Bonaventurae*, I *Sent.*, d. 14, scholion [I, p. 250].)

⁵³ I *Sent.*, d. 18, dub. 5 (I, p. 335): "Nullus habet *Spiritum sanctum, quantumcumque operetur sanctus in eo,* nisi qui potest eo frui." (Emphasis supplied.)

⁵⁴ *Ibid.*, d. 37, p. 1, a. 3, q. 2 (I, p. 648). Cf. II *Sent.*, d. 27, a. 1, q. 3 (II, p. 660): ". . homo habet Deum in ratione tendentis."

⁵⁵ I *Sent.*, d. 14, a. 2, q. 1 ad 3, 4 (I, p. 250).

⁵⁶ I *Sent.*, d. 15, p. 1, a. un., q. 4 (I, p. 265); d. 16, a. un., q. 1 (p. 279). Cf. *supra*, p. 101, note 69.

⁵⁷ *Ibid.*, d. 15, p. 2, a. un., q. 2 (I, p. 272): ". . . in missione invisibili est donorum collatio, in quibus est manifestatio et inhabitatio." *Ibid.*, d. 16, a. un., q. 1 (I, p. 279): "Missio autem com-

muniter dicta, ut dictum fuit supra in praecedenti distinctione, praesupponit circa missum emanationem et superaddit manifestationem. Et quoniam manifestatio emanationis, secundum quam attenditur missio, non fit nisi super eum, quem Spiritus sanctus inhabitat per effectum gratiae inhabitantis, hinc est, quod missio de ratione generali dicit manifestationem emanationis et inhabitationis." Cf. *ibid.*, d. 15, p. 2, a. un., q. 1 ad 4 (I, p. 271); d. 16, a. un., q. 2 ad 4 (I, p. 282).

[58] I *Sent.*, d. 15, p. 2, a. un., q. 2 (I, p. 272): "In habitibus pure affectivis datur sive mittiur Spiritus sanctus quia ei appropriantur. In habitibus pure cognitivis nec Filius nec Spiritus sanctus proprie, sicut dictum est, mittitur. In habitibus autem partim cognitivis partim affectivis, secundum quod diversa in se continent, et Filius mittitur et Spiritus sanctus. Nam cognitivi ducunt in manifestationem Verbi, affectivi in manifestationem Amoris."

[59] *Ibid.*, d. 16, a. un., q. 2 ad ult. (I, p. 282): " . . . sanctificatio appropriatur Spiritui sancto; unde sufficiebat, esse missionem visibilem ad manifestandam ipsius inhabitationem, cui sanctificatio appropriatur, cum inhabitatio Filii et Spiritus sancti sint indivisae. Manifestato quod in homine inhabitet Spiritus sanctus, sufficienter ostenditur quod et Filius." Previously (*ibid.*, d. 15, p. 2, a. un, q. 2; I, p. 272) he has pointed out that the missions are distinct not in their root (grace) but in respect to the habits which come from grace and the acts which spring from the different habits; hence the missions are *de facto* inseparable.

[60] *Ibid.*, d. 15, p. 2, a. un., q. 3 (I, 273): "Ad hoc dicunt aliqui, quod gratiam augeri est dupliciter, scilicet perceptibiliter et imperceptibiliter. Si perceptibiliter, tunc dicunt, in tali augmento dari vel mitti Filium et Spiritum sanctum; si autem imperceptibiliter, tunc dicunt, ipsum non mitti. Et ratio huius est, quia tunc dicitur dari vel mitti, cum mente percipitur."

"Sed aliter potest dici, quod augmentum gratiae est dupliciter: aut secundum profectum in gratia prius habita et eius usu, aut per collationem novi usus vel etiam doni gratuiti. Si solum per profectum, sicut ostendunt ultimae rationes, non dicitur mitti Spiritus sanctus. Si autem per collationem novi doni, sicut fuit in Apostolis in die Pentecostes, vel novi usus, sicut est in confirmatione; tunc potest dici vel dari Spiritus sanctus, quia aliquo modo est ibi de novo quantum ad illud donum vel usum doni, et quia abundantius est."

CHAPTER SIX

The Solution of St. Thomas

In the modern welter of a thousand and one variant theories on the divine indwelling, the invisible missions, the union of man with God by grace; in the bewildering conflict of innumerable "interpretations" of St. Thomas' utterances on these and similar subjects; in the daily proclamations, emanating from quite diverse and distant and contrary sources, of 'Behold, here he is,' or 'Behold, there he is' — can one be assured of giving a truly objective exposition of the solution of the Angelic Doctor to the problem of the inhabitation? An exposition free of preconceptions and predilections and prejudices? One untrammeled by polemics and party bias? The true thought of the Angel of the Schools, not that of his commentators and interpreters?

Such is the difficulty which now presents itself. After studying the scholastic tradition concerning the abiding presence of the Trinity, after seeing the first tentative efforts to solve the problem raised by this mystery, after considering the successes and failure of the *Doctor universalis* and the *Doctor seraphicus*, the task at hand is to examine the elucidations of him who is the providential culminating point of the theological renaissance of the Ages of Faith. The solution given by St. Thomas now must be disclosed.

Considering the violent disagreements, especially among modern theologians, as to what that solution is, an exposé of this answer must appear difficult in the extreme. In fact, however, the *determination* of St. Thomas' teaching on the indwelling (as distinguished from a comprehension of the profundities therein revealed) offers no major stumbling block to one willing to adhere to elemental exegetical principles. Confusion arises—and why not?—only when phrases are wrenched from their contexts, or texts are interpreted with bland disregard for principles elsewhere clearly enunciated, or a material identity of words and phrases is understood as formal avowal of a particular position—in short, when a writer or theologian finds what he wants to find (in many cases, what he *needs* to find), with scant concern for the doctrine of his authority.*

To *discover* St. Thomas' solution is by no means the purpose of this investigation: that answer clearly appears in both the *Scriptum super Sententiis* and the *Summa Theologiae,* provided they be interpreted by means of his own unequivocally stated principles; it has been pointed out, with greater or less clarity, by John of St. Thomas, Gardeil, Garrigou-Lagrange, Cuervo, Ciappi,† Morency[1] and many others; no original contribution by any theolo-

---

* Justification for such an attitude may be found, of course, when the authority in question is determinedly eclectic; toward one whose excelling genius is generally recognized as superlatively synthetic, this disregard of his principles and doctrine and his formal teaching is inexcusable, an appalling instance of serious intellectual injustice and, in some cases, of sheer charlatanism or dishonesty.

† For the works of the writers here noted see the Bibliography.

gian can reasonably be expected along the lines of discovery. Since, however, that explanation has been presented in completely different manners in the work of his youth and the masterpiece of his maturity,[2] it is necessary to determine how this difference is to be interpreted and explained. Such is the present purpose, let it be reiterated: through doctrinal analysis and historical comparison to reveal how and why St. Thomas' solution appears in various guises, to prove the identity of the answer underlying its diverse manifestations and to acquire in the process a deeper understanding of the position of the Angelic Doctor with regard to the indwelling of the Trinity.

The presentation of this definitive explanation of the mystery is not, then, an attempt to answer the question before it has been asked nor a prejudgment of the problem. On the contrary, it too provides necessary groundwork for the comparison of his theory with those of the other Schoolmen and hence for the later examination of the difficulty to which his solution in the two statements of it gives rise. Essentially the same answer in his earlier and his later works, howsoever different the forms under which it seems to appear, it will be unfolded *per modum unius*: illustrated by texts drawn impartially both from the *Summa*, where it is stated without equivocation, and from the *Sentences*.

This synthetic method of presentation should, first of all, indicate the doctrinal identity of these two works; but it will likewise bring into sharp relief the differences to be pointed out in the succeeding chapter. Such a procedure will have the further advantage of anticipating and answering the objections of adversaries of this theory, thus leaving the way clear for a positive consideration of St. Thomas' two distinct expressions of his doctrine. Finally, it will obviate the necessity for a later and more detailed analysis of the explanation offered by the Common Doctor of the mystery.

To render this exposé as objective as possible and its exegesis scientific, the facts with which St. Thomas worked—his acceptance of the common tradition of the Scholastics—will first be given. The second article will unfold the indisputable principles he has advanced which serve as his intellectual instruments for uncovering the true solution. Last of all, that solution itself will be set forth. In the interests of brevity, simplicity and clarity, these facts and principles and the solution will be enunciated in a series of propositions.

ARTICLE 1

The Facts of the Indwelling

1: *The existence of the divine Persons in the soul of the just is real and substantial.*

This fundamental teaching of divine revelation, attested to by the Fathers and by theologians, is many times affirmed by St. Thomas. It is the very basis of the mystery, of course, and determines the fact that St. Thomas, like his contemporaries, considers the invisible missions of the divine Persons as the extension or prolongation in time—in us—of the eternal processions of the Trinity. And as the Persons are really and substantially present in Their eternal processions, so are They really and substantially present in Their temporal processions.

"The Holy Spirit Himself proceeds in the temporal procession, or is given," he says in the *Sentences*, "and not only His gifts."[3] The phrase changes in the *Summa*, the truth is the same: "In the very gift of sanctifying grace, the Holy Spirit is had, and inhabits in man. So the Holy Spirit Himself is given and is sent."[4] The fact is universal and indisputable; it need not be insisted on.[5]

2: *This existence of the Trinity in the souls of the just is really distinct from the presence of immensity.*

Whereas God is present in all things as agent cause,[6] only in rational creatures does He dwell;[7] hence this presence constitutes a second *species* of God's presence,[8] *essentially* distinct from His common presence.[9] It is, then, a new way of being present,[10] presupposing the presence of immensity;[11] now God is present as man's end, not merely as His principle, as for other creatures.[12] For this reason, the just may be said to have and possess the divine Persons[13] as fruits for their enjoyment.[14]

3: *This new way of being present is realized by sanctifying grace.*

This is a central and conclusive fact for St. Thomas and admits of no dispute. It is stated as the significant conclusion of the pivotal third article of the tract on the divine missions in the *Summa* and of an equally important article in the *Sentences*, d. 14, q. 2, a. 2, as well as in numerous other places. So he expressly excludes the *gratiae gratis datae* from effecting a real presence of the divine Persons:[15] only the *gratia gratum faciens*, sanctifying grace as the root of the supernatural virtues and with its panoply of the gifts of the Holy Ghost, can give man the power to possess the Trinity as fruits of his enjoyment.

4: *This new presence of God, realized by sanctifying grace, is common to the three Persons.*

Not only does St. Thomas insist on the invisible missions of both the Holy Spirit and the Son and Their consequent indwelling, he also declares explicitly that while the Father is not sent, He yet comes to man to dwell in him.[16] So his direct affirmation that "the coming or inhabitation belongs to the entire Trinity"[17] and "the entire Trinity dwells in the mind"[18] must be understood as arguing not from the concomitance or circuminsession of the Persons, but from the fact that each in His own right comes to take up His abode with us.

5: *The inhabitation of the Trinity in the souls of those in a state of grace is the effect of the invisible missions of the Son and the Holy Ghost.*

Although St. Thomas briefly considers the inhabitation in the tract on the presence of God (I *Sent.*, d. 37, q. 2, a. 2; *Sum. Theol.*, I, q. 8, a. 3), his profess treatment of the mystery is reserved for the tracts on the divine missions, the culminating point of his Trinitarian theology. This fact is not unimportant, for it indicates the aspect under which the indwelling should be considered: as the prolongation in time of the intimate life of the triune God. So rich an understanding of the mystery, derived from St. Augustine (as noted previously) and eagerly received by the Scholastics, could not but result in a more profound appreciation of the problem and of its consequent solution.

If the indwelling should be conceived in reference to the invisible missions, then conversely the missions should be recognized as indissolubly linked with the real presence of the Trinity. The missions of the Son and Holy Ghost, therefore, include Their donation as an essential note[19]—in fact, between this concept and that of mission no real distinction can be made but only one of reason.[20] What this fact implies is well brought out by S. Thomas:

> As in the going forth of things from the principle, the divine goodness is said to proceed into creatures, inasmuch as it is represented in creatures by a similitude of the divine goodness received in the creature, so in the bringing back of the rational creature to God the procession of the divine Persons is understood, which is also called a mission, insofar as the proper relation of the divine Person Himself is represented in the soul by some similitude received, which is exemplified and originated by the very property of the eternal relation. So the proper way in which the Holy Spirit is referred to the Father is love, and the proper way of referring the Son to the Father is the fact that He is His word manifesting Him. Hence as the Holy Spirit proceeds invisibly in the mind by the gift of love, so the Son by the gift of Wisdom, in which there is a manifestation of the Father Himself, as the ultimate to which we recur.[21]

This remarkable passage merely enunciates the more remarkable fact: the divine missions continue in us the eternal processions: the Father is in the just soul in the eternal generation of the eternally begotten Son; Father and Son are there in the eternal spiration of the eternally proceeded Holy Spirit.[22] In the soul in grace the whole Trinity comes and dwells: the Son and Holy Spirit as sent, the Father and Son as sending, and Father, Son and Holy Ghost as donated and given that man may possess the divine Persons, in virtue of the divine missions, as fruits he has the power to enjoy.[23]

6: *The presence of the Trinity in the souls of the just, the result of the divine missions, involves the manifestation of the divine Persons.*

This notion of the inhabitation, universally accepted by the Schoolmen, is another of the contributions of Augustine to an understanding of the missions. How it is to be interpreted and applied lies at the crux of the problem, and it will have to be considered closely as St. Thomas' solution is unfolded. Here it suffices to note that he takes the notion from scholastic tradition and utilizes it, both in the *Sentences*[24] and in the *Summa*.[25] 'To be sent is to be known'—the Augustinian adage is too traditional and too important to be ignored. But it is in St. Thomas' interpretation of the phrase that his proper solution and his proper genius is found, as later examination of the point will disclose.

ARTICLE 2

The Principles of Solution

To say of St. Thomas that he is, intellectually, a man of principle, of theological principles and philosphical principles, is to state so obvious a truth for one who has considered his doctrine at all that the phrase may be considered only a useless platitude. Even those who do not have intimate knowledge of this truth from personal investigation of his works, nor of the intellectual consistency therein so frequently manifest, will recall the historic and historical consequences which demonstrate the fact: his unremitting war against the Averroistic dichotomy of science vs. faith, reason vs. revelation; his inauguration of a true science of theology (using the word 'science' in the proper sense, as a causal knowledge acquired through *propter quid* demonstration proceeding from principles—revealed or naturally known—to conclusions); and his genius at synthesis, before mentioned, which scorns a voluntarist eclecticism to construct deliberately and with the utmost inner harmony an ordered whole, uniting the most diverse material elements (Plato and Aristotle, the Greek Fathers and the Latin Fathers, for general examples) in a higher corpus of doctrine under the formal light of theology.

In practice, unfortunately, this obvious fact is all too frequently ignored. Individual doctrines, isolated texts, are considered self-explanatory, self-sufficient, a vivisection doomed to ultimate failure, since the excision of the part to be examined necessarily kills the living breath of the whole which was its form—one ends up with a generically different thing, only the names being the same. To avoid this error, peculiarly prevalent among modern theologians, it is necessary (even at the risk of trying the patience of a true student of St. Thomas) to point out those of his unswerving principles which have reference to the problem of the divine indwelling, most of which, in fact, he has explicitly applied. Only thus can one be certain that no violence is done to his living thought when the klieglight of analysis is focused on a particular doctrine, his solution to the problem at hand. These principles, which determine his resolution of the problem presented by the facts of scholastic tradition, are listed below in proposition form.

1: *The existence of God in things consists in a real relation of things to God and a relation of reason in God to things.*

Evidence of this fact was given in the introductory chapter, when the problem of the inhabitation in its scientific formulation was discussed. It is merely recalled here, as fundamental for any solution of the problem, and to point out that St. Thomas states the fact in his explicit treatment of the inhabitation.[26]

2: *God is present in all things in virtue of His action on the creature.*

The importance of this truth, not only in general, but for the solution of the problem of the inhabitation, may not be immediately apparent. But if one follows St. Thomas' profound metaphysical analysis of the fact, its significance in this question, especially illuminating as to the approach the Angelic Doctor will take to the problem, may perhaps be better appreciated.

Since it is necessary that every agent be united to the thing on which it acts immediately[27]—*actio in distans repugnat*—and since God is subsistent being, each and every creature to the extent that it participates being is in immediate contact with God, the immediate cause of being *qua* being. This is so on four counts: respecting the production of its being, the conservation of its being, the application to actual operation of its powers, and the production of the being of the effects of its operations.[28] On the one hand, moreover, God's operation is His substance, and on the other, nothing is more intimate to a thing than its being: so God is present in things most intimately, being by His essence the cause of that which is most intimate to them.[29]

The consequences of this profound doctrine are immediately apparent: wherever there is being, in any shape or form, God will be present as cause of that being, whether it is substance or accident, newly produced or long conserved in existence, static or dynamic. He will be there, not in virtue of His absolute attribute of immensity (for if nothing existed God would still be immense), but in virtue of His operation, an attribute relative to actually existing things.[30] But His operation is His essence, and His essence is common to all three divine Persons. So by reason of His operation He will be present as principle to all (created) things, as one in essence, not as three in Persons, *per se primo*.[31]

3: *God can be present to a creature in a way essentially distinct from His common presence only as the term of the creature.*

The validity of this principle rests on that of the preceding principle; and of the preceding principle St. Thomas never entertained the slightest doubt. Nevertheless, man knows from divine revelation that God is present to creatures in a manner essentially distinct from His presence of immensity—the singular union of the divine and human natures in the Person of the Son of God; and the union of the Trinity with the just soul, inchoate here on earth, perfect in heaven. Some principle must therefore be determined to explain the specific diversity of these various presences.

The common note of both of these special supernatural presences of God is that the creature in some way becomes God, is united with Him. But the difficulty in understanding how this can occur is enormous: as unique and perfect Being, as the plenitude of being itself, how can God give Himself to a creature—distinct from Him not by what it has of being but by what it has of non-being—in such a way as to become one with it?

St. Thomas solves the dilemma of the Incarnation by means of the concepts of nature and person. The human nature, not another being but a principle of being, receives its ultimate perfection in the line of essence in the hypostasis of the Second Person, and through this divine personality it receives its existence.[32] As a principle of being, the human nature is not a subsisting thing; it receives its subsistence from the being which terminates it. And since this ultimate perfection in the line of essence is the hypostasis of the Word, who possesses the fulness of the divine plentitude of being, divine and human natures are united in Christ as a term is united to that which it terminates,[33] not by any composition of parts or elements.

From the point of view of principle of this marvelous union, God as one in essence is present; from the point of view of term, the Second Person alone is present by proper right, the divine essence and the other Persons by reason of His presence; the three Persons produce this effect, that the human nature is united to the one Person of the Son.[34] It is thus that from the notion of term the explanation of the intellectual difficulties of the mystery of the Incarnation is determined, by means of the analysis of the notions of nature and person.

But the rational creature in the line of essence is a complete being, with his own subsistence, not merely a principle of being. One can, accordingly, find no explanation for his union with the Trinity in the line of nature: God cannot be present to him as a hypostatic term because his nature is closed by his own personality, whereas the human nature of Christ was open to the divine personality.[35] Only in the line of operation, then, can God exist as a term for the rational creature: "The grace of a creature makes a union with God: which is even a double one, that is, by operation, according to which we are united to God by knowing and loving Him; and in person."[36]

It is obvious from this analysis* that there will be three ways, and only three, in which God is present to His creatures: 1) as the cause of whatever of being is in them or from them: the presence of immensity, admitting only of accidental variations, God, one in essence, immediately present as agent cause; 2) as term of the creature in the line of nature, God, the Second Person, terminating a human nature He alone properly assumes (the

---

* In view of these frequent affirmations, one does not know what to make of Father Urdánoz's peculiar interpretation of I *Sent.*, d. 37, q. 1, a. 2 (cf. "La inhabitación del Espiritu Santo en el Alma del Justo," *Revista Española de teología*, 6 [1946], p. 502, note 61), according to which the operation of the creature cannot be the formal reason of the inhabitation but only a manifestive note, because the division of the different modes of God's presence cannot be understood "ex parte creaturae" *since the operation of the creature does not produce the presence of immensity nor that of the Incarnation.* And therefore the modes presuppose a difference "ex parte Dei."

It is a *change in the creature*, St. Thomas holds, which explains the various modes, and only in the second mode of presence, the inhabitation, is that change explained as an operation of the creature, not in the presence of immensity nor of the Incarnation. Cf. John of St. Thomas, *op. cit.*, I, q. 43, disp. 17, a. 3, n. 7 (ed. Solesmnes, IV, fasc. II, p. 470): "Omnis enim praesentia Dei ad creaturam fit per aliquem effectum seu mutationem ex parte creaturae, quo coniungitur Deo in se, sicut mediante esse quod recipit a Deo fit praesens ei praesentia communi immensitatis, et mediante assumptione unitiva et applicativa humanitatis ad personalitatem Verbi, fit ei coniuncta in Persona et specialissime praesens, et mediante gratia et lumine gloriae fit ei coniunctus et unitus Patri."

divine nature and the other Persons present by concomitance or perichoresis); 3) as term of the operation of the creature: God, the three divine Persons existing in the one divine nature, terminating as object of the creature's knowledge and love.

These are the three essential species of the presence of God; there are no others.*

ARTICLE 3

The Solution of St. Thomas

It is by the application of these principles to the facts of the inhabitation which he has accepted that the Angelic Doctor resolves the problem of the formal reason of the presence of the Trinity in the souls of the just. As with the facts and with the principles, which exist without variation of doctrine or understanding in both the early commentary and in his later work, so too the solution, so far as the doctrine is concerned.

This is the answer of St. Thomas:

In the divine indwelling, the Most Holy Trinity is really and substantially present in the souls of the just by reason of sanctifying grace: not precisely insofar as it is an effect of God, but by reason

* Christ's presence as God in the Holy Eucharist is explained by reason of the hypostatic union, and differs only accidentally (from the point of view of presence) from His presence in the flesh. The presence of God in the Beatific Vision — from the point of view of presence again — does not differ specifically from His presence in the inhabitation but is the perfection of that presence, only imperfectly realized here on earth.

of the operations (or habits) of love and knowledge of which grace is the root, the presence of immensity being presupposed.

In this statement the first part—'in the divine indwelling the Most Holy Trinity is really and substantially present by means of sanctifying grace'—constitutes the facts of the mystery, facts received without question by St. Thomas as the genuine interpretation of divine revelation by the Church. The latter part consists of separate propositions, each of which will be shown to be taught by St. Thomas both in the *Sentences* and the *Summa*.

1: *Considered as an effect of God, sanctifying grace does not constitute the formal reason of the inhabitation.*

On this point many modern theologians have impaled themselves in hopeless confusion, but St. Thomas' doctrine is clear, constant and certain, whatever they may make of isolated statements. Certainly grace is an effect of God, a proper effect in the common teaching of Thomists, which is above all the natural order as a participation of that which is connatural to God Himself.[39] And it is on this special divine character of grace that certain recent writers, such as Galtier,[40] Urdánoz[41] and Retailleau[42] —to cite only a few—wax eloquent, as if panegyrics could substitute for science: for because of the special nature of grace they wish to postulate a special causality of God which escapes the limitations of His ordinary efficient and exemplary causality and which founds on the part of God-principle the formal reason of the presence of the Trinity.

This theory has been well stated by Father Urdánoz, a Spanish Dominican, and his statement represents the view of his colleagues as well as his own, so that it is quoted as typical:

> ... in this expression, 'God operating as one and triune,' we have a denomination proper and sufficient to affirm that the causal operation of grace is likewise *assimilative* of the said supernatural effect to the three divine Persons, as the divine mark or engraving which bears impressed on it the image of the three divine engravers; that the said operation of God, one and triune, imprints on grace an intrinsic order to God as He is in Himself, therefore, to the divine Persons; that, moreover, it unites the soul in the closest conjunction with the divine Persons—*coniungit toti Trinitati,* St. Thomas says; a union supernatural and new, which is not so much by the attraction of the divine being for ourselves as by the elevation of our soul to It and an introducing into Its intimate, trinitarian life. Finally, that given the elements of the aforesaid operation, it is sufficient to make the three divine Persons present to the soul by the effect of grace. The reception of grace implies the visitation of the Trinity, complete and entire. To receive grace implies at the same time the reception of the three divine Guests. Their action and conjoined influence, *the bearer of their substantial presence,* is necessary to conserve that God-like seal of grace, the participation of the divine substance.[43]

But this is a theory entirely other than that of St. Thomas. He admits the marvelous character of sanctifying grace—indeed, who would dare to say that he rejoices less in it than do these moderns?—and he insists that only God can cause so exalted an effect, even that God must be present as efficient cause to produce the infinite proper effects of which grace is the formal cause, as will shortly be seen.[44] But never does he violate principles founded on the very nature of the Trinity itself and on the metaphysical necessities entailed in the divine activity *ad extra*. God as principle acts *in every order of causality* as one in essence;[45] and so His action, howsoever divine and efficacious, cannot be the proximate reason for the presence of the distinct Persons.

"Everything which has causality in the divinity," says St. Thomas, "pertains to the essence, since God by His essence is the cause of things. But the properties of the Persons are relations by which the Persons, not to creatures, but to one another are referred."[46] But since it is only by Their relations that the Persons are distinct from each other; and since they are referred *as Persons* only to one another, nothing outside of the Trinity Itself can be referred to Them as Persons except insofar as they are considered as terms: "all creatures *under one species of relation* are referred to God, as they are His creatures."[47] Sanctifying grace, no matter what the nobility of the participation, is still something created by God: to distinguish formalities here cannot change the causality involved, for it would change that which is by participation to that which is by essence. "The grace which is in us is an effect of the divine essence, not having relation to the distinction of Persons."[48]

So St. Thomas everywhere and always insists on the fundamental truth: *omniaque sunt unum, ubi non obviat relationis oppositio*.[49] All things outside of the Trinity Itself are beings by participation, dependent for their very existence on the productive and sustaining power of the subsistent Being. Even grace comes into existence and is conserved by God's efficient action;[50] and God as agent cause acts in virtue of His essence, as the one God without distinction of Persons.[51]

St. Thomas sums up this truth in one definitive passage in the *Sentences*:

> In all those things which are said of God in time and designate a relation of principle to principiated, it is true absolutely that they pertain to the entire Trinity. But if the relation of the creature to the Creator be considered as to a term, it is possible that such a relation be to something essential or to something relative. . . . But this relation by which the creature is referred to God as to a term includes in consequence in itself a relation which is to God as to a principle. Therefore in all things which are said of God according to a relation to a creature by the fact that the creature is referred to Him as to a term, it must be understood that so far as the relationship of term is concerned they can pertain to one Person alone, but the notion of principle, here included, pertains in consequence to the whole Trinity. So according to one relationship they can make a Person understood, and according to the other they make the essence understood; as it is plain that when He is called incarnate, this pertains to the Son alone, because the Incarnation is terminated at the Person of the Son alone, which, however, the whole Trinity produces.[52]

So it must be as term of the new relationship effected by grace that the presence of the Trinity be considered: in virtue of the operations of the just soul.*

---

* This is true of all orders of causality. When St. Thomas says that the divine processions are the idea and cause of the return of creatures to God as they are of the production of creatures by God (cf. I *Sent.*, d. 14, a. 2; d. 15, q. 4, a. 1), he is speaking of exemplary causality (*ibid.*, d. 30, q. 1, a. 2), which he explains in the *Summa* more precisely as follows: God is the cause of things by His intellect and will, as the artisan of the artifacts he makes (I, q. 45, a. 5); therefore, insofar as they *include* the essential attributes of knowledge and will, the processions of the Persons are the ideas

2: *A quasi-experimental knowledge, springing from the love and knowledge rooted in grace, is the proximate formal reason for the divine indwelling.*

Other creatures, although they follow the divine likeness because of the operation of God Himself, do not, however, attain God according to substance; and therefore although God is in them, they are not, nevertheless, with God. But the rational creature by grace attains God Himself, inasmuch as he loves Him and knows Him; and therefore he is said to be with Him, and on the same score he is called capable of God as His perfection, by way of object; and because of this he is even said to be the temple of God and to be inhabited by God.[53]

Since God's indwelling cannot be explained from His presence as efficient or exemplary cause—as principle—but only as term (as has been abundantly seen); and since God as object of man's operations is the Trinity as such, for which acts grace is necessary; one may legitimately

---

of the production of creatures (*ibid.*, a. 6) and are the cause and notion of creation in this manner (*ibid.*, a. 7, ad 3).

Moreover, since the three Persons subsist in the one divine essence, They are also in a certain way the causes of all that the essence produces, so that the Father as principle produces all that the Son as generated and the Holy Ghost as spirated produce, and vice versa, and hence there is a certain order in Their causality (*ibid.*, a. 6, ad 2). But since They cause not *in virtue of* or *by reason of* their distinctive properties, the intratrinitarian relations, but in virtue of Their common essence, the Persons as Persons are in no way causes *per se primo* in any order of causality (except final) of the effects created, produced or conserved by God, but only secondarily. Cf. Bañez' commentary on I, q. 45, a. 6.

So far as exemplary causality is concerned, then, the divine processions are, so to speak, on the third plane: the immediate exemplar is the divine essence (first plane) as imitable in this way (second plane: a divine attribute), which represents a divine procession (third plane).

inquire what operations radicated in sanctifying grace are involved. And the difficulty is compounded when one reflects that the presence is real and substantial, whereas the intellectual operations of man assure only an objective and intentional or moral presence. How, then, can man's operations account for this real and distinct presence of the Trinity?

St. Thomas proceeds logically from the facts concerning the mystery to a solution of these difficulties. From his analysis of the conceptually distinct notions of temporal procession, invisible mission and divine donation, he specifies exactly the object of the operations of the just soul, so that he can determine with equal precision what acts are necessary to attain such an object. The three distinct Persons, sending and sent, coming to the just, proceeding in him (so that the Father is present eternally generating the Son, and Father and Son eternally spirating the Spirit)—They are, on this account, *given, donated* to the just, with the result that They familiarly abide in him as in a temple. And in consequence of this divine coming and giving, man is inhabited by the Trinity: he has and possesses the Persons for his enjoyment.[54]

To have or possess a spiritual object requires an act of the intellect: that is certain from psychology and is brought out in respect to the missions and inhabitation by St. Augustine's notion of manifestation.[55] But obviously not any knowledge suffices, since it must be a knowledge uniting us with God Himself, establishing a real contact with the really present Trinity; it must be a knowledge springing from grace and intimately linked with love.[56] Natural gifts, no matter how perfect; unformed Faith, no matter how exalted; all the charismata, no matter how extraordinary—none of these enable man to possess the divine Persons, and in none of them are They sent or given, do They come or proceed, can They abide with us and dwell in us.[57]

Why cannot these effect what grace produces? Because none of these lesser gifts enters into contact with an object as had or possessed, that is, as really present to us. But the knowledge of grace is in every way special, because it is informed by love. It is a type of experimental knowledge, as St. Thomas states many times.[58] And it is necessary well to understand why he thus characterizes the knowledge involved in the missions and indwelling if one wishes to grasp his solution of the difficulties of the mystery. In this explanation the Augustinian insight comes to theological perfection.

> The experiencing of a thing is gained through the senses; but in one way, of a thing present, in another, of an absent thing. Of an absent thing, by reason of sight, smell and hearing; but of a thing present, by touch and taste—of a thing extrinsically present, by touch; by taste, however, of a thing intrinsically present. God, however, is not far from us nor outside of us but in us . . .; and therefore the experiencing of the divine goodness is called a tasting.[59]

The loving-knowledge rooted in grace which is implied by the inhabitation attains the Persons as objects *present* to us and *within* us. So it cannot be a discursive knowledge,[60] which by definition has no direct contact with the thing known. On the contrary, like sense experience it involves a sort of sympathy with the object, a similarity or affinity which inclines to the object; and since that object is the Holy Trinity, this is a judgment without reasoning caused by love:

> The gift of Wisdom has an eminence of knowledge, because of a kind of union with divine things,

to which we are not united except by love, so that he who adheres to God is one spirit, according to I Cor. And hence the Lord says in John 15:15 that He had revealed the secrets of the Father to His disciples, inasmuch as they were friends. And therefore the gift of Wisdom presupposes dilection as a principle, and so it is in the affection. But as to its essence it is in knowledge. Therefore its act seems to be, both here and in the future, to contemplate divine things loved, and by these to judge not only in speculative matters but even in things to be done, judgment on which is obtained from the end.[61]

We know God as present in us and with us without reasoning to this presence, by a sort of contact, or, better, a sort of tasting. This does not mean, however, that we have an *immediate* knowledge of the Trinity, such as in the Beatific Vision or with the immediacy of sense experience: "Wisdom, by which we now contemplate God, does not immediately regard God Himself, but the effects from which we contemplate Him as present."[62] In this respect our loving-knowledge is like that of Adam before the fall,[63] or like the natural knowledge the angels have of God:[64] we know God by means of an effect produced by God operating, intrinsic in our intellective powers, known without discursive reasoning: as the angels naturally grasp God in their very substances naturally known; as Adam before sin saw God by the light of contemplation,[65] "by an internal inspiration from the irradiation of divine Wisdom, in which manner he knew God not from visible creatures, but from a certain spiritual likeness imprinted on his mind."[66]

There is, then, a formal objective medium in this experiential knowledge, by which God is known;[67] and so it cannot be an immediate knowledge as Father Gardeil and other modern authors wish.[68] But not any effect of God suffices as a medium for the contuition of Him: it must be an effect within man, an effect to which **God** is immediately present, an effect immediately perceptible, an effect supremely expressive of God. And these conditions are realized only in the gifts of grace,[69] but especially in the gift of the Holy Ghost of Wisdom[70] and in the supreme theological virtue of Charity.[71]

One cannot know these effects, moreover, in a purely human way, in virtue of reasoning processes and the like; it is not by the indirectness of Faith but in a manner properly supernatural, suprahuman and God-like—that is, in a knowledge, affective and intimate, similar to the knowledge that God has of Himself—that these effects are grasped. Such a mode of operation, St. Thomas teaches, comes not only from the divine infusion of the gifts but includes as well the special motion or instinct of the Holy Ghost through operating grace;[72] so that God Himself is the rule and measure of these gifts[73] and is specially present as their "motor."

It is important to note, also, that love here functions not only as cause but as the *formal medium* and *rule* of Wisdom: we contemplate divine things *loved*:[74] the Spirit renders testimony "through the effect of filial love which He produces in us."[75] And the concepts of Faith and the inescapable material images man can never do without because of the very nature of human knowledge, these are present only as the material requisite as a condition for this suprahuman apprehension of the Trinity.[76] From every formal aspect, man knows the Persons as present within him, and (analogically) in the manner that They know Themselves:

> The movement of the intellect toward the image as image is identical with a movement to-

ward the thing imaged, although the movement toward the thing as it is a thing is different; and therefore when, through the likeness of a creature which the intellect has within itself, it is turned toward the creature, not as a certain thing but as a likeness of God, then immediately it thinks of God, even though it does not immediately see God.[77]

The just soul knows the Trinity by an affective and intimate knowledge in the supernatural effects of grace immediately produced in the mind by God. It knows these effects as experienced and tasted, by a sort of contact, not merely abstractly and speculatively; knows them without any reasoning process, in a suprahuman manner, as the angel seeing its own being knows the Author of that being. So in these supernatural and personal effects, precisely as they are the proper effects of God working in us, His sons, we attain, we touch God Himself, one in essence and three in Persons, as present within us, as had and possessed by us, as indwelling: our Guests, our Friends.

This is a direct knowledge, like our intellectual knowledge of this book present before our eyes; so it is called "experimental," a knowledge of a present thing without recourse to the exigencies of discursive procedures or scientific analysis. But like the book before us, which is not known without abstraction, the Persons are not grasped by us with the immediacy of sense knowledge nor as we shall know Them in heaven; so it is only a *sort* of experimental knowledge—imperfect, obscure, uncertain, incomprehensive. Yet by this loving-knowledge, product of the Wisdom and Love of grace, we know God, the Father and the Son and the Holy Ghost, as present, as in us, giving Their gifts and Themselves, working in us and with us—possessed and enjoyed by us: indwelling.

St. Thomas states these facts, if obscurely, nonetheless certainly, in his discussion of the divine missions in the *Sentences* and the *Summa*. Simply put, they come down to this: we know the gifts of the Trinity by experiencing them;[78] and by Their gifts, we know, we experience the divine Persons Themselves.[79] But this is to have and to possess and to enjoy (imperfectly) the Persons: God is present by this fact in a very special manner, utterly other than His common presence in all things. It is clear, then, that in the experimental knowledge which Wisdom gives birth to, whose cause and formal medium is divine Charity, the formal explanation of the Trinity in the souls of the just is found.

3: *This experimental knowledge presupposes God's presence of immensity.*

To place the formal reason of the inhabitation in a grace-given experience of the Trinity seems, at first sight, to fulfill a condition, not to explain a fact—how are the Persons physically, substantially present? Not by means of experimental knowledge, certainly, for this type of knowledge rather presupposes than constitutes such an immediate presence. So the problem remains unsolved.

This objection, a common one with modern theologians, represents a basic confusion. The problem of the triune presence, in truth, is not simply how God is present really and substantially in man but how He is present really and substantially in this *new way*, i.e., as newly related to the creature in virtue of some new real relation of the creature to Him: as possessed and enjoyed by the creature after the manner of a present object. Analogously, in the Beatific Vision the *reality* and *substantiality* of the presence of the divine essence as intelligible species of the elevated created intellect does not explain the immediate vision and union with the Trinity (for the divine essence is already really and substantially present as cause); what does explain this union is the fact that the divine essence is present as species. And this *new* presence or *way of being present* is accounted for by the *lumen gloriae*, a special gift which represents the perfection of grace; and yet the light of glory of itself cannot explain the reality and substantiality necessarily implied by God's new mode of presence in the beatified intellect.

St. Thomas therefore insists that the presence of immensity is prerequisite for that of the inhabitation: "The fact that God is in the saints by grace presupposes the fact that He is in all things by essence, presence and power."[80] The direct experience of any thing, in the material or spiritual order, presupposes its real or physical presence, a presence in virtue of the intrinsic qualities of the thing present, not accomplished by reason of the apprehension of that thing. And this is why the Scholastics unanimously demand as a presupposition the physical reality of God. From the point of view of the reality of the presence, however, no modal difference is implied: a thing is not really present in different species of reality: the book is as really present to the table as to the man reading it or the book worm digesting it. And this is why the Scholastics unanimously maintain that the presence of the inhabitation is not a physically different presence, but the same physical reality of God present in a different way: not a new presence, but a new way of being present.

In consequence, the explanation of this new way of being present *cannot* explain the physical, substantial reality of the presence: it must explain the difference involved, not what is constant. And, conversely, the explanation of the physical reality of the thing present *cannot* account for the difference of presence, because the difference does not consist in the physical nature of the presence, which by definition remains the same.

By the presence of immensity the Trinity is already physically or really present, for the divine essence exists only in the three divine Persons. Since They are identical with the essence, They do not exist in the soul as distinct from one another, but They are nonetheless present really and substantially. Because of this indistinctness, God as efficient cause is intelligible only as one in essence, not as three in Persons. But by reason of the new relation established by grace — the experimental knowledge through Wisdom and Love of a really present object who are the Three — the divine Persons, already really and substantially in the soul by the presence of immensity as identical with the essence of God, commence to exist in the soul really and substantially *in a new way*, as distinct among Themselves and as possessed in Their distinctiveness by the just.

The whole reality and substantiality of the divine Persons in the soul of the just is given by the presence of immensity. The operation of the creature in grace is no more — and no less — than the cause of the presence in the soul of this same substantial and physical reality of the Trinity in a new manner, as distinct among Themselves. Whence St. Thomas' insistence on the presence of immensity as a necessary prerequisite of the indwelling.

But this must be understood clearly. First of all, God is present in the inhabitation by the presence of immensity in virtue of His special operation in producing and conserving the effects of grace and in specially moving man through operating grace by means of these dispositions He has caused.[81] This is clear from the fact that the formal medium of the experimental knowledge of Wisdom and Love is His proper effects, i.e., the effects of grace. Knowing these as more express similitudes of God, the just soul without reasoning apprehends God as *their* cause and root, more intimately and fully present to them than they are to themselves, and more intimately and fully present to them than He is present to His ordinary effects.

It is necessary to insist on this point, somewhat obscured by John of St. Thomas,[82] for the following reasons. First, the question of fact: God as present by immensity in His natural effects in the soul is not known directly and experimentally, it would seem, but only reflexively and discursively, even though the *fact* of His presence in this way be beyond dispute and necessarily presupposed as grace necessarily presupposes nature.* Stressing this point, too, the exact nature of the knowledge implied by the inhabitation is more clearly indicated. Second, the intimate nature of this real presence of the Trinity is far better underlined: the Persons are present in and within *this* effect, here and now, of grace—not in some other thing (operation or habit or faculty or substance more or less removed from this effect), where They are not experienced but reasoned to. Third, it shows that if, *per impossibile*, God's presence of immensity in His natural effects were removed, He would still be present by the presence of immensity;[83] hence this necessary condition is verified whether one wishes to admit it or not.

Moreover, a fourth reason is not inconsiderable. God's presence as author of grace is a more perfect and higher presence of immensity than His presence as author of nature. This is an accidental difference, to be sure, for God is entire in every being and His entire immensity is

---

* Thus this loving-knowledge of the just differs *ex parte objecti* from the natural knowledge of the angels.

present in every place; and He is present by His essence, without distinction of Persons. But He is not entire in every effect *entirely*, i.e., in every way in which His essence and power can be applied and exist — just as we say the blessed in heaven know the whole essence of God, but not completely, one knowing Him better than another but all knowing His entire being. So understanding this presence as connoting the effect of grace, one may say that God is specially present there in a nobler, more intimate, more complete, more obvious manner.

There are varying degrees of the one specific kind of presence, then; but no matter how lofty the degree it cannot constitute the presence of the three Persons as distinct among Themselves and present in virtue of Their proper relations. It is well to point out, however, the more noble degree of the presence of God in the inhabitation — even though this more exalted presence of immensity by itself explains in no way the specific mode of the triune presence and enters into the formal explanation only as a condition. Still by this nobler presence one can undertsand the nature of the experimental knowledge of grace better, and its function as formal reason of the inhabitation;[84] and the intimacy of the union between God and man which is the formal characteristic of the inhabitation becomes clearer.

It is for these reasons, it would seem, that St. Thomas declares that in the inhabitation the Persons are present, even from the point of view of agent cause, in a new way, "as if leading or conjoining to the end";[85] and he says that "the divine Persons Themselves, by a certain sealing of Themselves on our souls, leave certain gifts by which we formally enjoy, that is, love and wisdom."[86] More clearly yet, in the following short passage he sums up this whole relationship between God's presence of immensity as the cause of grace and the knowledge which formally explains this essentially different presence of the indwelling:

> That knowledge from which love proceeds flourishes in those fervent in divine love, by which, namely, they know the divine goodness insofar as it is most liberally pouring forth its benefits in us.[87]

Is this not truly the complete picture of the indwelling of the Trinity in the souls of the just — to know Them in the wonders of grace as the source of these wonders?

One last point, which should be clear from what has gone before: the presence of immensity is presupposed not as an integral part of the formal reason of the inhabitation but as a necessary prerequisite, a condition *sine qua non*. And here one finds once more a curious misunderstanding among modern authors, who see in John of St. Thomas' interpretation a mean, or a middle theory, between that of Suarez and the (so-called) theory of Vasquez; or charge the eminent Thomist simply with following Suarez' Jesuit rival[88] — a confusion for which Gardeil is perhaps responsible.[89]

Such objections as that of Retailleau — that the presence of immensity is a 'presupposition of integration' and hence inadmissible[90] — cannot be maintained as valid if the precise function of this prerequisite is understood. As a condition *sine qua non* it is in no manner a cause nor a complementary or integral element; not in the slightest respect does it explain the present problem and it is not a part of its formal reason. Just as dryness is necessarily presupposed for the burning of wood but does not cause or explain that burning formally; just as the teaching of the Church is a necessary condition modifying the formal object of Faith, but does not cause or explain divine

Faith;[91] so the presence of immensity is necessarily presupposed, for the Persons are really and substantially present, but it in no way causes that They be present as objects of man's knowledge and love — nor does it explain that new manner of presence.

Far from being a return to Vasquez, this theory is antipodal to any explanation from the point of view of God as principle. Its whole bearing, in truth, is toward God as end, as object known and loved, as term. That this presupposes the reality of God's presence adds nothing to the newness of the presence: and the newness is the fact, and the problem, of the inhabitation.

> 4: *The experimental knowledge of Wisdom and Love, presupposing the presence of immensity, is necessary as a habit, not as act.*

"Most blessed are those for whom having God comes from the fact that they know Him."[92] But who actually know God in the way described in the third proposition? Certainly not those who are incapable of rational acts, children in the flesh; nor yet all, or even the majority of men, who do not attain to so lofty a state of contemplation, children in the spirit. Yet indubitably the Trinity dwells in these children when they are in the state of grace.

> God is said to dwell spiritually as in a familiar abode in the saints, whose mind is capable of God by knowledge and love, even if they do not know and love in act, so long as by grace they have the habit of Faith and Charity, as is evident in baptized children.[93]

Thus does St. Thomas constantly and universally determine the triune presence in virtue of man's *powers* to know and love the divine Persons,[94] even though for sake of clarity and analysis these habits are explained in terms of their perfections, their acts. And the reason is very clear. The presence to be explained is that of the Trinity as a non-distant object of man's operations. But habits are specified by their objects, and like all powers involve a real relation to these objects. Since God as He is in Himself, one in essence and three in Persons, is the object of the theological virtues;[95] and since the Trinity as really present is the object of the gift of Wisdom under the power of Charity, these gifts of grace, divinely infused, constitute and explain the indwelling of the divine Persons, even though no acts should ever flow from them. Upon their infusion the Trinity dwells within us.

Is this a "vain and illusory subterfuge" rather than a genuine explanation?[96] Only for those who do not understand the notion of habit in general and of the infused habits in particular. By its very nature a habit is an inclining toward its object and proper acts, as the inclination of a stone is the weight of the stone inhering in it, and not a movement of the stone. A habit or power is not a simple non-repugnance toward some act and object, nor a naked and indeterminate susceptibility of receiving something; it is a vital tending toward some object, even in first act, in virtue of its very form. In like manner someone holding a stone senses the real tending of that stone to a lower point of gravity — a tending which is not an operation of the stone, since it is felt when neither the stone nor the hand sustaining it is moving: it is not a motion but the very weight of the stone inhering in it in first act.

Similarly, the one possessing a habit or potency is weighted in this direction toward this object, which becomes connatural to the subject in virtue of the habit and draws the subject to it (in a metaphorical sense). And this real inclination precedes actual operation (although in natural habits it is caused by acts), is already there in first act and remains when the subject ceases to act. So between the soul who has the theological virtues (even when he cannot or does not use them) and the soul in a purely natural state (or the sinful soul) there is a chasm wider even than that between a baby and an animal (the difference between these last not being in their acts, which are similar, but in their powers to act).

The natural soul possesses a purely logical possibility of knowing and loving the Trinity; the soul in grace has a real relation to the divine Persons really present, a tending toward Them on the part of the intellect and will and a real capability of realizing this tendency in second act. It has the ultimate dispositions necessary for act, so that already, without any act ever being placed, the Persons are present to the just soul as a really present object, by reason of the gifts of Wisdom and Charity. The inclination of these supernatural habits explains the realness of this relationship; its specification, the fact that it is this kind of inclination and inclined in this way, comes from the objects themselves.

Those who possess these gifts are only *potentially* in second act respecting the love and knowledge of the divine Persons. But they bear a real respect to the Persons before any act on their part, since these habits are directly infused by God and not acquired by repeated acts. In first act, by the very form and being of these gifts, they know and attain the Trinity, and they have the power to receive the special instinct and motion of the Holy Ghost and so pass into actual operations of knowing and loving. Hence they have God within them, not only in potency, but *actually*, here and now, as the real and actual object of their knowledge and love. They are actually the temple of God, in whom the Trinity really and substantially dwells.

ARTICLE 4

Recapitulation

Since the Father and Son and Holy Ghost are present in the inhabitation as Persons distinct by reason of Their proper relations, the mystery can only be explained from the point of view of term, insofar as the Persons are the term of the operation of the just. Since They are present as possessed, as objects or fruits to be enjoyed, They can only be attained by sanctifying grace, for only in love is union with Them realized. Since They are present really and substantially (the presence of immensity, therefore, being presupposed), only such grace-acts as unite man with the divine objects as really present can explain their presence: the experiential knowledge of love. And since the objects of habits are already present to the subject in first act, it is in the truly divine habits of the gifts of Wisdom and Love that the Trinity comes to us and dwells in us.

Such is St. Thomas' explanation of the indwelling of the Most Holy Trinity in the souls of the just.

NOTES

[1] R. Morency, *L'union de grâce selon S. Thomas*. Montréal, 1950. This important work on questions allied with the present problem deserves particular consideration, although it is not, alas! impeccable. The author considers, in turn, the union of God with the soul and of the soul with God, terminating the work with a synthetic view of the whole. Under the first aspect Father Morency sees this union from four diverse vantages: union and habitation, in which the special presence of the Trinity manifests the double relations of assimilation and knowledge; union and mission, God as exemplary cause present by similitude and as term of the tendencies of the just soul present as the object of knowledge and love; union and love, likewise indicative of both assimiliation and operation; and union and adoption, where efficiency, similitude and finality come into play.

From the opposite point of view, the union of grace also enjoys a four-fold division: the union of *passio* (the correlative of the union of efficiency); the union of assimilation (which corresponds to exemplarity); the union of finalization, inasmuch as God is the final end of the just; the union of operation, insofar as God is the object of the knowledge and love of the just. For the author these are all "essential" parts of the union of grace, but the "formal and specific" constitutive of this union is none other, for St. Thomas, than the union of operation (p. 261). Cf. also his article, "L'union du juste à Dieu par voie de connaissance et d'amour," *Sciences ecclésiastiques*, II (1949), pp. 27-79. Thus his attempt is a synthesis of Chambat and Gardeil (p. 270).

[2] According to Mandonnet, the first book of the *Scriptum super Sententiis* was composed between 1254-1256 ("Chronologie sommaire de la vie et des écrites de Saint Thomas," *Revue des sciences philosophiques et théologiques*, 9 [1920], p. 147), the first part of the *Summa Theologiae* between 1267-1268 (*ibid.*, p. 151). M. Grabmann agrees on the date for the *Sentences* (*Thomas von Aquin Eine Einfuhrung in seine Personlichkeit unde Gedankenwelt*, p. 28), but gives a somewhat wider latitude for the *Summa* (first and second parts), 1266-1272.

[3] I *Sent.*, d. 14, q. 2, a. 1: ". . . ipsemet Spiritus sanctus procedit temporali processioni, vel datur, et non solum dona ejus."

⁴ *Sum. Theol.*, I, q. 43, a. 3: "In ipso dono gratiae gratum facientis, Spiritus sanctus habetur, et inhabitat hominem. Unde ipsemet Spiritus sanctus datur, et mittitur."

⁵ Cf. *Lect. super Joann.*, Chap. 14, lect. 5 and 6; *Exp. in I Epis. ad Cor.*, Chap. 3, lect. 3; IV *Con. Gen.*, Chap. 21.

⁶ I *Sent.*, d. 37, q. 1, a. 2 and 3: "Illi tres modi (per essentiam, praesentiam et potentiam) non sumuntur ex diversitate creaturae, sed ex parte Dei operantis in rebus; et ideo omnem creaturam consequuntur." *Sum. Theol.*, I, q. 8, a. 3: ". . . per modum causae agentis (Deus) est in omnibus rebus creatis ab ipso."

⁷ *Loc. cit.* ". . . Deus specialiter est in rationali creatura, quae cognoscit et diligit illum actu vel habitu." I *Sent.*, d. 15, q. 5, a. 1, sol. 1: ". . . ad omnes rationales creaturas potest fieri missio, nisi sint depravatae per obstinationem in malo, sicut daemones et damnati, et non ad irrationales creaturas." Cf. d. 37, q. 1, a. 2.

⁸ I *Sent.*, d. 37, q. 1, a. 2: "Distinctio istorum modorum partim sumitur ex parte creaturae . . . inquantum diverso modo ordinatur in Deum et conjungitur ei, *non diversitate rationis tantum, sed realiter*. Cum enim Deus in rebus esse dicatur secundum quod eis aliquo modo applicatur, oportet ut ubi est diversus conjunctionis vel applicationis modus, ibi sit diversus modus essendi. Conjungitur autem creatura Dei tripliciter. Primo modo secundum similitudinem tantum, inquantum invenitur in creatura aliqua similtudo divinae bonitatis, non quod attingat ipsum Deum secundum substantiam: et ista conjunctio invenitur in omnibus creaturis per essentiam, praesentiam et potentiam. Secundo creatura attingit ad ipsum Deum secundum substantiam suam consideratum, et non secundum similitudinem tantum; et hoc est per operationem: scilicet quando aliquis fide adhaeret ipsi primae veritati, et charitate ipsi summae bonitati: et sic est alius modus quo Deus specialiter est in sanctis per gratiam." (Emphasis added.) Cf. *Sum. Theol.*, I, q. 8, a. 3: ". . . Deus dicitur esse in re aliqua dupliciter. Uno modo, per modum causae agentis. . . . Alio modo, sicut objectum operationis est in operante. . . . Hoc igitur secundo modo, Deus specialiter est in rationali creaturae. . . ."

⁹ I *Sent.*, d. 37, q. 1, a. 2 ad 2: ". . . Deum esse in creaturis per se dividitur secundum diversos modos quibus creaturae attingunt Deum: et haec est divisio essentialis et formalis."

¹⁰ *Ibid.*, d. 15, q. 1, a. 1 ad 1: ". . . quod quamvis Spiritus sanctus, qui ubique est, non possit esse ubi fuerat, loci mutatione circa

ipsum intellecta; tamen potest esse aliquo modo quo prius non fuerat, mutatione circa illud in quo esse dicitur; et in hoc salvatur ratio missionis." *Sum. Theol.*, I, q. 43, a. 1 ad 2: ". . . Persona divina missa, sicut non incipit esse ubi prius non fuerat, ita nec desinit esse ubi fuerat." Cf. I *Sent.*, d. 14, q. 2, a. 1 ad 1; d. 15, q. 1, a. 1; q. 4, a. 3.

[11] *Ibid.*, d. 37, q. 2, a. 2 ad 3: "Illi tres modi non sumuntur ex diversitate creaturae, sed ex parte ipsius Dei operantis in rebus: et ideo sequuntur omnem creaturam et praesupponuntur in aliis modis. In quo enim est Deus per unionem, etiam est per gratiam, et in quo est per gratiam, est per essentiam, praesentiam et potentiam. Cf. *ibid.*, d. 14, q. 2, a. 1 ad 1; d. 15, q. 1, a. 1 and ad 1; *Sum. Theol.*, I, q. 43, a. 1 ad 2.

[12] I *Sent.*, d. 15, q. 5, a. 1, sol. 1 ad 3: ". . . missio pertinet ad reditum creaturae in finem: et ideo non potest esse missio, nisi secundum illa quae possunt dicere relationem in finem." Cf. *ibid.*, d. 14, q. 2, a. 2; d. 15, q. 4, a. 1.

[13] Cf. *ibid.*, d. 14, q. 2, a. 1 ad 2; a. 2 ad 2; d. 15, q. 4, a. 1; *Sum. Theol.*, I, q. 43, a. 2; a. 3 and ad 2, 3.

[14] I *Sent.*, d. 14, q. 2, a. 2 ad 2: "In processione Spiritus secundum quod hic loquimur, prout scilicet claudit in se dationem Spiritus sancti, non sufficit quod sit nova relatio, qualiscumque est, creaturae ad Deum: sed oportet quod referatur in ipsum, sicut ad habitum: quia quod datur alicui habetur aliquo modo ab illo. Persona autem divina non potest haberi a nobis nisi vel ad fructum perfectum, et sic habetur per donum gloriae; aut secundum fructum imperfectum, et sic habetur per donum gratiae gratum facientis. . . ." *Sum. Theol.*, I, q. 43, a. 3 ad 1: ". . . per donum gratiae gratum facientis perficitur creatura rationalis, ad hoc quod libere non solum ipso dono creato utatur, sed ut ipsa divina Persona fruatur. Et ideo missio invisibilis fit secundum donum gratiae gratum facientis, et tamen ipso Persona divina datur." Cf. corpus, and I, q. 38, a. 1 for a completer analysis of the notion: "Persona divina dicitur esse alicuius, vel secundum originem, sicut Filius est Patris; vel inquantum ab aliquo habetur. Habere autem dicimur id quo libere possumus uti vel frui, ut volumus. Et per hunc modum divina Persona non potest haberi nisi rationali creatura Deo coniuncta. Aliae autem creaturae moveri quidem possunt a divina Persona; non tamen sic quod in potestate earum sit frui divina Persona, et uti effectu eius. Ad quod quandoque pertingit rationalis creatura; ut puta cum sic fit particeps divini Verbi et procedentis Amoris, ut possit libere Deum vere cognoscere et recte amare."

¹⁵ I *Sent.*, d. 14, q. 2, a. 2 ad 1, 4; *Sum. Theol.*, I, q. 43, a. 3 ad 4.

¹⁶ I *Sent.*, d. 15, q. 3, a. 1; *Sum. Theol.*, I, q. 43, a. 4 ad 1.

¹⁷ I *Sent.*, d. 15, q. 2 ad 4.

¹⁸ *Sum. Theol.*, I, q. 43, a. 5; cf. a. 4 ad 2.

¹⁹ *Ibid.*, a. 3, obj. 1: "Divinam Personam mitti est ipsam donari." I *Sent.*, d. 14, q. 2, a. 2 ad 2: ". . . in processione Spiritus sancti, prout scilicet claudit in se dationem Spiritus sancti. . . ."

²⁰ Cf. I *Sent.*, d. 15, q. 1, a. 1.

²¹ *Ibid.*, q. 4, a. 1: ". . . sicut in exitu rerum a principio dicitur bonitas divina in creaturas procedere, in quantum repraesentatur in creatura per similitudinem bonitatis divinae in ipsa receptam; ita in reductione rationalis creaturae in Deum intelligitur processio divinae personae, quae et missio dicitur, inquantum propria relatio ipsius personae divinae repraesentatur in anima per similitudinem aliquam receptam, quae est exemplata et originata ab ipsa proprietate relationis aeternae; sicut proprius modus quo Spiritus sanctus refertur ad Patrem, est amor, et proprius modus referendi Filium est, quia est verbum ipsius manifestans ipsum. Unde sicut Spiritus sanctus invisibiliter procedit in mentem per donum amoris, ita Filius per donum sapientiae; in quo est manifestatio ipsius Patris, qui est ultimum ad quod recurrimus."

²² *Sum. Theol.*, I, q. 42, a. 2 ad 4: "Generatio vero Filii non est in *nunc* temporis aut in tempore, sed in aeternitate. Et ideo, ad significandum praesentialitatem et permanentiam aeternitatis, potest dici quod *semper nascitur*, ut Origines dixit. Sed, ut Gregorius et Augustinus dicunt, melius est quod dicatur *semper natus*: ut ly *semper* designet permanentiam aeternitatis, et ly *natus* perfectionem geniti."

²³ Man's possession is, of course, to be understood in a passive sense: he receives the divine processions, he does not produce them or cooperate in them in any active way. Cf. *Sum. Theol.*, I, q. 36, a. 1 ad 3: "Nulli autem creaturae competit esse principium respectu alicuius divinae personae, sed e converso. Et ideo potest dici *Pater noster*, et *Spiritus noster*: non tamen potest dici *Filius noster*." Cf. *Mystici Corporis* (ed. cit.), p. 35: "But let all agree uncompromisingly on this, if they would not err from truth and from the orthodox teaching of the Church: to reject every kind of mystic union by which the faithful would in any way pass beyond the sphere of creatures and rashly enter the Divine, even to the extent of one single

attribute of the eternal Godhead being predicated of them as their own."

[24] I *Sent.*, d. 14, q. 1, a. 2 ad 2; d. 15, q. 2 ad 2; q. 4, a. 1 and ad 1; d. 16, q. 1, a. 2.

[25] *Sum. Theol.*, I, q. 43, a. 3, obj. 3; a. 5 ad 1 and ad 2; a. 6 ad 2.

[26] I *Sent.*, d. 14, q. 1, a. 1: ". . . sic dicetur processio temporalis ex eo quod ex novitate effectus consurgit nova relatio creaturae ad Deum, ratione cujus oportet Deum sub nova habitudine ad creaturam significari, ut patet in omnibus quae de Deo ex tempore dicuntur." *Sum. Theol.*, I, q. 43, a. 2 ad 2: ". . . divinam Personam esse novo modo in aliquo, vel ab aliquo haberi, non est propter mutationem divinae Personae, sed propter mutationem creaturae: sicut et Deus temporaliter dicitur Dominus, propter mutationem creaturae."

[27] *Sum. Theol.*, I, q. 8, a. 1: "Oportet enim omne agens coniungi ei in quod immediate agit, et sua virtute illud contingere. . . ."

[28] *De Pot.*, q. 3, a. 7: "Sic ergo Deus est causa actionis cuiuslibet in quantum dat virtutem agendi, et in quantum conservat eam, et in quantum applicat actioni, et in quantum eius virtute omnia alia virtus agit. Et cum coniunxerimus his, quod Deus sit sua virtus, et quod sit intra rem quamlibet non sicut pars essentiae, sed sicut tenens rem in esse, sequetur quod ipse in quolibet operante immediate operetur, non exclusa operatione voluntatis et naturae." Cf. I *Sent.*, d. 37, q. 1, a. 1 and ad 4.

[29] *Sum. Theol.*, loc. cit.; I *Sent.*, d. 37, q. 1, a. 1 and ad 1.

[30] I *Sent.*, loc. cit.; *Sum. Theol.*, loc. cit.

[31] Cf. II *Sent.*, Prol.; *Sum. Theol.*, I, q. 45, a. 6; *De Pot.*, q. 9, a. 5 ad 20.

[32] Cf. Joannes a S. Thoma, *Cursus Theologicus* (ed. Vivès, 1883), III, q. 3, a. 2, n. 8: "Caeterum, tota haec terminatio existentiae, quam non negamus non fit per distinctam unionem, neque ad ipsam immediate existentiam, ut communis est totius Trinitatis, sed fit immediate, et per unicam unionem ad personam Verbi, et mediante ipso Verbo ad existentiam, ut est proprius actus personae."

[33] Cf. II *Sent.*, d. 6, q. 2, a. 3; *Sum. Theol.*, III, q. 2, a. 4 ad 2.

[34] *Sum. Theol.*, III, q. 3, a. 4: "Tres enim personae fecerunt ut humana natura uniretur uni personae Filii." III *Sent.*, d. 1, q. 2, a. 1: ". . . tota Trinitas univit humanam naturam Filio in persona."

[35] Cf. I *Sent.*, d. 17, q. 1, a. 1: "Dicunt enim [quidam] quod sicut Filius univit sibi naturam humanam solus, quamvis sit ibi operatio totius Trinitatis; ita Spiritus sanctus solus unit sibi voluntatem, quamvis ibi sit operatio totius Trinitatis. Sed hoc non potest stare; quia unio humanae naturae in Christo terminata est ad unum esse personae divinae: et ideo idem actus numero est personae divinae et naturae humanae assumptae. Sed voluntas alicujus sancti non assumitur in unitatem suppositi Spiritus sancti."

[36] III *Sent.*, d. 10, q. 3, a. 1, sol. 1: "Gratia autem creaturae facit unionem ad Deum. Quae quidem duplex est: scilicet per operationem, secundum quod nos unimur Deo cognoscendo et amando ipsum; et in persona. . . ." Cf. ad 3; I *Sent.*, d. 37, q. 1, a. 2; *De Ver.*, q. 29, a. 1; *Sum. Theol.*, I, q. 43, a. 3.

[37] I *Sent.*, d. 37, q. 1, a. 2: ". . . distinctio istorum modorum partim sumitur ex parte creaturae, partim ex parte Dei. Ex parte creaturae, inquantum diverso modo ordinatur in Deum et conjungitur ei, non diversitate rationis tantum sed realiter. Cum enim Deus in rebus esse dicatur secundum quod eis aliquo modo applicatur, oportet ut ubi est diversus conjunctionis vel applicationis modus, ibi sit diversus modus essendi. Conjungitur autem creatura Dei tripliciter. Primo modo secundum similitudinem tantum, inquantum invenitur in creatura aliqua similitudo divinae bonitatis, non quod attingat ipsum Deum secundum substantiam; et ista conjunctio invenitur in omnibus creaturis per essentiam, praesentiam et potentiam. Secundo creatura attingit ad ipsum Deum secundum substantiam suam consideratum, et non secundum similitudinem tantum; et hoc est per operationem: scilicet, quando aliquis fide adhaeret ipsi primae veritati, et charitate ipsi summae bonitati: et sic est alius modus quo Deus specialiter est in sanctis per gratiam. Tertio creatura attingit ad ipsum Deum non solum secundum operationem, sed etiam secundum esse: non quidem prout esse est actus essentiae, quia creatura non potest transire in naturam divinam: sed secundum quod est actus hypostasis vel personae, in cujus unionem creatura assumpta est: et sic est ultimus modus quo Deus est in Christo per unionem." Cf. *Sum. Theol.*, I, q. 8, a. 3 and ad 4.

[39] Cf., e.g., Petrus de Ledesma, O. P., *De Divina Perfectione*, q. 4, a. 6. concl. 1a (Neopoli, 1639): "Gratia est quaedam specialis participatio divinae naturae, secundum quod divina natura excedat omnem aliam naturam, et est expressior quaedam similitudo divinae naturae, quam quaecumque natura creata, aut creabilis ordinis naturalis quantumvis elecata sit. . . . . . . omnis creatura creata, et creabilis

ordinis naturalis est participatio quaedam Dei secundum rationem partialem, et consideratam ut finitam, et distinctam ab omnia alia ratione; caeterum, gratia est quaedam participatio Dei secundum illam amplissimam et totalem rationem, qua Deus excedit omnem creaturam, et est ipsum esse infinitum et amplissimum, excedens omne esse." Cf. 4um corollarium: ". . . gratia est proprius, et particularis effectus Dei, et veluti univocus, et Deus est propria et particularis causa gratiae. . . ."

[40] Paul Galtier, S.J., *De SS. Trinitate in Se et in Nobis*, n. 457, p. 319: "[Personae divinae] fiunt vere justorum, seu ita jam in eorum possessione constituuntur ut illas habeant jam vere suas. Ratio est ipsa natura effectus in eis producti. . . . Vi proinde solius status gratiae habetur mutua justi et personarum divinarum possessio, quae vere inchoet mutuam status gloriae possessionem."

[41] Teófilo Urdánoz, O.P., *op. cit.*, p. 524: "La gracia no es un *efecto muerto*, sino un principio vital que se inserta en la vida del hombre, haciéndole vivir una vida divina y sobrenatural, constituyéndole hijo de Dios, partícipe de su misma vida, de sus dones y su herencia eterna. Por la gracia, pues, Dios non viene a nosotros simplemente como causa, sino como un padre y amigo, uniéndonos a sí en abrazo intimo de hijos, dándose a neustra alma en posesion y prenda dichosa, como principio interno y objecto de conocimiento y amor divinos. Al considerar estos efectos y ostros muchos de la gracia, quién va a decir que Dios al dárnosla se comporta como en la producción de los efectos comunes, a que no tiene virtualidad suficiente para producir la inhabitación o presencia intima y sobrenatural de Dios en el alma?"

[42] Marcel Retailleau, *op. cit.*, pp. 225-226: "Il n'apparaît pas évidemment impossible que la grâce sanctificante qui sous un rapport est un dégré de l'être, mais sous un autre rapport, l'emporte sur l'être, et ses autres dégrés soutienne vis-à-vis de la Divine Substance une double relation "essentielle et formelle," l'une et l'autre des ces deux relations se situant neanmoins dans le même ordre de la causalité efficiente ou formelle-exemplaire. . . . de par la deuxième relation, la Trinité sainte descend dans la crèature formellement; l'Unité trinitaire descend formellement, en raison de l'oeuvre sanctificatrice, qui exige, à cause de son terme: la grâce, en tant que participation de la Deité, l'application immediate de la Deité, de la substance divine en son centre le plus intime, le centre où prend naissance la Trinité."

[43] *Op. cit.*, p. 529: ". . . en esa expresión: Dios operante como uno y Trino, tenemos una denominación propia y suficiente para

afirmar que la operación causador de la gracia es asimismo *asimiladora* de dicho efecto sobrenatural a las tres divinas personas, como la marco o grabado divino que lleva en sí impresa la imagen de los tres divinos grabadores. Que dicha operación de Dios uno y Trino imprime en la gracia un orden intrínseco a Dios como es en sí y, por lo tanto, a las divinas personas. Que ademas une en muy estrecha coyunda — *coniungit toti Trinitati,* dice Santo Tomás — en el alma con las divinas personas; unión sobrenatural y nueva, que no es tanto por atración en su vida intima, trinitaria. Por fin, que dados los elementos de dicha operación, es suficiente para hacer presentes al alma por el efecto de la gracia, las tres divinas personas. La recepción de la gracia implica la visita de la Trinidad toda entera. Recibir la gracia implica recibir a la vez los tres divinas Huespedes. Su acción e influencia conjuncta, *portadora de su presencialidad substancial,* es necesaria para conservar aquel sello deiforme de la gracia, participación de la substancia divina." (Emphasis in text.)

[44] Cf. also the criticism of St. Albert, *supra,* pp. 148-155, where Cajetan's explanation of these relations between created and Uncreated grace was set forth.

[45] Cf. Bañez, *op. cit.,* I, q. 15, a. 1 ad 3um argumentum Durandi (ed. cit., p. 375): ". . . quod Deus sit causa creaturarum, sive efficiens, sive exemplaris, sive formalis competit Deo, quatenus est unus ratione Divinae Essentiae, et non competit *per se primo alicui Divinae Personae.* . . ."

[46] *De Ver.,* q. 10, a. 13: ". . . omne illud quod in divinis causalitatem habet, ad essentiam pertinet, cum Deus per essentiam suam sit causa rerum. Propria autem personarum sunt relationes, quibus personae non ad creaturas, sed ad invicem referuntur."

[47] *Sum. Theol.,* q. 32, a. 2: "Omnes autem creaturae sub una specie relationis referuntur ad Deum, ut sunt creaturae ipsius."

[48] III *Sent.,* d. 4, q. 1, a. 2, sol. 1: ". . . nos dicimur per gratiam filii Trinitatis et tamen gratia quae in nobis est, est effectus essentiae divinae, non habens respectum ad distinctionem personarum."

[49] The classic phrase of St. Anselm (*De processione Spiritus Sancti,* Chap. 2; PL 158: 288), canonized by the Council of Florence (1438-1445) in the *Decree for the Jacobites* (Denz. 703).

[50] III *Sent.,* d. 32, a. 5, sol. 2 ad 5: "Deus non magis operatur in eo cui de novo infundit gratiam quam in eo quo eam continuat. . . . Nihil enim potest subsistere, nisi Dei operatio continuatur." St. Thomas

explains the difference of God's operation as principle, not from the point of view of the cause, but from that of the effect. Cf. *ibid.*, d. 19, a. 5, sol. 1: ". . . dilectio Dei ad nos secundum effectum judicatur. Cum enim ipse, quantum in se est, ad omnes aequaliter se habeat, secundum hoc aliquos dicitur diligere secundum quod eos suae bonitatis participes facit. Ultima autem participatio suae bonitatis et completissima consistit in visione essentiae suae secundum quam ei convivimus socialiter, quasi amici, cum in ea sua vita et beatitudo consistat. Unde illos simpliciter dicitur diligere quos admittit ad dictam visionem vel secundum rem vel secundum causam, sicut patet in illis quibus dedit Spiritum sanctum quasi pignus illius visionis."

[51] I *Sent.*, d. 5, q. 1, a. 1; d. 11, q. 1, a. 4 ad 2; d. 29, q. 1, a. 4 ad 2; II *Sent.*, Prol.; d. 1, a. 5 ad 11; *De Ver.*, q. 10, a. 13; IV *Con. Gen.*, Chap. 21; *Sum. Theol.*, I, q. 3, a. 3; q. 32, a. 1; q. 36, a. 4 ad 7; q. 45, a. 3 ad 1; a. 6 and a. 7; III, q. 3, a. 4 ad 3; q. 23, a. 2; *De Pot.*, q. 9, a. 5 ad 20; a. 9 ad 3; etc., etc.

It should be noted that these texts refer to God's creative causality: but as grace is an immediate effect of God, the same principle applies as for creation and conservation: God works outside Himself in virtue of His omnipotence, intellect and will; His activity, consequently, is His substance, since these are absolute attributes. Hence He can be present as principle and cause of things only as one in essence, without distinction of Persons.

[52] I *Sent.*, d. 30, q. 1, a. 2: ". . . in omnibus istis quae dicuntur de Deo ex tempore, et important habitudinem principii ad principiatum, simpliciter verum est quod conveniunt toti Trinitati. Si autem consideretur relatio creaturae ad Creatorem ut ad terminum, possible est quod talis relatio creaturae sit ad aliquid essentiale, vel ad aliquid personale . . . sed ista relatio qua creatura refertur in Deum ut ad terminum, includit ex consequenti in se relationem quae est ad Deum ut ad principium. Unde in omnibus quae dicuntur de Deo secundum habitudinem termini, possunt uni tantum convenire personae: sed ratio principii, quae ibi includitur, ex consequenti convenit toti Trinitati. Unde secundum habitudinem unam possunt facere intellectum personae, et secundum aliam faciunt intellectum essentiae; sicut patet, cum dicitur, incarnatus, hoc tantum Filio competit, quia ad solam personam Filii incarnatio terminata est, quam tamen tota Trinitas fecit."

[53] I *Sent.*, d. 37, Expositio Primae Partis Textus: ". . . aliae creaturae, quamvis consequantur divinam similitudinem per operationem

ipsius Dei, non tamen attingunt ad ipsum Deum secundum suppositum; et ideo quamvis Deus in eis sit, non tamen ipsae cum Deo sunt. Sed creatura rationalis per gratiam attingit ad ipsum Deum, secundum quod ipsum amat et cognoscit: et ideo, cum eo esse dicitur; et eadem ratione dicitur capax Dei, sicut suae perfectionis, per modum objecti; et propter hoc etiam dicitur templum Dei, et inhabitari a Deo."

[54] Cf. I *Sent.*, d. 14, q. 2, a. 2; *Sum. Theol.*, I, q. 43, a. 3.

[55] *Sum Theol.*, I, q. 43, a. 5 ad 2; I *Sent.*, d. 15, q. 4, a. 1 ad 3.

[56] I *Sent.*, d. 14, a. 2, a. 3 ad 2: ". . . in processione Spiritus sancti, prout scilicet, claudit in se dationem Spiritus Sancti, non sufficit quod sit nova relatio qualiscumque creaturae ad Deum, sed oportet quod referatur in ipsum sicut ad habitum; quia quod datur alicui habetur aliquo modo ab illo. Persona autem divina non potest haberi a nobis nisi vel ad fructum perfectum, et hoc habetur per donum gloriae, aut secundum fructum imperfectum, et sic habetur per donum gratiae gratum facientis, vel potius sicut id per quod fruibili conjungimur." *Ibid.*, ad 3: "Non qualiscumque cognitio sufficit ad rationem missionis, sed solum illa quae accipitur ex aliquo dono appropriato Personae, per quod efficitur in nobis conjunctio ad Deum, secundum modum proprium illius Personae." *Sum. Theol.*, I, q. 43, a. 3 ad 3: "Per aliquos effectus [distinctos a gratia] Filius cognosci potest a nobis, non tamen per alios effectus nos inhabitat, vel etiam habetur a nobis." *Exp. in I Epis. ad Cor.*, Chap. 3, lect. 3: "Cognitio sine dilectione non sufficit ad inhabitationem Dei. Inde est quod multi cognoscunt Deum, vel per naturalem cognitionem, vel per fidem informem, quos tamen non inhabitat Spiritus Dei." I *Sent.*, d. 15, q. 4, a. 1 ad 3: "Non habet Filium in se inhabitantem nisi qui recipit talem cognitionem [cum amore caritatis]. Hoc autem esse non potest sine gratia gratum faciente. Unde constat, quod simpliciter et proprie loquendo Filius nec datur nec mittitur nisi in dono gratiae gratum facientis."

[57] Cf. *Sum. Theol.*, I, q. 43, a. 3 ad 4; I *Sent.*, d. 14, q. 2, a. 2 ad 1; d. 15, q. 3, a. 1 ad 3.

[58] I *Sent.*, d. 14, q. 2, a. 2 ad 3; d. 15, q. 2 ad 5; d. 15, Expos. Secundae Partis Textus; d. 16, q. 1, a. 2; *Sum. Theol.*, I, q. 43, a. 5 ad 2.

[59] *Lectura in Psal.* 33, v. 9: "Experientia de re sumitur per sensum; sed aliter de re praesenti et aliter de absente: quia de absente per visum, odoratum et auditum; de praesenti vero per tactum et gustum, sed per tactum de extrinseca praesente, per gustum vero de in-

trinseca. Deus autem non longe est a nobis nec extra nos, sed in nobis, Ierem, 14, 9: tu in nobis es, Domine; et ideo experientia divinae bonitatis dicitur gustatio. . . ."

[60] Cf. *Sum. Theol.*, II-II, q. 9, a. 1 ad 1: ". . . in Deo est certum iudicium veritatis absque omni discursu per simplicem intuitum, ut in Primo dictum est; et ideo divina scientia non est discursiva vel ratiocinativa, sed absoluta et simplex. Cui similis est scientia quae ponitur donum Spiritus Sancti: cum sit quaedam participativa similitudo ipsius."

As Bañez here notes, what applies to the gift of Knowledge is even more applicable to that of Wisdom. Therefore St. Thomas will say that Wisdom judges of divine things not from the investigations of reason (as does the natural habit), but from a certain connaturalness with divine things, caused by Charity (*ibid.*, q. 45, a. 2), an affective or experiential knowledge of the divine goodness which one experiences in himself (*ibid.*, q. 97, a. 2 ad 2). In this experiencing we are more acted upon than active (*De Ver.*, q. 26, a. 3 ad 18), according to the words of St. Paul, Rom. 8:14: "Quicumque enim spiritu Dei aguntur, hi sunt filii Dei." (Cf. *Exp. in Epis. ad Romanos*, Chap. 8, lect. 3).

[61] III *Sent.*, d. 35, q. 2, a. 1, sol. 3: ". . . sapientiae donum eminentiam cognitionis habet, per quamdam unionem ad divina, quibus non unimur nisi per amorem, ut qui adhaeret Deo, sit unus spiritus: I Cor. Unde et Dominus, Joan., XV, 15, secreta Patris se revelasse discipulis dicit, inquantum amici erant. Et ideo sapientiae donum dilectionem praesupponit, et sic in affectione est. Sed quantum ad esesntiam in cognitione est. Unde ipsius actus videtur esse et hic [et] in futuro divina amata contemplari, et per ea de aliis judicare non solum in speculativis, sed etiam in agendis, in quibus ex fine judicium sumitur."

In other places St. Thomas describes this 'union with divine things' (cf. *Sum. Theol.*, II-II, q. 9, a. 2 ad 1; q. 45, a. 4), characteristic of the experimental knowledge of Wisdom, as an 'affinity' (III *Sent.*, *loc. cit.*, sol. 1) and 'connaturalness' (*ibid.*, d. 34, q. 1, a. 2; *Sum. Theol.*, II-II, q. 45, a. 2 and a. 4) with divine things.

[62] *De Virtutibus in Communi*, a. 12 ad 11: "Sapientia, qua nunc contemplamur Deum, non immediate respicit ipsum Deum, sed effectus ex quibus ipsum in praesenti contemplamus."

This is an important point that unfortunately seems to have been missed or misunderstood by Fr. Morency in his excellent study, *L'union de grâce selon S. Thomas*. Cf. pp. 228-229 where he states a "paradoxical" thesis: that grace unites the just to the divine essence itself, as the habitual object of knowledge, and thus we habitually bear in us God, *"objet de la vision intuitive."* This expression is, to say the least, unfortunate and inexact: materially permissible, it is formally untrue, inasmuch as grace is only the radical principle of the *vision* of God, and by grace God is in no way present *as* object of vision.

[63] *De Ver.*, q. 18, a. 2 ad 4.

[64] II *Sent.*, d. 23, q. 2, a. 1; *De Ver.*, q. 18, a. 1 ad 16.

[65] *De Ver.*, q. 18, a. 2 ad 8.

[66] *Ibid.*, a. 2: ". . . per inspirationem internam ex irradiatione divinae Sapientiae, per quem modum Deum cognoscebat non ex visibilibus creaturis, sed ex quadam spirituali similitudine suae menti impressa."

[67] *Ibid.*, a. 1 ad 1: "In statu ante peccatum indigebat duplici medio, scilicet medio quod est similitudo Dei et quod est lumen elevans vel dirigens mentem." Cf. *ibid.*, a. 3: "Deus interius inspirando non exhibet essentiam suam ad videndum, sed aliquod suae essentiae signum quod est aliqua spiritualis similitudo suae sapientiae."

[68] *La structure de l'âme et l'experience mystique* (Paris, 1927) II, pp. 259-263; "L'experience mystique pure dans le cadre des missions divines," *La Vie Spirituelle*, 32 (1932), suppl., pp. (1)-(28). Cf. also the unique theory of S. I. Dockx, O.P., *Fils de Dieu par grâce* (Paris, 1948), by which man would be immediately united to the divine essence in this life by Charity, as he is in the Beatific Vision by the light of glory, so that God would be not only what we know but that by which we know (pp. 95-101). (A just, if brief criticism of the contradictions of this thesis and its anti-Thomistic characteristics is given by Father Luigi Ciappi, O.P., "Una nova interpretazione dell'inhabitazione della SS. Trinità nell'anima," *Vita Cristiana*, 20 [1951], pp. 113-124.)

[69] Cf. Ledesma, *op. cit.*, 5um corollarium: ". . . effectu gratiae, et bonorum supernaturalium divini ordinis, multo melius et perfectius possumus cognoscere Deum quam ex effectibus ordinis naturalis. Ratio est aperta, gratia est quaedam participatio et quidem Dei effectus maxime illi similis, et eiusdem ordinis et rationis. Alii vero effectus naturales non sunt eiusdem ordinis et rationis, ergo. Imo existimo, quod ex gratia meliori et excellentiori modo possumus venire in Dei cognitione quam ex omnibus creaturis ordinis naturalis creatis et

creabilibus, quoniam gratia habet maiorem et expressiorem similitudinem cum Deo, cum sit eiusdem ordinis et rationis, quam omnes creaturae ordinis naturali simul sumptae."

[70] IV *Sent.*, d. 49, q. 2, a. 7 ad 2 (ed. Vivès): "Sanctorum mentes etiam in via, vitiis purgatae, Deum contemplantur adjutae divino lumine quod perfunduntur secundum quam quidem visionem quamvis divina natura ut est non videatur, quia illud lumen receptum non est similitudo sufficienter repraesentans divinam essentiam; tamen aliqua cognitio de Deo habetur, cum illud lumen sit expressior ejus similitudo quam lumen naturae aut creaturae sensibilis ex quibus homo naturali cognitione ducitur ad Dei cognitionem."

[71] *Lectura super Evan. S. Matt.*, V, n. 435 (ed. Cai, V revisa): "Sancti qui habent cor repletum iustitia, vident [Deum] excellentius quam alii qui vident per effectus corporales: quanto enim effectus sunt propinquiores, tanto Deus magis cognoscitur per illos. Unde sancti, qui habet iustitiam, caritatem et hujusmodi effectus qui sunt simillimi Deo, cognoscunt magis quam alii. . . ." Cf. *De Car.*, a. 1 ad 8.

[72] *Sum. Theol.*, II-II, q. 52, a. 2 ad 1: "In donis Spiritus Sancti, mens humana non se habet ut movens, sed magis ut mota." Cf. *ibid.*, a. 1; I-II, q. 68, a. 1. But such passivity is characteristic of man under the influence of *operating* grace: "Operatio alicujus effectus non attribuitur mobili sed moventi. In illo ergo effectu in quo mens nostra est mota non movens, solus autem Deus movens, operatio Dei attribuitur, et secundum hoc dicitur gratia operans. In illo autem effectu in quo mens nostra et movet et movetur, operatio non solum Deo attribuitur sed etiam animae, et secundum hoc dicitur gratia cooperans" (I-II, q. 111, a. 2). Cf. Cajetan on this article, and John of St. Thomas, I-II, disp. 5, a. 5, n. 43.

[73] III *Sent.*, d. 34, q. 1, a. 3; q. 2, a. 1, sol. 3; q. 3, a. 2, sol. 1; *Sum. Theol.*, I-II, q. 68, a. 1 ad 3.

[74] Johannes a S. Thoma, *Cursus Theologicus*, I-II, disp. 18, De donis, a. 4, n. 11 (ed. Lavalle, Québec; 1948): "Amor et affectus potest duplicem considerationem habere. Primo, ut applicat se et alias potentias ad operandum, et sic solum se habet effective et executive in ordine ad alias operationes, scilicet per modum applicantis ad agendum. Secundo, ut applicat sibi objectum et illud unit et inviscerat sibi per quamdam fruitionem et quasi connaturalitatem et proportionem cum tali objecto et quasi experitur illud experientia affectiva juxta illud: "Gustate et videte" (*Psalm.* XXXIII, 9). Et sic affectus transit

in conditionem objecti, quatenus ex tali experientia affectiva redditur objectum magis conforme et proportionatum et unitum personae eique magis conveniens; et sic fertur intellectus in illud ut expertum et contactum sibi, et hoc modo se habet amor ut praecise movens in genere causae objectivae." Cf. n. 15: ". . . voluntas non formaliter illuminat intellectum, sed potest causaliter majus lumen praebere seu perficere, quatenus reddit objectum magis unitum sibi per amorem et immediatius in se attactum et gustatum, et sic repraesentatur de novo intellectui cum diversa convenientia et proportione ad affectum."

[75] *Exp. in Epis. ad Romanos*, Chap. 8, lect. 3: ". . . hic autem testimonium reddit non quidem exteriore voce ad aures hominum; sicut Pater protestatus est de Filio suo, sed reddit testimonium per effectum amoris filialis, quem in nobis facit."

[76] *Sum. Theol.*, II-II, q. 180, a. 5 ad 2: "Contemplatio humana, secundum statum praesentis vitae, non potest esse absque phantasmatibus, quia connaturale est homini ut species intelligibiles in phantasmatibus videat, sicut Philosophus dicit (*De anima*, III). Sed tamen intellectualis cognitio non consistit in ejus phantasmatibus sed in eis contemplatur puritatem intelligibilis veritatis." Cf. *De Ver.*, q. 18, a. 5.

[77] IV *Sent.*, d. 49, q. 2, a. 7 ad 8 (ed. Vivès): "Idem est motus intellectus in imaginem inquantum est imago et in imaginatum, quamvis alius motus sit intellectus in imaginem in quantum est res quaedam et in id cuius est imago: et ideo quando per similitudinem creaturae, quam intellectus habet penes se, non convertitur in creaturam ut res quaedam, sed solum ut est similitudo Dei, tunc immediate de Deo cogitat, quamvis non immediate Deum videat." Cf. *De Ver.*, q. 8, a. 3 ad 18.

Thus St. Thomas anticipates Galtier's objection that such knowledge involves a double inference, from the phenomena of grace to the powers of grace responsible for them, from these powers to their exemplary and efficient principles, the Persons themselves (*L'habitation en nous des trois personnes*, ed. cit., p. 194). In another place the Angelic Doctor also solves the same difficulty: "Contingit ex effectu causam cognoscere multipliciter: uno modo secundum quod effectus sumitur ut medium ad cognoscendum de causa quod sit et quod talis sit, sicut accidit in scientiis, quae causam demonstrant per effectum. Alio modo ita quod in ipso effectu videatur causa inquantum similitudo resultat in effectu, sicut homo videtur in speculo propter suam similitudinem. Et differt hic modus a primo. Nam in primo sunt duae cognitiones, effectus et causae, quarum una est alterius causa: nam cognitio effectus est causa quod cognoscatur causa eius. In modo autem secundo, una est visio utriusque: simul enim dum videtur effectus, videtur et causa in ipso. . . . Substantiae autem separatae cognoscunt Deum per suas substantias sicut causa cognoscitur per effectum, non autem primo modo, quia sic eorum cognitio esset discursiva, sed secundo modo, inquantum una videt Deum in alia" (III Con. Gen., Chap. 49). Cf. Sum. Theol., I, q. 58, a. 3 and ad 1.

[78] I Sent., d. 15, Expositio Secundae Partis Textus: " 'Et tunc unicuique mittitur, cum a quoquam cognoscitur.' Hoc intelligendum est non tantum de cognitione speculativa, sed quae est etiam quodammodo experimentalis; quod ostendit hoc quod sequitur: 'Atque percipitur,' quod proprie experientiam in dono percepto demonstrat." Cf. Sum. Theol., II-II, q. 97, a. 2 ad 2.

[79] I Sent., d. 14, q. 2, a. 1, sol. 2; Sum. Theol., I, q. 43, a. 3. Cf. I Sent., d. 14, q. 2, a. 2 ad 2; d. 15, q. 4, a. 1 ad 1; Sum. Theol., I, q. 38, a. 1.

[80] III Sent., d. 18, a. 4, sol. 4: "Hoc quod Deus est in sanctis per gratiam praesupponit hoc quod est in omnibus per essentiam, praesentiam et potentiam."

The context of this particular excerpt *exactly* affirms the very point insisted on, namely, that the real and substantial presence of God in the soul is presupposed by the posterior (at least by nature) grace-state. St. Thomas here emphasizes that the later union (whether that of the indwelling or *even that of the hypostatic union of the Incarnation*) presupposes the real and substantial presence of God in the soul by essence, presence and power: ". . . *gloria animae* consistit in hoc quod anima ipsi Deo unitur per visionem et amorem. Et quia posterior unio praesupponit priorem, sicut hoc quod Deus est in sanctis per gratiam praesupponit hoc quod est in omnibus per essentiam, praesentiam et potentiam; ideo eadem ratione unio quae est in persona — quae est ultima et completissima — praesupponit omnem aliam unionem ad Deum. Unde ex hoc ipso quod anima Christi erat Deo in persona conjuncta, debebatur sibi fruitionis unio, et non per operationem aliquam est ei facta debita. Et ideo, quia meritum consistit in operatione quae facit nobis aliquid debitum, Christus fruitionem non meruit."

No doubt, so far as the Incarnation is concerned, this is a dangerous argument, since it seems at first to suggest that somehow or other the human nature of Christ is previously disposed for its union with the Second Person (in fact, St. Thomas does not employ this reasoning again, even though he affirms the same doctrine concerning Christ's possession of beatitude: *De Ver.*, q. 29, a. 6;

Comp. Theol., Chap. 231; *Sum. Theol.*, III, q. 19, a. 3). It can, however, be properly understood not as a priority of causality but as the order of perfection, in which the less precedes the greater (and is presupposed by it), the imperfect the perfect—this fact being clear from the words, 'quae est ultima et completissima.'

[81] Cf. Capreolus, *op. cit.*, I, d. 37, q. 1, a. 2 (II, p. 437): ". . . Deus in aliquo per gratiam, ut objectum dilectum et cognitum in diligente et cognoscente, non quocumque amore vel qualicumque notitia, sed quam ipse diligenti se et cognoscenti specialiter infundit, et infusam conservat; et ideo stant simul quod Deus sit per gratiam in aliquo per modum objecti, et per modum specialiter operantis."

[82] Although in the tract on the ubiquity of God he *always* speaks of God as present by immensity in producing grace (*op. cit.*, I, q. 8, disp. 8, a. 7, nn. 8-11; Solesmnes ed., II, pp. 38-39), in the tract on the divine missions he invariably speaks of the presupposition involved as one of God's presence in producing both natural being and supernatural being. On one occasion in this tract, however, he specifies this presence as that of God's production of sanctifying grace: "Non potest autem cognosci experimentaliter nisi ut habitus, et possessus et coniunctus intime, nec coniunctus esse intime nisi supponendo contactum immensitatis, quo influit esse in anima non solum esse naturale, quod est commune omnibus, sed etiam esse supernaturale gratiae, quo ita dat esse supernaturale, quod se manifestat ut obiectum ipsi praesens; atque ideo speciali modo dicitur ibi esse tanquam non solum vivificans influendo et agendo, sed etiam vivificatione ipsam praesentem producens et manifestans, nunc per indicia et experimentalem coniunctionem ad animam, licet obscuram, in patria per intuitionem."

[83] Cf. R. Garrigou-Lagrange, O.P., *L'amour de Dieu et la Croix de Jésus* (Paris, n.d.; *imprimatur* 1929), II, pp. 663-664: "Si donc par impossible Dieu n'était pas déjà réellement présent dans le juste, comme cause conservatrice de son être naturel, il deviendrait réellement present en lui, comme cause productrice et conservatrice de la grâce et de la charité, et par suite comme object de connaissance quasi expérimentale et d'amour surnaturel d'amitié."

[84] Similarly, the more noble the effect the better one can know God from it: "Quanto autem aliqua creatura est altior et Deo similior, tanto per eam Deus clarior videtur, sicut homo perfectius videtur per speculum in quo expressius imago ejus resultat. Et sic patet quod multo eminentius videtur Deus per intelligibiles effectus quam per sensibiles et corporeos" (*Sum. Theol.*, I, q. 94, a. 1).

⁸⁵ I *Sent.*, d. 15, q. 4, a. 1: ". . . in receptione hujusmodi donorum habentur personae divinae novo modo quasi ductrices in finem vel conjungentes."

⁸⁶ *Ibid.*, d. 14, q. 2, a. 2 ad 2: ". . . ipsae personae divinae quadam sui sigillatione in animabus nostris relinquunt quaedam dona quibus formaliter fruimur, scilicet amore et sapientia. . . ."

⁸⁷ *Ibid.*, d. 15, q. 4, a. 2 ad 4: ". . . illa notitia ex qua procedit amor, viget in ferventibus divino amore, qua scilicet cognoscunt divinam bonitatem inquantum est finis, et inquantum est largissime in eos profluens sua beneficia."

⁸⁸ See, for example, von Rudloff, "Des hl. Thomas Lehre von der Formalursache der Einwohnung Gottes in der Seele der Gerechten," *Divus Thomas* (Fr.), 8 (1930), p. 177: "Uns Scheint, dass der grosse Thomist bei genauerer Betractung in des Vasquez 'Ansicht zurücksinkt.' " Retailleau, *op. cit.*, p. vii and p. 272; Urdánoz, *op. cit.*, p. 514; Trütsch, *op. cit.*, pp. 17-18.

⁸⁹ Gardeil, *op. cit.*, II, p. 60: "Restent donc en présence deux facteurs positifs et solides de la présence effective de Dieu dans les justes: le facteur vasquézien . . . et le facteur suarézien. . . . Nous avons vu à quoi on aboutit en les opposant absolument, comme s'ils étaient exclusifs l'un et l'autre. Ne pourrait-on pas tenter de les compléter l'un par l'autre, le premier expliquant la caractére substantiel de la présence de Dieu l'âme due à la grâce; le second rendant compte de ce qu'il y a de spécial dans cette présence?" See also p. 66, where he calls his theory and that of John of St. Thomas a 'synthetic view of these complementary realities.' One can understand how the apparent equalizing of these elements leads to the belief that this presupposition of immensity enjoys a formal role. Gardeil himself, however, is under no such illusion: cf. p. 66: "La présence substantielle d'immensité est requise, non pas comme chez Vasquez, comme la raison adéquate et déterminante de la présence speciale à la grâce, mais comme une condition préalable et indispensable de cette nouvelle présence substantielle."

⁹⁰ *Op. cit.*, pp. 168-169: "On se souvient que la théorie présente inscrivait (au moins équivalement) dès son principe, une double présupposition de l'immensité au mode speciale de la présence de grâce: la présupposition pure et simple (celle que d'ordinaire nous appelons tout court: présupposition) et la présupposition d'intégration; la première nécessaire pour octroyer au nouveau mode être et consistance,

mais du dehors; la seconde nécessaire pour lui fournir, mais du dedans, ce caractère substantiel que le mode nouveau est impuissant, dit-on, à se procurer efficacement de lui-même. Or, de ces deux présuppositions, nous admettons la première, mais nous récusons la seconde."

[91] Cf. the commentaries of Cardinal Cajetan on II-II, q. 1, a. 1 and q. 5, a. 3.

[92] St. Augustine, *Epistula* 187, 6: 21 (PL 33:840): "Beatissimi autem sunt illi quibus hoc est Deum habere quod nosse."

[93] *Exp. in I Epis. ad Cor.*, Chap. 3, lect. 3: ". . . spiritualiter dicitur Deus inhabitare tamquam in familiari domo in sanctis, quorum mens capax est Dei per cognitionem et amorem, etiam si ipsi in actu non cognoscant et diligant, dummodo habeat per gratiam habitum fidei et caritatis, sicut patet in pueris baptizatis." Bañez describes this difference between act and habit in a graphic metaphor, which has its Scriptural and theological bases, as noted previously: "Spiritus Sanctus est in anima justi qui actu diligit Deum ex caritate, veluti cibus est in ore comedentis. In ea vero qui solum habitualiter diligit, est veluti cibus in ore ejus qui non coepit masticare" (*op. cit.*, I, q. 43, a. 3; ed. Salmanticae, 1585).

[94] Cf. *I Sent.*, d. 3, q. 4, a. 5; d. 15, q. 4, a. 1 ad; d. 17, q. 1, a. 1 ad 1 and ad 3; *Sum. Theol.*, I, q. 8, a. 3; q. 43, a. 3.

[95] Cf. *Sum. Theol.*, I-II, q. 62, a. 2; II-II, q. 1, a. 1; etc.

[96] Urdánoz, *op. cit.*, p. 612; quoted happily by Galtier, *L'habitation en nous des trois personnes*, pp. 176-177.

CHAPTER SEVEN

A Comparative Study of the Scriptum super Sententiis

All that has gone before — the determination of the common teaching of the Schoolmen on the indwelling of the Trinity and of this teaching's sources, remote and immediate; the explication of the various theories sponsored by the Scholastics to explain the problem these traditional facts occasion for the inquiring mind of Faith; the doctrinal exposition of the solution undeniably offered by the Angelic Doctor—all this long and sometimes tedious labor is but the necessary prelude for the investigations which will occupy the next two chapters: the comparison of the two diverse statements of Thomas' theory presented in the *Scriptum super Sententiis Magistri Petri Lombardi* and his *Summa Theologiae* with the explanations, and the statements of those explanations, produced by his predecessors.

It is clear from the preceding chapter that St. Thomas teaches the same doctrine on the inhabitation in both of these works. The triune presence in the souls of the just is explained on the basis of final causality; neither efficient nor exemplary causality (nor any combination of these types) can adequately account for this new union of Creator and rational creature caused by grace. The formal reason of the divine indwelling, then, cannot be the divine efficiency or the divine exemplarity, howsoever important those aspects of God's causality are in themselves, whatever ultimate significance must be accorded them in a total explanation (on human terms) of this mystery.

This conclusion was established by quoting from both works, impartially and indiscriminately, the facts, principles and explanations which constitute the principal elements of a theory founded in final causality. If this theory is then compared with the solutions given by the other Schoolmen, two facts are immediately apparent on *a priori* grounds. First, the answers of St. Thomas and St. Albert are antithetic and incompatible. Second, within the limits of the present problem, the solutions proposed by the *Summa Theologica* attributed to Alexander of Hales and by the *Commentarius in IV Libros Sententiarum* of St. Bonaventure are practically identical with that given by the Common Doctor, even though their final resolution of the difficulty is unsatisfactory on extrinsic principles and ultimately rejected by St. Thomas.

It is the burden of the next two chapters to illustrate these significant facts from another angle, on an *a posteriori* basis, by a textual comparison of the works of St. Thomas with those of the other medieval Masters. By a comparative examination of the scholastic texts involved, it will be proved — and as apodictically as such a procedure admits — that his doctrine in the *Sentences* follows the Halesian *Summa*, not the *Commentary* of St. Albert (Chapter Seven); it will further be shown that the revision advanced in Thomas' *Summa Theologiae* is also of

Franciscan origin, chiefly by suggestion from St. Bonaventure (Chapter Eight). Since the Franciscan works teach a theory of the inhabitation on the basis of final causality, the identification of both the earlier and later expositions of the Angelic Doctor with them (and his rejection in both works of the exemplary-efficient solution of St. Albert) conclusively shows the doctrinal identity of his two treatments of the problem of the divine indwelling.

This comparative study will thus not only serve the apologetic purpose of defending the exposition of St. Thomas' theory set forth in the preceding chapter (the determination of which was declared to be neither original nor intrinsically difficult). More importantly for the ends of this investigation, it will show that the divergencies between the two considerations of the mystery—divergencies briefly pointed out in the introductory chapter, to be examined more in detail in the chapters to follow—are essentially stylistic, a difference of expression, perspective, aspect and emphasis rather than of doctrine. And it will open the way for possible explanations of these considerable differences, as well as for a clearer and deeper penetration of his thought on a most difficult subject.

In this chapter, then, the earlier tract on the divine missions contained in the *Scriptum super Sententiis* will be studied comparatively. The study begins with a preliminary investigation of the possibility of St. Thomas' use of the works to be compared with his. From the strictly textual point of view, this explicit comparison will be treated in Article 2. Re-examination of the collation of St. Thomas' *Sentences* with the work of his predecessors, especially with the Franciscan *Summa,* this time from a textual-doctrinal aspect, will be accomplished in Article 3.*

ARTICLE 1

St. Thomas' Familiarity with the Works to be Compared

To establish specific relations between written works, one of which is presumed to be influenced by the others, certain conditions are obligatory. Obviously the author of the possibly derivative work must be capable of using the works to be compared with his: they must have preceded his efforts and have been widely enough disseminated to permit their use (or, this last condition unestablished, the fact of their specific availability to him proved on some other basis). Nor is this sufficient. To eliminate the possibility of coincidence or the employment of some common source—written or oral—the author must evidence direct familiarity with the other works. And the question of possible influence will be more certainly resolved if it can be shown that the author not only knew the other

* It will not be necessary to consider the solution of Peter Lombard, which is definitively rejected by St. Thomas, and hence connot influence his own thought or composition. The suggestions and tentations of William of Auxerre, the Codex Vaticanus latinus 691 and Eudes Rigaud are perfected in the Franciscan *Summa;* while St. Albert performs a similar task for the theories suggested by Alexander of Hales in his *Glossa* and *Quaestiones Disputatae.* Thus the explicit comparisons with the *Summa Alexandri* and the *Commentary* of Albert the Great implicitly concern these other works as well, but their influence may reasonably be supposed to have filtered through the more perfect expositions of their positions.

works but actually utilized them on the precise matter under discussion.

These conditions are amply fulfilled, relative to the works mentioned, by St. Thomas' tract on the divine mission in his commentary on the *Sentences* of Peter Lombard.

1. Possibility of Utilization

An early chapter has shown that all the works in question precede St. Thomas' youthful reading (and writing) of the *Sentences*. The tract on the divine missions of the Alexandrian *Summa* was finished by 1245; the first book of St. Albert's commentary was certainly completed before 1246; St. Bonaventure composes his first book in 1249 or 1250. The first book of the *Scriptum super Sententiis*, however, appears in 1253.[1] And since Thomas was a student of St. Albert at Cologne and his protégé, and a Bachelor at Paris (biblical and sententiary) from 1252-1256, the possibility of his acquaintance with the works of St. Albert and of the Franciscans is, on extrinsic grounds, firmly established.

2. Knowledge of the Works

An examination of St. Thomas' early work shows his intimate familiarity with the works that have been mentioned. In Table I this fact is clearly indicated with regard to the respective tracts on the divine missions.[2] Simply on the basis of material similarities, this Table, without any necessity for interpretation, shows that St. Thomas must have known the works of his predecessors. The same questions are asked, the same solutions given; similar objections are proposed, and they are resolved in a similar way. Thus not only the possibility but the fact of his acquaintance with the works of the Franciscans and of his Dominican master is abundantly demonstrable on intrinsic grounds, as even a cursory survey of Table I will manifest.

3. Use of the Works

Is the fact that St. Thomas knew these works sufficient to show they influenced his own labors? Obviously not: many possible explanations can be proposed for the manifest parallelism observable, and not one of these explanations need postulate the fact of direct influence. Moreover, since two of the works present antipodal theories of the inhabitation (the *Summa Alexandri*, of which St. Bonaventure's commentary is only a clearer statement, and the commentary of St. Albert), both of these should be shown to have been consulted by St. Thomas if one is to argue conclusively to the acceptance of one instead of the other. In fact, however, it is not difficult to prove that St. Thomas used all these works in writing his commentary; and hence all of them *may* be regarded as proximately possible sources for his theory of the indwelling in that work. This will be shown for each work in succession.

1) The *Summa Theologica* of Alexander of Hales.

The dependence of St. Thomas' commentary in the tract on the divine missions upon that of the Franciscan compilation has already been noted.[3] Although a difference of style and phraseology between the two is evident —St. Thomas already evidences that gift for precise, limpid, succint and lean presentation which reaches perfection in his *Summa*, but even here, in comparison with the prolixity of the *Summa Alexandri*, stands out—the fact is an obvious one. Not only are there innumerable similarities, but more than fifty times an absolute parallelism can be identified, identical all but to the word.* These points embrace questions, solutions, objections, responses, *auctoritates*, distinctions and explanations. It would be difficult, indeed, to imagine more conclusive evidence of the dependence of one work on another beyond an explicit acknowledgment by the author of the derivative work of his indebtedness to a predecessor.

Illustrative of this correspondence is Distinction 15, q. 1, a. 1 of Thomas' work ("Utrum missio conveniat divinis personis") which parallels all but verbally the first chapter of the tract on the divine missions in the Halesian *Summa* ("Utrum sit ponere missionem in divinis")[4]— the only notable difference being the fourth objection of the *Sentences* (from Dionysius) and its answer, an addition St. Thomas makes to the three he takes from the Franciscan *Summa*. A similar dependence is observed in the following article ("Utrum missio significat notionem"),† where St. Thomas' source for objections 2 and 4 and their responses, as well as for the solution of the question, is the third chapter of the *Summa Alexandri*

* Cf. Table I, pp. 362-371.

†*Scriptum*		*Summa Alexandri*
Obj. 1	=	p. 705, Contra, a.
Obj. 2	=	p. 700, Contra, 1.
Obj. 3	=	No parallel
Obj. 4	=	p. 700, Contra, 2.
Solution	=	p. 700, Sol. and ad 1
Ad 1	=	p. 706, a.
Ad 2	=	p. 701, ad 1.
Ad 3	=	No parallel
Ad 4	=	p. 702, ad 2.

Where the *Summa*, however, merely relates the two contrary opinions as to what is principally signified by a mission, the divine essence or the Person (p. 702, II), St. Thomas expilictly prefers the first (a position he will change in his own *Summa*).

("Quid significetur per mittere et mitti").[5] Although Thomas' third objection here (again drawn, significantly enough, from Dionysius) finds no parallel, the first objection and its response are found in the fourth chapter of the Franciscan *Summa*.[6]

An even more impressive proof is found in the second article of Question 3 of the same distinction. Here the solution is parallelled by two of Thomas' sources. Not only the *Summa Alexandri*[7] but also St. Albert (I *Sent.*, d. 15, a. 9, sol.) offer the same opinions, the same choice and the same explanation. But St. Thomas is obviously working from the Halesian *Summa* rather than from his master's commentary. The first objection and its answer and the two 'Sed contra' are not found in St. Albert but are identical with those of the *Summa Alexandri*. Moreover, St. Albert mentions the first opinion given as that of Altissiodorensis, while Thomas, like the Franciscan *Summa*, neglects to identify it; and St. Thomas quotes in his solution an *auctoritas* (Augustine, II *De Trin.*, Chap. 5) not used by Albert but cited by the Franciscan *Summa* as one of the affirmative proofs for its solution (p. 709, c).

All of these facts—and many more could be adduced —conclude to the fact it was expedient to prove: that St. Thomas not only knew but actually used the *Summa Alexandri* in composing his tract on the divine missions for his *Sentences*' commentary. The extent of that influence in regard to his theory on the inhabition remains to be determined; its possibility is beyond cavil.

2) The *Commentary on the Book of the Sentences* of St. Albert.

St. Thomas was, of course, no mere copyist of another man's thought: his criterion was truth. So it cannot be surprising that he differs (by addition, by precision, by contradiction) from the Halesian *Summa* on many points, howsoever much he is indebted to the Franciscan compilation. Nor can one be surprised to find that many of these differences find their source in St. Albert's *Commentary*.

Thus the important notion of the divine processions as the cause and reason both of the creation of things (a doctrine of Pseudo-Dionysius) and of the return of things to their final end—a notion which plays a very significant role in St. Thomas' treatment of the divine missions in the *Sentences*[8]—this finds no precedent in the *Summa Alexandri*, but it is explicitly taught by St. Albert.[9] St. Thomas' insistence on the divine missions as involving a new relation would also seem to derive from his mentor,[10] for the Franciscan *Summa* eschews this philosophical notion to describe the new presence simply as 'another way' of being present.[11] Like Albert, too, he solves the objection that certain effects are appropriated to the Father and therefore the Father can be sent by denying that the effects connoted by the missions can be appropriated to Him,[12] where the *Summa Alexandri* is content simply to affirm that the Father cannot be sent because He is not 'ab alio.'

The most conclusive illustration of St. Thomas' use of his patron's work, however, comes on those points where the doctrine of the Franciscan *Summa* is contradicted and the opposite doctrine affirmed in Albert's very words. The most notable instance of this concerns the notion of donation. For both Albert and Thomas, donation does not imply 'dominion' when referred to the divinity; St. Albert explicitly rejects the Halesian *Summa*'s teaching on this[13] to give his own solution,[14] and this solution St. Thomas follows verbally.[15] In the very same article, moreover, although both the *Summa Alexandri*[16] and Albert[17] list and reject the same opinions, the explanation which is adopted by St. Thomas[18] for the opinion chosen by both is precisely that of St. Albert—and this despite the fact that Thomas' final judgment on the propriety of the expressions 'mitti a se' and 'procedere a se'[19] is more closely connected with the Franciscan *Summa*[20] than with Albert's exposition of the same judgment.[21]

No less evidently than in the case of the *Summa Alexandri*, then, St. Thomas must have had the *Commentary* of his master and patron, St. Albert the Great, before him while writing the *Scriptum super Sententiis*.

3) The *Commentarius in IV Libros Sententiarum* of St. Bonaventure.

Although a quick glance at Table I will assure the reader that St. Bonaventure exercises far less influence on St. Thomas than the two earlier works, and any similarities might thereby be better explained on the grounds of a common source (in this case the *Summa Theologica* of the Franciscans or, certainly in some specific instances, St. Albert's work), there is yet indication that St. Thomas consulted the work of his Franciscan colleague. This occurs chiefly respecting the first article of the tract on the missions, "Ultrum aliqua processio Spiritus sancti sit temporalis." For this article, St. Thomas seems to take every one of his five objections from St. Bonaventure (I *Sent.*, d. 14, a. 1, q. 1), and while the answers to objections 2 and 3 (St. Bonaventure, ad 3 and 4) are only remotely similar, those to objections 1 and 5 (St. Bonaventure, ad 1-2 and 6) have close affinity. Moreover, the notion contained in the solution that the Holy Spirit proceeds toward two objects, one eternal and the other temporal, is an obvious parallel of Bonaventure's solution.

This article alone, without textual duplication in the *Summa Alexandri* or in St. Albert's *Commentary*, appears to argue for Thomas' use of the work of his Franciscan colleague. Yet since there is no other definite trace of Bonaventure's influence in all the rest of the tract (on some points of which one might expect that Thomas would prefer Bonaventure's statement of the case to that of the Halesian *Summa*), it is possible that both are working from a common source unknown to us, or that only this much of Bonaventure's work was available to Thomas. However this be, it may be safely stated that his influence on the *Scriptum super Sententiis* is slight, if present at all.

ARTICLE 2

Textual Determination of the Influence of These Works on St. Thomas' Theory of the Divine Indwelling

Being certain that these works (St. Bonaventure excepted) were known by St. Thomas and were utilized by him for his treatise on the divine missions in his *Scriptum super Sententiis*, the crucial question may now be posed: what was their respective contribution or influence on his doctrine of the inhabitation? The work of the Franciscan compilers and that of St. Albert are of deep interest, for both obviously exercised considerable influence on this tract and they teach theories of the triune presence antipodally different, however much some of the individual elements of these theories may be reconcilable and even complementary. Which has St. Thomas followed? Or is it either?

When two antipathetic notions are present in the works of authors definitively influential on the labors of a third, there are a certain limited number of possibilities open to that third writer, presuming that, in some way, he treats a subject common to them all. He may equably and equally present the opinions of both his predecessors, leaving the reader to choose between them. He may ignore both of the solutions to proffer an original solution of his own, or one derived from another source. Or he may choose one of the two opinions.

In this last case, his choice may take significantly diverse forms. At its most definitive, it will involve the explicit rejection of one opinion and the deliberate preference of its opposed number. Less definitively, it will consist in an avowed choice of one of the two: 'this seems the truer.' Still further removed from intellectual conviction will be a preference expressed either by way of default (the failure to include a known theory when conditions favorable to its utterance are present) or by way of emphasis (the development of one proposal at the expense of the other).

It is the contention of this collation of texts that, although St. Thomas may seem to express in the *Sentences* a theory which would reconcile the apparently contradictory theses of the Franciscan *Summa* and the *Commentary* of St. Albert, he actually prefers the theory of the former to that of the latter. And that, as shall be proved, his preference is as significant and definitive as possible: the rejection of one theory, the whole-hearted acceptance of its opposite. This conclusion will be demonstrated on a purely textual basis.

1. The Rejection of the Theory of the Inhabition Proposed by St. Albert

Since St. Thomas has followed Albert on so many important points in the tract on the divine missions, he may also be expected to reflect his master even so far as details are concerned. This expectation is justified on many occasions, one of which has special bearing on the present matter. On the vital question of whether the Holy Spirit is given to men or only His gifts (I *Scriptum Super Sententiis*, d. 14, q. 2, a. 1: "Utrum Spiritus sanctus temporaliter detur"), St. Thomas takes his first two objections directly from St. Albert (d. 14, a. 13: "Utrum Spiritui sancto convenit mitti, vel dari. . . .")—they are proposed neither by the Halesian *Summa* nor by St. Bonaventure. The first of these depends even verbally on St. Albert:

St. Albert: d. 14, a. 13, obj. 1	St. Thomas: d. 14, q. 2, a. 1, obj. 1
1. Primo; quia quod ubique totum est, nusquam deest: ergo nusquam mittitur: quia quod mittitur, de loco transit in locum: ergo videtur cum **Spiritus** ubique sit, ut dicit Ambrosius, quod nusquam mittatur.	1. Videtur quod ipse Spiritus sanctus non procedat temporaliter vel detur. Illud enim quod secundum se est ubique non videtur usquam secundum se procedere. Sed Spiritus sanctus, cum sit Deus, est ubique. Ergo non potest in quemquam procedere.

The very words used illustrate this dependence, which, in the absence of other sources, the nature of the objection itself would prove. 'Usquam,' an unfamiliar word in the Thomistic vocabulary, is an undoubted echo of the 'nusquam' of St. Albert's statement of the same fundamental and crucial difficulty.

That St. Thomas here depends on Albert is further confirmed by the second objection. Here the phraseology varies considerably, and Thomas quotes Dionysius where St. Albert does not. Yet in the face of their intellectual similarities and of the fact that no other source is found for the Thomistic objection, no one can deny the relation that exists between the two objections:

St. Albert, obj. 2	St. Thomas, obj. 2
2. Item, Si ante missionem ubique est essentialiter, et praesentialiter, et potentialiter, post missionem non videtur aliquid plus in isto esse ad quem mitti dicitur, nisi tantum donum creatum: ergo videtur, quod non ipse detur aliter, quam prius affuit, sed tantum donum ejus.	2. Si dicas, quod potest esse secundum aliquem modum in aliquo secundum quem prius non erat, adhuc habetur propositum; quia, secundum Dionysium, *De div. nom.* c. iii et philosphum, lib. *De causis,* prop. 24, Deus eodem modo se habet ad omnia, quamvis non omnia eodem modo se habeant ad ipsum. Sed iste modus diversus in creaturis est ex diversis perfectionibus quas ex Deo consequuntur. Ergo videtur quod hoc quod Spiritus sanctus dicatur aliter esse in isto quam prius, non sit propter aliud, nisi quia aliquem effectum consequitur iste quem prius non consequebatur: et sic tota datio vel processio refertur ad dona, et non ad ipsum Spiritum sanctum.

But the significant fact rests not in the certain dependence here on St. Albert for the objections; this is but the necessary preliminary for the comparison of the answers to those difficulties. And here St. Thomas definitely and definitively parts company with his master. They both begin their responses in the same way:

St. Albert, ad 1	St. Thomas, ad 1
Ad hoc ergo quod primo objicitur, dicendum quod Spiritus ubique est ut Deus, quia Deus est:	Ad primum igitur dicendum, quod cum dicitur Deus esse ubique, importatur quaedam relatio Dei ad creaturam, quae quidem realiter non est in ipso, sed in creatura.

Albert continues with his explanation, which we immediately recognize as a succint but clear statement of his doctrine on the inhabitation:

> ... sed tamen per hunc effectum quo manifestatur in Sanctis, non ostendit se ubique: et ideo quoad hoc mitti dicitur, quia ipse personaliter et essentialiter adest speciali modo ubi sic operatur: sed in omni loco modis generalibus est, scilicet praesentialiter, potentialiter, et essentialiter.

The Holy Spirit is present (*adest*) as a distinct person (*personaliter*) in a real and substantial presence (*essentialiter*) because of His operation (*quia ... sic operatur*).

St. Thomas rejects this solution. The Holy Spirit, who as God is everywhere by the presence of immensity, is by His temporal procession present in a new way: but not in virtue of His operation, on the basis of some special activity on the part of God; on the contrary, it is because of a difference *on the part of the creature*, who in virtue of the temporal procession of the Holy Spirit is differently assimilated to God. Because of this change in the creature, the Holy Spirit is signified as differently related to the creature, and *not because of His special operation*:

Contingit autem ex parte creaturae istas relationes multipliciter etiam diversificari secundum diversos effectus quibus Deo assimilatur; et inde est quod significatur ut aliter se habens ad creaturam quam prius. Et propter hoc Spiritus sanctus, qui ubique est, secundum relationem aliquam creaturae ad ipsum potest dici de novo esse in aliquod, secundum novam relationem ipsius creaturae ad ipsum.

Considering the identical nature of the objections from a doctrinal point of view, and St. Thomas' dependence on the objection of St. Albert from a textual point of view, no doubt can exist concerning the fact of St. Thomas' rejection of St. Albert's solution. Here St. Thomas finds his master inaccurate, if not in outright error. He *could* have substituted a different explanation which would not have so forthrightly contradicted him. He could have eliminated the objection altogether if he merely doubted his master's opinion. He does neither of these things; instead he proposes a solution which flatly contradicts that of St. Albert. Between an explanation which ultimately rests on the special activity of God and one which ultimately rests on the special change in the creature there is as much difference as between the infinite and the finite. The proposal of the second explanation in the very teeth of the first is as clear a rejection of it as an explicit condemnation would be.

This is not to say that St. Albert is so naive a philosopher or so obtuse a theologian as to teach a theory which predicates change in God. Any change must come in the creature, and by reason of that change the Holy Spirit is present as specially operating. Such is the way he immediately clarifies and amplifies the doctrine of the first response in his answer to the second objection:

> Ad aliud dicendum, quod post missionem specialiter est Spiritus sanctus in Sanctis: sed haec specialitas refertur ad opus: non ad diversum modum Spiritus, et quoad hoc quod Sancti aliter quam prius se habent ad ipsum, et aliter quam res aliae.

But if one compares this doctrine (which would seem to modify the doctrinal dichotomy noted in the diverse responses to the first objection) with St. Thomas' answer to the same second difficulty, the change of doctrine, more subtle than that pointed out in the first response, is equally fundamental. Thomas, too, states what Albert has insisted on: that the special presence of the Holy Spirit comes from the different gifts the creature has received, which place him in a different relation with the divine Person:

> ... quamvis ille modus aliter se habendi, diversificetur ex diversis donis receptis in creatura ...

More strongly than his master, however, he insists on the point that the new relation terminates not at the gifts but at the Holy Spirit Himself:

> ... tamen relatio creaturae non sistit in donis illis, sed ulterius tendit in eum per quem illa dona dantur.

Both agree that the creature is newly related, as a result of the temporal procession or mission, to Him who has caused that relation by infusing His special gifts. But what is the relation involved? Is it to the Person as cause? So St. Albert has said: to the Holy Spirit as specially operating. Hence in his third response he specifies the change on the part of the creature as referred by appropriation to the Third Person:

> ... effectus sanctitatis, inquantum effectus, communiter est Trinitatis: sed in quantum sanctitatis est, non est aequaliter appropriabilis Trinitati,

> sed potius ex ratione sanctitatis ponit convenientiam ad proprium Spiritus sancti, quod est donum vel amor in quo omnia dona donantur.

But St. Thomas rejects such an explanation. That is to say, he offers in this same second response his own explanation of the new relation, an explanation ultimately irreconcilable with that of St. Albert. For the Angelic Doctor, the creature 'has himself in a different way' to the Holy Ghost because by the gifts which flow from that temporal procession he *has* the Holy Ghost, and the Holy Ghost *is had* by him:

> Et ideo possumus significare, nos alio modo habere Spiritum sanctum, et Spiritum sanctum aliter a nobis haberi; et hoc significatur cum dicitur ipsemet in nos procedere vel nobis dari.

One does not have or possess something which operates on one. One cannot be said, in any proper meaning of the word, to *have* a principle of operation extrinsic to one, an efficient or exemplary cause. On the other hand, one does properly possess something which can be used at will, such as the gifts of grace; one does properly possess something one is capable of enjoying. So that when Thomas specifies this new relation as one in which we *have* the Persons and they *are had* by us, he effectively denies the explanation of Their presence as by way of principle and deliberately affirms the contrary, Their presence as object or end. This is a definitive rejection of St. Albert's theory, all the more impressive because it occurs precisely in regard to the very objections he has copied from his master, within solutions which on other points reproduce his master's doctrine and even his words.

Confirmation for this significant discarding of Albert's opinion comes from a further perusal of his own doctrine in this same key article. His fourth objection shows an acquaintance with current scholastic terms and solutions of the question of the indwelling, but a curious misunderstanding of this doctrine:

> 4. Item, Hoc datur proprie, quod habetur ad usum postquam collatum est: Spiritus autem sanctus nunquam habetur ad usum, sed ad fructum a viris sanctis: ergo Spiritus sanctus non datur vel mittitur, sed dona ejus tantum.

The pertinent terms here are, of course, 'use' and 'fruit'; St. Albert's peculiar opacity is the presumption that only things had *for use* are given, and the consequent denial that the Holy Spirit can be given, since He is had *as fruit*. Not only for the Franciscan *Summa*, but for Eudes Rigaud, for the anonymous compiler of Cod. lat. 691, even for William of Auxerre, as was previously determined, the Holy Spirit is given (and therefore sent) *precisely* because He is had as fruit. To offer as an unassailable principle the fact that donation only involves use and in no way enjoyment, is seriously to misunderstand the doctrine concerned. It is evidence of a fatal blind spot.

Yet it is on the basis of just such a false principle that Albert answers the objection. In effect, he concedes that the Third Person cannot be given as fruit, for he attempts to explain His presence in terms of use, as the necessary aid or adjunct to the gifts:

> ... hoc datur, quod habetur ad usum, et quod juvat ad usum: licet autem gratia effecta ad usum habeatur, tamen Spiritus juvat ad usum, quia aliter non valeret gratia aliquid efficere, nisi adesset Spiritus sanctus per seipsum. ...

It is clear that this equivalent denial of the specification worked out by his predecessors is deliberate. The Holy Spirit is not given as fruit but (in a manner) for use. It is equally certain that this denial springs from his own proper theory of this special presence of the Holy Ghost—from the point of view of operation, as principle of the new effect, as 'quod juvat ad usum.' So determinate will be this *idée fixe* that even when he explains the metaphorical expressions describing the Holy Spirit as 'food' and 'drink,' he will disregard the obvious exegesis (from the viewpoint of objects to be enjoyed) in order to offer an unconvincing interpretation from the aspect of principle: the Holy Ghost is food because He strengthens the heart in grace: He is drink because He restrains the ardor of worldly thirst—this last a notion derived from St. Augustine.[22]

But it is not only the Franciscans Albert contradicts by this denial of the presence of the Persons as fruits to be enjoyed, it is the future work of his disciple, the Bachelor of the *Sentences*. For St. Thomas, no less than for the other Parisian Masters and Bachelors, the presence of the Persons as objects of enjoyment is a determining characteristic of the new triune presence. The Persons are had. And why? Because They are given as fruits:

> . . . in processione Spiritus sancti secundum quod hic loquimur, prout scilicet claudit in se dationem Spiritus sancti, non sufficit quod sit nova relatio qualiscumque est, creaturae ad Deum: sed oportet quod referatur in ipsum sicut ad habitum: quia quod datur alicui habetur aliquo modo ab illo. Persona autem divina non potest haberi a nobis nisi vel ad fructum perfectum, et sic habetur per donum gloriae; aut secundum fructum imperfectum, et sic habetur per donum gratiae facientis. . . .*

A divine Person, says St. Thomas, *cannot* be had except by way of fruit. The Holy Spirit, says St. Albert, is had as aiding for use.

* I *Sent.*, d. 14, q. 2, a. 2 ad 2.

Precisely here, however, an almost insuperable difficulty looms up, and it would be intellectually dishonest to minimize it. For immediately following the apparent modification of St. Albert's proper theory just pointed out, a modification which is fundamental and essential, St. Thomas seems to reverse his position in order to accept whole-heartedly the explanation of his master. Thus the last part of his answer to Objection 2 reproduces this efficient-exemplary solution of the problem:

> Persona autem divina non potest haberi a nobis nisi . . . aut secundum fructum imperfectum . . . vel potius sicut id per quod fruibili conjungimur, inquantum ipsae personae divinae quadam sui sigillatione in animabus nostris relinquunt quaedam dona quibus formaliter fruimur, scilicet amore et sapientia; propter quod Spiritus sanctus dicitur esse pignus haereditatis nostrae.

Rather than being possessed as fruits to be enjoyed (perfectly in glory, imperfectly by grace), the divine Persons are possessed as the efficient and exemplary causes of man's union with God, because They imprint Their own seal on the soul, namely the gifts of love and Wisdom by which man is united formally to God. Not as end, in short, but rather as principle (and, in some sense, as means) are the Persons present in the indwelling. And the ultimate explanation of this fact lies in appropriation and efficient-exemplarity, since the gifts constitute a likeness of the Persons who cause them.

Moreover, this elucidation is not an isolated instance of adherence to the doctrine of St. Albert. Several times in the course of his treatment of this mystery St. Thomas explicitly declares that the effects of grace are caused immediately by a divine Person, by the divine Person to whom they correspond by appropriation.[23] And so in the indwelling They are present as in a similitude,[24] They are had by us as "leading and conjoining to the end."[25] Even if the phraseology differs, who can deny that these are the ideas specific of St. Albert's solution to the problem? Who would be so bold or so foolish as to maintain that St. Thomas *rejects* that position to affirm an antithetic one?

But the point at issue, for the moment, is just this: is there such a textual similarity with St. Albert's presentation that the Common Doctor may be said to have fathered the explanation of his son? And to this question an unequivocal *no* must be answered.

St. Thomas *admits* in the passage quoted what St. Albert has equivalently denied, the presence of the Persons as fruits. He *eliminates* the phrases characteristic of his master's description of this new presence, the Persons as 'specially operating,' the gifts containing 'God operating.' He *changes* the specifying expression: the divine Persons are not 'quod juvant ad usum' but 'sicut id per quod fruibili conjungimur.' He *adds* the scriptural and Patristic metaphors, expressing the causality of the Persons 'as a kind of sealing of Themselves,' and of the Holy Ghost as 'the pledge of our inheritance'—and thus he *reduces* St. Albert's formal expression of appropriation as an ultimate solution (answer to the third objection) to the vague and non-formal terms of a figure of speech.

Finally, the Angelic Doctor *insists,* and the strength of this insistence must be significative, on the fact that the indwelling constitutes a 'conjunction with the ultimate end,' with the truly enjoyable, with ultimate perfection, with God: five times in this article alone (twice in the solution and once in each of the first three responses) and so many times in the tract on the divine missions that the idea becomes its theme.[26] And he also *emphasizes* that it is by the gifts, not by the Persons, that we *formally* enjoy the truly enjoyable, Almighty God. *Neither of these last two important points is so much as mentioned by St. Albert.*

This passage owes nothing, on textual grounds, to the Universal Doctor. On the contrary, if it is presumed that St. Thomas consulted his master's work, this answer constitutes a rejection of his master's statement in favor of a formulation of his own, one which, moreover, plays down St. Albert's notions and underlines expressions diametrically opposed to them. This must surely suggest that the apparent identity of doctrine may be less real than first believed; that the description of the Persons present in the inhabitation as efficient and exemplary principles has a somewhat different role in St. Thomas' theory than that which it plays in the solution of his mentor. And even were absolute doctrinal identity finally agreed upon (and further investigation of the point will show that this is far from the case), this similarity will not be derivative on Thomas' part but coincidental.

What thus first appears as destructive of the conclusion that St. Thomas, working with the text of his master at hand, rejects the solution of St. Albert, now serves as a corroboration, from the textual point of view, of that very fact. For what are surface doctrinal similarities differ so seriously and significantly in their manners of presentation that the later work can only be described as a correction of the former. And suspicion grows upon reflection that difference of form here also reflects difference of material—a point to be confirmed in a later doctrinal examination of this same difficulty.

Abstracting for the moment from the as yet undetermined doctrinal significance of the disputed passage, one may safely state, on the basis of the other evidence adduced, that St. Thomas in his tract in the *Scriptum super*

Sententiis completely and definitely discards the answer of St. Albert. For in the very article where he has drawn so freely from his mentor, he denies what St. Albert, *precisely on the grounds of his inhabitation theory,* affirmed; and he affirms exactly what St. Albert had denied *in virtue of his inhabitation theory.* Thus the denial and the affirmation of the Angelic Doctor are an equivalent but clearcut rejection of that solution. And if the contradiction is not explicit and pointed, that will be not only out of reverence and affection for his mentor and friend, but, more importantly, because the fact of God's presence as specially operating is an important truth, one of the elements of a complete delineation of the divine indwelling (as noted in Chapter Six), even when it cannot ultimately explain, nor be the formal reason for, that special presence of the three distinct Persons. As *the* theory it is inadequate, and St. Thomas discards it.

But this rejection of St. Albert is not made in favor of a new and original solution. He chooses, and his choice is as deliberate as his rejection, the theory proposed by the *Summa Theologica* of Alexander of Hales. Textual proof of this choice will be offered in the following section.

2. The Choice of the Theory of the Inhabitation Proposed by the *Summa Alexandri*

1) *First example.*

Both the Franciscan *Summa* and St. Thomas pose the vital question, according to what gifts is the Holy Spirit sent to us?[27] That St. Thomas, in attempting to solve the problem, had the *Summa Alexandri* before him is certain: where only remote parallels are found with St. Albert and St. Bonaventure,[28] both the two 'Sed contra' of St.

Thomas' article and the fourth objection with its response are found in the Halesian *Summa*,* similar even to the words used.

Yet the actual solutions to this pivotal problem seem disparate enough to discountenance any actual influence of the Franciscan work on the doctrine of St. Thomas. The Angelic Doctor uses the principle that the divine processions are the reason and cause of the return of things to their end (a principle inherited from Pseudo-Dionysius by the agency of St. Albert) to conclude that such divine processions can only be causes of *this* type in virtue of the gifts which join us to our ultimate end, the gifts, that is, of grace and glory.[29] The Franciscan *Summa*'s solution, on the other hand, works from the fact that the Persons are given as well as Their gifts, given as fruits, given in a more special way as inhabiting; and this can only take place by reason of the gifts of sanctifying grace.[30]

But the difference is more apparent than real. In the second of the 'Sed contra' St. Thomas has likewise pointed out the fact that the procession of the Holy Spirit means His indwelling in the just soul as in a temple, which can only be by reason of sanctifying grace.[31] In the objections he emphasizes the fact that the gifts of grace unite us to our end; and that for this reason the procession of the Holy Spirit can only be found in virtue of such gifts as these. Even the basis of the analogy which concludes his solution[32] is used (in another context) by the *Summa Alexandri*.[33]

These facts show that St. Thomas is not antipathetic to the Halesian *Summa*'s solution. It is in the parallelism

Scriptum		*Summa Alex.*
Obj. 4	=	p. 732, obj. 2.
Contra	=	p. 731, II, a.
Praeterea	=	p. 733, II, ad 1.
Ad 4	=	p. 733, ad 2.

of the answer to the second objection (an answer which is the explanation of the reasoning given by St. Thomas in the solution) to the teaching of the *Summa Alexandri* that one finds textual proof of St. Thomas' acceptance of that work's theory on the inhabitation. This response is a succint synthesis of various elements distributed in different answers to objections in the Franciscan *Summa,* but all contained in the very same article St. Thomas uses on other points in his own discussion of this question.

The parallelism follows:

I Sent., d. 14, q. 2, a. 2 ad 2	Summa fratris Alexandri
. . . in processione Spiritus secundum quod hic loquimur, prout scilicet claudet in se dationem Spiritus sancti, non sufficit quod sit nova relatio qualiscumque est, creaturae ad Deum: sed oportet quod referatur in ipsum sicut ad habitum: quia quod datur alicui habetur ab illo.	. . . licet timor servilis et alia dona gratis data sint dona Spiritus Sancti, non tamen in illis vel cum illis datur Spiritus Sanctus, similiter n e c Filius ratione cognitionis informis: et hoc est quia per illa dona non efficitur anima templum sive habitaculum Filii vel Spiritus Sancti . . . nec etiam dona illa faciunt Filium v e l Spiritum Sanctum esse nostrum. . . . (p. 733, II, ad 1)*
Persona autem divina non potest haberi a nobis nisi v e l ad fructum perfectum, et sic habetur per donum gloriae; aut se-	[Filius] non dicitur mitti nisi ratione illius doni ratione cuius dicitur inhabitare vel esse in anima sicut donum et fructus

* Cf. p. 730, c, where the words 'to have' and 'to be had' are used: "Verum est etiam quod ille alius modus attribuitur Spiritui Sancto, non ratione sui, sed ratione effectus; non tamen sequitur quin aliud sit illud quod hoc modo haberi dicitur et illud ratione cuius haberi dicitur, etc."

cundum fructum imperfectum, et sic habetur per donum gratiae gratum facientis:	eius, quod non contingit nisi ratione gratiae gratum facientis. (p. 732, ad 2)
vel potius sicut id per quod fruibili conjungimur,	No parallel.
inquantum ipsae personae divinae quadam sui sigillatione in animabus nostris relinquunt quaedam dona quibus formaliter fruimur, scilicet amore et sapientia;	... donum sapientiae et donum intellectus dicuntur dona Spiritus Sancti, non ratione actus proprii, sed communis, sive ratione finis, qui est unire animam Deo. . . . (p. 732-733, ad 3) si datur gratia gratum faciens ad sanctificandam animam v e l gratificandam vel accendendam ad amorem, cum huiusmodi actus sint appropriati Spiritui Sancto et in illis habeat cognosci, dicitur mitti Spiritus Sanctus. Si vero detur gratia ad illuminandam animan vel instruendam vel ad aliquos actus pertinentes ad sapientiam, quae appropriatur Filio, cum in huiusmodi effectibus habeat cognosci Filius, dicitur mitti Filius. . . . (p. 732, ad 3)
propter quod Spiritus sanctus dicitur esse pignus haereditatis nostrae.	No parallel.

The phrases and the words may vary, but that is purely accidental; the essential facts are the same and the expressions are at least equivalent. St. Thomas includes one notion which is not present in the Franciscan *Summa* (nor in St. Albert or St. Bonaventure, for that matter), that of the Persons as sealing or signing; and he adds a description not found in the *Summa Alexandri* (nor in St. Albert or St. Bonaventure, for that matter), the presence of the Holy Ghost as pledge of our inheritance—both of them, however, familiar Patristic expressions. Otherwise the identity, even if not strictly verbal, is certainly evident, the expressions far too similar to be explained on the basis of coincidence.

The essential elements of the answer of St. Thomas are taught many times by the Alexandrian *Summa*—for this *is* the solution it offers to the problem of the inhabitation. The Persons are present as fruits to be enjoyed (pp. 721, Resp. I; 730, c; 732, Sol. I-II, I, ad 2; 733, II, ad 1); sanctifying grace and its gifts are necessary dispositions for the presence of the Persons as 'ours,' as 'fruits' (pp. 729, Resp. I; 729, ad 3; 729, a, b; 730, c; 732, Sol. I-II; 732, I, ad 1, 2 and 3; II, ad 1); Their missions are distinguished by the effects of grace appropriated to them, love and Wisdom (pp. 714, ad 4; 732, ad 3 and 4).

With such an array of texts to choose from, it cannot be thought strange that St. Thomas rephrases these essential facts when he summarizes the doctrine in his response. But the facts are in both works, and the key words are in both works, and the doctrine is the same. So one can only conclude, simply on a textual basis which abstracts from the doctrinal identity, that here, too, St. Thomas depends on the *Summa Alexandri*, that he deliberately and consciously chooses and follows the theory it proposes.

The answer St. Thomas gives to the third objection is likewise derived from the *Summa,* even though here again the words may differ. Both insist that not just any knowledge suffices for a divine mission:

I Sent., d. 14, q. 2, a. 2 ad 3	Summa fratris Alexandri
... non qualiscumque cognitio sufficit ad rationem missionis	... non ratione cuiuscumque effectus sive doni, in q u o cognoscitur Filius vel Spiritus Sanctus.... ... Augustinus non intelligit de cognitione qualicumque.... (p. 714-715, ad 5)

The knowledge must be that of a gift which is appropriated to a person:

sed solum illa quae accipitur ex aliquo dono appropriato personae,	... mitti non dicitur de Filio vel Spiritu Sancto ratione cognitionis actualis, sed ratione alicuius effectus appropriabilis Filio vel Spiritu Sancto, in quo potest cognosci Filius vel Spiritus Sanctus esse ab alio. (p. 714, ad 4)

a gift, morever, which effects conjunction with God:

per quod efficitur in nobis conjunctio ad Deum,	... exigitur quod ille effectus sive illud donum pertinet ad gratiam gratum facientem, quia solum secundum illam inhabitant animam et sunt in ea modo speciali quo Deus dicitur habitare in iustis.... (p. 714, ad 5)[34]

The gift will be one of sanctifying grace, then; and it will be one representing (and therefore capable of being appropriated) the *proper* mode of this particular person:

secundum modum proprium ipsius Personae,	. . . cum dicitur "mitti est cognosci," etc., ibi dicitur cognitio non actus ipsius cognitivae, sed repraesentatio ipsius processionis in effectu, ordinata ad actum cognitivae. . . . (p. 714, ad 2)[35]

In the case of the Holy Spirit, this will be by love:

scilicet, per amorem, quando Spiritus sanctus datur.	si vero [effectus] approprietur personae Spiritus Sancti et per illum effectum, sic ei appropriatum, potest cognosci Spiritus Sanctus esse ab utroque, ut donum amoris, dicitur mitti Spiritus Sanctus. (p. 714, ad 4)

Once again, on the basis of a purely textual comparison, one can see how St. Thomas has collected various elements from the *Summa Alexandri* for his answer, reshaped and rephrased them, and given a more precise synthesis to the Halesian responses. But here also his indebtedness seems evident, even though his genius has transformed the scattered facts of the earlier work into a more succint and coherent whole. One new fact appears: St. Thomas calls the knowledge derived from the temporal procession *quasi-experimentalis*. Otherwise the significant elements are those contained in the Franciscan *Summa*, deliberately chosen, carefully restated, textually parallel.

Confirmation of this dependence on the *Summa Alexandri* comes when one compares Thomas' response with a somewhat similar passage in St. Albert:

> ... in veritate optime determinat Augustinus missionem, quando dicit, quod "mitti est cognosci quod ab alio sit": et bene concedo quod hoc fit per effectum, sed non quemlibet: sed duo exiguntur, scilicet appropriabilitas ad proprium, et quod sit effectus gratiae gratum facientis, cui conjuncta semper sit processio personae, et persona ipsa: oportet enim ipsam personam cum effectu suo praesentem novo modo monstrari, si debeat dici temporaliter procedere....*

The facts of this answer are similar to those of Thomas' on two points: the effect to be known must be one of sanctifying grace; and it must be appropriable to the property of a Person. But aside from the fact that St. Thomas includes many other elements in his response (only some of which can be found in Albert's commentary, and in widely separated parts), the very style of Thomas' answer, the words he employs, the turns of phrase, are obviously more similar to those of the Franciscan *Summa* than to those of Albert.

From this textual similarity between the responses of the *Scriptum super Sententiis* and the Franciscan compilation, several important facts can be gleaned. The first is that Thomas is accustomed to mine the *Summa Alexandri* for its ideas and phrases, which he then fuses into a new and more significant whole for answers to important questions not so directly or pointedly or clearly asked by that work. This is a process which will reach perfection in his own *Summa*, where he will pick and choose from his own works, rework language and doctrine into a more concise,

---

* I *Sent.*, d. 14, a. 3, sol.

thought-packed summary. The process is the same here regarding these second and third answers, only his source is not himself but the Alexandrian *Summa*.

Important, too, is the fact that the present parallelism shows that Thomas' doctrine on *appropriation* in respect to the divine missions is anticipated, textually as well as factually, in the earlier Franciscan work. To be sure, the emphasis of St. Albert on this notion is perhaps more notable. But the *Summa Alexandri* contains, in much the same language, the elements of appropriation utilized by St. Thomas in the *Sentences*. His indebtedness to the Franciscan tract, if one can believe one's eyes, is as great in this respect as it is in regard to the theory of the presence of the Persons as objects to be enjoyed by love and Wisdom. Since that work does not see anything contradictory in the two notions, nor regard them as if they were disparate and complementary elements of a single whole, St. Thomas likewise can avail himself of both without thereby conceding anything to an 'ontological' view of the missions and inhabitation from the aspect of principle, a position he unequivocally rejects, textually as well as doctrinally, in discarding the theory of St. Albert the Great.

From this study of the answers to the second and third objections of this important article, the conclusion that St. Thomas follows, by deliberate choice and intellectual preference, the theory of the inhabitation proffered by the *Summa Theologica* of Alexander of Hales seems definitely certain, so far as textual comparison can give such certainty. This important fact rests on the similarity of phrases and equivalence of statement between Thomas' answer to the second objection and the solution given by the Franciscans to the difficulties proposed by the necessity of determining by what gifts the mission of the Holy Spirit takes place. Rather than a literal copying of the Halesian answer, however, the Angelic Doctor utilizes a selective and transforming procedure. But such a process rather proves than damages the conclusion, since it emphasises the deliberateness of his choice and the explicitness of his preference. The comparison of the third response with the *Summa Alexandri* shows the same method of composition at work and the same adherence to the Franciscan statement of the 'intentional' theory on the inhabitation; it is a convincing confirmation of the previous judgment that the second response represents a deliberate choice of that theory.

2) *Second example.*

One of the major difficulties in showing the doctrinal identity of St. Thomas' two statements of the divine indwelling is offered by the first article of Distinction 15, q. 4. To the question whether the Son is sent invisibly St. Thomas answers that by the reception of the gifts of grace the property of the divine Persons is represented in us, and hence They are there present "as a thing is present in its similitude."[36] Such a solution, on the face of it, offers solid support for the sponsors of an 'ontological' element in the theory of the inhabitation. Their position is further strengthened by St. Thomas' description, in the last part of the solution, of the Persons as present from the viewpoint of principle, as leading and joining us to our end.[37]

For these doctrines and these phrases no parallel can be expected in the *Summa* of Alexander; nor can any be found. On the other hand, there apparently is doctrinal similarity, at least, with the teaching of St. Albert.

The explanation given in the solution is clarified and amplified, as almost always in St. Thomas' method, by the answers to the objections. Thus the first of these explains that the knowledge required for the missions is a habitual knowledge, insofar as the gifts themselves represent as in a similitude the properties of the divine Persons, and hence the Persons *can* be known. The second points out that the property of the Son can serve as exemplary principle of the effect, and hence He can be said to be sent. The likeness of the Son necessary for the mission, the third response clarifies, is that which involves a knowledge from which love naturally flows; and this requires a gift of sanctifying grace.

Nothing here appears to contradict the first impression of St. Thomas' conclusion; quite the contrary, all is deliberately destinated and designed to clarify the meaning of similitude for the missions and strengthen the value of the theory proposed. The Persons are present in a similitude which properly represents them.

But if one turns to the *Summa fratris Alexandri,* the first interpretation of this article is quite rudely shocked out of its smugness. For contrary to what one has a right to anticipate, the same doctrine seems to be taught by that work. And against all expectation, the definitive clarification of St. Thomas' first response is textually parallelled by a series of responses in the Franciscan *Summa* which bear on the same difficulty. And this parallelism is so similar as to elements, words and phrases that the earlier work may be justly cited as the source of Thomas' answer.

In this response St. Thomas first points out that actual knowledge is not required for the notion of a mission; the *Summa Alexandri* says exactly the same:

I Sent., d. 15, q. 4, a. 1 ad 1	Summa Alex., p. 714, a. 2
. . . ad rationem missionis non requiritur quod sit ibi cognitio actualis personae ipsius, sed tantum habitualis,	. . . cum dicitur "mitti est cognosci" etc., ibi dicitur cognitio non actus ipsius cognitivae,

And the reason given by both is the same: because the gift *represents* the Person:

	p. 714, ad 2
inquantum scilicet in dono collato, quod est habitus, repraesentatur proprium divinae personae	sed repraesentatio ipsius processionis in effectu, ordinata ad actum cognitivae: unde illud cognosci est repraesentari in effectu sive per effectum aliquid per quod potest cognosci Filium vel Spiritum Sanctum esse ab alio.

... represents the property of a Person as a habit, as that from which knowledge of the Persons *can* be obtained:

	p. 714, ad 3
... inquantum scilicet in dono collato, quod est habitus,	... etsi nunquam cognosceretur ille effectus vel per illum effectum processio Filii vel Spiritus Sancti, nihilominus p e r illum effectum repraesentatur illud per quod potest cognosci. ...

... inasmuch as the effect represents the *property* of the divine Person:

	p. 714, ad 2
... repraesentatur proprium divinae Personae.	... repraesentatio ipsius processionis in effectu.

... as in a similitude:

	p. 714, ad 3
sicut in similitudine.	... hoc modo dicitur hic cognosci, scilicet signo aliquo spirituali cognoscibiliter repraesentari.

... just as something is said to manifest itself or cause knowledge of itself insofar as it represents itself in its likeness:

	p. 714, ad 2
... et ita dicitur quod mitti est cognosci quod ab alio sit per modum repraesentationis, sicut aliquid dicitur se manifestare vel facere cognitionem de se, inquantum se repraesentat in sui similitudine.	Et est talis modus loquendi, sicut cum dicitur 'in hoc opere cognoscitur sapientia vel bonitas artificis,' id est in hoc opere repraesentatur aliquid per quod potest cognosci sapientia vel bonitas artificis....

Drawing all these elements which he unites in a single whole from the same place in the Franciscan *Summa*, St. Thomas works in his usual manner—select, eliminate, rephrase, summarize, collate. But the parallelism is unmistakable, the textual similarity undeniable, the indebtedness of St. Thomas to the *Summa Alexandri* unavoidably evident. Here again he has deliberately chosen and preferred the theory and the expression of the Franciscan compilation.

Chosen, perhaps, you admit; but why preferred? Because St. Albert presents an apparently identical doctrine in a concise and precise manner; and yet it is obviously not Albert's solution which appears in the *Scriptum super Sententiis*, it is the Franciscan answer. Even a superficial reading of Albert's text makes this self-evident:

> Cognitio exigitur ad missionem, ut mihi videtur, sed non omnis, sed triplex, scilicet una quae est ex parte cogniti, scilicet ut sentiam in me donum in quo ut in signo cognoscibilis sit persona missa: *signum* autem voco id quod habet actum gratiae facientis gratum, et appropriabile est Filio vel Spiritui sancto. Secunda est habitualis cognitio.

> Tertia est conjecturalis ex signis, sicut si videam me posse de facili facere quae non habens gratiam vel non potest, vel cum magna difficultate potest: si videam spiritum meum esse liberum a vana spe, et vano amore, et vano gaudio, et caduca tristitia, et timore mundano, et hujusmodi. Et illam triplicem cognitionem puto sufficere secundum habitum ad missionem, et dico non oportere adesse cognitionem secundum actum.*

But, you object, St. Albert includes the fact that this knowledge is only conjectural, a fact not mentioned in the tract on the divine missions either by the Franciscan *Summa* or by St. Bonaventure, yet included by St. Thomas as the last part of this very response:

> Sed tamen me habere actuale donum, in quo persona divina detur, non possum scire certitudinaliter in actu, propter similitudinem actuum naturalium ad actus meritorios, etsi possim ex aliquibus signis conjicere, nisi per revelationem fiat certitudo; et ideo dicit Job: 'Si venerit ad me, non videbo eum; si abierit, non intelligam'; quia certitudinaliter gratia gratum faciens, in qua est adventus divinae personae, cognosci non potest; quamvis ipsum donum perceptum sit in se sufficienter ductivum in cognitionem advenientis personae.†

Does this not argue for St. Albert's influence on this particular answer of St. Thomas?

The answer is no. There is not a single textual parallel between the two explanations; quite the reverse, the textual differences are considerable. The doctrine is a common teaching among the Schoolmen, affirmed as certainly by the Halesian *Summa*[38] and St. Bonaventure[39] as by

---

* St. Albert, I *Sent.*, d. 15, a. 17, sol.

† St. Thomas, I *Sent.*, d. 14, q. 4, a. 1 ad 1.

St. Albert. In consequence of these facts one need admit only that his master's commentary suggests the addition to St. Thomas, or presents to him the occasion of deciding on such an addition. And in this case, the coincidence works against the objector, for it shows that the Angelic Doctor has not only preferred the Franciscan presentation (a certainty on textual grounds so far as the first part of the response is concerned) but rejected the answer and presentation of his master.

A further indication of this preference for the doctrine of the *Summa Alexandri*, specifically on the point in question, is given in the answer to the third objection. Here one can discover no parallel in Albert's *Sentences*, but there is patent similarity with the Franciscan *Summa*'s response to the fifth objection in the same chapter whose second, third and fourth answer Thomas uses for his first response. The first part of the Thomistic answer is strictly original, but the last part finds a fundamental similarity with the Alexandrian fifth response, so that St. Thomas' statement seems a true echo of the earlier work:

I Sent., d. 15, q. 4, a. 1 ad 3	p. 714, ad 5
Quandocumque igitur habetur cognitio ex quo non sequitur amor gratuitus, non habetur similitudo Verbi, sed aliquid illius. Sed solum tunc habetur similitudo V e r b i , quando habetur cognitio talis ex qua procedit amor, qui conjungit ipsi cognito secundum rationem convenientis. Et ideo non habet Filium in se inhabitantem, nisi qui	. . . non ratione cuiuscumque effectus sive doni, in quo cognoscitur Filius vel Spiritus Sanctus, dicitur mitti Filius vel Spiritus Sanctus, sed exigitur quod ille effectus sive illud donum pertineat ad gratiam gratum facientem, quia solum secundum illam inhabitant animam et sunt in ea modo speciali quo Deus dicitur habitare in iustis.

recipit talem cognitionem. Unde constat quod, simpliciter et proprie loquendo, Filius nec datur nec mittitur, nisi in dono gratiae gratum facientis; sed in aliis donis quae pertinent ad cognitionem, participatur aliquid de similitudine Verbi.	... unde ratione fidei informis non dicitur mitti, licet per fidem informem possit aliquo modo cognosci processio Filii vel Spiritus Sancti, quia Augustinus non intelligit de cognitione qualicumque, sed de cognitione coniuncta affectioni amoris, quae, cum est in homine, dicitur Deus inhabitare, et cum de novo est, dicitur mitti.

The necessity for St. Thomas's more profuse explanation, found in the first part of the response which has been omitted, arises from his use of the concept of similitude, the solution he offers in the body of the article. This additional explanation aside, the parallelism of the two answers clearly stands out, even though, as usual, the Angelic Doctor does not simply copy his predecessor's response but refashions it for his own uses. Of the dependence of one on the other there can hardly be doubt.

The example given in this section of St. Thomas' preference for the *Summa Theologica* of Alexander of Hales is very important. It shows that on the exact point which most explicitly appears to inculcate an ontological doctrine of the inhabitation—God present in some way as operating, from the point of view of principle—the Angelic Doctor chooses to use a preceding work in which such a theory is rejected and an opposing and incompatible theory is advanced. And he makes his choice of this work despite the fact that the theory purportedly taught in the article is proposed explicitly, vigorously and intelligently in the work of his master and friend.

These facts should at least give pause to the sponsors of the 'ontological' interpretation of St. Thomas' solution. They certainly must preclude, on all the canons of sound exegesis, the facile and smug assumption of such a theory merely on the superficial basis of the words and expressions employed: which might be a sound *a priori* ground, were this contrary derivation not so unequivocally established. These facts, however, urgently support as they urgently suggest the need of a re-examination and reconsideration of St. Thomas' explanation in this article in the light which the equivalent statements of the Alexandrian *Summa* can furnish. But that is the burden of another time.

3. Conclusions

This textual study of the relations between the theories of the divine indwelling proposed by the *Summa Theologica* of Alexander of Hales and the *Commentarium in Libros Sententiarum* of St. Albert the Great with the early *Scriptum super Sententiis* of St. Thomas shows his absolute and definite rejection of St. Albert's doctrine, a rejection proven not on a doctrinal basis but simply from the examination of the texts. It shows, next, St. Thomas' acceptance of the Franciscan solution, not only on the points certainly proper to that explanation but even on matters which to some seem elements of a contradictory or at least a contrary solution; this, too, was established on the basis of a critical textual comparison.

This being so, and it being equally certain that the overt rejection of one theory and the deliberate selection of its contrary represent the strongest intrinsic proof of the determinate influence of a particular doctrine and work, the following conclusion, which can be regarded as proven and as certain, even without recourse to doctrinal considerations, can be unhesitatingly offered: <u>the theory of the *Scriptum super Sententiis* on the divine indwelling is identical with the theory of the *Summa Theologica* of Alexander of Hales.</u>

Now is not the time to develop the consequences such a fact implies nor to solve the difficulties it deliberately ignores and others it inevitably presents. But even to the casual reader its significance will be apparent.

ARTICLE 3

Textual-doctrinal Comparisons

In this section the tract on the indwelling of the Trinity in St. Thomas' *Sentences* will be studied from a slightly different aspect than has heretofore been the case, one neither strictly textual nor formally and exclusively doctrinal. What is meant by this type of comparison is that the various doctrinal elements comprising the theory of the earlier work will be examined comparatively. As a result, they will be found to be parallelled in the *Summa Alexandri*, a parallelism which extends to a textual similarity, even if not to complete identity of words and phrases, such as would be required for a comparison of an exclusively textual type. The combination of these two parallelisms, however, leads to the same degree of certainty enjoyed by a more rigorous method which would be strictly doctrinal or strictly textual.

This textual-doctrinal comparison concerning the theory of the inhabitation as taught by Thomas' *Sentences* and the Franciscan *Summa* (chiefly, but not exclusively) will be summarized in the examples to follow, which are taken as illustrative of the principal points on the subject taught by the two works. But first it is necessary to see the general facts concerning the divine missions taught by both authors. These are the common store of the Schoolmen, of course, constituting their scientific analysis of the theology of the mystery which has been revealed by Scripture and proclaimed by Tradition.

1. The Divine Missions: A Scholastic Analysis

Since God cannot change, nor the processions and relations of the Persons escape the exigencies of the exhaustive fecundity which restricts their real differences to their intratrinitarian operativity, the new and different reality evoked by the notion of mission can implicate the divinity only when, God remaining Himself immutable, the notion connotes some created effect or some new and different created effect. Hence this tract will be entitled in the Halesian *Summa,* "De notionibus connotantibus effectum in creaturae," and the fact announced will be numberlessly insisted on.[40] St. Thomas also will recognize the fact as the basis of any theological investigation of the mystery.[41]

What does this mean, a divine personal procession or relation connoting an effect? For St. Thomas, the philosophical notion of a new relation of the Godhead to the creature and of the creature to the Persons, necessarily only a relation of reason on the part of God but a real relation on the part of the creature.[42] For the *Summa Alexandri*, speaking less metaphysically, a new way of God's being present in the works He has made.[43] St. Thomas does not reject this manner of expressing the new fact presented by the mystery, whatever his philosophical predilections;[44] in truth, they are but two aspects of the same reality, one considered more from the aspect of Creator, the other viewing the reality rather from the change in the creature. Ultimately, then, they say the same thing, and the Angelic Doctor does not hesitate to identify them:

> . . . missio, quia ponit missum esse in aliquo eo modo quo prius non erat et sic fieri in illo secundum illum modum, importat quamdam factionem, sed rationis tantum, quae determinatur ad relationem rationis, et non rei, sicut dicitur Deus factus est refugium. Sensus ergo est: "Spiritus sanctus est missus," id est, factus est ens ab alio existens in creatura per gratiam. Unde oportet ad hoc ut dicatur missus, quod et sit ab alio, et fiat in aliquo secundum novam habitudinem.*

For him, as for his Franciscan predecessors, the presence of the Persons in the creature which the divine missions imply is not an utterly new presence, but instead a new manner, a new realization of this presence in a different way.[45] In the classic scholastic phrase,† the presence of the Persons which here is signified 'presupposes' Their presence as the immediate and intimate cause of all being and all modes of being.

What does it mean for the Persons to be present in a new manner, according to a new relation between God and rational creature? In what does this new relation and the new presence consist?

* *Ibid*, d. 15, q. 3, a. 1, sol.
† Cf. *supra*, p. 81.

2. The Divine Missions: The Theory of the Inhabitation

The reason for the divine missions, visible and invisible, was recognized by Augustine,[46] whose obvious interpretation is accepted simply and without comment by the Halesion *Summa*[47] and St. Thomas:[48] to sanctify the rational creature and bring him back to God. From this notion to the pertinent scriptural texts concerning the indwelling is no step at all, and hence both Thomas and the Franciscan compilator presume rather than attempt to prove that the obvious newness implied by the missions is that of the dwelling of the divine Persons in the soul:

I Sent., d. 14, q. 2, a. 2 Praeterea	Summa Alex., p. 733, II, ad 1
Spiritus Sanctus non procedit in aliquem nisi quem inhabitat Deus, sicut in templo suo: quia per Spiritum sanctum efficitur quis templum Dei, I Corinth., vi. Sed in nullo dicitur habitare Deus nisi per gratiam gratum facientem.	... [non datur] Filius ratione cognitionis informis: et hoc est quia per illa dona non efficitur anima templum sive habitaculum Filii....

From the point of view of the creature, this means that the Persons (from the awfulness of this conclusion the Schoolmen do not shrink, for its foundation is the revealed word of God) are 'ours,' that we 'have,' that is *possess* them:

d. 14, q. 2, a. 2, sol. 1 ad 2	p. 733, II, ad 1
... in processione Spiritus secundum quod hic loquimur, prout scilicet	... [non datur Filius ratione cognitionis informis] quia ... nec etiam

claudit in se dationem Spiritus sancti, non sufficit quod sit nova relatio qualiscumque est, creaturae ad Deum: sed oportet quod referatur in ipsum sicut ad habitum: quia quod datur alicui habetur aliquo modo ab illo.	dona illa faciunt Filium vel Spiritum Sanctum esse nostrum....

In what manner can God be ours? In what way does God dwell within us so that we may truly be said to possess the Father and the Son and the Holy Ghost? Is it because They work differently in us by their missions (for surely They do work a different work in us)? Such is apparently the answer of St. Thomas, at least, as it was the answer of St. Albert. The Persons are possessed by man rather 'as that by which we are conjoined to the enjoyable'; They are had by the reception of Their gifts in a new way, 'as leading to, or conjoining with, the end.'[49] To have or possess the divine Persons may thus be defined in terms of Their special operation which characterizes Their indwelling.

But to accept this obvious interpretation of St. Thomas' statements one must ignore both the immediate context of the answers wherein they are contained and the entire bearing of the tract on the indwelling of the Trinity. Negatively, he explicitly excludes the possibility of the presence of the distinct Persons as principles. Such a presence is impossible from the point of view of efficiency, since the gifts by means of which the Persons are present is the result of Their common operation and common power.[50] Thus not only can the Holy Ghost give Himself to others, but because of the created effect which is the reason of His mission and temporal procession and which

He, together with the Father and the Son, has produced in the creature, He may even be said to send Himself and proceed (temporally) from Himself.[51] In the strict sense of the word, then, there is no such thing as a special operation on the part of God or one of the Persons: "by one and the same operation God acts on all things"—even though there may be a purely rational distinction, insofar as the operation proceeds from the exemplar of diverse attributes or diverse ideas.[52] Hence although the effects of grace may be described as coming immediately from a divine Person,[53] there can be no *real* distinction among Them based upon Their power or Their activity, and the only distinction at all will be a distinction of reason based on exemplarity: the effects of grace proceed in us immediately from God,[54] not from one or other Person as They are really distinct among Themselves.

Not only is efficiency or 'special operation' eliminated as an explanation; appropriation (and its correlative, exemplary causality) cannot explain the real presence of really distinct Persons either. For the gifts of grace, which do reflect the distinct properties of a Person inasmuch as they image divine attributes attributed to one or other Person, are by no means exclusively *appropriable* to one Person rather than another, but only so more or less.[55] Thus the grace of experimental knowledge appropriated to the Son can likewise represent the Holy Ghost,[56] as, in fact, every gift of grace.[57] And appropriation can in no wise explain the presence of the Father, since the notion of power which is appropriated to Him pertains to creation rather than to sanctification.[58] So intellectually unstable and indistinct a principle cannot account in any formal manner for the distinct reality to be explained.

Thus St. Thomas, like the *Summa Alexandri*,[59] teaches that it is the Godhead as such, the Persons as indistinct, which causes all things, all differences outside of Themselves. They are ours as distinct Persons, and we may have Them, only insofar as now, by Their missions, They are objects we possess, fruits to be enjoyed:

d. 14, q. 2, a. 2 ad 2	p. 732, Sol. I-II
Persona autem divina non potest haberi a nobis nisi vel ad fructum perfectum, et sic habetur per donum gloriae; aut secundum fructum imperfectum, et sic habetur per donum gratiae gratum facientis....	... solum dicitur missio ratione ipsorum donorum ratione quorum dicuntur inhabitare animam et esse ibi secundum alium modum quam prius, ut in missione eorum non solum dona eorum sint nostra, sed etiam ipsi: quod est solum per gratiam gratum facientem, secundum quam ipsi sunt in anima in ratione fructus.

Such a determination of what it means for the divine Persons to dwell in us by no means ultimately solves the question. But considering the denial just pointed out, it narrows the possibilities down. For if They are present in a new way identified as Their inhabitation and that newness is characterised and specified as a presence after the manner of a fruit to be enjoyed by the rational creature, then Their presence as specially operating on or in the creature (however true and necessary that may be) is not the central fact of the mystery nor the new reality to be explained. The relation involved is not that of the creature to the principle, as it is in the case of the presence of immensity; rather it is of the creature to his end.

This fact, implicit only in the *Summa Alexandri* where the notion of relation has no functional role, is variously insisted on by St. Thomas. It appears as the necessary and essential postulate of the two key articles dealing most specifically with the inhabitation, "Whether the temporal procession of the Holy Spirit is attended according to all gifts" (d. 14, q. 2, sol. and ad 1 and 2) and "Whether the Son is sent invisibly into the soul" (d. 15, q. 4, a. 1, sol.). Temporal procession and divine mission, St. Thomas maintains, are essentially concerned with the return of man to his end, with the bringing back of the rational creature to God. As a result, the Father cannot be sent (even aside from the fact that He is not 'ab alio'), because the attribute of power appropriated to the Father pertains to the going forth of creatures from their principle, not to their return to their end; hence a created similitude representing the attribute of power cannot represent the Father as sent.[60]

If it is under the aspect of end that the missions must be considered, then the specific note of the indwelling of the Persons must appear under that aspect also: as our end, in some manner already possessed by us; not as principle, in some manner acting differently on us. The conclusion seems fair and logical, but St. Albert, as a matter of fact, who readily admits the premise,[61] draws quite the opposite conclusion:

> ... illa [dona naturalia] data sunt et dicuntur: et non secundum quod donatio quaeritur hic, scilicet in qua et cum qua donum primum sit per praesentiam effectus alicujus operantis ad reductionem naturae rationalis aberrantis ad sanctificationem.*

But St. Thomas' viewpoint differs essentially from this of St. Albert. The fact is indicated in the very notion which the Angelic Doctor takes from his master and uses as a principle of solution of the mystery, the idea that the

* I *Sent.*, d. 14, a. 4 ad obj.

divine processions are the cause and *ratio* of the effects of grace as they are of the effects of nature. Comparing the parallel passages, the difference, if subtle, is nevertheless significant:

St. Thomas: I Sent., d. 14, q. 2, a. 2, sol.	St. Albert: I Sent., d. 14, a. 1 ad 3
Sicut igitur dictum est, quod processio personarum est ratio productionis a primo principio, ita etiam est eadem processio ratio redeundi in finem, quia per Filium et Spiritum sanctum sicut et conditi sumus ita etiam et fini ultimo conjungimur. . . . Secundum hoc ergo processio divinarum personarum in creaturas potest considerari dupliciter. Aut inquantum est ratio exeundi a principio; et sic talis processio attenditur secundum dona naturalia, in quibus subsistimus, sicut dicitur a Dinyosio. . . . Sed de tali processione non loquimur hic. Potest etiam attendi inquantum est ratio redeundi in finem, et est secundum illa dona tantum quae proxime conjungunt nos fini ultimo, scilicet Deo, quae sunt gratia gratum faciens et gloria. . . .	. . . duplex est processio bonitatis divinae in entia: quaedam enim est boni, secundum quod bonum est diffusivum sui et esse per actum creationis, secundum quem modum vocat ea quae non sunt tamquam ea quae sunt: et sic procedit in omnia bonum . . . et huic processioni non est conjuncta processio Spiritus sancti ut in qua manifestetur. Sed est iterum processio boni in effectibus gratiae gratum facientis rationalem naturam, sicut est charitas, et hujusmodi: et quia talia manifestant amorem gratuitum ad nos, ideo in his manifestatur collatio doni primi: et hoc est Spiritus sanctus: ergo in his manifestatur processio Spiritus sancti.

St. Thomas deliberately stresses the aspect of end; but this is, at best, only implicit in St. Albert, insofar as he concentrates on the fact of sanctification. It is *possible* that the two notions are equivalent: to sanctify the creature, to confer on him the gifts of grace, is to bring the creature to his end. Albert's omission of the aspect emphasized by Thomas *may*, in consequence, be indeliberate and without significance. On the other hand, St. Thomas' emphasis *may* have no relevance to that omission.

These possibilities are eliminated, however, if we consider their respective doctrines on this point. And in that light, this small and subtle difference acquires a significance out of proportion to its apparent value, for it epitomizes and signifies the essential and contradictory diversity of their two points of view. St. Thomas explicitly teaches what has previously been regarded as the legitimate conclusion of this preoccupation of the missions with the return of the creature to its end, the conclusion—denied by Albert's contradictory affirmation of the presence of the Persons as operating, as principle—that the new existence in the creature to whom the divine Persons are sent is as end:

> . . . missio pertinet ad reditum creaturae in finem; et ideo non potest esse missio, nisi secundum illa quae possunt dicere relationem in finem. Sed generatio Filii, inquantum Filius est, dicitur tantum secundum exitum a principio, et ideo secundum rationem illam non pertinet ad missionem, set magis ad creationem, secundum quod res educuntur in esse, prout dicitur, quod per Filium omnia facta sunt. Sed ratio verbi et amoris possunt se habent ad utrumque; et ideo ratio verbi et amoris pertinet ad creationem et ad missionem.*

* I *Sent.*, d. 15, q. 5, sol. 1 ad 3.

There *cannot* be a mission, St. Thomas insists, except according to those things which can say a relation to the end; but St. Albert has said, in the text just quoted, that the mission is concerned with a difference of cause, inasmuch as God now causes in man the gifts of grace, which manifest His gratuitous love.

For both the *Summa Alexandri* and St. Thomas' *Sentences* the divine indwelling, result of the divine missions, has been defined and specified in a definitive manner. The Persons are present as had or possessed, as fruits to be enjoyed, as man's end or term, in this life somehow even his. But both must now face a crucial question: what is the formal reason of the inhabitation? What explains, *formally*, the presence of the Persons in the way they have specified?

As their previous determination was doctrinally identical while being verbally but similar (and sometimes diverse), so their answers to this question are theologically twin, despite a difference of presentation. The formal reason of the divine indwelling is the gifts of sanctifying grace, explained by the Franciscan *Summa* as the dispositions necessary to possess the Persons as fruits, and by St. Thomas as that by which we are conjoined to God as our end:

I Sent., d. 14, q. 2, a. 2 ad 2	Summa Alex., p. 729, Resp. I
Persona autem divina non potest haberi a nobis nisi vel ad fructum perfectum, et sic habetur per donum gloriae; aut secundum fructum imperfectum, et sic habetur per donum gratiae gratum	. . . in missione Spiritus Sancti non solum datur Spiritus Sanctus nec solum dona eius, sed etiam utrumque: unde datur Spiritus Sanctus in se et in donis suis. Et ratio huius est: quia Spiritus

facientis . . . quibus formaliter fruimur. . . .

Sanctus est in iustis in ratione fructus, quia eo fruuntur iusti; dona autem Spiritus Sancti in iustis sunt, non sicut fructus, sed sicut dispositiones mentis vel liberii arbitrii ad fruendum: anima enim de se non habet virtutem fruendi bono increato, sed per gratiam et virtutes.

By sanctifying grace and its gifts, St. Thomas repeats over and over,[62] we are conjoined with God, with the divine Persons. With God as principle, as specially operating? Such is not the ordinary meaning of the word. We usually speak of 'conjoin' as uniting something to an object or an end; we do not speak of being 'conjoined' to an efficient cause, nor yet of something intrinsic in us effecting such a union with a principle, since the disposition results from the cause and does not precede it (at least according to the order of nature).

But St. Thomas eliminates the need of such a philosophical analysis of the phrase, for he states precisely that we are conjoined to God by grace *as to our end*:

> Sicut igitur dictum est, quod processio personarum est ratio productionis creaturarum a primo principio, ita etiam est eadem processio ratio redeundi in finem, quia per Filium et Spiritum sanctum, sicut et conditi sumus, ita etiam et fini ultimo conjungimur. . . . Potest etiam attendi [processio] inquantum est ratio redeundi in finem, et est secundum illa dona tantum quae proxime conjungunt nos fini ultimo, scilicet Deo. . . .*

* *Ibid.*, d. 14, q. 2, a. 2, sol. Cf. ad 1 and ad 2.

By sanctifying grace and its gifts, the *Summa* of Alexander of Hales repeats over and over,[63] we are properly disposed for the inhabitation of the divine Persons. For Them to dwell in us as principles, as specially operating? Obviously not: for Them to dwell in us as fruits to be enjoyed:

> ... Spiritus Sanctus in missione alio modo est in creatura quam prius, quia prius habebatur in quantum Spiritus, sed non in quantum Sanctus nec per modum fructus. Verum est etiam quod ille alius modus attribuitur Spiritui Sancto, non ratione sui, sed ratione effectus sive doni; non tamen sequitur quin aliud sit illud quod hoc modo haberi dicitur et illud ratione cuius haberi dicitur. Non enim sequitur si gratia sit illud ratione cuius inhabitat Spiritus Sanctus vel hoc modo est in anima tamquam medium ex parte animae, disponens ipsam ad fruendum ipso, quin aliud sit gratia existens in anima et Spiritus Sanctus existens in ipsa vel quod in se ipso non habeatur ab anima.*

Both St. Thomas and the *Summa Alexandri*, this verbal similarity and doctrinal identity being recognized, will naturally teach the same doctrine on the relations between created and uncreated grace: that the Persons, in the order of nature, precede the gifts from the point of view of agent and final cause, but follow them from the aspect of the subject and the material cause.[64] And both state, unequivocally and beyond argument, that it is *by reason of* the gifts that the divine Persons dwell in us:

I Sent., d. 15, q. 2 ad 4	**Summa Alex., p. 732, ad 2**
... adventus vel inhabitatio convenit toti Trinitati: quae non **dicuntur nisi ratione effectus** con-	... licet illuminatio possit esse ex gratia gratis data sine gratum faciente, nunquam tamen ratione

---

* P. 732, c. Cf. pp. 732, sol. I-II and ad 2; 733, II, ad 1.

jungentis ipsi Trinitati, quamvis ille effectus ratione appropriationis possit ducere magis in unam personam quam in aliam.

illius illuminationis dicetur Filius mitti vel dari, quia non dicitur mitti nisi ratione illius doni ratione cuius dicitur inhabitare vel esse in anima sicut donum et fructus eius, quod non contingit nisi ratione gratiae gratum facientis.

Sanctifying grace and its gifts explain the special presence of the Trinity which results from the missions and donation of the divine Persons. For both the *Sentences* of Thomas and the *Summa Theologica* of Alexander of Hales herein lies the formal reason of the divine indwelling.

To this point the two works keep doctrinal and textual company. But when it comes to the further specification necessary to account fully on a theological basis for the mystery of the indwelling, they come to a parting of the ways, and their adieus are final, definitive, forever. The Franciscan *Summa*, as shown in Chapter Four, will situate the proximate formal reason in the supernatural habit of Charity. This is not expressly stated in the tract on the missions, but it is an inevitable consequence of the general teaching of that work.

For St. Thomas, as Chapter Six has shown, the final explanation of the inhabitation lies in the quasi-experimental knowledge of the divine Persons, a supernatural contuition or intuition which presupposes supernatural Charity and from which supernatural love inevitably flows. It is in the gift of Wisdom, then, which gives man the capacity for such knowledge, that the formal reason of the divine indwelling is ultimately and definitely placed by St. Thomas. And in this solution is found the perfect theological flowering of the Augustinian insight: *mitti est cognosci.*

3. Conclusion

The study of the Franciscan *Summa* and St. Thomas' early work under the peculiar aspect of this section shows again the identity of the two respecting the theory of the inhabitation. It has served as a confirmation, from a more textual point of view, of the doctrinal similarity observable from the analysis of the two theories in Chapters Four and Six, which has seemed obvious enough to make explicit comparison redundant. It also serves as a confirmation, from a more doctrinal point of view, of the fact of St. Thomas' rejection of St. Albert's theory and his choice of the Halesian *Summa's* theory, facts previously established largely on a textual basis in this chapter.

Again, then, the former conclusion may be affirmed; and were it possible to state it more forcefully, it should be done. <u>It is an indisputably proven fact that the theory of the divine indwelling of St. Thomas' *Scriptum super Sententiis* and that of the *Summa Theologica* of Alexander of Hales are identical up to the point of the final particularization of the formal reason for this new divine presence.</u> Minor and unessential differences between the two statements of this theory need not detain one; the difficulties it raises in regard to St. Thomas' statement of it are left to the last chapter to explain.

NOTES

[1] Cf. A. Walz, "Ecrits de Saint Thomas," *Dict. théol. cath.*, XV, 1, coll. 639-640.

[2] Cf. pp. 362-371.

[3] Cf. P. Minges, "Abhangigkeitsverhältnis zwischen der Summe Alexanders von Hales und dem hl. Thomas von Aquin," *Franziskanische Studien*, 3 (1916), pp. 60-62.

[4] N. 495, ed. cit., I, pp. 697-698. All subsequent citations of the *Summa Alex.* are from this edition and this volume.

[5] N. 497, pp. 700-702.

[6] P. 705, Contra, a (objection) and p. 706, a (response).

[7] N. 501, pp. 709-710.

[8] Cf. I *Sent.*, d. 14, q. 1, a. 1, sol.; q. 2, a. 2; d. 15, q. 4, a. 1.

[9] I *Sent.*, d. 14, a. 1 ad 3. The passage is quoted *infra*, p. 278. There is little doubt that St. Thomas' respect and love for the Pseudo-Areopagite was a direct inheritance from his master, whose great commentary on the *De Divinis Nominibus* he may have transcribed ('reported'). Cf. L. H. Petiot, *San Thommaso d'Aquino* (Italian trans.; Torino, 1924), pp. 29-30. St. Thomas uses four objections from the works of Dionysius in Distinctions 14 and 15 which are without parallel in the works of his precedessors: he also quotes him twice in responses.

[10] Cf., e.g., Albert the Great, I *Sent.*, d. 14, a. 7, sol.: ". . . in veritate aeterno substantialiter et accidentaliter nihil addi potest: sed tamen aliquid se ad ipsum aliter habere potest, quam ante habuit: et ita dico hoc, quod processio temporalis claudit in se intellectum aeternae processionis, et addit respectum qui causatur ex hoc quod creatura rationalis ex dono Dei aliter se habet ad ipsum in gratiam, quam ante habuit." Cf. also *ibid.*, a. 13 ad 2 and 3.

[11] This is a note as characteristic of the *Summa Alex.*'s doctrine as that of relation is of St. Thomas' doctrine. Cf. pp. 704, ad 3; 722, n. 2; 723, ad 3; 725, b; 728, c; 729, ad 2; 731, d; 734, Con. 1.

[12] St. Thomas, I *Sent.*, d. 15, q. 2 ad 3 equals St. Albert, I *Sent.*, d. 14, a. 13, q. 2 ad obj.

[13] P. 709, II.

[14] St. Albert, *ibid.*, d. 15, a. 2, sol.

[15] St. Thomas, *ibid.*, d. 15, q. 3, a. 1, sol., first part. Similarly the first objection and its response will be precisely those of St. Albert (*ibid.*, obj. 5 and ad 5) rather than those of the *Summa Alex.* (p. 708, Contra 3 and p. 709, ad 3).

[16] Pp. 708-709, sol. I.

[17] I *Sent.* d. 15, a. 5, sol.

[18] I *Sent.*, d. 15, q. 3, a. 1, sol., second part ("Sed circa missionem. . . .").

[19] *Loc cit.*, third part ("Ulterius. . . .").

[20] P. 709, II.

[21] *Ibid.*, d. 15, a. 5, sol. ad q. 2.

[22] *Ibid.*, d. 14, a. 14, sol.: ". . . in veritate Spiritus metaphorice potest dici cibus, et potus. Potus dicitur, ut innuit hic Augustinus, in quantum saecularis sitis restringit ardorem. . . . Panis autem dicitur in quantum confortat cor in gratia." Significantly, St. Bonaventure uses this first explanation, derived from St. Augustine (I *Sent.*, d. 14, Dub. V), but does not give the second at all.

[23] Cf. I *Sent.*, d. 15, q. 1, a. 1 ad 4; d. 16, q. 1, a. 4.

[24] *Ibid.*, d. 15, q. 4, a. 1.

[25] *Loc. cit.*

[26] *Ibid.*, d. 14, q. 2, a. 1, sol. and ad 4; q. 3, Praeterea and sol.; d. 15, q. 2 ad 4; q. 4, a. 1 ad 3; q. 4, a. 2 ad 5.

[27] *Summa*, n. 512, pp. 730-733; St. Thomas, *ibid.*, d. 14, q. 2, a. 2.

[28] Cf. Table I, p. 364.

[29] I *Sent.*, d. 14, q. 2, a. 2, sol.: ". . . processio divinarum personarum in creaturas potest considerari dupliciter. Aut inquantum est ratio exeundi a principio; et sic talis processio attenditur secundum dona naturalia, in quibus subsistimus, sicut dicitur a Dionysio, IV *De div. nom.*, cap. IV, col. 694., t. I, divinia sapientia vel bonitas in creaturas procedere. Sed de tali processione non loquimur hic. Potest etiam attendi inquantum est ratio redeundi in finem, et est secundum illa dona tantum quae proxime conjungunt nos fini ultimo, scilicet Deo, quae sunt gratia gratum faciens et gloria, et de ista processione loquimur hic."

³⁰ P. 732, Sol. I-II: ". . . loquendo proprie de missione non dicitur mitti Filius vel Spiritus Sanctus nisi ratione alicuius effectus pertinentis ad gratiam gratum facientem nec dari similiter. Nam in missionibus eorum non solum dantur dona eorum, sed etiam ipsi, et inhabitant animam et sunt ibi specialiori modo quam prius. Unde solum dicitur missio ratione ipsorum donorum ratione quorum dicuntur inhabitare animam et esse ibi secundum alium modum quam prius, ut in missione eorum non solum dona eorum sint nostra, sed etiam ipsi: quod est solum per gratiam gratum facientem, secundum quam ipsi sunt in anima in ratione fructus."

³¹ I *Sent.*, d, 14, q. 2, a. 2, Praeterea: "Spiritus sanctus non procedit in aliquem nisi quem inhabitat Deus, sicut in templo suo: quia per Spiritum sanctum efficitur quis templum Dei, I Corinth., vi. Sed in nullo dicitur habitare Deus nisi per gratiam gratum facientem. Ergo secundum hoc donum tantum temporalis processio Spiritus sancti attenditur."

³² *Loc. cit.*, sol.: "Sicut enim in generatione naturali generatum non conjungitur generanti in similitudine speciei nisi in ultimo generationis, ita etiam in participantibus divinae bonitatis non est immediata conjunctio ad Deum per primos effectus, quibus in natura subsistimus, sed per ultimos quibus fini adhaeremus. . . ."

³³ Cf. p. 712, ad 3: ". . . non est simile de luce et calore corporali et de luce et calore spirituali, quae est gratia. . . . Tertio, propter continuitatem materiae et propter symbolum: nam in habentibus symbolum facilior est transitus; sed in animabus non est continuitas materiae, secundum quam una possit agere in aliam; ideo praedictis rationibus non est simile de infusione gratiae et illuminatione corporali."

This notion of 'symbol' (similitude) is directly drawn from Aristotle (*De generatione et corruptione*, II, Chap. 4; *Opera Omnia S. Thomae*, ed. Leonina, III, p. XXXIV, with the commentary of an unknown author, drawn largely from St. Albert's commentary), where it signifies the necessary physical similarity requisite for direct generation. When von Rudloff elaborately argues on this very passage in St. Thomas (cf. *supra*, p. 30, note 39) to the fact of a merely logical similarity, he does violence to St. Thomas' most obvious meaning by neglecting to distinguish between the logical and ontological orders. Just as there is no logical similarity between generator and generated except on the basis of an ontological (physical) similarity of species, so there is no logical similarity between God-Idea and the creature in grace except on the basis of an ontological assimilation— grace as the root of operations whose proper objects are the divine

Persons, as the divine nature is the root of divine operations whose object is God in Himself. Not only would von Rudloff's theory make of St. Thomas a Platonist of the most rigorously idealistic stripe; inferentially, he would do the same violence to Aristotle, from whom St. Thomas borrows the analogy.

[34] Cf. pp. 732-733, I, ad 3, where this inhabitation and the presence of the Persons as fruits is specified as a union: ". . . si daretur aliquod donum aeque principaliter ad utrumque actum appropriatum Filio et Spiritui Sancto, diceretur mitti sivi dari Filius et Spiritus Sanctus, et ideo donum sapientiae et donum intellectus dicuntur dona Spiritus Sancti, non ratione actus proprii, sed communis, sive ratione finis, qui est unire animam Deo . . . ."

[35] In another place this is more precisely specified as not any effect which makes the procession of the Person known, but such an effect as is, in some way, predicated of the *Person*. Cf. p. 710, ad 2: ". . . [Filium cognosci esse a Patre] est Filium mitti, quia illa cognitio est a Spiritu Sancto, ideo missio Filii est aliquo modo a Spiritu Sancto. Sed hoc non est verum de quocumque effectu in quo cognoscitur processio Filii, sed de tali effectu qui aliquo modo praedicatur de persona Filii Dei, ut est incarnatio . . . ."

[36] I *Sent.*, d. 15, q. 4, a. 1: ". . . quia secundum receptionem horum donorum [amor et sapientia] efficitur in nobis similitudo ad propria personarum; ideo secundum novum modum essendi, prout res est in sua similitudine, dicuntur personae divinae in nobis esse, secundum quod novo modo eis assimilamur, et secundum hoc utraque processio dicitur missio."

[37] *Loc. cit.*: "Ulterius, sicuti praedicta originantur ex propriis personarum, ita etiam effectum suum non consequuntur ut conjungantur fini, nisi virtute divinarum personarum; quia in forma impressa ab aliquo agente est virtus imprimentis. Unde in receptione hujusmodi donorum habentur personae divinae novo modo quasi ductrices in finem vel conjungentes. Et ideo utraque processio dicitur datio, inquantum est ibi novus modus habendi."

[38] Ed. cit., III, pp. 488 ff.

[39] I *Sent.*, d. 17, I, a. 1, q. 3.

[40] Cf. pp. 699, ad 1; 700, sol.; 702, a; 714, ad 3 and 5; 706, a, c, d; etc.

[41] Cf. I *Sent.*, d. 14, a. 1, sol. and ad 3; a. 2, sol. and ad 2 and 3; d. 15, q. 1, a. 2, sol.

[42] *Ibid.*, d. 14, q. 1, a. 1, sol. and ad 2; a. 2, sol. and ad 1 and 3; q. 2, a. 1, sol. 1 and ad 1 and 3; d. 15, q. 1, a. 1, sol.; q. 3, a. 1, sol. and ad 3 and 5; etc.

[43] Pp. 704, ad 3; 722, 2; 723, ad 3; 725, b; 728, c; 729, ad 2; 731, d; etc.

[44] Cf. I *Sent.*, d. 15, q. 1, a. 1, sol. and ad 1; q. 3, a. 1, sol.; q. 4, a. 3, sol. and ad 3.

[45] I *Sent.*, d. 14, q. 2, a. 1, sol. 1 equals p. 725, b. Cf. p. 708, sol.; 725, ad 2; 726, b. This is found implicitly many times in Thomas' *Sentences*, inasmuch as a new *mode* of existence implies a previous presence.

[46] XV *De Trin.*, Chap. 27, n. 48 (PL 42: 1095).

[47] P. 731, II, a.

[48] I *Sent.*, d. 15, q. 4, a. 2, contra; q. 5, q1a. 4, obj. 2.

[49] I *Sent.*, d. 14, q. 2, a. 2 sol. 1 ad 3: ". . .potius sicut id per quod fruibili conjungimur"; *ibid.*, d. 15, q. 4, a. 1: ". . . in receptione hujusmodi donorum habentur personae divinae novo modo quasi ductrices in finem vel conjungentes."

[50] *Ibid.*, q. 3, a. 1: ". . . quia tota Trinitas facit Spiritum sanctum esse in aliquo secundum novam habitudinem, propter donum collatum totius Trinitatis . . . ." Cf. *ibid.*, Expositio Primae Partis Textus; d. 17, q. 1, a. 1; q. 2, a. 2 ad 2; d. 18, q. 1, a. 1 ad 1.

[51] *Ibid.*, q. 3, a. 1 and a. 2.

[52] *Ibid.*, d. 17, q. 2, a. 2 ad 2: ". . . Deus una et eadem operatione agit in omnia quae sunt, quamvis forte illa operatio differat solum secundum rationem, secundum quod exit a ratione diversorum attributorum, vel diversarum idearum."

[53] Cf. *ibid.*, d. 15, q. 1, a. 1 ad 4; d. 16, q. 1, a. 4.

[54] *Ibid.*, d. 14, q. 3: "Et quia per gratiam efficimur ipsi Deo conjuncti, et non mediante aliqua creatura; ideo oportet quod gratia immediate a Deo in nos procedat."

[55] Cf. *ibid.*, d. 15, q. 2 ad 2 and 4.

[56] *Ibid.*, ad 5.

[57] *Ibid.*, ad 6.

[58] *Ibid.*, ad 3.

[59] Cf. pp. 705-707; 700, sol.; and, definitively, p. 720, ad 2: ". . . nec ratione operationis dicitur mitti persona, sed ratione repraesentationis in effectu sibi appropriato."

[60] I *Sent.*, d. 15, q. 2 ad 3.

[61] St. Albert, however, never precisely mentions the term 'end' in connection with the divine missions or inhabitation, even though he readily agrees that they are concerned with, and have as *their* end, the sanctification of the creature. Cf. I *Sent.*, d. 14, a. 1, sol.; a. 2 ad 3; a. 4 ad aliud; a. 13, sol. and q. 2 ad obj.; d. 15, a. 11 ad obj.; a. 16 ad 2.

[62] *Ibid.*, d. 14, q. 2, a. 1, sol. 1 and ad 4; a. 2 ad 3; q. 3, sol.; d. 15, q. 2 ad 4; q. 4, a. 1 ad 3; a. 2 ad 5.

[63] Pp. 728, II, contra; 729, ad 3.

[64] P. 730, sol. II equals I *Sent.*, d. 14, q. 2, a. 1, sol. 2.

CHAPTER EIGHT

A Comparative Study of St. Thomas' Solution in the Summa Theologiae

The tract on the divine missions in that masterpiece of St. Thomas' maturity, the *Summa Theologiae,* is one of innumerable examples, each remarkable, of how this work fulfills the ends he set for himself in writing it. He has eliminated superfluous questions and unnecessary repetitions; he proceeds logically, according to a scientific order; briefly and clearly he presents the profundities explained by Sacred Doctrine in the matter of the mystery of the divine missions.*

This can be fully appreciated, of course, only by comparing St. Thomas' treatment of a particular question in his *Summa* with parallel considerations in his previous works and in the writings of his predecessors. While it is not the primary intention of this study to point up the considerable theological improvements such a comparison reveals, these will yet be illuminated by the necessity of a brief comparative consideration of the relations between

---

* Cf. *Sum. Theol.,* Prologus.

his *Summa* and his *Commentary on the Sentences*, between his *Summa* and the *Summa* of Alexander of Hales and the commentaries of St. Albert and St. Bonaventure. From this study the primary purpose will be to reach conclusions concerning the influence of these previous works on the tract on the divine missions in St. Thomas' *Summa Theologiae*.

ARTICLE 1

The Summa Theologiae and the Scriptum super Sententiis

A casual glance at the two major explicit treatments the Angelic Doctor has given to the question of the divine missions confirms beyond question the *a priori* judgment that the greatest influence on his *Summa* comes from his own earlier works.* Indirectly, of course, since the *Scriptum super Sententiis* shows in varying degrees and in different places the influence of his predecessors, the *Summa Theologiae* will canonize certain of the doctrines and even the presentations of the other Schoolmen. But, in the main, the later treatment is immediately and directly dependent on his own previous consideration of the matter.

There are considerable differences to be expected between the two works because of the difference of literary genre to which each pertains and because of the special aims inspiring the composition of the *Summa*. Such differences are, in fact, present. They may be considered un-

---

* Cf. Table II, pp. 372-373.

der three heads: logical differences; stylistic differences; doctrinal differences.

1. Logical Differences

Since the *Summa* proceeds *secundum ordinem disciplinae* whereas the *Sentences* must follow the text of Peter Lombard, the treatment of the former is much more orderly and logical than that of his earlier writing. There is, for example, no separate consideration of the notion of temporal procession, because this differs only logically from the concept of a divine mission; so the repetitions occasioned by the divisions of the Master of the Sentences are eliminated.* Similarly, the scientific approach guarantees the discarding of superfluous questions and the incorporation of two or several of the earlier points as parts of one article, either within the corpus or as objections and responses. This process of shuffling, elimination, re-arrangement, summarization — its comparison with the schema of the *Sentences* and with those of the other works — is illustrated in Table III and Table IV.†

The net effect of this logical revision of the matter more diffusively covered by the *Sentences* is directly in line with St. Thomas' stated purpose: a simplification, clarification and intensification in which essential issues stand out, superfluities are dismissed and scientific investigation is unhampered, yet without any sacrifice of vital material or necessary comprehension.

* E.g., a. 1 equals both d. 14, q. 1, a. 1 and d. 15, q. 1, a. 1; a. 2 equals both d. 14, q. 1, a. 2 and d. 15, q. 1, a. 3.

† Pp. 374-377. St. Albert's commentary is not included among these outlines because it proceeds strictly as a commentary, without any inner logic of its own, its questions being determined simply by the necessity of explaining the text.

The resultant logic of this more scientific consideration can be represented schematically as follows:

```
                    ⎧ Utrum conveniat (art. 1)   (AN SIT)
In genere: missio   ⎨
      sec. se       ⎩ Utrum aeterna vel temp. (art. 2) (QUID SIT)

                                  ⎧ sec. quid attenditur (art. 3)
                                  ⎪              ⎧ Patris (art. 4)
              ⎧ missio in-        ⎨ cuius sit    ⎨
              ⎪   visibilis       ⎪              ⎩ Filius (art. 5)
In specie     ⎨                   ⎩ ad quos (art. 6)
              ⎪
              ⎩ missio visibilis Spiritus Sancti (art. 7)
Ex parte mittentis (missio active considerata)   (art. 8)
```

Two points appear from this outline. First, the importance of Article 3, the initial consideration of the difficulties involved in the invisible missions, i.e., the inhabitation. Its place in the schema shows that it serves as a definition of those missions and of the inhabitation, equivalent to the *quid sit* of the invisible missions. Second, the unimportance of Article 8 is indicated, for it is added as a sort of afterthought or corollary; properly its logical location is under the first division. This accents the fact that St. Thomas has already solved the problem raised by the article ("Who can send a divine person?") by the determination of the first two articles that the mission is chiefly a notional concept rather than an essential one. The contrary opinion admitted in this last article is thus seen to be a concession made to the authority of others and not the proper and scientific view of the mystery.

The other articles, of course, indicate what scientific importance is to be attached to the questions raised, and by comparison with the *Sentences* the respective value of the difficulties brought up (and of their solutions) becomes apparent. The advantages of this method over the less concise, more confused procedure necessitated by following another's text are sufficiently evident to go without further comment. So far as the question of the inhabitation is concerned, the two previously mentioned points are the most important differences which are revealed by the diverse logics of the two works.

2. Stylistic Differences

A simple numerical count of words and pages would show how the mature writer has sifted the material of his previous labor for its doctrinal core and expressed these theological essentials in the briefest, most precise manner compatible with the profundities of the mystery to be explained. Compared with the simplicity, conciseness and clarity of the *Summa,* the *Scriptum super Sententiis* seems prolix, indeed, and diffuse, repetitious, imprecise, confused.

But these general qualities of the mature work have little immediate bearing on the question at hand. On other points—which one may designate as at least stylistically different, although these differences may possibly express more important doctrinal divergences—the changes are significant and noteworthy.

In the first article of the tract of the *Summa Theologiae* the divine missions are analyzed in virtue of a comparison with human missions, which imply a relation both to the one sending and to the term to which he is sent. St. Thomas simply *eliminates* the distinctions between the notions of procession, mission and donation which introduced the parallel analysis in the *Sentences* (d. 15, a. 1). He *adds* the notion that there are three ways in which a person can be sent: by command, by counsel or by origin—only the last of these applicable to a divine mission, since it alone does not imply inferiority. When he considers the relation of the one sent to the term, he *changes* his point of view, preferring to describe this not as a new real relation of the creature to God and a new relation of reason of God to the creature (the key words of the *Sentences*), but as a new way of being present in someone.

These differences—the elimination, the addition, the change—are connected and interdependent. It suffices to note them now; their significance and explanation will be later determined.

In the second article the doctrinal identity of the analyses made by both works of the temporal nature of the divine missions is accompanied by a procedural diversity. In the *Summa* St. Thomas sees fit to analyze the notion of the missions in comparison with other names pertaining to the origin of the Persons, a procedure more clearly illuminative of the similarities and differences, and more certainly specifying the characteristic of the mission as connoting a temporal term. Moreover, while showing the difference between mission and donation, he considers them together, in virtue of their common concern with a temporal term; and he defines both from the point of view of the Person involved, as existing in a new way in a creature (mission) or as had by the creature (donation). This he explains, as in the *Sentences*, by reason of a change in the creature (ad 2); the notion of relation, implicit in the comparison given by the response, is not explicitly expressed.

The changes included in Article 3 are considerable. He *eliminates* entirely the notion of the divine processions as the cause and idea of the return of the creature to God.

He *emphasizes* the necessary connection between the divine mission and the divine donation; by implication, at least, this connection is not simply a logical one but a real interdependence. He also *emphasizes* the fact that the mission is a new and special way of being present, presupposing the common presence of immensity. He *changes* the formula describing this presence: 'sicut cognitum in cognoscente et amatum in amante' replaces 'sicut res est in similitudine sua'; and the creature's power to have the Godhead so present is explicitly advanced as the reason for the inhabitation. His *emphasis* on the possession of the Persons by the creature (the brief factual statement here presupposes the longer analysis of donation of Question 38, Article 1) brings out the same fact. And he merely *adds*, without special consideration, the essential fact that this means that the Holy Spirit, not only His gifts, is sent and is given.

These important differences—elimination, change, addition, emphasis—are surely significant. But of what? Merely of a difference of presentation, or of a deeper doctrinal divergence necessitating stylistic changes? This is the problem with which this study began, but it is not now to the point to solve it nor even to account for the divergences. The task of simple comparison is to indicate the similarities and differences of the tract in the *Summa* with the treatments of the other works and, in the case of St. Thomas' *Sentences*, to show where that work is not a direct source of the later presentation. To attempt to explain these facts at this time would carry this analysis beyond its proper scope.

In the fourth article the differences are less noteworthy and more subtle. In the *Sentences* the fact that the notion of giving cannot imply dominion in the divinity is insisted on; here (ad 1), without stressing the point, St. Thomas concedes that if donation be understood as signifying the authority of origin, then the Father cannot be given—a change of emphasis directly attributable to the insistence of the article on the fact that the Father is not 'ab alio' as explaining the fact that He is not sent. From this insistence, which follows his determination of the primary significance of a mission as notional, implying procession, also comes the elimination of the previous explanation—in terms of appropriation—of the Father's inability to be sent. On the other hand, the article gives more prominence to the fact that the Father is actually given and to the specification of this donation as 'for enjoyment' — both the result of the new importance the concept of donation receives in the *Summa*.

Article 5 is most notable for its shift of emphasis. Whereas the corresponding article in the *Sentences* (d. 15, q. 4, a. 1) stresses the notion of similitude in affirming the invisible mission of the Son and only indirectly and implicitly touches the notion of inhabitation, the situation is reversed in the *Summa*. It is because the Son and Holy Spirit can both dwell by grace in the soul and do receive their origin from another that They can both be sent. Appropriation and assimilation appear in the answers to the objections as connected or sequent notions, but not as the fundamental explanation of the invisible missions. Here again the fact that the missions primarily signify a notional concept rather than an essential one plays an important role: it explains why the Father, who, St. Thomas here explicitly affirms, also dwells in the soul by grace, cannot be sent; He is not 'ab alio.'

A double affirmation—the new mode of this indwelling and the renovation of the creature by grace are intimately connected; the divine presence *is* the divine indwelling by means of grace—is the basis for the response of the sixth article. Such a way of stating the matter is a much more direct and simple presentation of the essential and complementary facts of the divine missions than can be found in any comparable place in the *Sentences*. There can be no doubt, however, that the doctrine of this article is the same as that of the earlier work, even though the previous expression of it is more obscure and diffuse.

No significant changes which bear on the question of the divine indwelling occur in Article 7, which deals with the visible mission of the Holy Ghost. Nor does the eighth article offer any stylistic divergence not accountable for by the doctrinal change to be considered.

The noteworthy differences between the *Summa* and the *Sentences*, from the point of view of—at the least—style, are the following:

1) *Total elimination*: the notion of the processions as cause and *ratio* of the return of the creature to God; the formula describing the presence of the Persons as the presence of a thing in its similitude; the explanation on the grounds of appropriation of the fact that the Father cannot be sent.

2) *Partial elimination* (de-emphasis): the missions as a new relation between God and creature; the distinction between mission and donation; the notion of assimilation and appropriation as explanatory of the missions.

3) *Emphasis*: the missions as a new way of being present, presupposing a previous presence; donation implies possession for use and enjoyment; the intimate connection between mission and donation; inhabitation as the effect of the missions; the fact that the Father is given and inhabits.

4) *Change*: substitution of the formula 'sicut cognitum in cognoscente et amatum in amante' for the formula 'sicut res est in similitudine sua.'

3. Doctrinal Differences

The chief of the differences between the tracts of the *Summa* and the *Sentences* which can be called indubitably doctrinal has already been mentioned several times. In the first and second articles of Question 43 of the *Summa*, St. Thomas distinctly teaches that a divine mission implies a procession by way of origin from the sender, this relation then connoting a temporal term. This is a simple reversal of his opinion in the *Sentences*, where the mission is described as principally signifying the divine essence (because of the temporal effect it connotes) and secondarily a divine notion or Person (d. 15, q. 1, a. 2).

The consequences of this view are considerable. It means the practical elimination of the question of the missions *ex parte mittentis*, for if the mission primarily signifies a notion, only one who can be the principle of the personal procession can send a divine Person. Hence the matter of the 'active' missions, which occupies a prominent role in the earlier tract, is simply appended in the *Summa* at the end of all other considerations (Article 8). What there is of truth in the opposite opinion is pointed out, the opinion itself admitted because of the authorities maintaining it, but it is clear that St. Thomas regards it as an improper or less formal manner of speaking and not one to which he himself adheres.

The same doctrine means the outright elimination of the question, "whether a saint can send a divine Person." The question is redundant now, since obviously no creature can be the principle of a divine Person. In the *Sentences*, on the other hand, it was necessary also to point out that the creature could not be a true principle of the effect caused by the divine essence, sanctifying grace (d.

14, q. 3). That task would be superfluous here and is omitted.

Last of all, the insistence on this personal signification of the divine mission as primary brings into clear light the fundamental reason why the Father cannot be sent: because He is without a principle of origin. Here, too, there is no need to consider the effect connoted by the mission; and the possibility of appropriating an effect to the Father is not even raised.

The only other difference clearly and unequivocally doctrinal concerns the question of new missions due to an increase of sanctifying grace. In the *Sentences* St. Thomas mentions and admits that a new mission is possible by simple increase of grace (d. 15, q. 5, a. 1, sol. 2), but he can hardly be said to sponsor such a notion. But in the answer to the second objection of Article 6 of the *Summa* he teaches it as an undeniable fact, even though he adds that this new mission will occur chiefly when there is such a progress in grace as to indicate a new act or a new state of proficiency. The difference here is not fundamental, of course, merely one of emphasis; it would be difficult to see any significant conclusion in the shift of viewpoint.

4. Conclusion

What a comparison of St. Thomas' two treatments of the divine missions shows, then, is the consistent doctrinal dependence of the later work on the earlier one and a group of interesting differences which are certainly stylistic and may be indicative of deeper divergencies on the doctrinal plane. In the sections to follow which compare the *Summa* with the works previously studied in connection with the *Scriptum super Sententiis*, the main object will be to see if these divergencies manifest any parallel with these other works. For on points where St. Thomas' *Summa* and his *Sentences* agree, one may safely assume that the earlier work is his source and the labors of his predecessors influential only as filtered through his previous exposition.

ARTICLE 2

The Summa Theologiae and the Summa Theologica of Alexander of Hales

1. Logic

The most obvious influence which the Franciscan *Summa* may have exercised on St. Thomas' work is logical. With two notable exceptions, the order established by the earlier *Summa* is followed by the later one, as a comparison of their outlines shows.* The exceptions are the question of the active missions, relegated by St. Thomas to the end of the tract as a casual appendix (for reasons sufficiently noted) and the question of the gifts constituting the invisible missions, which St. Thomas places at the beginning of his consideration of the invisible missions as tantamount to their 'quid sit.' Thus he gives the determination of this important point its merited prominence, whereas the *Summa Alexandri* considers the matter at the end of the tract on the invisible missions, the 'quid sit' having been already discussed. Otherwise the general order of the Franciscan compilation has been observed. When one

*Cf. Table III, p. 374 with p. 376.

reflects that this order is not followed by St. Bonaventure but, within the restrictions imposed by the nature of the work, is maintained in St. Thomas' *Sentences,* the logical influence of the earlier *Summa* on St. Thomas' work seems certain.

Both St. Thomas' *Summa* and Alexander's eliminate the separate discussion of the temporal procession which was necessitated by commenting on Peter Lombard's work. But this elimination is an obvious one, inasmuch as there is only a conceptual difference between mission and procession, a fact recognized by the Master of the Sentences himself. On this point there seems no need to speak of the influence of the Halesian *Summa,* even though it is the first to dispose of the superfluous and repetitious consideration.

2. Style

Concerning the stylistic differences of St. Thomas' two works, the example of the earlier *Summa* and its influence —either direct or through the intermediary of St. Bonaventure's commentary—are clearly recognizable. The Franciscan *Summa* prefers to describe the new reality of the missions as a new and other mode of God's presence which presupposes a previous divine presence rather than to explain this newness on the basis of a new relation—as has already been pointed out.* It stresses the presence of the Persons by Their missions and donation as possessed, as fruits to be enjoyed,† a presence which is essentially the divine indwelling. But it is *exactly* on these same points that St. Thomas places the emphasis in the *Summa,* whereas they are not so significantly stressed in the *Sentences.* Especially with regard to the Halesian description of the

---

* Cf. *supra,* p. 272 and Chapter Seven, note 43.
† Cf. *supra,* pp. 111, 273-274.

mode of the divine presence does the stylistic influence seems direct and immediate; for this description, characteristic of St. Thomas' tract in his *Summa,* finds no parallel in any of the other works. Stylistically as well as logically, then, the older *Summa* appears to have been used by St. Thomas in revising his tract on the divine missions.

ARTICLE 3

The Summa Theologiae and St. Albert's Commentarium

The relation of St. Albert's commentary to the *Summa Theologiae* of his protégé is less than negative. Not only are there no traces of his influence, logical, stylistic or doctrinal; what is more, the very things eliminated from the former tract by the *Summa,* or most radically altered in emphasis, are precisely those elements for which St. Thomas was most deeply and directly indebted in his earlier work to his master's commentary. The notion of the divine procession as cause completely disappears; the explanation of the new presence as a new relation yields to the Halesian description; assimilation and appropriation enjoy only a secondary role.

Yet these are the very points of the tract in the *Sentences* that St. Thomas took from St. Albert and incorporated into his own explanation. The new working of this material for his *Summa* significantly rejects or de-emphasizes the Albertinian elements sponsored by the earlier commentary. The fact is inescapable.

ARTICLE 4

The Summa Theologiae and the Commentarius of St. Bonaventure

Although St. Thomas prefers the logical order and completeness of the Franciscan *Summa* to St. Bonaventure's truncated treatment of the same matter, the commentary of his colleague has exercised definite and important influence on his own revision of the tract on the divine missions. This influence is certainly rather one of suggestion than of wholesale incorporation of ideas or style, but it is no less determinate or significant because of that. First of all the evidence of this influence on St. Thomas' tract in the *Summa* will be examined in general before considering it in respect to the special question of the inhabitation.

1. General Influence

The fact that St. Thomas uses Bonaventure's commentary seems clear on several scores, although the nature and extent of that influence is considerably more difficult to determine and assess. In the first article the logical exposition of the notion of the divine missions, for example, would appear to be suggested by the same *manner* of proceeding adopted by St. Bonaventure in his parallel exposition (d. 15, I, a. 1, q. 1). Both consider the various relations of the one sent to the sender and the term, and in virtue of this analysis determine the nature of a divine mission. There is no substantial borrowing of Bonaventure's development—in fact there are considerable doctrinal differences; but the inner logic of St. Thomas' exposition, his method of procedure, is a not distant parallel of the manner of exposition followed by the Franciscan, and has no other precedent.

In the second article, also, there is significant similarity, this with the second question of St. Bonaventure (d. 15, I, a. 1, q. 2). Both insist—the parallelism is verbal here—on the relation of the mission to its temporal term. On doctrinal grounds the similarity is, perhaps, slight and insignificant; its importance, instead, rests on a stylistic similarity, even though St. Thomas brings up the question of the other names referring to divine notions, a point totally omitted by Bonaventure.

The influence of St. Bonaventure is perhaps also present in respect to the important doctrinal change effected in the *Summa Theologiae,* namely, that the mission primarily signifies a divine Person. As a matter of fact, the Franciscan does not embrace this explanation but adheres to the contrary opinion. His reason for doing so, however, is founded simply on authority: "alia positio tum ob reverentiam Sanctorum tum ob reverentiam Magistri videtur magis esse tenenda."* And he declares that the opinion later adopted by St. Thomas appears more reasonable and easier to sustain†—in other words, a more scientific view of the question.

St. Bonaventure, then, yields to the authorities in adopting an opinion which seems less reasonable to him. St. Thomas, on the contrary, adopts the 'more reasonable' view as his own, and merely admits the contrary opinion because of the authorities sponsoring it, showing what it possesses of truth (Article 8). Under the circumstances,

* I *Sent.,* d. 15, I, a. 1, q. 4, resp.

† *Loc. cit.*: "Sed licet haec positio rationabilior videatur et facilior ad sustinendum, tamen. . . ."

St. Bonaventure's influence cannot be considered as determinate; yet it can hardly be doubted that his analysis of the problem must have influenced, in some degree, St. Thomas' decision to change his doctrine on this point.

These examples are sufficient to indicate, it would seem, that St. Bonaventure's *Commentarius in IV Libros Sententiarum* was utilized by St. Thomas when he prepared his tract on the divine missions for his *Summa*. But they likewise show that that influence is rather more subtle than the kind commonly attributed to a true source or font of a work. St. Thomas has not simply incorporated parts of the work of the Seraphic Doctor in his masterpiece (a common practice of the Schoolmen, and clearly the case for much of Thomas' *Sentences*) nor reworked and transformed previous material as suits his purpose and inclination. Rather he finds in the Franciscan certain hints as to procedure, mode of expression, even doctrine, which he develops in his own way and perfects by his own proper genius. In a word, here the influence of St. Bonaventure is *suggestive* rather than determinate. But it is very real.

2. Influence on the Statement of the Theory of the Divine Indwelling

What would most recommend itself to St. Thomas in St. Bonaventure's treatment of the inhabitation is the simplicity and lucidity of his style, which fundamentally expresses the same truth and explanation as that advanced by the *Summa* of Alexander but without the confusions, repetitions, prolixity and superfluities of that work, in language at once more scientific and simpler to understand. This is evident on three important points, concerning which one may classify St. Bonaventure's influence as, respectively, determinate, suggestive and remote.

1) *Determinate influence.*

St. Bonaventure's scientific analysis of the notion of donation and of its correlative, possession, is, from the point of view of style, ease of comprehension and of logical procedure, a considerable improvement over the expression of the same doctrine and its elements by the Franciscan *Summa*. It is undoubtedly the direct source of St. Thomas' own analysis of the concept,* this analysis being obviously presupposed to his brief repetition of the essential elements of donation in Article 3 of the tract on the divine missions.

Comparing the two passages, one cannot but be struck by their parallelism, despite the difference of purpose and the diverse phrases employed:

St. Thomas, Sum. Theol., I, q. 38, a. 1	**St. Bonaventure, I Sent., d. 14, I, a. 2, q. 1**
. . . in nomine *doni* importatur aptitudo ad hoc quod donetur. Quod autem donatur, habet habitudinem et ad id a quo datur et ad id cui datur: non enim daretur ab aliquo nisi esset eius; et ad hoc alicui datur, ut eius sit. Persona autem divina dicitur esse alicuius, vel secundum originem, sicut Filius est Patris; vel inquantum ab aliquo habetur. Habere autem dicimur id quo libere possumus uti vel frui, ut volumus. Et per hunc modum divina Persona non	. . . dare est ad aliquid habendum vel possidendum, habere autem aliquid vel possidere est, cum aliquid est in facultate habentis vel possidentis. Esse autem in facultate habentis vel possidentis est esse praesto ad fruendum vel utendum. Perfecta autem possessio est, cum homo habet illud, quo possit uti et quo possit frui. Sed recte frui non est nisi Deo, et recte uti non contingit nisi per gratiam gratum facientem: ergo perfecta possessio est, in qua Deus ha-

---

* *Sum. Theol.*, I, q. 38, a. 1.

potest haberi nisi a rationali creatura Deo coniuncta. Aliae a u t e m creaturae moveri quidem possunt a divina Persona; non tamen sic quod in potestate earum sit frui divina Persona, et uti effectu eius. Ad quod quandoque pertingit rationalis creatura; ut puta cum sic fit particeps divini Verbi et procedentis Amoris, ut possit libere Deum vere cognoscere et recte amare. Unde sola creatura rationalis potest habere divinam Personam. Sed ad hoc quod sic eam habeat, non potest propria virtute pervenire: unde oportet quod hoc ei desuper detur; hoc enim dari nobis dicitur, quod aliunde habemus.

betur et eius gratia. Sed perfectum donum est ad perfectam possessionem: ergo non est *datum optimum et donum perfectum*, nisi detur Donum increatum, quod est Spiritus sanctus, et donum creatum quod est gratia.

Here there is more than coincidence of doctrine or logical similarity. The difference of presentation (although much of this is accounted for by the difference of purpose, St. Bonaventure seeking to prove that the divine Person is given and not only His gifts, St. Thomas that the name 'gift' properly pertains to the Holy Spirit) may be freely admitted, without the stylistic parallelism becoming thereby less impressive. Equivalent expressions, in fact, insist on the same significant truths. To have something is to be 'in the power' of the possessor, to be 'his'; it is 'to be able to use and enjoy,' 'when we will.' It is 'to enjoy a divine Person' and 'to use His effect.' And hence it is only 'when

His grace is had,' 'is given from above,' that a divine Person 'is given.'

The relation here between Bonaventure's analysis and that of St. Thomas cannot be denied. The importance of this doctrine for the theory of the inhabitation is paramount and evident.

2) *Suggestive influence.*

Commenting on the Augustinian phrase, 'when we seize something by our mind we are not in this world,' St. Bonaventure offers the following objection. What is known and loved, he points out, is either drawn to the one knowing or loving or draws the knower and lover to itself; but when we love God and know Him we do not draw God to ourselves but are drawn to God. Hence we are not in this world but in heaven—which is absurd.*

To this St. Bonaventure responds:

> Et secunda ratio intelligitur, quod amatum trahit, non localiter mutando, sed sibi conformando, quia amans transformatur in amatum, et cognoscens conformatur cognito.†

Is this not an adumbration of the key phrase of St. Thomas' presentation in his *Summa*? St. Bonaventure does not explicitly offer it as an explanatory formula expressive of God's presence in the inhabitation. But two small things, nevertheless, point to the fact that from this passage in St. Bonaventure comes the suggestion for a formula the pertinent value of which St. Thomas was quick to see, perfect and utilize.

* *Ibid.*, d. 15, II, Dub. V: ". . . quod cognoscitur et amatur, aut trahitur ad cognoscentem et amantem aut e converso; sed dum Deum amamus et cognoscimus, non trahimus Deum ad nos sed nos ad Deum. . . ."

† *Loc. cit.* Cf. *ibid.*, d. 14, a. 1, q. 1 ad 5.

In St. Thomas' own treatment in the *Sentences* of this Augustinian phrase (d. 15, q. 5, a. 3), no such manner of explaining the matter as this of St. Bonaventure is given, although the doctrine is substantially identical. On the other hand, in his *Summa*, where a similar expression occurs, no treatment of the matter is offered at all. The reason for this omission would seem to be that the formula 'sicut cognitum, etc.' already perfectly expresses the conformity with God implicit in the phrase of St. Augustine and renders further explication superfluous. Considering these two facts—the omission of the expression in the *Sentences*, on the one hand, and the omission of the doctrine in the *Summa*, on the other—one receives the definite impression that the inspiration for the characteristic and significant Thomistic formula comes from St. Bonaventure's comment on the words of Augustine. For in that comment the same phrase as Thomas' formula serves to explain the notion of conformity.

Knowing that St. Thomas has used the Bonaventuran commentary for his revision, and that the phrase there appearing is admirably adapted to his purpose, there is a strong probability that the suggestion for the Thomistic formula comes from the Franciscan work. The evidence is nebulous, to be sure; the fact impossible to prove; and yet the relationship seems highly probable.

3) *Remote influence.*

On another important point the influence of St. Bonaventure, if more remote and indirect, is even more important. This is the manner in which the Seraphic Doctor, without retreating from the doctrine taught by the Alexandrian *Summa*, has given a far clearer and simpler explanation of the twin notions of inhabitation and manifestation, the last implied by St. Augustine's definition 'mitti est cognosci.' Where the *Summa Alexandri* seems to offer two theories (or two elements of a single theory) to explain the inhabitation, one by the notion of similitude and appropriation (an effect representing the property of a Person), the other by the notion of final causality (the Person as fruit to be enjoyed in virtue of the dispositions of grace), St. Bonaventure permits no such ambiguity. The Persons inhabit because They are possessed as fruits to be enjoyed; and They are possessed as fruits to be enjoyed by reason of the gifts of grace (d. 14, a. 2, q. 1, resp.); to be sent is to be given, and to be given absolutely is to be given not only for use but as fruit, and this is only by the gifts of sanctifying grace (d. 15, II, a. 1, q. 1). Such a forthright explanation of the mystery tolerates no possible confusion nor does it admit of any interpretation other than that from the aspect of final cause.

The *function* of these two articles as an exact definition of the nature of the triune presence caused by the divine missions and as an unequivocal specification of the formal reason of this new mode of presence is precisely paralleled by the famous third article of St. Thomas' tract in the *Summa*. This, too, in regard to the obscurities, confusions and apparent contradictions of an earlier attempt at explanation (his own tract in the *Sentences*), presents a lucid, unambiguous statement on the divine indwelling.

Like St. Bonaventure, the Angelic Doctor closely unites the double notion of mission and donation. But where the Franciscan makes this an absolute connection—*mitti est dari*—on the basis of their real identity, St. Thomas preserves the logical distinction between the two and defines the nature of the inhabitation from these logically diverse aspects. To be sent is to be present in a new way: and this he specifies as a special presence (the common mode of the divine presence being presupposed) by which God is present as the thing known in the knower and the thing loved in the lover. To be given is to be had: and this he specifies as the presence of the divine Persons as a thing freely to be enjoyed.

Under both aspects, therefore, the distinct Persons are present as objects or terms of the acts or powers of the rational creature; such a special manner of being present is called Their inhabitation. Obviously to possess the Persons in this way, to have Them so present in us, can only come from the gifts of grace: God is attained as He is in Himself and God is freely enjoyed by man by powers man freely uses and possesses—and neither of these things is possible by the powers of nature alone. Man, in consequence, by the divine missions receives sanctifying grace and its gifts; not only that, the Persons Themselves come to him, for by reason of these gifts he possesses Them.

This article, then, serves the same purpose for St. Thomas' tract on the missions as it does for St. Bonaventure's. In both cases an unambiguous definition of the vital reality effected by the missions is given; and this fact once clearly established, further questions can be dealt with. Hardly on this point alone could any influence attributable to St. Bonaventure be legitimately established, nor is the verbal similarity of the texts such as to warrant an assumption of influence. Yet the key phrases of the article—the Thomistic formula and the specification of donation—definitely suggest the earlier work of the Franciscan. And the intellectual *procedure* followed by St. Thomas is a clear parallel of the method of the Seraphic Doctor. Moreover, the relation of this article to St. Thomas' earlier consideration of the same facts is a perfect analogue of the relations between Bonaventure's treatment and that of the Alexandrian *Summa*. Considering all these facts together, it is difficult to avoid the conclusion that St. Bonaventure's *Commentarius* suggested to St. Thomas the changes to be made in his revision of his earlier work, and the manner in which these improvements and clarifications could best be realized.

The 'remote' influence of the Franciscan Doctor is further exemplified by the parallelism of treatment of the invisible mission of the Son. In the *Sentences* (d. 15, q. 4, a. 1), St. Thomas had explained this on the basis of similitude, an explanation entirely analogous to the Halesian notion of manifestation and, in respect to the doctrinally important answer to the first objection, even textually similar. But in his *Summa* (Article 5), the Angelic Doctor drops this way of explaining the mystery to insist on the two essential dogmatic facts of the mystery: that an invisible mission implies both a divine procession and the divine inhabitation, both of which properly pertain to the Son. This explanation having been given in the body of the article, he then proceeds in the responses to the objections to clarify the notions of assimilation and appropriation as they apply to the missions.

Since the formal reason of the divine indwelling has already been defined in Article 3, there is now no possibility of misconstruing the role attributed to similitude (that is to say, to assimilation, appropriation or what the Schoolmen more generally term the manifestation of the Persons). Formally speaking, this manifestation by similitude is *not* the reason of the inhabitation, not a constituent but a consequence. Because the gifts conjoin us to the Persons as objects known, loved and enjoyed, they are the formal reason of the divine indwelling; but because of this power they possess, precisely because they have this kind of supernatural capacity for real contact with the distinct Persons, they are also capable of manifesting one or other of the Persons sent. And yet their invisible missions are inseparable, howsoever distinct, just as, and because of, the fact that the gifts of Charity and Wisdom are inseparable.

St. Bonaventure has already explained the confused and confusing Alexandrian notion of manifestation in precisely the same way. Having defined the formal reason of the inhabitation as the power to enjoy the Persons as fruits in virtue of the gifts of grace (d. 15, II, a. 1, q. 1), he then, in the next article, takes up the question of the invisible missions of the Son and the Holy Spirit. At the very beginning he points out a key fact: that the gifts of grace really involve two things, the inhabitation of the Persons and Their manifestation. It is a distinction which enables him to restate the notions of the Franciscan *Summa* without confusing the issues.

Thus it is clear that the Persons do not dwell in the just *by reason of* Their manifestation or the similitude. But the formal reason of Their indwelling is also the formal reason of Their manifestation: the gifts of sanctifying grace. Because the gifts are of such a nature as to give man the power to possess the Persons as fruits of enjoyment, they explain both the inhabitation of the Persons and Their manifestation. Hence these gifts are similitudes properly representative (by appropriation) of one or other Person; but since the gifts are necessarily connected, the divine missions, although distinct, are necessarily inseparable. By love and wisdom, the *illuminatio intellectus* and *inflammatio affectus*,* the Son and Holy Ghost are sent and given, and inhabit and made manifest.

The procedural parallelism here with St. Thomas' article is remarkable. The relations between St. Bonaventure's tract in his *Sentences* and the early Franciscan *Summa* are exactly the same as those between St. Thomas' tract in

---

* The very same words are employed by St. Bonaventure (d. 15, I, a. 1, q. 2, resp.) and by St. Thomas (I, q. 43, a. 5, ad 3).

the *Summa* and his early *Sentences*. The *same* confusions of the two early works (the notion of similitude, appropriation, manifestation) are clarified in the *same* manner; the *same* imprecisions are rendered definite by the *same* manner of presenting the *same* doctrine. Verbal similarity is certainly also present, but it is far from striking; on the deeper level, however, the similarities of problem and presentation, of solution and procedure, point to as definite an influence as would be indicated by strict verbal parallelism.

Again, one can but conclude that the changes to be made in his earlier work and the manner in which these changes could best be realized are suggested to the Angelic Doctor by St. Bonaventure's revision of the tract on the divine missions of the *Summa Theologica* of Alexander of Hales.

3. St. Bonaventure's Influence: An Appraisal

In attempting to assess the effect of St. Bonaventure on the revision St. Thomas makes of his own earlier tract, one must keep certain facts in mind. The first is that St. Thomas has re-examined *all* of the sources of his earlier explanation when he prepared to revise it. This is evident for the Alexandrian *Summa* in that its logical order is followed, and its insistence on the mission as another mode of the divine presence is repeated—neither of these found so emphatically in St. Thomas' own *Sentences,* nor in St. Albert, nor in St. Bonaventure. It is evident for St. Albert's work precisely because all former traces of his influence now disappear, a fact difficult to account for unless it is presupposed that Thomas studies the Albertinian notions (appropriation, procession as cause and *ratio*) in their original source and, seeing them in context, recognizes their pejorative force for the theory proper to St. Albert. For the *Commentarius* of St. Bonaventure, the same examination or re-examination (for it is possible that St. Thomas did not previously use this work) is proven by the facts considered in the first section of this article.

St. Thomas re-examines his former sources, then. The result is a new influence from both the Alexandrian *Summa* and St. Bonaventure, and the elimination of that of St. Albert. But there is more than addition and subtraction in his revision, there is a consistent restatement of the essential doctrine of the *Sentences,* clarifying the factors which are likewise most obscure in the Franciscan compilation. This is a second fact to consider. For in this respect St. Thomas' labor is a remarkable parallel of the same task that St. Bonaventure performs for the *Summa* of his colleagues. It is hardly mere coincidence that St. Thomas recognizes as faults of his earlier treatment the same faults of the *Summa Alexandri* recognized by St. Bonaventure, and that he changes his presentation to clarify the earlier work in the same manner that St. Bonaventure clarifies the earlier Franciscan presentation. Given the fact of his re-examination of the Franciscan *Summa* and of St. Albert, and the fact of his consultation of St. Bonaventure, and the fact of Bonaventure's perception of the faults of the Franciscan work and his simple, scientific restatement of its doctrine: these facts, plus the evident parallelism of St. Thomas' revision and St. Bonaventure's revision indubitably declare the indebtedness of the Dominican doctor to his Franciscan colleague for the major changes that occur in the *Summa Theologiae* compared with the *Scriptum super Sententiis,* in the tract on the divine missions.

This influence is not, however, verbal; on this score the similarities are few. As was stated in the beginning, it is rather a *suggestive* influence, which indicates to Thomas what changes should be made and how they can best be realized. All in all, on the matters concerning the inhabitation, it is the *determinate* source of the considerable stylistic changes existing between Thomas' two treatments. But it will be left to Thomas' own genius to develop and perfect the hints of the *Commentarius* of St. Bonaventure to a more perfect statement of the same theory; and, of course, left to him also the ultimate answer to the 'how' of the divine indwelling, the ultimate perfection of the Augustine insight on the manifestation of the Persons: the gift of Wisdom.

CHAPTER NINE

Conclusion

The investigation of the sources of scholastic teaching on the indwelling of the Trinity in the souls of the just revealed the dependence of the medieval theologians on the revealed data of Sacred Scripture as that revelation had been authentically interpreted by the Church in the person of the Fathers, both Greek and Latin. Thus a common fundamental view of the mystery is disclosed by the Schoolmen's analysis, and it is on this inviolable substratum that individual theologians attempt a theological construction which will, in human terms, explain the inhabitation.

St. Thomas' doctrine on this vital and central revelation represents the high water mark of an intellectual tide which has swelled through the centuries. In the brightly obscure light of theological wisdom he sees the indwelling of the Trinity as a possession of the distinct Persons by those in the state of grace, a vital and dynamic contact with God as He is in Himself which is realized by that higher, more direct knowledge of supernatural Wisdom grounded in supernatural love. So is the theological problem of the inhabitation resolved, the formal reason for this new presence of God within man finally specified. Sanctifying grace, precisely as the principle of God-like operations of knowing and loving the distinct Persons really present in the soul, is the basic formal specification of this new supernatural union. And the proximate explanation will be found in those supernatural properties of grace, the habits of Wisdom and Charity, by which grace becomes so operative.

This masterpiece of theological analysis and synthesis, however, does not spring full-grown from the mind of the Angelic Doctor without precedent or antecedent; on the contrary, it is the fruit, the final perfection, of the approaches, discoveries, experiments, tentations and trials of his predecessors. By comparing his works with the efforts of those who have gone before him, it is clear that he is profoundly influenced, not only as to doctrine but even as to style, by the labors of other theologians. This fact establishes the justification for the comparative study undertaken in the last two chapters, the attempt to determine from a historical point of view, on the basis of textual and textual-doctrinal parallelisms and antitheses, the relations which prevail between St. Thomas' two major treatments of the inhabitation and the writings of the Schoolmen who influenced him. And in accomplishing this task, the expectation was to extend this determination to the relations which obtain between the tract in his *Scriptum super Sententiis* and the tract in his *Summa Theologiae*.

The comparisons thus instituted in the preceding two chapters reveal the following conclusions:

    1. Respecting the *Scriptum super Sententiis*:

        1) In composing the tract on the divine missions, St. Thomas actually had available to him and

used as sources (in varying degrees) the *Summa fratris Alexandri*, the *Commentary* of St. Albert, and (possibly) the *Commentary* of St. Bonaventure.

2) St. Thomas rejects the theory of the inhabitation proposed by St. Albert but incorporates in his presentation certain notions taught by his Master.

3) St. Thomas deliberately chooses the theory of the Franciscan *Summa*, following its doctrine and presentation. This is evident both on textual grounds and on textual-doctrinal grounds.

4) St. Bonaventure's influence on the *Sentences*, if present at all, is negligible.

2. Respecting the *Summa Theologiae*.

1) Although his own earlier work is St. Thomas' principal source for the tract on the divine missions in his *Summa*, there are important logical and stylistic differences between the two presentations, and at least one doctrinal difference.

2) The Alexandrian *Summa* seems to be the main source of the scientific order of the tract and of a major stylistic change.

3) St. Albert exercises no influence on the *Summa*. On the contrary, the notions of the tract in the *Sentences* traceable to him are eliminated or given much less importance.

4) For the emphasis on certain elements relative to the theory of the inhabitation and for certain specific phrases, St. Thomas seems to have relied, at least by way of suggestion, on the *Commentary* of St. Bonaventure. This work, indeed, in its revision of the *Summa fratris Alexandri* sets St.

Thomas the example for the revision of his own previous presentation and gives him the procedure to follow in clarifying and simplifying the *Scriptum super Sententiis*.

It is from the foregoing facts, firmly established by all the preceding labor, that one can now at last draw some pertinent conclusions, the determination of which, as set forth in the introductory chapter, constituted the ends of this investigation and prompted its prosecution. The first of these conclusions is primary and principal, the other two subsidiary and derivative but of greater moment and more profound consequence.

FIRST CONCLUSION:
St. Thomas teaches an identical doctrine on the inhabitation in the Scriptum super Sententiis **and the** Summa Theologiae.

1) *Doctrinal basis for this judgment.*

Chapter Six of this book presented St. Thomas' theory by quoting impartially from both of his major treatments of the divine indwelling in the souls of the just. The net result of this presentation was to show that the essential elements of an 'intentional' explanation are equally present in both these major considerations of the mystery. Implicitly the chapter teaches an obvious fact, but one all too often forgotten or ignored: the necessity of understanding and interpreting a particular aspect or presentation of St. Thomas' doctrine in the light of that doctrine.

In the present case, St. Thomas can only be rightly understood if his teaching on grace, on the gifts of the Holy Ghost, the divine causality, the ubiquity of God is also known and used in interpreting his statements on the divine indwelling. It is also helpful, if not as essential, to recall his doctrine on the Trinity, on the Incarnation and on the Beatific Vision. Teaching more directly philosophical, especially Thomistic metaphysics and psychology, must be well grasped before a true comprehension of his theory can be obtained.

If the recognized canons of sound exegesis are followed, however, his teaching on the inhabitation in the *Sentences* becomes as clear and as unequivocal as that of the tract in his *Summa*: and it is the same doctrine in both instances. For the kind of presence which specifically characterizes the indwelling, which is *essentially* different from the presence of immensity,[1] it is necessary that God be known and loved.[1a] And from this fact proceeds two determining consequences: first, to be known and loved God must be present *in ratione objecti*;[2] second, the union of the just with God is not merely by likeness but with God as He is in himself—a contact and conjunction which takes place only *per operationem creaturae*.[3] Thus a purely assimilative union on the ontological plane (as distinguished from the intentional) cannot explain this new presence which specifies the mystery, since on that level man is not united to God Himself but only to a similitude of Him.[4]

If these particular facts advanced explicitly in the *Sentences* are taken into account, together with such general principles likewise expressed in the same work as the common efficiency of the Trinity,[5] the instability

[1] I *Sent.*, d. 37, q. 1, a. 2 ad 2.
[1a] *Ibid.*, d. 15, q. 4, a. 1 ad 3; a. 2 ad 4 and 5.
[2] I *Sent.*, d. 3, q. 1, a. 2 ad 3; q. 4, a. 5; d. 15, q. 5, a. 3 ad 2; d. 17, q. 1, a. 4 ad 4; IV *Sent*, d. 49, q. 2, a. 6 ad 4.
[3] I *Sent.*, d. 37, q. 1, a. 2. Cf. II *Sent.*, d. 1, q. 2, a. 2; III *Sent.*, d. 2, q. 1, a. 3 sol. 1 ad 3; d. 10, q. 3, a. 1, sol. 1 and ad 2 and 3. Cf. Morency, *op. cit.*, pp. 257-261 for a summary analysis of all the pertinent texts.
[4] III *Sent.*, d. 13, a. 3, sol. 1 ad 2. Cf. II *Sent.*, d. 1, q. 2, a. 2.
[5] I *Sent.*, d. 15, Exp. Primae Partis Textus; q. 3, a. 1; d. 17, q. 1, a. 1; q. 2, a. 2 ad 2; d. 18, q. 1, a. 1 ad 1.

and inadequacy of appropriation and exemplarity as functional explanations,[6] the specification of the missions and inhabitation from the point of view of final causality[7]—if, in other words, St. Thomas is permitted to tell us himself what he meant to say in his elucidation of this mystery, then the doctrinal identity of the earlier and later considerations must be rigidly affirmed. There remains no room for qualification and quibbling, minimizing or depreciation, difficulty or equivocation. The theory stated in the *Scriptum super Sententiis* concerning the formal reason of the inhabitation is uniquely an intentional one.

Such being the case, it is clear that the formula of the *Sentences* which describes the Persons as present "as a thing is in its likeness" must be interpreted in a deeper and less obvious sense than the material signification of those terms suggests. But the truth of this *a priori* judgment is no less certain from an *a posteriori* approach to the exegetical problem. For St. Thomas carefully specifies in the proximate and remote contexts from which the formula is drawn that the similitude he has in mind is of such efficacy that it not only assimilates us to God but actually conjoins us with God.[8]

Thus he states that by the visible mission the Holy Spirit is present *only* as in a sign, but in His invisible mis-

---

[6] Cf. *supra.* pp. 275-276.

[7] Cf. *supra*, pp. 276-283. Although we have preferred to designate the specifying presence of the Trinity as objects known and loved as that from the point of view of final cause, this could also be termed formal extrinsic causality; since, however, God is the end of the just only insofar as He is also the object of their knowledge and love, it does not matter which designation is used: the distinction between the Persons as ends, as objects, as terms is purely logical.

[8] I *Sent.*, d. 14, q. 2, a. 1 and ad 4; q. 2, a. 2 and ad 1, 2, 3; q. 3, Praeterea and sol..; d. 15, q. 2 ad 4; q. 4, a. 1 ad 3; q. 4, a. 2 ad 5; d. 18, q. 1, a. 5 ad 6.

sion He is truly present in a new way (and therefore not only as in a sign).⁹ He distinguishes carefully between the unitive aspect of the effect of grace *by reason of which* the missions and indwelling take place (which unitive function conjoins the just to the whole Trinity, and the entire Trinity thereby dwells in the soul) and the assimilative aspect of the same effect (the function of which is to lead the just more to one Person than to another by appropriation).[10] In short, as he explicitly points out with respect to Charity, it is necessary to consider these supernatural effects not only as the term of the operations of the Persons but also as the medium of operation of the creature,[11] precisely as the form which is the principle of the acts by which man is con-formed to the Persons.[12]

Why the emphasis on similitude? First of all, because every *per se* agent produces acts similar to its nature: so that the just man must possess an intrinsic supernatural principle of action which is similar to those supernatural operations by which he knows and loves and rejoices in God as God knows, loves and rejoices in Himself:[13] supernatural powers, consequently, which mirror the Son and the Holy Ghost. Secondly, this conjunction with God as object and end is by means of a quasi-experimental knowledge grounded in supernatural love,[14] by which an 'assimilation' of knower to thing known, a conformity of lover and thing loved, is produced.[15] In this life, however, God is not immediately joined to the soul *in ratione ob-*

[9] *Ibid.*, d. 16, q. 1, a. 1.
[10] *Ibid.*, d. 15, q. 2 ad 4.
[11] *Ibid.*, d. 17, q. 1, a. 1 ad 1 and 3.
[12] *Ibid.*, sol.
[13] *Ibid.*, d. 14, q. 3.
[14] *Ibid.*, d. 15, q. 4, a. 1 ad 3; d. 16, q. 2, a. 2.
[15] *Ibid.*, d. 15, q. 5, a. 3.

jecti,[16] and hence He must be known in the effects He has produced. But for the type of knowledge which characterizes the indwelling, this effect must more perfectly represent Him as He is in Himself, an effect which images the property of one or other Person, a similitude which can be appropriated to the Son or Holy Ghost.[17] In that supernatural likeness man knows and loves God in His trinity of Persons, not, however, by discursive processes or simply as a cause is known by its effects, but as something imaged is known in the image: and St. Thomas therefore specifies these effects as signs,[17a] for the precise role of a sign is to make something other than itself known. Wisdom and Charity are similitudes of this kind, signs of the Persons. And why? *Because* they are principles of divine operations, of God-like knowledge and God-like love, and thus in the self-reflective knowledge and love of these supernatural powers God is known and loved as He is in Himself.

In brief, the divine Persons by Their indwelling are said to be in us 'as in a likeness' because *by* these gifts of grace They are known *in* these gifts of grace which mirror the Persons by their power to reproduce actions reflecting Their personal properties. And in this context, without any violation of the specification of the indwelling by reason of operation (from the point of view of end and formal extrinsic causality), without any contradiction of the determination of the new presence of the Persons as objects of man's knowledge and love, fruits to be enjoyed, St. Thomas can speak of these grace-effects 'as originated and exemplified by the personal property of a divine Person'; he can describe the Persons 'as lead-

[16] *Ibid.*, d. 15, q. 5, a. 3 ad 1 and 2; d. 17, q. 1, a. 4 ad 4.
[17] *Ibid.*, d. 15, q. 4, a. 1 ad 1.
[17a] *Ibid.*, d. 14, q. 1, a. 2 ad 2; d. 16, q. 1, a. 2 ad 3.

ing and conjoining us to our end'; he can speak of Their 'imprinting a seal on our souls.'

For through Wisdom and Charity, which are truly the seals of the Persons, we are assimilated by the Persons to Themselves: in a new manner,[18] as to the proper terms and objects of those supernatural powers, as to fruits to be enjoyed, as to our end. And thus the concept of similitude acquires its full meaning for St. Thomas only insofar as it is informed and specified by its terminal relationship to the objects known and loved, only in the light of his 'intentional' explanation of the divine indwelling.[19]

[18] *Ibid.*, d. 15, q. 4, a. 1: ". . . secundum novum modum essendi, prout res est in sua similitudine, dicuntur personae divinae in nobis esse, *secundum quod novo modo eis assimilamur.* . . ." Cf. *ibid.*, d. 14, q. 2, a. 2 ad 2. In these texts where the Persons are described as the means by which the creature is conjoined to God, the activity implied can only be explained insofar as Their gifts are considered as principles of activity rather than as representations; or likenesses which are what they are because they actually *unite* the creature to God.

[19] *Ibid.*, d. 30, q. 1, a. 2.

The term 'similitude' has a very special meaning for the Schoolmen, signifying the perfection by grace of the image of God in man: "imago quantum ad naturalia, similitudo quantum ad gratuita" (Petrus Picaviensis, II *Sent.*, Chap. 9 [PL 211: 966]; Haymo, *In. Gen.*, I, Chap. 7 [PL 117: 459 f.]; Peter Lombard, II *Sent.*, d. 16, Chap. 3; *Summa Alex.*, II, p. 411, II). This meaning, product of the medieval exegesis of Genesis, although found in a few of the Fathers, is preserved by St. Thomas (I *Sent.*, d. 3, q. 2, a. 3; q. 4, a. 1 ad 7; *De Ver.*, q. 22, a. 1 ad 2; *Sum. Theol.*, I, q. 93, a. 9). In the first two references he gently corrects the *Summa Alex.* (II, p. 412, III, Resp.) and Hugh of St. Victor (*De Sacr. Chris. fidei*, I, Part 6, Chap. 2 [PL 176: 934]; *De arrha Sponsae* [PL 176: 934]), who interpret St. Augustine (*De spiritu et anima*, Chap. 10 and 139 [PL 40: 786 and 809]) as applying 'image' to knowledge and 'similitude' to love by pointing out simply that the words should be understood of nature and grace— an interesting commentary on their *a priori* psychological positions. In this tract, however, St. Thomas does not seem to be using the word in this technical sense—even though such an interpretation would easily solve the difficulties it causes.

2) *Historical basis for this judgment.*

In Chapters Seven and Eight—the comparison of St. Thomas' presentations in his *Sentences* and his *Summa* with those of his predecessors—the long investigations of Chapters Two and Three (the tradition of the Scholastics) and Chapters Four and Five (an analysis of scholastic solutions) bore fruit. In the *Sentences,* as the textual and textual-doctrinal evidence demonstrates, St. Thomas rejects St. Albert's solution and follows, even to details, that of the *Summa fratris Alexandri.* The fact is very important. For Chapter Four showed that the Franciscan *Summa* definitively teaches, despite its obscurities and confusions, a strictly intentional theory of the inhabitation, in which no formal role is played by an ontological element; whereas the case is the exact reverse for St. Albert, who both in his *Sentences* and his *Summa* teaches an ontological theory in which no essential part is enjoyed by an intentional element. St. Thomas' *Sentences,* therefore, which rejects St. Albert's theory and adopts the Franciscan theory, must be a rejection of the ontological theory and the acceptance of the intentional theory. Since this latter theory is also taught by the *Summa Theologiae*—as is generally admitted and as was shown in Chapter Six— the two works teach the same doctrine on the inhabitation, though the two presentations of that doctrine differ.

Confirmation for this conclusion is given, again on a historical and textual basis, by a comparison of the *Summa Theologiae* with the earlier works, including Thomas' own. This comparison (Chapter Eight) reveals that St. Thomas performs the same *task* of clearing up the confusions of his earlier treatment in the same *manner* in which St. Bonaventure clarifies similar confusions in the Alexandrian *Summa.* The Seraphic Doctor accomplishes his task by re-presenting the theory of the earlier work in clearer language which emphasizes essentials and discards repetitions, superfluities and confusing elements. St. Thomas' labor is the same: a restatement of the doctrine he taught less clearly in the *Sentences,* without essential change of that doctrine.

What, in this case, of the statements in the *Sentences* which seem to favor an ontological theory or element, notably the concepts of similitude and exemplary causality? The answer can only be—on textual grounds as well as on doctrinal—that they must be interpreted on the lines of a purely intentional theory.

This is clearly the case for the notion of similitude, for that is specifically drawn from the *Summa* of Alexander. If St. Thomas follows the theory of the Halesian *Summa,* then this idea can only play in his theory the role it enjoys in his source. And that role, as evidenced in Chapter Four, is perfectly consonant with an exclusively intentional theory. As a matter of fact, the function of similitude with respect to the inhabitation is perfectly expressed by the Franciscan work, and serves as a definitive interpretation both of its own use of the idea and of St. Thomas' borrowing it:

> [God to be present by grace] necessarily places created grace in the creature, which created grace is, indeed, a similitude by which the soul is an image in act, that is in actual imitation; and since the soul is referred to God in an express similitude, God is said to dwell in it by grace.... From this it is apparent that created grace is a similitude by which the soul is an image in act; hence to be [present] by grace puts in the soul a habit assimilating to God.[19a]

[19a] *Suma Alex.,* ed. cit., I, p. 77: "[Deum esse per gratiam] ponit necessario gratiam creatam in creatura, quae quidem gratia est simili-

One must interpret St. Thomas' concept of similitude in the same way, since he has adopted, even textually, the same doctrine and rejected the theory explaining the divine indwelling from the aspect of principle. Similitude for him, as for the *Summa Alexandri,* is not just any similitude, but a dynamic, practical likeness—the image of conformity. And if one turns to St. Thomas's teaching on the image of God in man, which in the *Sentences* (Distinction 3) precedes and is presupposed to the tract on the missions (Distinctions 14 and following), the full meaning of assimilation becomes clear. For the similitude of the gifts of grace which constitute the image of conformity assimilates man to God by giving him the capacity to know and love God as He is in Himself; and in virtue of this image, because the gifts are what they are, man contacts the properties of the Persons, the distinct Persons Themselves.

It is clear from this doctrine that the formula 'the Persons are present by the missions as a thing is present in its similitude' is equivalent to the formula 'the Persons are present as the object known is present in the knower and the object loved in the lover.' For the similitude of grace is constituted by the presence of the Persons as objects known and loved—exactly what St. Thomas less indirectly says in his *Summa.* Such an image is not only a mere representation by appropriation of the Persons caus-

tudo, qua anima est imago actu, id est in imitatione actuali; et cum se habet anima per conformitatem ad Deum in similitudine expressa, dicitur Deus inhabitare in ipsa per gratiam. . . . Ex hoc patet quod gratia creata est similitudo qua anima est imago in actu; unde esse per gratiam ponit in anima habitum assimilantem Deo." The part omitted is a confirmatory quotation from St. Augustine, *Epist.* 187, Chap. 5, n. 17 (PL 33:838).

It should be underlined that St. Thomas himself makes the same identification of 'operation' and 'assimilating habit.' Cf. III *Sent.,* d. 10, q. 3, a. 1, sol. 2: ". . . pràedestinatio autem nostra est ad unionem per operationem aut per habitum assimilantem."

ing the effect (by appropriation, since God operates as one, not as distinct Persons), but, far more importantly, a conformity which regards God Himself, one and triune, as an object known and loved *as He is in Himself*—not analogical only, therefore, nor by mere appropriation, but an object attained by real contact with the properties of each and every Person, in the presence of whom man rejoices, even on this earth, because he is conjoined with Them really present, howsoever imperfect this conjunction be.

As in the Halesian *Summa*, so the notion of similitude and assimilation in the *Sentences* of St. Thomas teaches a purely intentional theory of the divine indwelling.

The idea that the divine processions are the cause and the *ratio* of the return of the rational creature to God also inculcates the same doctrine. Although this notion is textually derived from St. Albert, it is interpreted by St. Thomas from the aspect of end, in contradistinction to his master's understanding of the doctrine, as may be seen in Chapter Seven. Where Albert visualizes the Dionysian concept from the point of view of the Persons as cause, efficient and exemplary, St. Thomas sees the same idea from the aspect of term. This significant difference, implicit in the tract on the divine missions, is explicitly stated in the *ex professo* treatment of the relations between God and His creatures:

> ... in all those things which are said of God temporally, and signify a relation of principle to principiated, it is absolutely true that they pertain to the entire Trinity. If, however, the relation of creature to Creator is considered [a relation] *as to a term*, it is possible that such a relation of the creature be to something essential or to something personal. This, however, happens in three ways. Either according to operation. . . . *Or according to exem-*

plarity, as in the creation of things there is a termination in the similitude of essential attributes and in the infusion of Charity there is a similitude of the personal procession of the Holy Spirit. Or there is termination according to being. . . .[20]

To Thomas' mind, therefore, the divine processions are cause and *ratio*—exemplars and exemplary cause—of the return of the creature to God which is effected by the divine missions, not so far as They are *principles* causing this exemplary relationship but inasmuch as They are the *terms* to which the relationship of similitude refers. A small and subtle change of aspect, you may say. But it accounts for the fact that this particular notion harmonizes perfectly with an exclusively intentional theory of the inhabitation, an explanation of the mystery solely from the aspect of end. And it indicates, moreover, on a deeper level, the single-mindedness of Thomas' view of the whole mystery of the divine missions, his 'obsession' with the presence of the Persons as objects, ends, terms; his 'contempt' for the view which sees the Persons present as causes and principles.

It is beside the point to object that this relationship to the Persons by exemplarity (the correlative of which is assimilation) cannot, according to St. Thomas' principles, explain by itself alone Their new manner of being present which is specific of the indwelling. The reason

---

[20] I *Sent.*, d. 30, q. 1, a. 2, sol.: "'. . . in omnibus istis quae dicuntur de Deo ex tempore, et important habitudinem principii ad principiatum, simpliciter verum est quod conveniunt toti Trinitati. Si autem consideretur relatio creaturae ad Creatorem ut ad terminum, possibile est quod talis relatio creaturae sit ad aliquid essentiale, vel ad aliquid personale. Contingit autem hoc tripliciter. Aut secundum operationem. . . . Vel secundum exemplaritatem, sicut in creatione rerum est terminatio in similitudinem essentialium attributorum, et in infusione charitatis est terminatio in similitudinem processionis personalis Spiritus sancti. Vel est terminatio secundum esse. . . ." (Emphasis added.)

why this exemplarity respects the Persons from the aspect of term rather than from the aspect of principle is precisely the reason why They are present in this new way. It is because the supernatural powers of Wisdom and Charity are capable of knowing and loving the Persons Themselves that these effects regard the Persons not as They are their cause (efficient-principle or exemplary-principle) but as They are their objects, formally specifying these supernatural habits, determining them to be what they are: images and signs and likenesses of the distinct Persons. Thus, for example, Wisdom is a more express similitude of the Son (and not merely of the essential attribute of intellectuality or knowledge) precisely because it is a power by which man can have a certain experimental knowledge of God in His trinity of Persons, thus producing a 'word' which 'reproduces' by way of knowledge, like the Word of God, the divine essence as it is in itself: by Wisdom man images the eternal procession of the Son.

But it should not be forgotten—St. Thomas himself never did so—that this assimilation is only by appropriation, and so even from the aspect of term the Persons are not the *immediate* exemplars of Their gifts. Evident as this fact is from the point of view of exemplar-principle, it is no less certain from the aspect of exemplar-term. For, as stated in the preceding paragraph, the specification of this type of exemplarity is by reason of the objects which specify the gifts, and all three Persons can be known and loved by the just and are so present in dwelling within the soul.[20a] Hence Wisdom is not only a power *by* which each and every Person can be known; by this very fact, it is also a sign and image *in* which each and every Person

[20a] I *Sent.*, d. 15, q. 2 ad 4; *Sum. Theol.*, q. 3, a. 4 ad 3.

can be known. It is in no manner *exclusively* representative of the Son, although by appropriation (as is obvious) it 'can lead more to one Person than to another.'[21]

St. Thomas' notion of appropriation-exemplarity as revealed by his own explications in the Scriptum super Sententiis differs:

    a) from St. Albert, by affirming a terminal rather than an efficient exemplarity by reason of the objects specifying the effects of the missions, and by denying any formal role in the indwelling to assimilation;

    b) from the *Summa Alexandri*,[22] by denying the separability of the missions of the Son and Holy Ghost[23] which that work professed on the basis of exclusivity of appropriation;

    c) from St. Bonaventure,[24] in not only denying the separability of the missions and pointing out the necessity for both knowledge and love, but also in specifying the basic reason for that denial by distinguishing explicitly between the effects as assimilative likenesses and as unitive powers[25] and and by destroying the fundament of the Halesian distinction, namely that a grace-effect can be appropriated exclusively to the Son alone or to the Holy Ghost alone.[26]

Thus the ideas of similitude, assimilation, appropriation and exemplarity acquire even in the *Sentences* a clarity and a precision which correct the errors, discrepancies

[21] I *Sent.*, d. 15, q. 2 ad 4.
[22] *Op. cit.*, I, p. 720, ad 2; p. 732, ad 3.
[23] I *Sent.*, d. 15, q. 4, a. 2.
[24] I *Sent.*, d. 15, p. 2, a. un., q. 2 (ed. cit., I, p. 272).
[25] I *Sent.*, d. 15, q. 4, a. 2 and ad 5; q. 2 ad 4.
[26] *Ibid.*, d. 15, q. 2 ad 4.

and inexactitudes of his predecessors at the same time as they preserve the truth of their conceptions and perfect their insights. And all this not only in remaining faithful to his intentional explanation but by reason of that very specification of the formal reason of the divine indwelling: consonance and harmony because of consistency in applying principles.

3) *Conclusion*

If these notions square so easily with St. Thomas' doctrine on the indwelling, why does he discard them in his *Summa?* The answer seems obvious. From a practical point of view, there is no doubt that such ideas offer grave difficulty for the correct interpretation of St. Thomas' theory unless they be perfectly understood. That much is certain from the subsequent history of St. Thomas' solution, and it is especially accentuated by the numerous unhappy attempts at explaining his ideas on the indwelling to which we are today subjected. It seems more than probable, also, that the fact of the difficulties and confusions of this way of stating the theory is brought home to St. Thomas when he re-reads the Alexandrian *Summa* in the light of St. Bonaventure's revision of it. When he writes for students and novices in theology, in consequence, he will be anxious to remove all possible obstacles to a comprehension of the essential facts of the mystery, even though the obstructing notions may—as in the present case—be in themselves profound and fruitful, and should—in any case—be capable of being properly understood.

A second reason for the change is doctrinal. In the *Sentences*, St. Thomas has already explained the doctrine of the image of the Trinity in man, so that when he comes to explain the inhabitation he can use the notion of similitude as the key of his exposition, without having to give a long theological analysis of it. The situation is quite the reverse for the *Summa,* where the doctrine of image is not examined until Question 93 of the First Part. It would be unscientific, as well as woefully impractical, to employ as an explanatory principle a profound doctrine as yet scientifically unknown.

Finally, it is these particular ideas which are most derivative, the common theological currency, so to say, recognized as legal tender for the inhabitation in the period when St. Thomas first taught and wrote. Deference toward the great Parisian Masters, and in particular toward his own mentor, would inevitably be demanded by public opinion of the young theologian; St. Thomas' own humility and docility would assure a cheerful compliance, and his charity a benignity of interpretation: his intellectual acumen and theological ingenuity would perceive that these traditional notions and expressions, properly modified, could serve his own purposes. To scandalize his auditors by forthright rejection of the neo-Platonic elements which were so entwined in the Augustinian and scholastic tradition would have served no purpose except to discredit himself, alienate his colleagues and prejudice the cause of Aristotelianism. Forebearance, in this as in any case, does not constitute condonation.

When he speaks as Master, however, he speaks as Master: the tone firm, the manner definite, the unvarnished truth plainly announced: charity remains, but he no longer defers.[26a] And thus the *Summa* clearly defines what was before obscure, synthesizes the diffuse, eliminates the

---

[26a] This is illustrated exactly by St. Bonaventure's attitude toward a position he does not think reasonable but accepts on authority (I *Sent,* d. 15, I, a. 1, q. 4) and St. Thomas' rejection of the very same authority and condescension to it (*Sum. Theol.,* I, q. 43, a. 8).

confused, perfects the approximate. The theory expressed in the *Sentences* is restated with the precision, the authority and the clarity of one whose mastery of the Queen of Sciences still knows no challenge. If something of mellifluousness is lost, something of emotional fire, in this transmutation to a more technical, more exact expression of doctrine, the ultimate gain for his readers in science and wisdom must forever balance the scales in favor of the *Summa*. Light the *Scriptum super Sententiis* undoubtedly possesses, a brilliance that illuminates the entire theological landscape, and especially the problem of the divine indwelling; and it flickers and sputters in dark corners and unforeseen depths. But on essentials this is but the shimmer of pearl compared to the hard blaze of diamond, of this diamond, the *Summa*, which Thomas has polished to such perfection that its myriad facets are so many windows to the burning heart within: the Truth who is.

SECOND CONCLUSION:

> All theories of the indwelling which explain the triune presence from the formal point of view of God as cause, principle or 'operating' are irreconcilable with the theory of St. Thomas. None of the proponents of these proposals is justified, therefore, in quoting passages from St. Thomas in authoritative support of their peculiar ideas.

This sweeping statement—which applies as well to those who advance 'original' theories on the indwelling as to those who seek merely to interpret St. Thomas— is a by-product of this study. It is, however, certain on several grounds. First of all, Chapter Five showed that St. Albert's theory, an ontological explanation, contradicts on a doctrinal basis certain and unequivocal principles of philosophy and theology expressly taught by St. Thomas; and this analysis likewise disclosed, in some specific modern proposals unconsciously Albertinian, the doctrinal errors which spring from an ignorance of, an ignoring of, a misinterpretation of, or a rejection of Thomistic principles.

Secondly, foundation for this conclusion is found in the exposition of St. Thomas' true doctrine in Chapter Six. Here it was demonstrated that no ontological element, no possible consideration from the point of view of God-principle, enters into the *formal* reason for the indwelling, which in St. Thomas' mind is fully and adequately explained from an exclusively intentional viewpoint, God as object, as term, as end. It was pointed out, moreover, that the proper role which the notion of God as operating and as principle enjoys in the Thomistic explanation is from the aspect of efficient cause, but that this function does not concern the formal elements of the 'how' of the divine indwelling. Finally, certain classical and certain modern objections against St. Thomas' theory, all of which spring from an ontological predisposition or presupposition, were sucessfully resolved.

The conclusion is founded, last of all, on the textual and textual-doctrinal comparison of Thomas' works with those of his predecessors, a task effected in Chapters Seven and Eight. There we saw that St. Thomas definitively rejects St. Albert's theory, which works from the aspect of God-principle, and explicitly follows the avowedly incompatible theory of the Halesian *Summa;* and that he revises his own work along the lines pointed out to him by St. Bonaventure, who also teaches an unequivocally intentional theory.

To interpret St. Thomas in a manner inconsistent with a theory exclusively intentional is, in consequence, a doctrinal absurdity and an historical injustice. To quote St. Thomas in confirmation of a theory not exclusively intentional is an exegetical crime and a scientific error—when it is not intellectual charlatanism.[27]

THIRD CONCLUSION:

> The presentation of the solution of the problem of the inhabitation given in the Scriptum super Sententiis is an invaluable commentary on the solution presented in the Summa Theologiae.

Although this fact has not been explicitly stressed in the examination of St. Thomas' doctrine in its two statements, nor has it been possible to develop it as fully as the matter warrants, the conclusion yet remains valid—it only makes explicit what lies beneath the surface of the doctrinal consideration of St. Thomas' theory. In Chapter Six, for example, where an analysis of his doctrine was effected, it was frequently the earlier work which was chosen to illustrate one or another point, since its treatment is more complete and in some ways more profound.

---

[27] One is amazed to find Father Morency, whose whole labor has been to show that the formal and specifying union of grace is, for St. Thomas, one of operation, conceding that a direct union to one individual Person by means of exemplarity and assimilation would be in perfect conformity with Thomistic principles (*op. cit.*, pp. 133-135). If it is a Thomistic principle that union with the Persons is achieved by operation, how can there be a contradictory union in line with Thomistic principles by reason of exemplarity? The only 'principle' advanced in support of this unfortunate concession is the obscure text, I *Sent.*, d. 30, q. 1, a. 2, previously commented on in this chapter. But the Petavian interpretation of this text would be in direct contradiction of St. Thomas' well-established notions of appropriation, as well as of Father Morency's well documented and profoundly argued thesis.

This is especially true of the notion of similitude. Thus the *Summa* teaches more clearly by its formula, *sicut cognitum*, etc., that the Persons are present as objects known and loved; but the *Sentences* inculcates the same truth on a yet deeper level by its concept of the image of God in man. Hence the earlier work shows not only what is the exact doctrinal key to the mystery but also tells us in what manner the indwelling affects man: for the triune presence conforms and assimilates man to God by making him a true image of the three divine Persons, an image which is what it is because man is conjoined to the really present Trinity not merely by appropriation but by a real union.

A brief consideration of St. Thomas' teaching on the image of God in man will illustrate this fact, even though its brevity runs the risk of over-simplifying a profound doctrine and thereby falsifying it. The salient points of St. Thomas' teaching, relevant to the interrelations of the two mysteries are these:

First: man at the summit of his intellectuality will image God.[28] On the one hand, the image should be found in that which is most noble in us, our supreme perfection;[29] on the other, God, who is to be imaged, is subsistent intellectuality, "Ipsum intelligere et Ipsum amare actualissimum." God most actually knows Himself by Himself and most actually loves Himself by Himself, and this love and knowledge is not only essential but notional, and notional primarily:[30] the generated Word is the Father's awareness of and by Himself, and the spirated Spirit His love of and by Himself (and the mutual love of Father

---

[28] I *Sent.*, d. 3, q. 3, a. 1.
[29] *Loc cit.*, q. 4 ad 1.
[30] *Sum. Theol.*, I, q. 39, a. 7 ad 3.

and Son), a unique divine Word and a unique divine Love in which His essence and all other things are known and loved.[31] Hence this image exists in the 'mind' (the superior part of the soul as it embraces both intellect and will),[32] primarily according to our acts of knowing and loving (the processions of the word according to the intellect, of love according to the will),[33] but secondarily according to the powers of the soul and especially its intellectual habits, insofar as our acts already exist in them virtually.[34]

Second: the perfection of the image will be proportionate to the object known and loved. Unlike God, whose knowing and loving is not specified by their objects (for in both knowledge and love His essence is the principle of specification, whatever be the object known and loved),[35] man's acts, habits and powers are determined and specified by their proper objects. Naturally, then, the most perfect image will be found in man's knowledge and love of God: knowledge and love of sensible reality constitutes only a 'vestige' of the divine essence; knowledge and love of one's own soul more perfectly represents God objectively (the soul being both *principium quod* and *principium quo*),[36] but on the natural plane it is not formally a knowledge of the soul as an image of God.[37]

[31] *Ibid.*, q. 37, a. 2; *De Pot.*, q. 9.
[32] *Ibid.*, III, q. 93, a. 6.
[33] I *Sent.*, d. 3, q. 4, a. 2.
[34] *Sum. Theol.*, I. q. 93, a. 7 ad 4.
[35] Cf. *Ibid.*, q. 14, a. 4 and a. 5 ad 3; q. 19, a. 1 and a. 2.
[36] *De Ver.*, q. 10.
[37] I *Sent.*, d. 3, q. 4, a. 4. It is interesting (and ultimately confirmatory of the interpretations of the medieval theories on the indwelling and the relations between the various medieval theologians which have been established in this work) that St. Albert insists more on the knowledge and love of self than on knowledge and love of God

Third: the more intimate the presence of the object known and loved the more perfect will be the image of God. In God the *principium quod* and the *principium quo* of His knowlege and love (both essential and notational) are absolutely identical: His essence is not only that which knows and loves and that which is known and loved but *that by which* He knows and loves.[38] This absolute identity by which God is most actually always present to Himself, the three Persons subsisting perfectly consubstantial in one and the same divine nature and distinct only by reason of Their opposed relations, can only be most imperfectly reflected in the created order. Thus the soul is intimately present to itself and can know and love itself as a *quo* and not merely as a *quod* (and this respecting the 'quid sit' as well as the 'an sit') :[39] as God knows and loves Himself (and in Himself knows and loves perfectly all other things) by Himself, so the soul knows and loves itself (and all things in a certain *most imperfect* manner in it),[40] by its own essence—not 'by acquisition,' by species or similitude. Yet this is only a 'potential' or 'habitual' knowledge and love, and on this score fundamentally differs from that most actual and always actualized knowledge and love of God.

(I *Sent.*, d. 3, a. 22; ed. cit., XXV, p. 122) as constituting the image, whereas the *Summa Alexandri* flatly holds that only in the knowledge and love of God does any true image exist at all (*op. cit.*, II, p. 413, ad 1; p. 414, Contra, a, where he cites St. Augustine's explicit affirmation of the same truth, XIV *De Trin.*, Chap. 12, n. 15 [PL 42: 1048]), a position St. Thomas apparently makes his own in the *Summa*, I, q. 93, a. 8 (by default, at least, not mentioning any other object), having previously refuted Albert's teaching in *De Ver.*, q. 10, a. 7 ad 5 (cf. ad 3).

[38] *Sum. Theol.*, I, q. 14, a. 4 and a. 5 ad 3; q. 19, a. 1 and a. 2.
[39] *De Ver.*, q. 10, a. 8.
[40] *Ibid.*, ad 7 in contrarium; a. 9 ad 2.

Again, even though man's natural knowledge and love of God is of an object really present ("eo quod ipse est per essentiam in anima, et tenetur ab ipsa non per acquisitionem"),[41] the image thereby realized is seriously deficient. God is known not only as giving being to the essence of the soul (the common presence of immensity) but especially as giving to the soul the proper intellectuality of a rational creature, since the mind is a participated similitude of the divine light (the special presence of immensity),[42] and so man can truly be said to know and love God by Himself as God knows and loves Himself by Himself. But his is specifically a *habitual* knowledge of God *operating*, of God as efficient and exemplary cause. God is known and loved only from and in His effects *as the cause of* these effects, and therefore neither *in* His essence nor *by* His essence, but by His causality.

This image, as is evident, is more perfect than that by which the soul knows and loves itself. Knowledge and love of self is an 'image of representation,' imitating the Trinity only by analogy; by his knowledge and love of God, however, man is *assimilated* to God, not merely by analogy but by intentional identity—and this is the greater, the more express likeness, the 'image of conformity.'[43] Howsoever deficient this 'image of creation'[44] is (an image "secundum exitum a principio," according to the gifts of nature),[45] it indicates exactly man's natural aptitude for knowing and loving God,[46] and consequently a natural

---

[41] I *Sent.*, d. 3, q. 4, a. 4.
[42] *De Ver.*, q. 10, a. 9 ad 2; *ibid.*, a. 11 ad 8.
[43] *Ibid.*, a. 7; *De Pot.*, q. 9, a. 9.
[44] I *Sent.*, d. 3, Divisio Secundae Partis Aextus; *De Ver.*, q. 27, a. 6 ad 5.
[45] I *Sent.*, d. 14, q. 2, a. 2.
[46] *Sum. Theol.*, I, q. 93, a. 4; cf. *De Ver.*, q. 10, a. 12 ad 1, 3, 5, *Sum Theol.*, III, q. 4, a. 1 ad 2.

desire (inefficacious and conditioned, no doubt, but nonetheless real) for attaining God as He is in Himself by knowledge and love.[47] *By the fact that he is an image of God,* man is capable of the very life and happiness of God,[48] for that life and that beatitude consist in operations of the intellect and will.

The triune image of creation is not *by nature* ordained to this supernatural participation; such a transcendent elevation is in no manner owed to it, nor was it intended by the Author of nature. Yet its very imperfection pleads mutely for the complementary supernatural realization of union with God which will bring it to the perfection it so obviously lacks: the human soul ever restless, incessantly uneasy, seeking always "the more noble things," with vehemence tending of its nature toward the known God Unknown, hoping beyond hope that God can and will somehow raise its insufficiency, its too feeble powers, to that splendor and glory of real union with Him which it dimly perceives and desperately initiates.

And such actually is the intention of Love: in the divine creative act which diffuses His goodness God envisions man as made by nature to His image and likeness, in order that he might be brought to perfection supernaturally (in a manner utterly beyond his needs and exigencies and powers). And for this purpose He will send His Word and His Love, that He and They might take up Their abode in the heart of man and transform him into Their knowledge and love.

In the theological perspective of St. Thomas, the image of creation is thus the *punctum insertionis* of the divine life and works, a real and positive similitude which will

---

[47] *Ibid.,* I-II, q. 5, a. 1.
[48] III *Sent.,* d. 28, q. 1, a. 2 ad 3; *Sum Theol.,* I-II, q. 113, a. 10; *ibid.,* III, q. 9, a. 2 and ad 3.

be the passive root, the aptitudinal capacity, the providential inchoation of the 'reformation' and 're-creation' by grace. The soul is the *forma beatificabilis,* in Bonaventure's phrase,[49] which returns to the end who was the principle of its coming forth through the gratuitous gifts by which alone the image of the Trinity in man attains its predestined perfection.[50] "Anima dicitur imago," says the Angelic Doctor, "secundum hoc quod Deum imitatur; sed gratia dicitur imago, sicut illud quo anima Deum imitatur."[51]

What is lacking to the perfection of the image of creation and how will this be supplied by grace? It is just at this point where these questions come up that the doctrines of the indwelling and of the image complement and perfect one another, for it is the inhabitation which brings the natural image in man to that inchoate conformation with the Most Blessed Trinity which is the prelude of beatitude. The most perfect of the images of creation does not possess God as present by His essence, i.e., as He is in Himself. Hence the natural man knows and loves Him not as He is, in His trinity of Persons, *in* His essence, but in His effects; nor does man know and love God *by* His essence: it is by His causality. On both counts, then, the natural image falls seriously short of realization.

But the supernatural man, even while *in via,* knows and loves God in His essence and by His essence, and thus this image infinitely transcends the image of creation, even though it remains imperfect when compared with the image of glory. This perfection, which is, so to

---

[49] *Breviloquium,* Part II, Chap. 9; ed. cit., V, p. 227.
[50] St. Thomas, I *Sent.,* d. 14, q. 2, a. 2.
[51] II *Sent.,* d. 26, q. 1, a. 2. Cf. the similar statement of St. Bonaventure: "Gratia ex hoc solo dicitur imago, quia est imaginis reformatio" (II *Sent.,* d. 26, a. un., q. 4 ad 1; ed. cit., II, p. 640).

speak, the indwelling from the point of view of the creature, elevates the soul with respect to each of the constitutive elements St. Thomas has insisted are requisite for the perfection of the image of the Trinity in man.

With respect to intellectuality: man's supreme intellectual perfection is realized in this participation of God's very nature and powers, supernatural effects which are most similar to God Himself,[52] proper to the divine order and connatural to God alone.[53] These are, therefore, more express likenesses,[54] surpassing in explicit resemblance the entire natural order simultaneously considered; so they are infinitely more capable of giving man a knowledge of God, since the more noble the effect the better can God be known in or from it.[55] So perfect are these effects, in fact, that by appropriation they represent the distinct Persons, images of Their proper relations; their exemplars and causes (not primary, of course, but secondary) are the divine processions themselves.[56] In this manner man is assimilated to the Persons as agent and exemplar principles, a prerequisite[57] for the formal union of conformity with the same Persons as objects substantially and really present to the soul which is realized by the operations of knowledge and love.

With respect to the object known: by grace man knows and loves the very essence of God, one in nature and three in Persons. "The rational creature is perfected by the gift of sanctifying grace," St. Thomas states, "to this end: that he may not only freely use the created gift

---

[52] *Lectura super Evan. S. Matt.*, V, n. 435.

[53] Cf. Cajetan, *Comm. in II-II*, q. 23, a. 2; Ledesma, *De divina perfectione*, q. 4, a. 6, 5um corollarium.

[54] IV *Sent.*, d. 49, q. 2, a. 7 ad 2.

[55] *Sum. Theol.*, I, q. 94, a. 1.

[56] I *Sent.*, d. 15, q. 4, a. 1.

[57] *Ibid.*, d. 15, q. 5, a. 3 ad 3; d. 17, q. 1, a. 1; a. 4 ad 4.

but even freely enjoy the divine Person Himself."[58] Thus the missions of Son and Holy Ghost and the donation of the Father, which are realized by the grace of the virtues and gifts, bring the image of the Trinity in man to its *ultimate* perfection, so far as the specifying object is concerned. It is the divine essence in its most proper and intimate nature which is known and loved. The *manner* of this union remains imperfect, but its object infinitely transcends the object of man's natural knowledge and love of God, as the supernatural which is connatural and proper to the divine order transcends the order of nature. This is the true *contemplatio divinorum* of the Wisdom of the Spirit[59] which the Angelic Doctor demands for the perfection of the image of the Trinity.[60]

With respect to the presence of the object: in the image of re-creation God is not merely present as cause and principle, even of the supernatural effects which assimilate man to Him, but specifically as the proper object and term of man's supernaturalized powers and acts, known and loved according to Himself, even though not clearly seen. God, to be sure, is not present as intelligible form as in the Beatific Vision: this is not an immediate knowledge.[61] But neither is He known *by means of* His effects, through the analogical notion of concepts, by discursive reasoning. Rather, under the inspiration of the Holy Ghost the 'mens,' by a kind of experiential apprehension according to the connaturality of love which springs from Wisdom, *experiences* God as really and substantially present, in a manner similar to the way in which the soul by which we live and sense is directly experienced. And therefore

[58] *Sum. Theol.*, I, q. 43, a. 3 ad 1.
[59] *Ibid.*, II-II, q. 45, a. 3 ad 3.
[60] I *Sent.*, d. 3, q. 3, a. 1 ad 3.
[61] *De Ver.*, q. 10, a. 11 ad 11.

God is known and loved not 'by acquisition' but as an object really present, and this not by causality but by His essence. So in this respect also the image of grace, inchoate though it be, infinitely transcends the image of creation, which knows and loves God only by His causality. The just know and love the *very essence* of God *by* the very essence of God, as God knows and loves, both essentially and notionally, His essence by His essence.

This image will reach perfection in glory, when the obscure is transmuted into vision, the habitual is always actual and God's essence is not only experienced but clearly seen. Nevertheless, St. Thomas' doctrine on the image of grace clearly shows that its perfection demands the real presence of the Trinity as objects of knowledge and love, and that conformity thus constitutes, as it does for his theory of the indwelling, the specifying and formal reason of this image; assimilation by representation and all that it implies—appropriation, exemplarity, etc.—is undoubtedly necessary, but in no sense the aspect of the gifts of grace which 'explains' these mysteries to us. Moreover, this doctrine admirably synthesizes the *Weltanschauung* of the wisdom of the Angelic Doctor, and brings into clear perspective the vital importance of the missions and indwelling of the divine Persons.

Difficulties there well may be in understanding two such profound doctrines as the image of the Trinity in man and the indwelling of the Trinity in man, and their mutual relations. It is reward enough if this long and exhaustive study shows that St. Thomas' theory on the inhabitation, uniquely an intentional one, is explicitly taught by the work which uses the notion of image as the key of the solution of the problem, and thus leads to the conclusion that the doctrines of image and indwelling are complementary, that the task of investigating one in the light of the other is possible and desirable. The present analysis can but suggest the rich intellectual rewards that can be anticipated by such a study.

l' envoi . . .

. . . no one by his own thinking can find out all that pertains to wisdom and, therefore, no one is so wise that he cannot learn from another.[62] And in this way, additions are made to knowledge. In the beginning a little bit was discovered; then, later, through different people it began gradually to increase into a great quantity: for it is everyone's concern to add what was lacking in the preceding additions to knowledge.[63]

In this study of the origins and sources of St. Thomas' doctrine on the indwelling of the Most Holy Trinity in the souls of the just, a classic example of theological evolution and progress is slowly unfolded before our eyes.

The essential elements of this tremendous mystery are revealed to man by Holy Scripture. But in what sense, literal or metaphorical, material or formal, are its astounding words to be understood? It is the primary contribution of the Greek Fathers to witness for us the Church's undeviating interpretation of the texts of Sacred Scrip-

---

[62] *Expositio in Psalmum 43;* n. 1 (*Omnia Opera,* ed. Parma, 1893, XIV, p. 315): ". . . nullus est sufficiens ad excogitanda omnia quae ad sapientiam pertinent: et ideo nullus ita sapiens est quin instruatur ab alio. . . ."

[63] *Expositio . . . Ethicorum Arist. ad Nicomachum,* Bk. I, lect. xi, n. 133 (ed. Spiazzi, Rome-Turin, 1949): "Et per hunc modum facta sunt additamenta in artibus, quarum a principio aliquid modicum fuit adinventum, et postmodum per diversos paulatim profecit in magna quantitate, quia ad quemlibet pertinet superaddere id quod deficit in consideratione praedecessorum."

ture: the inhabitation is 1) a special real presence, 2) of the three distinct Persons, 3) realized in the grace-state, 4) appropriated to the Holy Spirit, and 5) connected in some manner with the divine missions. Besides these basic scriptural facts, the Fathers of the East adumbrate two theological notions, those of the manifestation of the Persons and of a connection between the image of the Trinity and the indwelling.

This group of facts is unquestioningly accepted by the Latin Fathers and incorporated into their trinitarian doctrine. One among them, however, does more than simply repeat the asseverations of the eastern theologians: St. Augustine enriches the theological deposit. For he perfects the notion of manifestation, and by its means he becomes the first to offer a thorough analysis and a theological synthesis of the divine missions and the divine indwelling. Thus his explanation perceives a new and important fact, that the creature's knowledge of the Persons is necessarily implied by the divine missions. And he emphasizes the connection between mission and inhabitation, a point not so emphatically made by his predecessors.

The perception and presentation of these facts by the great Father of the Western Church does not, however, really explain the mystery. There still remain many important questions as yet unasked, and more satisfactory answers to be found—the very clarification of the facts of the mystery bring these to the fore. Hence when the theologians of the Middle Ages receive (without reservation) the body of doctrine concerning the inhabitation of the Trinity from St. Augustine, their logical and scientific minds perceive the difficulties raised by Augustine's presentation. And to the already considerable store of knowledge on this dogma they add a number of significant truths.

The missions imply some created effect, they agree: a change in the creature; this change their more precise understanding of grace enables them to distinguish as an effect of *sanctifying* grace. They insist in concert that the Holy Spirit is given as well as His gifts, and that all three Persons dwell in the soul. The specialness of this new divine presence, distinct from but presupposing the presence of immensity, is a cardinal tenet of their teaching. And they conclude that the invisible missions imply a divine procession, the indwelling of the Persons and Their manifestation by some created effect of sanctifying grace.

These further clarifications of the elements of the mystery clearly illuminate the central problem: how do the Persons dwell in man? what is the *formal reason* of Their inhabitation? Given the facts accepted about the mystery and the elements added by scientific analysis, the chief difficulties in answering this question revolve about two points: the specification of the special presence of the indwelling Trinity; and the relation of the manifestation of the Persons to Their inhabitation.

It is the great contribution of the Franciscan *Summa* on this matter to have solved successfully the first of these difficulties. Earlier scholastic attempts had been either fruitless, like those of Peter Lombard or of Alexander of Hales (who was followed by St. Albert), or merely suggestive, like that of Altissiodorensis. For the first time the nature of this presence is clearly and definitely stated: the Persons are present as possessed by the just as fruits to be enjoyed. This solution is accepted unreservedly by St. Bonaventure and St. Thomas, as it will be by their followers. And once this answer has been given, the problem of the inhabitation solves itself, for only by reason of the gifts of grace can the rational creature possess the Persons as fruits to be enjoyed. By reason of the gifts of grace, then, the three divine Persons come to the just and dwell in them.

All this wealth of theological analysis of the mystery —the facts of Scripture, the witness of the Fathers, the development of St. Augustine, the additions of the Schoolmen, the critical determination of the Halesian *Summa*— is gratefully received by St. Thomas. But he recognizes that the last word has yet to be said, for this theological tradition has not specified the proximate reason of the inhabitation. And without this ultimate specification no true understanding of the mystery can be said to have been attained: the revealed facts will be affirmed but not grasped; the theological investigations will possess but nominal value until they can be formally, not merely materially, understood.

Is it by Charity that the Persons dwell in the soul, as a logical development on Franciscan lines would teach? Not for Thomas, whose noetic is a historical turning-point in the evolution of scientific theology. Not for Thomas, whose profound Aristotelian psychology teaches that love is indifferent to the presence or absence of its object, whereas the Persons are contacted in the indwelling as objects really present. *Experimental* knowledge, on the other hand, is a direct experience of reality, of a reality physically present: a touching or tasting, in the intellectual order as well as in the physical order.

But is an experimental knowledge of the divine Persons possible? In answering this question St. Thomas has at his disposal the deep scholastic analysis of mystical knowledge, the tradition inaugurated by St. Augustine which reaches a scientific apogee in Richard of St. Victor; and he has, besides, his own thorough and original comprehension of the gifts of the Holy Spirit. The grace-gift of Wisdom, founded in supernatural Charity, gives man the power to know God as He is in Himself in a quasi-experimental manner. The formal reason of the indwelling of the Father and the Son and the Holy Spirit is this gift of the Holy Spirit, which presupposes the supernatural habit of Charity and issues in supernatural love.

So if this study has shown St. Thomas' indebtedness to his predecessors—and his debt is great—it also illuminates the originality of his contribution, and its value. Over the course of centuries man's knowledge of this mystery grows bit by bit, but it is left to the Angel of the Schools to offer the ultimate solution, the last and crowning achievement of a collective human effort to search the deep things of God by reason Faith-illumined.

St. Thomas has brought to perfection the special insight of St. Augustine: by reason of Their manifestation —by reason of Their gift by which man can know the distinct Persons in Their gifts as objects really present— the Persons are sent and given, and dwell in the soul. Thus is finally and profoundly clarified the relation between manifestation and inhabitation, a fact brilliantly perceived by St. Augustine, dimly understood by the Scholastics, but never before satisfactorily analyzed. For the Franciscan *Summa* and St. Bonaventure, manifestation was a consequence of the divine missions—it did not mean man's ability to contact God in Himself by direct experience but the representation of the Persons in the gifts of grace. Much the same was implied by the Augustinian fact for St. Albert and the school of which he was the chief representative: by appropriation, grace and its gifts make known the divine Persons, being similitudes of Their properties.

St. Thomas sees much more in the notion than his predecessors. The gifts of grace, especially Charity and

Wisdom, are more perfect images of the Trinity, to be sure, but not in that fact alone does the manifestation of the Persons (nor Their inhabitation) consist. The vital fact is that these same gifts give man the capacity to possess the Persons as really present, and Thomas' explanation of this shows how much deeper he plunged than his fellows, how much more profound was his comprehension of the mystery, how much more fruitful the hints of the past were for him. In a supernatural knowledge of which supernatural love is the formal medium, man can see these more perfect images of God, the gifts, and, in that vision, grasp without inference God Himself there imaged. And by such a direct contact man thereby possesses the Persons as really present.

Manifestation, in the eyes of the Angelic Doctor, means not only the representation of the Persons in their gifts but the quasi-experimental knowledge of the Persons represented in Their gifts by virtue of these gifts. And this, if not the knowledge of the Beatific Vision, is yet an immediate thinking of God without reasoning process, and a direct contact with the Persons as distinct and as really present. Hence the Augustinian notion, so understood in its formal sense, formally explains the divine indwelling; and it explains the mystery not in terms of appropriation but in terms of real contact with the properties of the Person. In the strictest sense of the word, this is a true 'proprium' theory—and the only one.

Is there need to remark on the value of this contribution? It is not a simple mathematical addition to past knowledge but a binominal theorem which explains all the facts and resolves all difficulties. It is not a simple limning in of a missing part of an unfinished canvas, it is an Angelico supplying the central figure in virtue of which the colors, the composition, the design, the perspective of the rest of the picture come to life, each element in this new light enhanced, intensified, perfected. In the groping of the ages in the bright-obscure of this mystery, many depths had been plumbed, many heights had been scaled. But it is St. Thomas' contribution to have gone to the heart of the mystery and, deeply searching, to have found the solution in whose light profundities and sublimities are, for the first time, seen in mutual relation; and, because of that, in true perspective. For the master alchymist at last discovers the secret sought by the ages, the elusive alkahest which catalyzes the unstable and discordant elements and transmutates the raw, unwrought matter into pure gold: the hidden *elixir vitae* of this supernature which is man's participation, even as he trods the clay, of the intense and fecund and blessed life of the Three-in-One.

Heir of, and debtor to, a vast and profound theological study of the divine missions, St. Thomas subsumes in himself the loving labor of centuries, and in and by it brings man's stutterings to their perfect conclusion. Beyond this we can say nothing essential, until such time as there shall no more be need of words.

APPENDIX

Transcriptions of Pertinent Manuscripts

For the transcriptions of the following manuscripts, the author is deeply indebted to the learning and the kindness of the Very Rev. L. B. Gillon, O.P., S.T.M., Vice-Rector of the Pontifical Athenaeum "Angelicum" and Professor of Moral Theology in the Pontifical Faculty of Theology of that institution. It should be noted, however, that since they have not been collated with other manuscripts some of the readings are doubtful; also only those parts which directly concern the present investigation are reproduced.

Alexander of Hales: *Quaestiones Disputatae de Missionibus.*

Cod. Vat. lat. 782: saec. XIII, membran., mm. 274 x 205 (f. 154^a mm. $\pm$ 175 x $\pm$ 185), ff. II. 186 (-103, + 154^a) coll. 2.*

f° 7 vb. Circa primum quid sit missio, NOTANDUM quod sicut dicit AUG., IV *De Trin.*, quod sicut generari est

* A Pelzer, *Codices Vaticani latini*, II, pars prior: Codd. 679-1134 (*Città del Vaticano*, 1931), p. 96. A complete description of the manuscript is here given, pp. 96-110.

Filio esse a Patre, ita mitti est cognosci esse a Patre, et sicut Spiritui Sancto donum dei esse ex Patre procedere, ita ipsum Spiritum cognosci quod a Patre procedit, est mitti.

Ex his duabus propositionibus sumitur haec propositio: mitti est cognosci esse a Persona alterius. Sed cognitio non est aeterna, ergo nec mittere.

. . . .

Rio/ Temporale dicitur dupliciter; uno modo quod est in tempore, licet non sit ex tempore. Hoc autem quod est cum tempore et non est ex tempore, est quod non habet causam suam in tempore, licet effectus temporalis sit.

Alio modo dicitur temporale quod est in tempore, in quantum manifestatur a tempore et hoc proprie dicitur temporale. — Primo modo dicitur missio temporalis, sive dicatur Spiritum S.tum mitti, sive Filium, quia non habet causam in tempore, vel est ibi aliquid quod est in tempore, quia cum dicitur: Spiritus S.tus mittitur, intelligitur gratiam infundi que est in tempore. Sed totum hoc quod est procedere ab alio ad demonstrationem, non est temporale, quia non habet initium in tempore, nec finem, licet demonstratio in creatura, que intelligitur, habeat initium et finem in tempore. Unde bene dico quod missio hoc modo temporalis est.

Rio/ Ad hoc quod obiicitur quod mitti est cognosci, sed cognosci est temporale, ergo etc., si recte definimus missionem sic dicemus: missio est processio manifestativa in creatura corporaliter vel spiritualiter. Sed cum dicitur: Spiritus S.tus mittitur [a] se, numquid hec est processio manifestativa, cum Spiritus S.tus non procedit a Spiritu S.to? Dico quod semper est processio manifestativa, quia semper est ibi ratio per quam potest manifestari. Sed non omnis creatura manifestat, sed creatura que est appropriata Filio et Spiritui Sancto, quia sapientia est effectus appropriabilis Filio, licet sit communis Tribus, similiter columba. . . .

Circa 2m, NOTANDUM est quod tria vocabula sunt que temporaliter dicuntur, licet intelligatur eternum: apparitio, missio, et datio. Et differentia est inter haec tria: essentia enim divina incognoscibilis est, quantum est de se et persona procedens. Sed divina persona communicat aliquid creature, quia Filius sapientiam, Spiritus S.tus, amorem. Est ergo ibi essentia et processio, que eterna est, que, quantum est de se, incognoscibiles sunt, sed cognoscibiles sunt in effectibus.

Sunt ergo tria secundum rationem dicendi: apparitio, que manifestat essentiam, missio que processionem, datio que manifestat circumstantiam qua nobis Filius communicat sapientiam, Spiritus Sanctus, amorem, et non est possibile plura esse. Omnia enim facta sunt propter hominem, ut homo cognoscat, quia apparitio facta est ut homo essentiam cognosceret, missio ut processionem, datio ut cognoscamus potentiam communicandi. Hec est ergo differentia eorum. Datio ergo est communicatio manifestativa in effectu. . . .

f⁰ 8 va. De missione spirituali. NOTANDUM quod missio spiritualis Filii sive Spiritus S.ti est manifestatio processionis eterne in creatura spirituali, data creature rationali ad remotionem ipsius a sensibilibus ad eterna. Hec diffinitio potest colligi ex diversis textibus Augustini in I *De Trin*. Est ergo missio spiritualis ad ostendendum spiritualiter processionem eternam et utilitas est ad revocandum creaturam a sensibilibus ad eterna.

Hec manifestatio est per duos modos in genere, quia una est eo quod pertinet ad veritatem, alter in eo quod pertinet ad bonitatem. Utroque modo est manifestatio Spiritus S.ti. Uno istorum modorum est manifestatio Filii, scl. quoad veritatem. Processio autem

Spiritus S.ti preintelligit processionem Filii, propter hoc illud manifestat processionem Spiritus S.ti, quod manifestat processionem Filii. Unde duobus modis manifestaur processio Spiritus S.ti. Unde dicuntur hi *filii adoptionis*, alii *filii veritatis*. Item manifestatio quoad veritatem et quoad bonitatem est per gratiam; manifestatio ergo primo est per gratiam. Gratia autem est duplex. . . .

Eudes Rigaud: *Commentarium in Libros Sententiarium.*

Cod. Vat. lat. 5982: membran., saec. XIII, foll. 171, mm. 305 x 235.*

f⁰ 24v. Si queratur que necessitas sit ut simul dentur ipse [Spiritus Sanctus] et dona eius et quomodo differentur dantur, DICENDUM quod ipse Spiritus Sanctus datur tamquam panis ad reficiendum. Gratia et virtus sunt quasi virtus faciens nos degustare et refici ex illo. Sicut enim homo, habens cibum, si non habeat virtus degustandi non reficeretur ex illo, sic et anima que de se non erat apta degustare et refici tanto pane, necesse habuit ut daretur ei gratia et cetera dona per que disponeretur et habilitaretur ad reficiendum et que essent ei quasi virtus ad degustandum.

f⁰ 24. Circa tercium queritur utrum processio temporalis sit nature vel persone. Et quod sit nature sive essentie et non persone VIDETUR sic. Procedere temporaliter dicit effectum in creatura, sed regula est quod omne dictum de deo convocans (connotans?) effectum in creatura, presupponit divinam essentiam et ratio hujus regule quia opera Trinitatis respectu creature sunt indivisa. Ergo procedere temporaliter dicit essentiam, ergo non est proprium alicujus persone solum, sed dicit quod est essentie vel nature.

* B. Pergamo, "De quaestionibus ineditis fr. Odonis Rigaldi. . . .", *Archivum Franciscanum historicum*, 29 (1936), p. 48, note 1.

CONTRA. Omne quod dicitur de essentia vel natura convenit toto Trinitati, ergo si procedere de essentia vel natura et ei convenit, convenit toti Trinitati et ita Patri quod falsum est, ergo et primum.

Ad hoc DICENDUM quod hujusmodi verba: temporaliter procedere et mitti convocant effectum in creatura qui in quantum effectus est totius Trinitatis. Unde quantum ad hoc dant intelligere essentiam, non quod ipsum mitti vel procedere sit essentie, sed quia effectus convocatus essentie est sive totius Trinitatis et non mitti vel procedere prout dicunt respectum ad illum *a quo,* quia omnis qui procedit vel mittitur, ab aliquo est. Esse autem ab alio, importat distinctionem. Ideo praedicta verba per comparationem ad illum a quo dicunt notionem, non essentiam, et dicuntur proprie de persona, [non] de essentia. Per respectum igitur ad illum a quo dicunt notionem et conveniunt potentie, non essentie, sed per respectum ad effectum in creatura, sive ad illud in quod est missio vel processio, verum est quod dant intelligere essentiam, sicut primo obiicitur, non quod procedere vel mitti conveniat toti Trinitati, sed quia effectus in creatura totius Trinitatis.

Anonymous: *Codex Vaticanus latinus 691.*

Saec. XIII, membran., mm. 289 x 190, ff. II. 178 (70ª-79ª), coll. 2.*

f⁰ 17 ra. Queritur utrum Spiritus S. infundatur mentibus nostris vel eius dona solum vel utroque modo? Cum enim Spiritus S. in nobis possit quidquid dona eius et amplius, videntur dona superfluere. . . . Sto. Spiritus S. utroque modo datur, in se et in suis donis et potest dici quod in iustis est Spiritus S. sicut fructus: omnis enim fruuntur eo. Dona autem sua sive gratie sunt sicut dispositiones mentis nostre ad fruen-

---

* Pelzer, *op. cit.,* p. 11.

dum. Quod obiicitur quod Spiritus S. sufficienter facit nos Deo gratos *effective*, gratie et virtus *formaliter*, quia informant mentem ad hoc quod sit templum Dei. Dicimus etiam quod licet sine suis donis possit agere, tamen nos *sine suis donis* aliquid meritorium non possumus agere. Et licet ab eo habeamus quod operemur, tamen non est forma mentis nostre.—Ad aliud dicimus quod S.S. in impio non est ut Sanctus, sed ut Spiritus et cum justificatur, sic est ut Sanctus.

TABLE I

Comparison of the Scriptum Super Sententiis With Possible Sources

The following Table is a schematic comparison of the tract on the divine missions in the *Scriptum super Sententiis* with the works which may have influenced its composition; it gives the references to the passages in these works which parallel, more or less perfectly, all of the elements of the Thomistic tract. It does not show, however, more than material identity or near-identity; that is, it does not of itself show that the passages referred to, howsoever parallel, are *in fact* sources of the Thomistic passage—it merely indicates that they are, to this or that degree, textually and doctrinally similar.

In the last column of this Table the passages in the *Summa Theologiae* of St. Thomas which parallel those of his earlier work have also been indicated.

For the Table, the following symbols are used:

<u>precise</u> parallelism (textual and doctrinal): **bold face type**

<u>approximate</u> parallelism (largely doctrinal): *italic type*

<u>remote</u> parallelism (textual or doctrinal or both): Roman type

<u>doctrinal differences:</u> brackets: [ ]

TABLE I

SCRIPTUM	SUMMA ALEXANDRI*	ALBERT: SENTENCES	BONAVENTURE: SENTENCES	SUMMA I, Q. 43
Distinction 14, Question 1, Article 1				
Obj. 1			14 a. 1 q. 1 obj. 2	
Obj. 2			" obj. 3	
Obj. 3			" obj. 4	
Obj. 4		14 a, 10 obj. 2	" obj. 5	
Obj. 5			" obj. 6	
Sol.	704 *ad* 3	14 a. 10 obj. 2	14 a. 1 q. 1 resp.	
Ad 1	703 ad 2	" ad 2	" ad 2	*a. 2 ad 2*
Ad 2		" ad 2	" ad 3	
Ad 3		" ad 2	" ad 4	
Ad 4			" ad 5	
Ad 5	703 ad 1		" ad 6	
Distinction 14, Question 1, Article 2				
Obj. 1		14 a. 7 Sed Con. 1		
Obj. 2				
Obj. 3				
Obj. 4			14 a. 1 q. 2 ad 4	
Con. 5				
Prae. 6				
Sol.	699 *sol.*	14 a. 7 obj. 1 & sol.	14 a. 1 q. 2 resp.	
Ad 1				
Ad 2	714 ad 2			
Ad 3		14 a. 7 obj. 1 & sol.		*a. 2 ad 3*
Ad 4		14 a. 10 sol.		
Ad 5			14 a. 1 q. 2 ad 1	
Ad 6			14 a. 1 q. 2 ad 2 & 3	

*Citations for this work are by page number from the first volume of the Quaracchi edition. Those from the commentaries of St. Albert and St. Bonaventure are from Bk. I, the first number given being that of the Distinction.

SCRIPTUM	SUMMA ALEXANDRI	ALBERT: SENTENCES	BONAVENTURE: SENTENCES	SUMMA I, Q. 43
Distinction 14, Question 2, Article 1, Questiuncula 1				
Obj. 1		14 a. 13 obj. 1		
Obj. 2		14 a 13 obj. 2		
Obj. 3				
Obj. 4		15 a. 16 obj. 5		
Contra				
Praet.				
Sol.	729 Cf. 704 ad 3; 722 n. 2 etc.		14 a. 2 q. 1 ad 2	a. 3 sol. & a. 2 sol
Ad 1		[14 a. 13 ad 1]	14 a. 2 q. 1 ad 2	
Ad 2		[14 a. 13 ad 2]	"	a. 2 sol.
Ad 3		15 a. 16 ad 5	"	
Ad 4				
Distinction 14, Question 2, Article 1, Questiuncula 2				
Obj. 1	728 II a			a. 3 obj. 2
Contra	728 Contra 1			
Sol.	730 II			a. 3 ad 2.
Distinction 14, Question 2, Article 2				
Obj. 1				
Obj. 2			15 II a. 1 q. 1 obj. 4	
Obj. 3				a. 3 obj. 3
Obj. 4	732 obj. 2		15 II a. 1 q. 1 obj. 1	a. 3 obj. 4
Contra	731 II a			
Praet.	733 II ad 1			
Sol.	cf. 712 ad 3		14 a. 2 q. 1 ad 3 & 4	a. 3 sol.
Ad. 1			"	
Ad. 2	See note 1	[14 a 13 ad 4]	15 II a. 1 q. 1 sol.	a. 3 ad 1
Ad 3	See note 2	14 a. 3 sol. & 15 a. 17 sol.	15 II a. 1 q. 1 ad 2 & 3 & 4	a. 3 ad 3
Ad 4	733 ad 2			a. 3 ad 4

NOTE 1: Cf. 732 ad 2; 732-733 ad 3; 733, II, ad 1. Also *supra,* pp. 255 f.
NOTE 2: Cf. 714 ad 2, ad 4, and ad 5. Also *supra,* pp. 258 f.

TABLE I

SCRIPTUM	SUMMA ALEXANDRI	ALBERT: SENTENCES	BONAVENTURE: SENTENCES	SUMMA I, Q. 43
Distinction 14, Question 3				
Obj. 1		14 a. 16 obj. 1		
Obj. 2	711 obj. 2	" obj. 3	14 a. 2 q. 2 obj. 2	
Obj. 3	711 obj. 3	" obj. 2		
Contra				
Praet.				
Sol.	711 sol.	14 a. 16 sol.	14 a. 2 q. 2 resp. & ad 1	
Ad 1	[712 ad 2]	" ad 1		
Ad 2	712 ad 3	" ad 3	14 a. 2 q. 2 ad 2	
Ad 3		" ad 2		
Expos. Textus		[14 a. 11 sol.]	14 Dubium III	
Distinction 15, Question 1, Article 1				
Obj. 1	697 obj. 1	15 a. 7 obj. 2		a 1 obj. 3
Obj. 2	697 obj. 2	15 a 7 obj. 1	15 I a. 1 q. 1 obj. 1	a. 1 obj. 2
Obj. 3	697 obj. 3		15 I a. 1 q. 1 obj. 3	a. 1 obj. 1
Obj. 4				
Sol.	698 sol.	14 a. 4 ad 2 & 14 a. 5 sol.	15 I a. 1 q. 1 sol.	a. 1 sol.
Ad 1	698 ad 1	15 a. 7 ad 2		a. 1 ad 2
Ad 2	698 ad 2	15 a. 7 ad 1	15 I a. 1 q. 1 ad 1	a. 1 ad 2 & ad 3
Ad 3	608 ad 3		15 I a. 1 q. 1 ad 3	a. 1 ad 1
Ad 4				

SCRIPTUM	SUMMA ALEXANDRI	ALBERT: SENTENCES	BONAVENTURE: SENTENCES	SUMMA I, Q. 43
Distinction 15, Question 1, Article 2				
Obj. 1	704 Contra 4			
Obj. 2	700 Contra 1			
Obj. 3				
Obj. 4	700 Contra 2			*a. 4 obj. 3*
Sol.	700 sol. & ad 1			
Ad. 1	706 a			
Ad 2	701 ad 1			
Ad 3				
Ad 4	701 ad 2			*a. 4 ad 3*
Distinction 15, Question 2				
Obj. 1	715 obj. 1		15 I a. 1 q. 3 obj. 1	
Obj. 2	715 obj. 3			*a. 4 obj. 2*
Obj. 3	715 obj. 2	14 a. 13 q. 2 obj. & 15 a. 21 Sed C. 2		
Obj. 4	716 II	15 a. 7 ult. Sed C. 2 & obj. 3	15 I a. 1 q. 3 obj. 4	
Obj. 5	718 II obj. 2			
Obj. 6		15 a. 16 obj. 3		*a. 5 obj. 1*
Sol.		15 a. 7 sol. ult & 14 a. 13 sol. ad q. 2		*a. 4 corp.*
Ad 1	716 *ad 1*			
Ad 2	716 ad 2 & 3		15 I a. 1 q. 3 ad 1 & 2	*a. 4 ad 2*
Ad 3	716 *ad 2*	14 a. 13 q. 2 ad obj.		
Ad 4	716 II sol.	14 a 13 q. 2 ad obj. & 15 a. 7 ad 3	15 I a 1 q. 3 ad 4	
Ad 5	719 II *ad 1*			
Ad 6	718 a & b	15 a. 16 ad 13		*a. 5 ad 1*

TABLE I

SCRIPTUM	SUMMA ALEXANDRI	ALBERT: SENTENCES	BONAVENTURE: SENTENCES	SUMMA I, Q. 43
Distinction 15, Question 3, Article 1				
Obj. 1		15 a. 2 obj. 5	*15 I a. 1 q. 4 obj. 1*	a. 8 obj. 2
Obj. 2	**708 Contra 2**			a. 8 obj. 3
Obj. 3				
Obj. 4	**707 Contra 1**	*15 a. 5 obj. 3*	15 I a. 1 q. 4 obj. 4	
Obj. 5		*15 a. 5 q. 1*		
Contra	**707 b & a** ..			
Sol. 1)	[*709 sol. II*]	15 a. 2 sol. See note 3	[15 I a. 1 q. 4 sol.]	*a. 4 ad 1*
2)	*708 sol. I*	15 a. 5 sol.	[15 I a. 1 q. 4 sol.]	
3)	*709 sol. II*	*15 a. 5 sol. ad q. 2*	[15 I a. 1 q. 4 sol.]	
Ad 1		15 a. 2 ad 5	15 I a. 1 q. 4 ad 1	
Ad 2				
Ad 3				
Ad 4		*15 a. 5 ad 3*	15 I a. 1 q. 4 ad 1	
Ad 5		[15 a. 5 sol. ad q. 2]		
Distinction 15, Question 3, Article 2				
Obj. 1	*709 contra 1*			
Obj. 2				
Contra	*709 a*			
Item	*709 b*			
Sol.	*710 sol.*	*15 a. 9 sol.*		
Ad 1	*710 ad 1*			
Ad 2				
Expos. Textus		**15 a. 4 obj. & sol.**	*15 Dubium III*	

NOTE 3: Cf. also *d. 14, a. 4 ad 2 and a. 5, sol.; d. 15, a. 21, sol.*

SCRIPTUM	SUMMA ALEXANDRI	ALBERT: SENTENCES	BONAVENTURE: SENTENCES	SUMMA I, Q. 43
Distinction 15, Question 4, Article 1				
Obj. 1			15 II a. 1 q. 1 obj. 4	
Obj. 2	718 Contra a			a. 5 obj. 2
Contra				
Item				
Sol.				
Ad 1	714 ad 2, 3, 4	15 a. 17 sol.	15 II a. 1 q. 2 sol.	
Ad 2				
Ad 3	714 ad 5; cf. note 2		15 II a. 1 q. 2 sol.	
Distinction 15, Question 4, Article 2				
Obj. 1				
Obj. 2				
Obj. 3				
Obj. 4				
Contra				a. 5 obj. 3
Sol.	720 sol.		15 I a. 1 q. 2 resp.	a. 5 ad 3
Ad 1				
Ad 2				
Ad 3				
Ad 4				
Distinction 15, Question 4, Article 3				
Obj. 1	703 obj. 2	15 a. 1 obj. 2		a. 2 obj. 1
Obj. 2	703 obj. 3			a. 2 obj. 3
Obj. 3	703 obj. 4	15 a. 1 obj. 3		
Contra		15 a 16 obj. & sol.		
Praet.				
Sol.	703 sol.	15 a. 1 sol.	15 I a. 1 q. 2 resp.	a. 2 sol.
Ad 1	703 ad 2	15 a. 15 sol. & 15 a. 1 ad 2	15 I a. 1 q. 2 ad 1	a. 2 ad 1
Ad 2	703 ad 3			a. 2 ad 3
Ad 3	704 ad 4	15 a. 1 ad 3		

TABLE I

SCRIPTUM	SUMMA ALEXANDRI	ALBERT: SENTENCES	BONAVENTURE: SENTENCES	SUMMA I, Q. 43
Distinction 15, Question 5, Article 1, Questiuncula 1				
Obj. 1	722 obj. 1			
Obj. 2	723 ad 2			*a. 6 obj. 4*
Obj. 3	722 obj. 3			
Contra				
Sol.	723 *sol.*			a. 6 corp.
Ad 1	723 ad 1			
Ad 2	723 ad 2			*a. 6 ad 4*
Ad 3	723 ad 3			
Distinction 15, Question 5, Article 1, Questiuncul a2				
Obj. 1	734 **Contra 1**		15 II a. 1 q. 3 obj. 1	
Obj. 2	722 *Contra c*	15 a. 19 obj. 2		
Contra	724 obj. 3			
Sol.	734 **resp.**	15 a. 19 sol.	15 II a. 1 q. 3 sol.	*a. 6 ad 2*
Ad 1	734 **ad 1**		15 II a. 1 q. 3 ad 1	
Ad 2	724 **ad 3**	15 a. 19 ad 2		
Distinction 15, Question 5, Article 1, Questiuncula 3				
Obj. 1				
Obj. 2	723 obj. 1	15 a. 19 obj. 1		
Sol.	724 *sol.*	15 a. 19 sol.	15 Dubium IV	*a. 6 ad 3*
Ad 1				
Ad 2	724 ad 1	15 a. 19 ad 1		

SCRIPTUM	SUMMA ALEXANDRI	ALBERT: SENTENCES	BONAVENTURE: SENTENCES	SUMMA I, Q. 43
Distinction 15, Question 5, Article 1, Questiuncula 4				
Obj. 1	725 **Contra b**			a. 6 obj. 3
Obj. 2	725 **Contra a**	15 a. 12 obj.		
Obj. 3	724 obj. 1			
Obj. 4	725 obj. 2			
Sol.				a. 6 ad 3
Ad 1	725 ad 2 & 726 b			
Ad 2	726 a			
Ad 3	[725 ad 1 & 2]			
Distinction 15, Question 5, Article 2				
Obj. 1				
Obj. 2	721 obj. 2	15 a 12 sol.		
Contra	721 c			a. 6 obj. 1
Praet.	721 a			a. 6 ad 1
Sol.	721 sol.	[15 a. 18 sol.]	15 Dubium III	
Ad 1				
Ad 2	721 ad 2			
Distinction 15, Question 5, Article 3				
Obj. 1		15 a. 20 obj. 4		
Obj. 2		15 a. 20 obj. 4		
Obj. 3				
Obj. 4				
Contra		15 a. 20 Sed C.		
Sol.		15 a. 20 sol.	15 Dubium V	
(Ad 1)				
Ad 2		15 a. 20 ad 4		
Ad 3				
Ad 4				
Expos.				
Textus		15 a. 21 Sed C.	15 Dubium VI	

TABLE I
SUMMARY

SIMILARITIES	SUMMA ALEX.	ALBERT	BONAVENTURE:
Precise parallelisms	53	15	9
Approximate parallelisms	21	28	28
Remote parallelisms	18	11	17
[Differences]	5	6	3

TABLE II

Comparison of the *Summa Theologiae*, I (Question 43), with the *Scriptum super Sententiis* (Book I)

Since St. Thomas revises his original treatment of the divine missions to a considerable extent in his *Summa*, the parallelisms here listed are largely (although not exclusively) *doctrinal*, and not *textual* as well as doctrinal. Where even this parallelism is remote, the reference to the *Sentences* is enclosed in parentheses. In some cases the only parallel will be one of subject-matter.

Article 1

Obj. 1 = d. 15, a. 1, q. 1, obj. 3
Obj. 2 =   ″   obj. 2
Obj. 3 =   ″   obj. 1
Corpus=   ″   sol.
Ad 1 =   ″   ad 3
Ad 2 =   ″   ad 1 & 2
Ad 3 =   ″   ad 2

Article 2

Obj. 1 = d. 15, q. 4, a. 3, obj. 1
Obj. 2 =   no parallel
Obj. 3 = d. 15, q. 4, a. 3, obj. 2
Corpus= (d. 14, q. 2 a. 1, sol. 1 & ad 2; d. 15, q. 4, a. 3, sol.)
Ad 1 = d. 15, q. 4, a. 3, ad 1
Ad 2 = d. 14, q. 1, a. 1, ad 2
Ad 3 = d. 14, q. 1, a. 2, ad 3 (d. 15, q. 4, a. 3, ad 2)

Article 3

Obj. 1 =   no parallel
Obj. 2 = (d. 14, q. 2, a. 1, q1a. 2, con.)
Obj. 3 = d. 14, q. 2, a. 2, obj. 3
Obj. 4 =   ″   obj. 4
Corpus= d. 14, q. 2, a. 1, sol. 1; a. 2, sol.
Ad 1 = (d. 14, q. 2, a. 2, ad 2)
Ad 2 = d. 14, q. 2, a. 1, sol. 2
Ad 3 = d. 14, q. 2, a. 2, ad 3
Ad 4 = d. 14, q. 2, a. 2, ad 4

Article 4

Obj. 1 =   no parallel
Obj. 2 = (d. 15, q. 2, obj. 2)
Obj. 3 = d. 15, q. 1, a. 2, obj. 4
Corpus= d. 15, q. 2, sol.
Ad 1 = (d. 15, q. 3, a. 1, sol. 1)
Ad 2 = d. 15, q. 2, ad 2
Ad 3 = d. 15, q. 1, a. 2, ad 4

TABLE II

Article 5
Obj. 1 = d. 15, q. 2, obj. 6
Obj. 2 = d. 15, q. 4, a. 1, obj. 2
Ob.j 3 = d. 15, q. 4, a. 2, con.
Corpus=   no parallel
 Ad 1 = d. 15, q. 2, ad 6
 Ad 2 = d. 15, q. 4, a. 1, ad 2
 Ad 3 = d. 15, q. 4, a. 2, sol.

Article 6
Obj. 1 = d. 15, q. 5, a. 2, con.
Obj. 2 =   no parallel
Obj. 3 = d. 15, q. 5, a. 1, q1a. 4, obj. 2
Obj. 4 = d. 15, q. 5, a. 1, q1a. 1, obj. 2

Corpus= (d. 15, q. 5, a. 1, sol. 1)
 Ad 1 = (d. 15, q. 5, a. 2, sol.)
 Ad 2 = d. 15, q. 5, a. 1, sol. 2
 Ad 3 = d. 15, q. 5, a. 1, sol. 3
                                 & sol. 4
 Ad 4 = d. 15, q. 5, a. 1, sol. 1
                                 ad 2

Article 7
(Distinction 16)

Article 8
Obj. 1 =   no parallel
Obj. 2 = d. 15, q. 2, obj. 1
Obj. 3 =   "   obj. 2
Corpus= (d. 15, q. 3, a. 1, sol.)

TABLE III

Outlines

Summa Fratris Alexandri, Book I, Part II, Inquisitio II, Tractatus I, Sectio II, Quaestio II: De notionibus connotantibus effectum in creatura

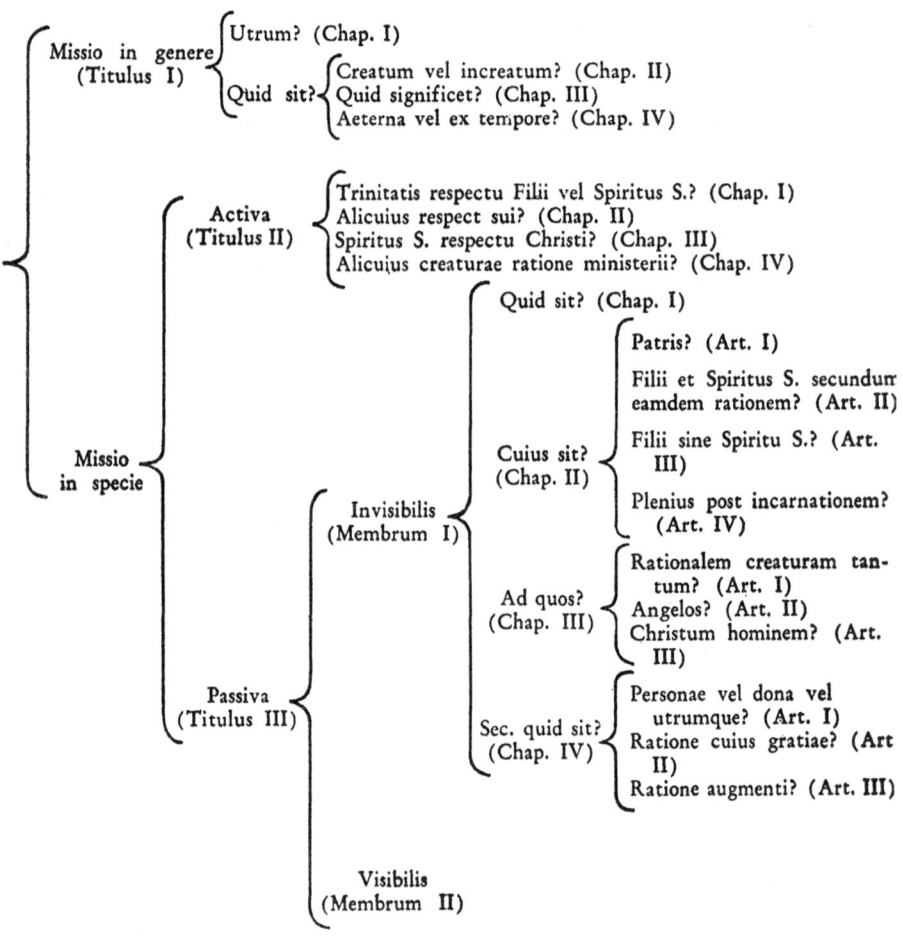

TABLE III

St. Bonaventure: *Commentarius in IV Libros Sententiarum*, Book I

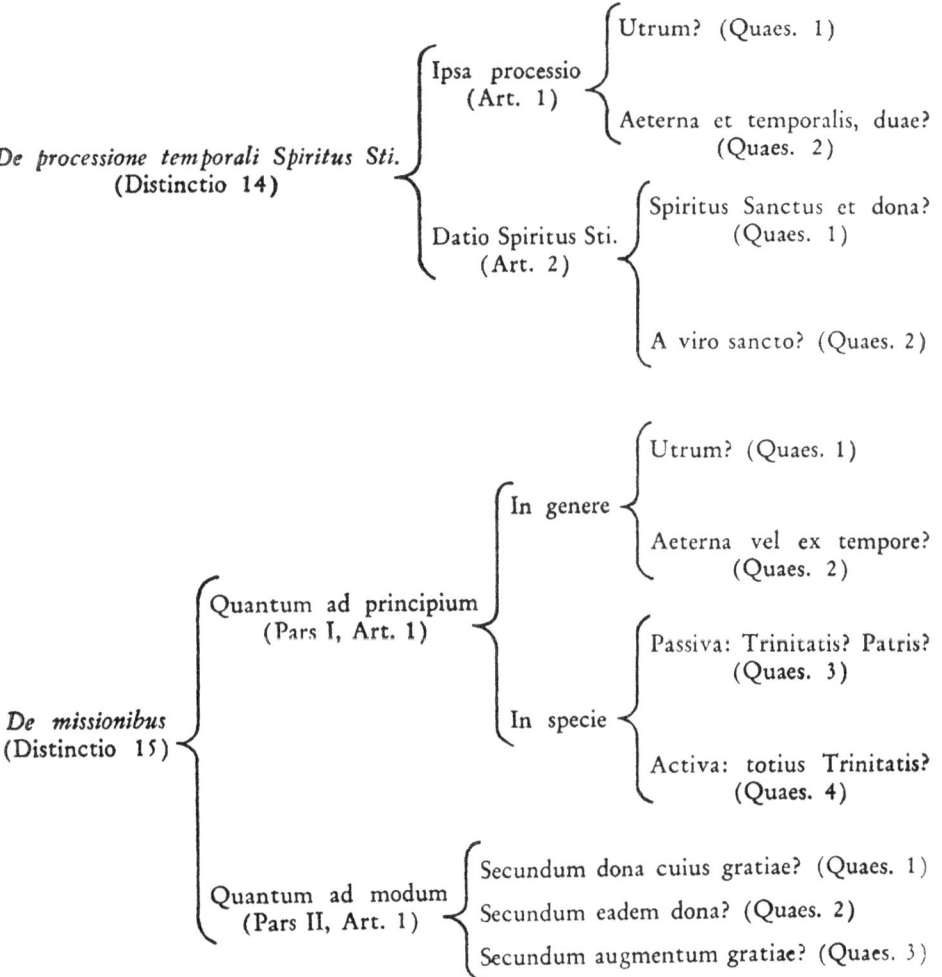

De processione temporali Spiritus Sti. (Distinctio 14)
- Ipsa processio (Art. 1)
  - Utrum? (Quaes. 1)
  - Aeterna et temporalis, duae? (Quaes. 2)
- Datio Spiritus Sti. (Art. 2)
  - Spiritus Sanctus et dona? (Quaes. 1)
  - A viro sancto? (Quaes. 2)

De missionibus (Distinctio 15)
- Quantum ad principium (Pars I, Art. 1)
  - In genere
    - Utrum? (Quaes. 1)
    - Aeterna vel ex tempore? (Quaes. 2)
  - In specie
    - Passiva: Trinitatis? Patris? (Quaes. 3)
    - Activa: totius Trinitatis? (Quaes. 4)
- Quantum ad modum (Pars II, Art. 1)
  - Secundum dona cuius gratiae? (Quaes. 1)
  - Secundum eadem dona? (Quaes. 2)
  - Secundum augmentum gratiae? (Quaes. 3)

TABLE III

St. Thomas: *Scriptum super Sententiis Magistri Petri Lombardi*, Book I

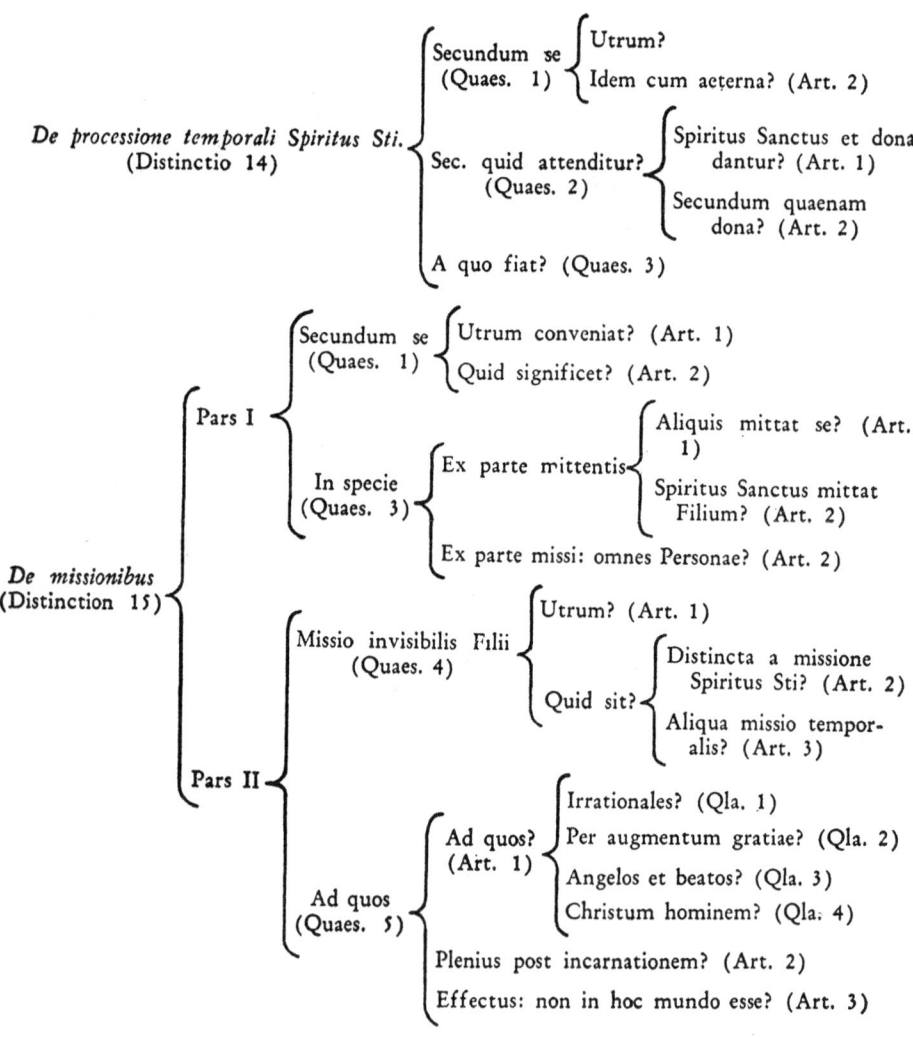

TABLE IV

The Economy of the Summa Theologiae

Summa Theologiae, I, Q. 43		Scriptum	Summa Alexandri	Bonaventure
Missio secundum se	Utrum sit (a. 1)	d.14, q.1, a.1 d.15, q.1, a.1 & a.2	Tit.1, Chap.1 & 3	d.14, a.1, q.1 d.15, I, a.1, q.1
	eliminates	d.14, q.3 d.15, q.3, a.1 & a.2	Tit.2 Tit.2, Chap.4	d.14, a.2, q.3 d.15, I, a.1, q.4
	Quid sit (a. 2)	d.14, q.1, a.2 d.15, q.1, a.3		d.14, a.1, q.2 d.15, I, a.1, q.2
In specie — Invis.	Sec. quod (a. 3)	d.14, q.2, a.1 " a.2	Tit.3, Chap.4, Art.1 & Art.2	d.14, a.2, q.1 d.15, II, a.1
	Cuius { Patris (a. 4)	d.15, q.2	Tit.3, Memb.1, Chap.2 Art.1	d.15, I, a.1, q.3
	Filii (a. 5)	d.15, q.4, a.1 " a.2	Tit.3, Memb.1, Chap.2 Art.2 & Art.3	d.15, II, a.1, q.2
	Ad quos (a. 6)	d.15, q.5, a.1 qla. 1, 2, 3, 4, d.15, q.5, a.2	Tit.3, Memb.1, Chap.2 Art.4; Chap.3, Art.1 & 2 & 3; Chap. 4, Art. 3	d.15, II, a.1, q.3 Dubia 3 & 4
Visibilis	(a. 7)	d.16	Tit. 3, Memb. 2	d.16
Ex parte mittentis	(a. 8)	d.15, q.3, a.1 d.15, q.3, a.2	Tit.2	d.15, I, a.1, q.4

BIBLIOGRAPHY

I. Sources

Biblia Sacra. Ed. Colunga-Tarrado; Matriti: 1946.
SS. *Patrum Apostolicorum Opera.* Ed Colombo; Torino: 1949.
Patrologia Orientalis. Ed. Griffin-Nau; Paris: 1903 ff.
Patrologia Graeca. Ed. Migne; Paris: 1857 ff.
Patrologia Latina. Ed. Migne; Paris: 1844 ff.
Enchiridion Patristicum. Ed. de Journel, 14th edition; Barcelona: 1946.
Enchiridion Symbolorum. Ed. Denziger-Bannwart-Umberg; Freiburg-im-B.: 1937.
Divinum Illud Munus. A.S.S., 29 (1896-1897), pp. 644-658.
Mystici Corporis, A.A.S., June 29, 1943.
Peter Lombard, *Libri IV Sententiarum.* Ad Claras Aquas: 1916.
Alexander de Hales, *Glossa in IV Libros Sententiarum Petri Lombardi,* I. Ad Claras Aquas: 1951.
———, *Summa Theologica.* Ad Claras Aquas: 1924 ff.
St. Albert the Great, *Opera Omnia.* Ed. Borgnet; Paris: 1890 ff.
St. Bonaventure, *Opera Omnia.* Ad Claras Aquas: 1882 ff.
St. Thomas Aquinas, *Opera Omnia.* Leonine edition; Rome: 1882 ff.
———, *Opera Omnia.* Parma (Fiaccadori): 1852 ff.
———, *Opera Omnia.* Paris (Vivès): 1871 ff.
———, *In Decem Libros Ethicorum Aristotelis ad Nicomachum.* Ed. Spiazzi; Turin-Rome: 1949.

―――――, *In Duodecim Libros Metaphysicorum Aristotelis Expositio.* Ed. Cathala-Spiazzi; Turin-Rome: 1950.

―――――, *In Omnes S. Pauli Apostoli Epistolas Commentaria.* 7th edition; Turin: 1929.

―――――, *Opuscula Omnia.* Ed. Mandonnet; Paris: 1927.

―――――, *Quaestiones Disputatae.* Ed. Spiazzi, 8th edition revised; Turin-Rome: 1948.

―――――, *In Librum Beati Dionysii de Divinis Nominibus Expositio.* Ed. Pera; Turin-Rome: 1950.

―――――, *Lectura super Evangelium S. Matthei.* Ed. Cai, 5th edition revised; Turin-Rome: 1951.

―――――, *Quaestiones Quodlibetales.* Ed. Spiazzi, 8th edition revised; Turin-Rome: (1949).

―――――, *Scriptum super Sententiis (super Libros Sententiarum) Petri Lombardi.* Ed. Mandonnet-Moos; Parisiis: 1929–.

II. Commentaries on St. Thomas Aquinas

Bañez, Dominicus, *Scholastica Commentaria in Primam Partem Summae Theologicae S. Thomae Aquinatis*, I, De Deo Uno. Ed. F.C.U.A.; Madrid-Valencia: (1934).

―――――, *ibid.*, I usque ad q. 64. Salmanticae: 1585.

Billuart, C. R., *Cursus Theologiae juxta Mentem Divi Thomae.* Parisiis: 1895.

Cajetanus, Thomas de Vio, *Commentaria in Summam Theologicam.* Leonine edition, *Opera Omnia S. Thomae Aquinatis;* Romae: 1888-1906.

Capponi a Porrecta, Seraphinus, *Elucidationes formales in Summam Theologicam S. Thomae de Aquino.* Venetiis: 1598.

Capreolus, Johannes, *Defensiones Theologicae Divi Thomae Aquinatis.* Ed. Paban-Pègues; Turonibus: 1900 ff.

Ferrariensis, Franciscus de Silvestris, *Commentaria in libros quatuor Contra Gentiles S. Thomae de Aquino.* Leonine edition, *Opera Omnia S. Thomae Aquinatis;* Rome: 1918-1926.

Gonet, Joannes Baptista, *Clypeus Theologiae Thomisticae.* Antwerpiae: 1753.

de Ledesma, Petrus, *Tractatus de Divina Perfectione.* . . . Neapoli: 1639.

Joannes a Sancto Thoma, *Cursus Theologicus,* Solesmnes edition; Parisiis: 1934 ff.

————, *ibid.* Paris (Vivès): 1883 ff.

————, *ibid.,* "*De donis.*" Laval edition; Québec: 1948.

Nazarius, J. P., *Commentaria et Disputationes in I Partem S. Thomae.* Bononiae: 1620.

Salmanticenses, *Collegii Salmanticensis Cursus Theologicus.* . . . Paris (Palmé): 1877 ff.

Suarez, Franciscus, *Opera Omnia.* Parisiis: 1856 ff.

Sylvius, Franciscus, *Commentaria in Summa S. Thomae.* Venetiis: 1726.

Vásquez, Gabriel, *Commentariorum ac disputationum in I P. S. Thomae tomus primus et secundus.* Compluti: 1598.

III. Other Works

1. BOOKS

Arintero, J. G., *Evolución Mistica, Libro III Desenvolvimiento y Vitalidad de la Iglesia.* 3rd edition; Salamanca: 1930.

Bardy, E., *Le Saint-Esprit en nous et dans l'Eglise d'après le Nouveau Testament.* Albi: 1950.

Bissen, J., *L'exémplarisme divin selon S. Bonaventure.* Paris: 1929.

Bouillard, H., *Conversion et grâce chez S. Thomas d'Aquin.* Paris: 1944.

Brunet, A. (with G. Paré and P. Tremblay), *La Renaissance du XIIe siècle, les écoles et l'enseignement*. Paris-Ottawa: 1933.

Cayré, F., *Manual of Patrology and History of Theology*. English trans. by H. Howitt; Paris, Tournai, Roma: 1936.

Ceuppens, F., *Theologica Biblica*. Turin-Rome: 1948 ff.

Chambat, L., *Présence et union: Les missions des Personnes de la Sainte Trinité, selon saint Thomas d'Aquin*. Editions de Fontenelle Abbaye S. Wandrille: 1945.

Chardon, L., *La Croix de Jésus*. . . . Ed. and Introduction by F. Florand; Paris: (1937).

Chenu, M.-D., *Introduction à l'étude de Saint Thomas d'Aquin*. Paris-Ottawa: 1950.

Copleston, F., *A History of Philisophy*. Revised ed.; London: 1951 ff.

Cuervo, M. *La inhabitación de la Trinidad en toda alma in gracia según Juan de Santo Tomás*. Salamanca: 1946.

Deferrari, R. (with Sister M. Inviolata and I. McGuiness), *A Lexicon of St. Thomas Aquinas*. Washington: 1948-1949.

Denifle, H., *Chartularium Universitatis Parisiensis*. Paris: 1889.

Dockx, S. I., *Fils de Dieu par grâce*. Paris: 1948.

Dorsaz, A. *Notre parenté avec les personnes divines*. St. Etienne: 1921.

Durantel, J., *S. Thomas et le Pseudo-Denys*. Paris: 1919.

Fabro, C., *La nozione metafisica di partecipazione secondo S. Tommaso*. Revised and augmented ed.; Torino: 1950.

Faraon, M. J., *The Metaphysical and Psychological Principles of Love*. Dubuque: 1952.

Fitzgerald, T. J.: *De Inhabitatione Spiritus Sancti Doctrina S. Thomae Aquinatis*. Mundelein, Illinois (U.S.A.): 1949.

Froget, B., *De habitation du Saint-Esprit dans les âmes justes*. 6th ed.; Paris: 1929.

Galtier, P., *De SS. Trinitate in Se et in Nobis*. Paris: 1933.

————, *Le Saint Esprit en nous, d'après les Pères Grecs*. Analecta Gregoriana XXIV. Romae: 1946.

————, *L'habitation en nous des trois personnes*. Rome: 1949.

Gardeil, A., *La structure de l'âme*. 2nd edition; Paris: 1927.

Garrigou-Lagrange, R., *De Beatitudine*. Torino: (1951).

————, *De Christo Salvatore*. Torino: (1945).

————, *De Deo Trino et Creatore*. Paris: (1943).

————, *De Deo Uno*. Paris: (1938).

————, *De Gratia*. Torino: (1946).

————, *De Virtutibus Theologicis*. Torino: (1948).

————, *L'amour de Dieu et la Croix de Jésus*. Paris: (1929).

Geiger, L.-B., *La participation dans la philosophie de S. Thomas d'Aquin*. Paris: 1942.

de Ghellinck, J. *Le mouvement théologique du XII*^{e} *siècle*. 2nd ed.; Paris: 1948.

Gilson, E., *La philosophie au moyen âge*. Paris: 1930.

————, *L'esprit de la philosophie médiévale*. Paris: 1932.

————, *La philosophie de S. Bonaventure*. Paris: 1925.

————, *Introduction à l'étude de S. Augustin*. Paris: 1929.

Glorieux, P., *Repertoire des Maîtres en théologie de Paris en XIII*^{e} *siècle*. Paris: 1933-1934.

Grabmann, M., *Einführung in die Summa theologiae des hl. Thomas von Aquin*. 2nd ed.; Fribourg: 1928.

Gratien de Paris, *Histoire de la fondation et de l'évolution de l'Ordre des Frères Mineurs au XIII*^{e} *Siècle*. Paris: 1928.

Gross, J., *La divinisation du chrétien d'après les Pères grecs*. Paris: 1939.

de Guibert, P., *Les doublets de Saint Thomas d'Aquin*. Paris: 1926.

Haskins, C., *The Renaissance of the Twelfth Century.* Cambridge (Mass.): 1927.

Joannes a Sancto Thoma, *Cursus Philosophicus Thomisticus.* Ed. Reiser; Taurini: 1930 ff.

Joret, J.D., *La contemplation mystique, d'après saint Thomas d'Aquin.* New ed.; Paris: 1927.

Koenig, H., *De Inhabitatione Spiritus Sancti Doctrina Sancti Bonaventurae.* Mundelein, Illinois (U.S.A.): 1934.

Kolipinski, S., *Le Don de l'Esprit-Saint. Don incréé et don créé, selon la doctrine de S. Thomas d'Aquin.* Fribourg (Suisse): 1924.

Lagrange, M.-J., *L'Evangile selon S. Jean.* Paris: 1925.

Lebreton, J., *Histoire de la dogme de la Trinité.* 8th ed.; Paris: 1910.

Lottin, O., *Psychologie et morale aux XIIe and XIIIe siècles.* Louvain: 1942 ff.

Lozano, S. M., *Unidad de la Vida Santa y de la Ciencia Sagrada.* 2nd ed.; Salamanca: 1942.

Manoir de Juaye, H., *Dogme et spiritualité chez S. Cyrille d'Alexandre.* Paris: 1944.

Maritain, J. *Les degrés du savoir.* Paris: 1932.

Marrou, H., *S. Augustin et la fin de la culture antique.* Paris: 1938.

Noble, H.-D., *L'amitié avec Dieu.* Essai sur la vie spirituelle d'après S. Thomas d'Aquin. New ed.; Paris: 1932.

Pelzer, A., *Codices Vaticani Latini,* II, pars prior: Codd. 679-1134. Città del Vaticano: 1931.

Petavius, *Dogmata Theologica.* Paris (Vivès): 1865 ff.

Petitot, L. H., *San Tommaso D'Aquino.* Italian transl., Torino: 1924.

Prat, F., *La théologie de Saint Paul.* 7th edition; Paris: 1920.

Primeau, J., *Doctrina Summae Theologicae Alexandri Halensis de Spiritus Sancti apud Justos Inhabitatione.* Mundelein, Illinois (U.S.A.): 1936.

Matthijs, M., *De Imagine Dei in Homine.* Rome: 1952.

Menendez-Reigada, I. G., *Las dones del Espiritu Santo y la perfección Christiana por el Ven. P. Maestro Fray Juan de Santo Tomás, O.P. Traducción, Introducción y Notas Doctrinales del* ———. Madrid: 1948.

Ramirez, J., *De Hominis Beatitudine.* Salmanticae-Matriti: 1942 ff.

de Régnon, T., *Etudes de théologie positive sur la S. Trinité.* Paris: 1898.

Retailleau, M., *La Sainte Trinité dans les âmes justes.* Université Catholique d'Angers: 1932.

Rondet, H., *Gratia Christi.* Essai d'histoire du dogme et de théologie dogmatique. Paris: 1948.

Schauf, H., *Die Einwohnung des Heilige Geistes.* Die Lehre von nichtapproprierten Einwohnung des Hl. Geistes als Beitrag zur Theologiegeschichte des XIX. Jahrhunderts unter besonderer Berücksichtigung der beiden Theologen Carl Passaglia und Clemens Schrader. Freiburg-im-B.: 1941.

Scheeben, M. J., *The Mysteries of Christianity.* English trans.; St. Louis-London: 1946.

———, *Handbuch der katholische Dogmatik.* Freiburg-im-B.: 1941.

Schütz, L., *Thomas-Lexicon.* 2nd ed.; Paderborn: 1885.

Sparks, T., *De Divisione Causae Exemplaris apud S. Thomam.* Somerset, Ohio (U.S.A.): (1936).

Spicq, C., *Esquisse d'une histoire de l'exégèse latine au moyen âge.* Paris: 1944.

Sullivan, L., *Justification and the Inhabitation of the Holy Ghost, the Doctrine of Father Gabriel Vásquez, S.J.* Rome: 1940.

Taymans d'Eypernon, F., *Le mystère primordial: La trinité dans sa vivante image.* Paris: 1941.

Terrien, J. B., *La grâce et la gloire.* Paris: 1901.

Tromp, S., *De Mystico Jesu Christi Corpore.* "Textus et Documenta," Pontificia Universitas Gregoriana, Series Theologicae, XXVI. Roma: 1943.

Trütsch, J., SS. *Trinitatis Inhabitatio apud Theologos Recentiores.* Trento: 1949.

Van Steenberghen, F., *Aristote en Occident.* Louvain: 1946.

Waffelaert, G. J., *L'union de l'âme aimante avec Dieu.* Paris: 1916.

Walz, A., *San Tommaso d'Aquino.* Roma: 1945.

Weigl, P., *Die Heilslehre des hl. Cyrillus von Alexandrin.* Main: 1905.

de Wulf, M., *Histoire de la philosophie médiévale.* 6th ed.; Louvain: 1936.

Zubiri, X., *Naturaleza, Historia, Dios.* Madrid: 1944.

2. ARTICLES

Alonzo, J., "Naturalez y fundamentos de la gracia de la Virgen," *Estudios Marianos,* 5 (1946), pp. 11-110.

—————, "Relación de causalidad entra la gracia creada e increada," *Revista Española de Teología,* 6 (1946), pp. 1-60.

Anciaux, F., "La cause exémplaire: notion de cette cause et nature de sa causalité," *Revue Augustinienne,* 2 (1907), pp. 685-704.

Bittremieux, J., "Utrum unio cum Spiritu Sancto sit causa formalis filiationis adoptivae iusti," *Ephemerides Theologicae Lovanienses,* 10 (1933), pp. 427-440.

Bourassa, F., "Les missions divines et le surnaturel chez saint Thomas d'Aquin," *Sciences ecclésiastiques,* 1 (1948), pp. 41-94.

—————, "Dom Chambat et l'habitation des Personnes divines," *Sciences ecclésiastiques,* 3 (1950), pp. 194-198.

—————, "Adoptive Sonship: Our Union with the Divine Persons," *Theological Studies,* 13 (1952), pp. 309-335.

Bruneau, A.-J., "Dieu, terme immanent de la charité?" *Revue Thomiste,* 52 (1952), pp. 225-233.

Callebaut, A., "L'entrée de S. Bonaventure dans l'ordre des Frères Mineurs," *La France Franciscaine,* 5 (1921), pp. 41-51.

Catherinet, F., "La Sainte Trinité et notre filiation adoptive," *La Vie Spirituelle*, 39 (1934), pp. 113-128.

Cavallera, F., "S. Augustin et le Livre des Sentences de Pierre Lombard," *Archive de philosophie*, 7 (1930), pp. 438-451.

Chenu, M.-D., "Maîtres et bacheliers de l'Université de Paris vers 1240," in *Etudes d'histoire litteraire et doctrinale du XIIIe siècle*. Paris-Ottawa: 1932.

Ciappi, L., "Una nova interpretazione dell' inhabitazione della SS. Trinità nell' anima," *Vita Christiana*, 20 (1951), pp. 113-124.

————, "The Presence, Missions, and Indwelling of the Divine Persons in the Just," *The Thomist*, 17 (1954), pp. 131-144.

Delaye, E., "Le Christ mystique," *Nouvelle Revue Théologique*, 53 (1926), pp. 721-733.

————, "L'onction du Saint Esprit," *Nouvelle Revue Théologique*, 53 (1926), pp. 641-656.

————, "La vie de la grâce," *Nouvelle Revue Théologique*, 53 (1926), pp. 561-578.

Dockx, F., "Du fondement propre de la présence réelle de Dieu dans l'âme," *Nouvelle Revue Théologique*, 72 (1950), pp. 673-689.

Dondaine, H., *La trinité*. Appendix II. *Somme Théologique;* ed. Revue des Jeunes. Paris: 1946.

Donnelly, M., "The Theory of R. P. Maurice de la Taille, S.J., on the Hypostatic Union," *Theological Studies*, 2 (1941), pp. 510-526.

————, "The Inhabitation of the Holy Spirit. A Solution according to de la Taille," *Theological Studies*, 8 (1947), pp. 445-571.

————, "The Inhabitation of the Holy Spirit," in *Proceedings of the IV Annual Meeting of the American Theological Society* (1949), n. p.

Doucet, V., "Maîtres Franciscaines de Paris," *Archivum Franciscanum Historicum*, 27 (1934), pp. 529-541.

Dumont, P., "Le caractère divin de la grâce d'après la théologie scholastique," *Revue des sciences religieuses*, 14 (1934), pp. 62-95.

Enrico di S. Teresa, "Dio in noi secondo i Salmanticensi," *Vita Carmelitana*, 1943, pp. 64-78.

Eröss, A., "Die Lehre über die Einwohung des Hl. Geistes bei M. Jos. Scheeben," *Scholastik*, 11 (1936).

Ferrero, M., "Existencia de los dones y presencia de Dios en el alma justa," *Revista Española de Teología*, 5 (1945), pp. 561-590.

Fries, A., "De Commentario Guerrici de S. Quintino in Libros Sententiarum," *Archivum Fratrum Praedicatorum*, 5 (1935), pp. 326-340.

Gabriel de Sainte-Marie-Madeleine, "De unione animae cum Deo per charitatem perfectam secundum D. Thomam et S. Joannem a Cruce," in *Acta Pontificiae Academiae Romanae S. Thomae Aquinatis et Religionis Catholicae*, 2 (1935), pp. 102-139.

Galtier, P., "Temples du Saint-Esprit," *Revue d'ascétique et de mystique*, 7 (1926), pp. 365-413; 8 (1927), pp. 40-76, 170-179.

Gardeil, A., "La perception expérimentale de l'âme par elle-même d'après saint Thomas," in *Mélanges Thomistes*. Paris: 1923.

———, "L'habitation en nous et la structure intime de l'âme," *Revue Thomiste*, 28 (1923), pp. 238-260.

———, "La structure de la connaissance mystique," *Revue Thomiste*, 29 (1924), pp. 109-126, 225-242, 340-369, 429-459.

———, "L'âme, sujet recepteur de la grâce," *Revue Thomiste*, 30 (1925), pp. 417 ff., 534 ff.

———, "Examen de conscience," *Revue Thomiste*, 33 (1928), pp. 156-180; 34 (1929), pp. 70-84, 270-287, 381-399, 520-532; 36 (1931), pp. 727-748, 840-864; 37 (1932), pp. 226-250, 379-393.

——————, "L'expérience mystique pure dans le cadre des missions divins," *La Vie Spirituelle*, 31 (1931), Suppl., pp. (120)-(146); 32 (1932), Suppl., pp. (1)-(21), (65)-(76).

Gachter, P., "Unsere Einheit mit Christus nach dem hl. Irenaeus," *Zeitschrift für Katholische Theologie*, 58 (1934), pp. 503-532.

Garrigou-Lagrange, R., "La grâce est-elle une participation de la Deité telle qu'elle est en soi?" *Revue Thomiste*, 41 (1936), pp. 470-485.

——————, "L'habitation de la Sainte Trinité et l'expérience mystique," *Revue Thomiste*, 33 (1928), pp. 449-474.

Geenen, G., "The Place of Tradition in the Theology of St. Thomas," *The Thomist*, 15 (1952), pp. 110-135.

——————, "St. Thomas et les Pères," *Dictionnaire de théologie catholique*, XV, 1, coll. 738-761.

——————, "L'usage des 'auctoritates' dans la doctrine du baptême chez S. Thomas d'Aquin," *Ephemerides Theologicae Lovanienses*, 15 (1938), pp. 279-329.

de Ghellinck, J., "Pierre Lombard," *Dictionnaire de théologie catholique*, XII, 2, coll. 1941-2019.

Gillon, L.-B., "Signification historique de la théologie de Saint Thomas," *Dictionnaire de théologie catholique*, XV, 1, coll. 651-693.

Gilson, E., "Le christianisme et la tradition philosophique," *Revue des sciences philosophiques et théologiques*, 30 (1941), pp. 249-266.

Glorieux, P., "Sentences (Commentaires de)," *Dictionnaire de théologie catholique*, XIV, 2, coll. 1860-1884.

González Ruiz, J., "La semenjanza divina de la gracia, explicación de una inhabitación formalmente trinitaria," *Revista Española de Teología*, 8 (1948), pp. 565-600.

Greenstock, D., "Exemplar Causality and the Supernatural Order," *The Thomist*, 16 (1953), pp. 1-31.

Hayen, A., "S. Thomas a-t-il édité deux fois son Commentaire sur le livre des Sentences?" *Recherches de théologie ancienne et médiévale*, 9 (1937), pp. 219-236.

Henquinet, F., "Les manuscripts et l'influence des écrits théologiques d'Eudes Rigaud," *Recherches de théologie ancienne et médiévale*, 11 (1939), pp. 324-350.

Hocedez, E., "L'habitaation en nous de la Sainte Trinité," *Nouvelle Revue Théologique*, 55 (1928), pp. 641-650.

Hislop, I., "Man, the Image of the Trinity, according to St. Thomas," *Dominican Studies*, 3 (1950), pp. 1-9.

J. J. de la Immaculada, "Acción Hipostatica del Espiritu Santo en la Sanctificatión del Alma," *Revista de Espiritualidad*, 4 (1945), pp. 440-445.

Joret, F.-R., "Seigneur, où demeurez-vous?" *La Vie Spirituelle*, 26 (1931), pp. 13-26.

———, "Les missions divines," *La Vie Spirituelle*, 26 (1931), pp. 113-128.

Landgraf, A., "Bemerkingen zum Sentenzkommentar des Cod. Vat. lat. 691," *Franziskanische Studien*, 28 (1939), pp. 183-190.

de Lanversin, F., "Le concept de présence et quelques-unes de ses applications théologiques," *Recherches de science religieuse*, 23 (1933), pp. 58-80.

Lebreton, J., "S. Augustin et la Trinité. Son exégèse des théophanies," in *Miscellanea Agostina*. Roma: 1930.

de Letter, P., "Sanctifying Grace and Our Union with the Holy Trinity," *Theological Studies*, 13 (1952), pp. 33-58.

———, "Sanctifying Grace and the Divine Indwelling," *Theological Studies*, 14 (1953), pp. 142-172.

Lottin, O., "*Commentaire des Sentences* et *Somme Théologique* d'Albert le Grand," *Recherches de théologie ancienne et médiévale*, 8 (1936), pp. 117-153.

———, "Notes sur les premières ouvrages théologiques d'Albert le Grand," *Recherches de théologie ancienne et médiévale*, 4 (1932), pp. 77-82.

Mahé, J., "La sanctification d'après S. Cyrille d'Alexandre," *Revue d'histoire ecclésiastique*, 9 (1909), pp. 475-480.

Mandonnet, P., "Chronologie sommaire de la vie et des écrits de S. Thomas," *Revue des sciences philosophiques et théologiques*, 9 (1920), pp. 142-152.

————, "Albert le Grand," *Dictionnaire de théologie catholique*, I, 1, coll. 666-674.

Martinez-Gómez, J. C., "El Misterio de la Inhabitación del Espiritu Santo," *Estudios Eclesiasticos*, 13 (1934), pp. 287-315.

————, "Relación entre la Inhabitación del Espiritu Santo y los Dones Creados de la Justificatión," *Estudios Eclesiasticos*, 14 (1935), pp. 20-50.

Masure, E., "La révélation du mystère de la Sainte Trinité et de l'habitation du Saint-Esprit dans nos âmes," *Revue Apologétique*, 46 (1928), pp. 161-173.

Menendez-Reigada, J., "Compte-Rendu de duobus voluminibus 'Structure' et 'Examen de conscience,'" *Revue Thomiste*, 34 (1929), pp. (421)-(430).

Mennessier, I., "Trinité et missions divines," *La Vie Spirituelle*, 43 (1935), pp. (176)-(183).

Mersch, E., "Filii in Filio," *Nouvelle Revue Théologique*, 65 (1938), pp. 551-582, 681-702, 809-830.

Michel, A., "Trinité (Missions et habitation des personnes de la)," *Dictionnaire de théologique catholique*, XV, 2, coll. 1830-1855.

Minges, P., "Abhängigkeitsverhältnis zwischen Alexander von Hales und Albert den Grossen," *Franziskanische Studien*, 2 (1915), pp. 208-229.

————, "Die theologischen Summen Wilhelms von Auxerre unds Alexanders von Hales," *Theologische Quartalschrift*, 97 (1915), pp. 508-529.

————, "Abhängigkeitsverhältnis zwischen der Summe Alexanders von Hales und dem hl. Thomas von Aquin," *Franziskanische Studien*, 3 (1916), pp. 58-76.

————, "Die psychologische Summe des Johannes von Rupella und Alexander von Hales," *Franziskanische Studien*, 3 (1916), pp. 365-378.

Monsegú, B., "Unidad y trinidad, propriedad y apropriación en las manifestaciones trinitarias, seqún la doctrina de San Cirilo Alejandrino," *Revista Española de Teología*, 8 (1948), pp. 1-57, 275-328.

Morency, R., "L'union du juste à Dieu par voi de connaissance et d'amour," *Sciences ecclésiastiques*, 2 (1949), pp. 27-79.

Mullaney, T., "The Incarnation: de la Taille vs. Thomistic Tradition," *The Thomist*, 17 (1954), pp. 1-42.

Nicholas, J.-H., "Présence trinitaire et présence de la Trinité," *Revue Thomiste*, 50 (1950), pp. 183-191.

Noble, H.-D., "La connaissance affective," *Revue des sciences philosophiques et théologiques*, 7 (1913), pp. 637-662.

———, "S'unir à Dieu dans la charité," *La Vie Spirituelle*, 13 (1925), pp. 129-141.

O'Connor, W., "A New Theory of Grace and the Supernatural," *American Ecclesiastical Review*, 98 (1938), pp. 401-413.

———, "The Theory of the Supernatural," *Theological Studies*, 3 (1942), pp. 403-412.

Pace, E., "Assimilari Deo," *The New Scholasticism*, 2 (1928), pp. 342-356.

Palucsák, P., "Imago Dei in Homine," in *Xenia Thomistica*, II. Rome: 1925.

Pergamo, B., "De quaestionibus ineditis fr. Odonis Rigaldi. . . .," *Archivum Franciscanum Historicum*, 29 (1936), pp. 3-54.

Philips, G., "Les mystères de la Sainte Trinité et de la grâce," *Revue ecclésiastique de Liège*, 27 (1935-1936), pp. 163-176.

———, "La présence des personnes divines par la grâce," *Revue ecclésiastique de Liège*, 27 (1935-1936), pp. 237-243.

———, "Le Saint-Esprit en nous. A propos d'un livre récent," *Ephemerides Theologicae Lovanienses*, 24 (1948), pp. 127-135.

———, "La Sainte Trinité dans la vie du chrétien," in *Etudes religieuses*. Liège: 1949.

Rahner, K., "Zur scholastichen Begrifflichkeit der ungeschaffene Gnade," *Zeitschrift für Katholische Theologie*, 63 (1939), pp. 137-156.

Rolland-Gosselin, M.-D., "De la connaissance affective," *Revue des sciences philosophiques et théologiques*, 27 (1938), pp. 5-26.

Rondet, H., "La divinisation du chrétien," *Nouvelle Revue Théologique*, 71 (1949), pp. 449-476, 561-588.

von Rudloff, L., "Des heiligen Thomas Lehre von der Formalursache der Einwohnung Gottes in der Seele der Gerechten," *Divus Thomas* (Fr.), 8 (1930), pp. 175-191.

Sagües, J. F., "El modo de Inhabitación del Espiritu Santo según Santo Tomás d'Aquino," *Miscelánea Comillas*, 2 (1944), pp. 160-201.

————, "El Espiritu Santo en la sanctificatión del hombre según la doctrina de San Cirilo de Alejandria," *Estudios Eclesiasticos*, 21 (1947), pp. 35-84.

Salman, D., "Albert le Grand et l'averroïsme latin," *Revue des sciences philosophiques et théologiques*, 24 (1935), pp. 38-64.

Squire, A., "The Doctrine of the Image in the *De Veritate* of St. Thomas," *Dominican Studies*, 4 (1951), pp. 164-177.

Stevaux, A., "La doctrine de la charité dans les commentaires des Sentences de S. Albert, S. Bonaventure, S. Thomas," *Ephemerides Theologicae Lovanienses*, 24 (1948), pp. 59-97.

de la Taille, M., "Actuation créée par l'Acte incréé," *Recherches de science religieuse*, 18 (1928), pp. 253-268.

————, "Entrétien amical d'Euxode et de Palamède sur la grâce d'union," *Revue Apologétique*, 48 (1929), pp. 5-26.

————, "The Schoolmen," in *The Incarnation*. Cambridge: 1926.

Urdánoz, T., "Influjo causal de las divinas Personas en la inhabitación en las almas justas," *Revista Española de Teología*, 9 (1949), pp. 141-202.

———, "La Inhabitación del Espiritu Santo en el Alma del Justo," *Revista Española de Teología*, 6 (1946), pp. 466-533.

Van Der Meersch, J., "Grâce," *Dictionnaire de théologie catholique*, VI, 2, coll. 1554-1687.

Van Hove, A., "De modo quo Deus inhabitat in animabus justis," *Collectanea Mechliniensia*, 28 (1948), pp. 289-295.

Vauthier, E., "Le Saint-Esprit, principe d'unité de l'Eglise, d'après saint Thomas d'Aquin. Corps mystique et inhabitation du Saint-Esprit," *Mélanges de science religieuse*, 5 (1948), pp. 175-196; 6 (1949), pp. 57-80.

Waffelaert, G., "Prospectus syntheticus vitae supranaturalis et porro mysticae: II. Qua ratione vitae divinae participies efficimur," *Ephemerides Theologicae Lovanienses*, 2 (1925), pp. 169-180.

Walz, A., "Saint Thomas (Ecrits de)," *Dictionaire de théologie catholique*, XV, I, coll. 639-640.

———, "Chronotaxis Vitae et Operum S. Thomae," *Angelicum*, 16 (1939), pp. 463-473.

Wébert, J., "L'image dans l'oeuvre de S. Thomas et spécialement dans l'exposé doctrinal sur l'intelligence humaine," *Revue Thomiste*, 31 (1926), pp. 427-445.

Zielsinki, T., "Doctrina Salmanticensium de modo inhabitationis SS. Trinitatis in anima justi," *Divus Thomas* (Pi.), 45 (1942), pp. 373-394.

INDEX OF SUBJECTS

Abstraction, 201; *see also* Reasoning
Act, pure, 152
Action; *see* Operation
Actual grace, 82, 152
  operation of, 152; *see also* Operating grace
Actual knowledge of Trinity, 53, 68, 118, 208, 258, 263, 266
Angels, knowledge of, 199, 201, 205
Apparitions, 163; *see also* Theophania
Appropriation, 12, 36, 39-40, 43, 45, 59, 61, 63, 64, 83, 97, 98, 99, 106, 111, 112, 113, 114, 115, 117, 118, 120, 125, 126, 127, 128, 145, 146, 147, 148, 150, 151, 154, 156, 160, 161, 164, 170, 238, 246, 250, 251, 258, 259, 260, 261, 275, 277, 283, 298, 299, 301, 304, 312, 314, 315, 316, 324, 325, 326, 327, 330, 331, 333, 334, 339, 346, 348, 349, 353, 354; *see also* Representation
Aristotelianism, 141, 163, 166
Assimilation, 12, 170, 193, 212, 244, 287, 298, 299, 304, 314, 323, 324, 325, 329, 330, 331, 332, 333, 334, 339, 346, 347, 348; *see also* Conformity, Union with God
Attribute of God
  essential, 47, 146, 150, 170, 188, 195, 196, 216, 220, 275, 332, 333
  personal, 146; *see also* Properties of Persons
Augustinism, 141, 163, 166; *see also* Franciscan tradition

Beatific Vision, 25, 37, 106, 119, 122, 129, 175, 191, 199, 202, 223, 323, 347, 354
Beatitude, 115, 129, 136, 175, 226, 345; *see also* Beatific Vision

Cause
  efficient, 9, 16, 18, 95, 107, 111, 113, 122, 125, 127, 136, 144, 145, 146, 148, 149, 150, 153, 154, 155, 159, 160, 162, 167, 171, 192, 193, 194, 196, 204, 212, 231, 232, 247, 250, 252, 275, 281, 282, 331, 333, 338, 343; *see also* Principle
  exemplary, 9, 16, 95, 113, 124, 125, 142, 146, 147, 148, 163, 169, 192, 195, 212, 231, 247, 250, 252, 275, 329, 331, 332, 333, 343; *see also* Exemplarism, Exemplarity, Exemplary idea *(ratio)*
  final, 9, 18, 128, 142, 163, 196, 212, 231, 282, 312, 324, 326
  formal, 98, 107, 109, 136, 151, 163, 162, 171, 193
  formal extrinsic, 148, 324, 326
  God as, 95, 111, 113, 122, 144, 145, 146, 149, 150, 152, 153, 154, 155, 160, 164, 167, 182, 188, 190, 193, 194, 195, 196, 203, 204, 205, 212, 220, 227, 231, 276, 280, 322, 337, 343, 345, 347, 358; *see also* God as operating, God as principle
  Persons as, 195, 196, 206, 225, 246, 247, 250, 251, 252, 262, 272, 274, 277, 279, 282, 296, 299, 304, 316, 331, 332, 333, 346; *see also* Trinity as
  relation between, and effect, 145
  Trinity as, 7, 152, 195, 196, 207; *see also* Persons as
Charismata, 82, 197; *see also gratia gratis data*
Charity, 37, 39, 98, 99, 108, 116, 120, 121, 123, 125, 131, 143, 150, 151, 158, 164, 175, 200, 202, 208, 209, 210, 222, 223, 278,

283, 315, 320, 325, 326, 327, 332, 333, 352; *see also* Love
Peter Lombard on, 83, 86, 98, 99, 106-107
Christ; *see* Son of God
Church 1, 7, 40
   teaching of, 5, 34, 45, 47, 80, 103, 163, 192, 207, 215, 319, 349
Circuminsession; *see* Perichoresis
Common teaching; *see* Tradition
Comprehension, 175
Concomitance, 84, 99, 147, 183, 191
Conformity, 310, 311, 325, 330, 331, 339, 343, 345, 346, 348; *see also* Assimilation
   image of; *see* Image of re-creation
Conservation, 220
Conjectural knowledge, 266
Contemplation, 4, 50, 199, 208, 347
Contrition, 200
Creation, 9, 196, 220, 238, 275, 278, 279, 332, 348
   image of, 123, 343, 345, 348
Creatures, 99, 107, 122, 123, 126, 184, 187, 188, 189, 190, 191, 194, 196, 199, 202, 204, 231, 244, 245, 255, 271, 272, 273, 274, 276, 277, 290, 296, 309, 329, 346, 351
   relations of:
      to God, 9, 107, 164, 187, 194, 195, 202, 204, 245, 246, 249, 255, 274, 296, 304, 331
      to Trinity, 12, 15, 44, 194

Dating of scholastic works on Indwelling
   Albert the Great, St.:
      Commentarium in Libros Sententiarum, 76-78, 79, 91, 92, 93, 234
      Summa Theologica, 78, 79
   Alexander of Hales:
      Glossa in Libros Sententiarum, 75, 79
      Quaestiones Disputatae de Missionibus, 75, 79
      Summa Theologica (*Summa Alex.*), 74-77, 79, 89, 90, 91, 127, 234
   Altissiodorensis; *see* William of Auxerre

Bonaventure, St.: *Commentarius in Libros Sententiarum*, 78, 79, 93, 234
Codex Vaticanus latinus 691, 76, 79
Eudes Rigaud (Odo Rigaldus): *Commentarium in Libros Sententiarum*, 75, 76, 79, 90, 92
Jean de la Rochelle (Joannes de Rupella); *see* Alexander of Hales, *Summa Theologica*
Peter Lombard: *Libri Sententiarum*, 73, 79
Thomas Aquinas, St.:
   Scriptum super Sententiis, 212, 234
   Summa Theologiae, 212
William of Auxerre (Altissiodorensis): *Summa Aurea*, 73, 74, 79
Definition
   of Indwelling (Inhabitation):
      of St. **Albert, 84, 85**
      of St. Augustine, 50-55, 100, 101, 112, 311, 312
      of St. Bonaventure, 84, 85, 96, 157, 159
      of *Summa Alex.*, 84, 111, 119
   of divine missions, 50-55, 84, 85, 96, 100, 101, 111, 112, 119, 311, 312

Delectation; *see* Enjoyment
Desire, natural, 344; *see also* Beatitude
Dilection; *see* Charity, Love
Divinization, 42, 43, 63; *see also* Union with God
Doctrine
   of Indwelling (Inhabitation), 6, 22, 40, 41, 46, 70, 230, 345
   of Fathers; *see* Fathers
   of Schoolmen; *see* Facts of **Indwelling**, Theories of **Indwelling**
Dogma, evolution of, 104
Donation ("Giving")
   of Father, 298, 299, 347
   of Persons, 37, 80, 81, 82, 95, 96, 106, 107, 111, 121, 122, 124, 125, 126, 143, 157, 164, 184, **185, 197, 201, 238, 242, 247,** 248, 249, 254, 255, 166, 274, 280, 283, 295, 296, 297, 298, 299, 308, 312, 313, 347, 351; *see also* Enjoyment of Persons,

Possession of Persons, Use of Persons
end of, 125, 126, 143, 157

Effect
  infinite, 95, 144, 150, 153
  of God, 114, 139, 191, 192, 196, 199, 200, 205, 220, 227, 245, 246, 300, 309, 325, 331, 343, 346, 347
  of grace, 15, 85, 86, 112, 113, 115, 116, 117, 118, 121, 122, 125, 126, 127, 132, 143, 144, 145, 146, 147, 149, 151, 152, 153, 157, 160, 164, 193, 201, 204, 205, 206, 207, 238, 250, 256, 257, 260, 267, 275, 278, 325, 326, 334, 350, 351

Efficient cause, 9, 16, 18, 95, 107, 111, 113, 122, 125, 127, 136, 144, 145, 146, 148, 149, 150, 153, 154, 155, 159, 160, 162, 167, 171, 192, 193, 194, 196, 204, 212, 231, 232, 247, 250, 252, 275, 281, 331, 333, 343; *see also* Principle

End (Purpose)
  of divine missions, 125, 126, 273
  of donation of Persons, 125, 126, 143, 157
  of this work, 17-20

End (Term)
  God as, 129, 152, 182, 208, 212, 335, 338; *see also* God as fruit, as gift, as object, as term
  Trinity as, 129, 159, 324, 327, *see also* Trinity as fruit, as object, as term

Elements of tradition concerning Indwelling, 80-87

Enjoyment (Delectation, Fruition) of Persons, 111, 112, 114, 119, 120, 121, 122, 123, 125, 128, 129, 130, 131, 132, 157, 158, 159, 160, 162, 164, 175, 182, 183, 185, 197, 201, 202, 211, 247, 248, 249, 250, 251, 252, 256, 257, 261, 276, 279, 280, 281, 282, 298, 299, 308, 309, 312, 313, 315, 326, 347, 351
  love and, 119, 120, 121, 158, 162

Essence, 108, 115, 153, 167, 189, 342, 343
  divine, 45, 118, 126, 131, 144, 145, 146, 148, 149, 150, 151, 152, 154, 188, 189, 190, 194, 195, 196, 201, 202, 203, 204, 206, 209, 220, 222, 236, 300, 333, 340, 342, 343, 345, 346, 347, 348

Eternal procession; *see also* Relations of Trinity
  of Holy Ghost, 50, 51, 84, 85, 112, 113, 115, 116, 121, 144, 239, 268, 332; *see also* Eternal procession of Persons
  of Persons, 50, 85, 88, 112, 116, 119, 123, 126, 142, 160, 181, 184, 195, 196, 215, 238, 254, 259, 264, 270, 278, 281, 288, 296, 298, 299, 300, 304, 316, 331, 332, 346, 351
  of Son, 50, 51, 85, 112, 113, 115, 121, 268, 314, 333; *see also* Generation of Son, Eternal procession of Persons

Evolution
  of dogma, 104
  of theology, 86, 104, 141, 162, 163, 164, 349

Exegesis, 59, 110, 113, 124, 269, 323
  of Sacred Scripture, 35, 57, 327
  of St. Thomas, 181

Exemplarism, 147, 163; *see also* Assimilation, Conformity, Representation

Exemplarity, 146, 150, 212, 230, 250, 275, 331, 333, 334, 339

Exemplary cause, 9, 16, 95, 113, 124, 125, 142, 146, 147, 148, 163, 169, 192, 195, 196, 212, 231, 247, 250, 252, 275, 329, 331, 333, 343

Exemplary idea *(Ratio)*, 145-150, 195, 275, 296, 299, 316, 331, 332, 333, 346

Facts of Indwelling (Inhabitation)
  for Fathers, 40, 45, 51, 56, 88
  for Nominalists, 93-94
  for St. Thomas, 180-185
  for Schoolmen, 73, 80-88

in Sacred Scripture, 36, 39, 40, 56, 88, 351, 352
Faith, 3, 4, 6, 8, 47, 103, 121, 123, 200, 207, 208, 230, 353
 unformed, 82, 119, 197, 268, 273
Father (First Person), 2, 6, 7, 123
 donation of, 298, 299, 347
 Indwelling of, 37, 38, 39, 42, 49, 83, 106, 183, 201
 union with, 37
Fathers of Church, 34, 35, 36, 57-59, 61, 63, 70, 80, 87, 103, 149, 181, 327, 351
 doctrine of:
  on Indwelling, 35, 40-56, 349, 350
  facts of, 40, 45, 51, 56, 88
  summary of, 55, 56
  on image of God in man, 45, 46, 48, 54, 55, 87
 Greek, 22, 35, 36, 40-46, 47, 48, 54, 56, 65, 87, 88, 319, 349, 350
 Latin, 22, 35, 36, 40, 46-56, 65, 88, 319, 350
 tradition of, 26, 40-56, 63, 87
Final cause, 9, 18, 128, 142, 163, 196, 212, 231, 282, 312, 324, 326; *see also* God as end, Trinity as end
Fear, servile, 255
Form
 accidental, 63, 151, 188
 participated, 151, 153
Formal cause, 98, 99, 107, 119, 136, 151, 153, 162, 171, 193
Formal extrinsic cause, 148, 324, 326
Formal medium of knowledge, 199, 200, 354
 love as, 200, 202, 205
Formal reason of Indwelling (Inhabitation), 8-10, 16-18, 23, 32, 103, 112, 113, 114, 118, 120, 121, 122, 128, 130, 154, 155, 157, 158, 160, 164, 190, 191, 192, 202, 206, 207, 211, 230, 253, 279, 283, 284, 312, 314, 315, 318, 320, 324, 335, 338, 348, 351, 353, 354
 love as, 108, 118, 119, 122, 123, 129-130, 158, 161, 162, 164, 283

Formulas of St. Thomas on Indwelling
 of *Scriptum super Sententiis*, 11, 16, 18, 30, 297, 299, 324, 330
 of *Summa Theologiae*, 12, 16, 19, 30, 297, 299, 310, 311, 313, 330, 339
Franciscan tradition, 109, 110, 130, 141, 159; *see also* Augustinism
Fruition; *see* Enjoyment
Fruits of enjoyment; *see also* Donation, Possession, Use
 God as, 111, *see also* God as object, God as term
 Holy Ghost as, 108, 112, 116, 120, 248, 281, 282
 Persons as, 111, 115, 119, 126, 128, 132, 139, 182, 185, 211, 249, 250, 251, 254, 255, 257, 276, 279, 282, 288, 303, 312, 315, 326, 351; *see also* Persons as object
 Trinity as, 10, 12, 17, 30, 108, 111, 112, 117, 123, 164, 197, 198, 200, 209, 324, 348; *see also* Trinity as end, as object, as term

Generation of Son, 184, 196, 197, 279, 339; *see also* Eternal procession, Relations of Trinity
Gift
 God as, 111
 of grace, 80, 81, 83, 115, 116, 117, 118, 121, 124, 143, 145, 148, 150, 151, 153, 154, 160, 161, 164, 182, 198, 202, 206, 209, 210, 254, 257, 262, 263, 268, 274, 275, 279, 280, 281, 282, 283, 309, 312, 314, 315, 326, 330, 345, 347, 348, 351, 353, 354
 of Holy Ghost, 4, 7, 80, 81, 113, 124, 130, 144, 158, 182, 183, 200, 242, 243, 246, 250, 256, 280, 281, 297, 322, 352
 of Knowledge, 160, 222
 of Love, 160, 184, 250, 256
 of Persons, 51, 80, 81, 98, 106, 159, 164, 182, 201, 242, 274, 297, 309, 310, 351, 353; *see also* Donation

INDEX OF SUBJECTS   399

of Understanding, 118, 256
of Wisdom, 118, 121, 126, 150, 184,
  198, 199, 200, 201, 205, 206,
  208, 209, 210, 211, 222, 250,
  256, 257, 261
"Giving" of Persons; see Donation
Goodness, divine, 108, 184, 207, 222,
  344
God
  as cause, 95, 111, 113, 122, 145,
    146, 149, 150, 152, 153, 154,
    155, 160, 164, 167, 182, 188,
    190, 193, 194, 195, 196, 203,
    204, 205, 212, 220, 227, 231,
    276, 280, 322, 337, 343, 345,
    347, 348; see also God as principle, Trinity as cause
  as end, 129, 152, 182, 208, 212,
    325, 338; see also God as fruit,
    as gift, as object, as term
  as fruit, 111
  as gift, 111
  as object, 10, 12, 30, 94, 111, 120,
    158, 191, 196, 202, 208, 209,
    210, 212, 223, 323, 324, 325,
    331, 338, 343, 347, 348
  as operating, 95, 113, 131, 143, 144,
    146, 152, 187, 193, 194, 199,
    201, 204, 244, 245, 251, 253,
    268, 274, 275, 281, 337, 343;
    see also God as cause, God as
    principle
  as principle, 111, 126, 151, 154,
    182, 188, 189, 192, 194, 195,
    196, 208, 220, 268, 281, 337,
    338, 347; see also God as cause,
    God as operating, Operation of
    God
  as term, 94, 188, 190, 191, 195, 196,
    208, 212, 324, 338, 347; see also
    God as end, as fruit, as gift, as
    object
  Author:
    of grace, 151, 152, 205
    of nature, 152, 205, 343
  effects of, 114, 139, 191, 192, 196,
    199, 200, 205, 220, 227, 245,
    246, 309, 325, 331, 343, 346,
    347
  immensity of, 188
  operation of, 114, 143, 144, 152,
    154, 163, 187, 188, 196, 204,
    220, 288

  presence of, 36, 37, 38, 42, 48, 49,
    53, 66, 129, 131, 143, 144, 152,
    157, 158, 159, 163, 164, 167,
    182, 187, 188, 189, 190, 191,
    193, 196, 199, 200, 201, 202,
    205, 206, 210, 220, 223, 226,
    253, 258, 267, 272, 298, 303,
    304, 310, 312, 320, 329, 343,
    345, 347; see also Presence of
    immensity, Ubiquity of God
  relations of to creatures, 9, 44, 146,
    187, 195, 202, 244, 245, 271,
    272, 296, 314, 331
  union with, 57, 104, 106, 118, 119,
    120, 122, 144, 189, 190, 197,
    199, 206, 212, 231, 250, 251,
    256, 258, 278, 280, 281, 309,
    319, 323, 324, 327, 344; see
    also Assimilation, Conformity
Grace
  actual, 82, 152
    operation of, 152
  created, 7, 10, 36, 41, 45, 48, 49,
    50, 80-83, 84, 107, 108, 117,
    118, 119, 122, 123, 124, 125,
    131, 139, 142, 143, 151, 152,
    153, 158, 159, 175, 178, 184,
    192, 193, 194, 195, 196, 198,
    201, 203, 204, 205, 207, 208,
    220, 222, 225, 227, 231, 248,
    249, 272, 275, 281, 282, 298,
    309, 310, 320, 327, 329, 345,
    346, 348
  effects of, 15, 85, 86, 112, 113, 115,
    116, 117, 118, 121, 122, 125,
    126, 127, 132, 143, 144, 145,
    146, 147, 149, 151, 152, 153,
    157, 160, 164, 193, 201, 204,
    205, 206, 207, 238, 250, 256,
    257, 260, 267, 275, 278, 325,
    326, 334, 350, 351; see also
    Operations of
  gift of, 80, 81, 83, 115, 116, 117,
    118, 121, 124, 143, 145, 148,
    150, 151, 153, 154, 160, 161,
    164, 182, 198, 202, 206, 209,
    210, 254, 257, 262, 263, 268,
    274, 275, 279, 280, 281, 282,
    283, 309, 312, 314, 315, 326,
    330, 345, 347, 348, 351, 353,
    354

God as Author of, 151, 152, 205
gratia gratis data, 82, 83, 152, 182, 255, 282
gratia gratum faciens, 82, 117, 118, 182, 249, 256, 258, 260, 265, 266, 267, 268, 273, 276, 278, 280, 282, 283, 308; *see also* Sanctifying grace
increase of, 161
knowledge of, 112, 115, 117, 196, 197, 198, 200, 201, 206, 225, 346, 354; *see also* Faith, Wisdom (Gift of)
operating, 200, 204
operations of, 193, 287, 288
sanctifying, 7, 10, 38, 59, 82, 83, 86, 88, 113, 115, 120, 130, 131, 143, 157, 182, 183, 191, 192, 193, 194, 197, 211, 227, 254, 257, 259, 260, 263, 280, 281, 282, 283, 300, 301, 312, 313, 315, 320, 346, 350, 351; *see also Gratia gratum faciens*
—state, 8, 38, 44, 53, 82, 88, 121, 128, 183, 208, 226, 319, 349
uncreated, 10, 151, 182
Gratia gratis data, 82, 83, 152, 182, 255, 282
Gratia gratum faciens, 82, 117, 118, 182, 249, 256, 258, 260, 265, 266, 267, 268, 273, 276, 278, 280, 282, 283, 308; *see also* Sanctifying grace
Greek Fathers, 22, 35, 36, 40-46, 47, 48, 54, 56, 65, 87, 319, 349, 350

Habitual knowledge, 53, 68, 208, 262, 263, 265, 342, 343
"Having" of Persons; *see* Possession
Holy Ghost (Third Person)
as fruit, object, term, 108, 112, 116, 120, 248, 281, 282
Gifts of, 4, 7, 80, 81, 118, 124, 136, 144, 158, 182, 183, 200, 242, 243, 246, 250, 256, 280, 281, 297, 322, 352; *see also* Faith, Love (Charity), Understanding, Wisdom
indwelling of, 2, 4, 6, 7, 26, 27, 36-40, 41, 42, 43, 47, 48, 49, 52, 58, 61, 80-82, 83, 105, 106, 112, 116, 117, 122, 143, 158, 159, 182, 183, 201, 249, 254, 282, 352
instinct of; *see* Motion of, Operation of
missions of:
invisible, 26, 38, 48, 50, 52, 68, 74, 84-85, 114, 115, 116, 117, 118, 121, 122, 125, 147, 183, 184, 197, 246, 259, 261, 267, 274, 280, 282, 294, 298, 315, 324, 325, 347; *see also* Indwelling of
visible, 26, 51, 52, 74, 294, 299, 324
motion of, 200, 210; *see also* Operation of, Operating grace
operation of, 144, 150, 189, 196, 197, 244, 249, 339; *see also* Motion of, Operating grace
power of, 144
processions of:
eternal, 50, 51, 84, 85, 112, 113, 115, 116, 121, 144, 239, 268, 332
temporal, 84, 105, 106, 182, 184, 239, 242, 244, 246, 249, 254, 273, 274, 277, 278; *see also* Indwelling of, Missions of
temples of, 37, 41, 81, 100, 254, 255
union with, 63, 98, 99
Hypostatic Union, 58, 152, 188, 189, 191, 226; *see also* Incarnation

Illapsus, 143, 167
Image, 12, 175, 200, 326, 327, 329
of God in man, 5, 19, 45, 48, 55, 327, 330, 339-349, 354
and Indwelling, 19, 45, 46, 48, 54, 55, 86-87, 345-349, 354
Fathers on, 45, 46, 48, 54, 55, 87
St. Thomas on, 327, 330, 335, 336
Summa Alex. on, 86, 87, 117, 122, 123, 137, 327
Christ as, 44
of creation (nature), 123, 343, 344, 345, 348
of Persons, 46, 55, 112, 117, 121, 123, 149, 193, 333, 339, 344, 345, 346, 347, 353
of re-creation, 122, 345, 347, 348

Immediate knowledge, 199, 201, 347
Immensity
  God's, 188
  presence of, 7, 8, 36, 37, 49, 81, 82, 111, 131, 143, 144, 146, 147, 152, 182, 188, 190, 192, 202, 203, 204, 205, 206, 207, 208, 211, 226, 227, 228, 242, 243, 244, 245, 276, 297, 312, 323, 343
Incarnation, 3, 38, 51, 98, 152, 171, 189, 190, 195, 226, 322
  term of, 189; *see also* Hypostatic Union
Increase of grace, 161
Indwelling (Inhabitation) (*besides the subjects listed here, consult the Table of Contents*)
  and Image of God in man, 19, 45, 46, 48, 54, 55, 69, 86-87, 345-349, 354
  definitions of:
    of St. Albert, 84-85
    of St. Augustine, 50-55, 100, 101, 112, 311, 312
    of St. Bonaventure, 84, 85, 96, 157, 159
    of *Summa Alex.*, 84, 111, 119
  doctrine of, 6, 22, 40, 41, 46, 70, 230, 345
  facts of:
    for Fathers, 40, 45, 51, 56, 88
    for Schoolmen, 73, 80-88
    in Sacred Scripture, 36, 39, 40, 56, 88
    in St. Thomas, 181-185
  formal reason of, 8-10, 16-18, 23, 32, 103, 112, 113, 114, 118, 120, 121, 122, 128, 130, 154, 155, 157, 158, 160, 164, 190, 191, 192, 202, 206, 207, 211, 230, 253, 279, 283, 284, 312, 314, 315, 318, 320, 324, 335, 338, 348, 351, 352, 354
  formulas of, St. Thomas':
    of *Scriptum super Sententiis*, 11, 16, 18, 30, 297, 299, 324, 330
    of *Summa Theologiae*, 12, 16, 19, 30, 297, 299, 310, 311, 313, 330, 339
  of Father, 37, 38, 39, 42, 49, 83, 106, 183, 201, 275, 298, 352
  of Holy Ghost, 2, 4, 6, 7, 26, 27, 36-40, 41, 42, 43, 47, 48, 49, 52, 58, 61, 63, 80-82, 83, 105, 106, 112, 116, 117, 122, 143, 158, 159, 182, 183, 201, 249, 254, 282, 352; *see also* Invisible mission of Holy Ghost
  of Persons, 36, 37, 38, 41, 57, 62, 63, 145, 160, 198, 209, 254, 273, 274, 276, 277, 282, 314, 315, 333, 348, 351, 353
  of Son, 36-40, 42, 49, 52, 83, 106, 112, 115, 117, 122, 183, 201, 255, 267, 283, 314, 352; *see also* Invisible mission of Son
  problem of, 6, 8-11, 17, 20-23, 34, 59, 86, 87, 88, 103, 104, 107, 123, 128, 131, 141, 142, 154, 161, 164, 175, 183, 185, 186, 187, 191, 202, 207, 208, 230, 232, 248, 251, 257, 320, 348, 350, 351,
    in St. Thomas:
      difference (apparent) of doctrine, 12, 13, 14, 15, 16, 17, 18, 73, 293, 295, 297, 299, 300-302, 321
      dissimilarity of statement, 11-15, 20, 21, 23, 72, 180, 230, 232, 262, 292, 295-299, 301, 303, 317, 318, 321, 339
      identity of doctrine, 11-15, 19, 21, 24, 180, 232, 262, 322-337
  revelation of, 2, 3, 5, 35, 48, 80, 88, 163, 181, 192, 271, 273, 319, 349, 352
  term of, 10, 107, 108, 112, 130, 131, 154, 155, 157, 161, 164, 324
  theories of, 16, 59, 60, 153, 155, 178, 273
    of Alexander of Hales, 124, 128, 155, 163, 164, 233, 351
    of Altissiodorensis; *see* Theory of William of Auxerre
    of Codex Vaticanus latinus 691, 124, 127, 131, 163, 233
    of early Scholastics, 130-139
    of Eudes Rigaud (Odo Rigaldus), 127, 131, 163, 233
    of Fathers, 35, 40-56, 349, 350

of modern theologians, 16, 17, 18, 32, 33, 58, 59, 146, 171, 192, 193, 199, 207 (*for individual theologians, consult Index of Names*)
of Peter Lombard, 105-107, 233, 351
of St. Albert, 23, 95, 140-156, 163, 164, 231, 232, 235, 240, 241, 242, 247, 251, 252, 253, 261, 269, 317, 321, 328, 337, 338, 351, 353
of St. Augustine, 48-55, 66, 85, 350, 354
of St. Bonaventure, 23, 140-142, 156-162, 163, 231, 232, 235, 318, 338, 353
of St. Thomas, 2, 5, 10, 11-15, 20, 21, 23, 35, 58, 72, 73, 88, 104, 111, 142, 162, 164, 178-211, 230, 231, 232, 235, 252, 254, 284, 305, 307, 319, 321, 322, 328, 329, 337, 338, 348, 349, 352, 353, 354, 355
"intentional" theory of, 16, 322, 324, 327, 328, 329, 331, 332, 335, 338, 339, 348
"ontological" theory of, 16, 18, 268, 269, 328, 338
of Scholastics, 73, 79, 88, 132, 162, 180, 230, 231, 248, 328, 341
of *Summa Alex.*, 109-132, 155, 159, 162, 231, 232, 235, 240, 241, 255, 257, 261, 269, 270, 271, 284, 321, 328, 338, 351, 352, 353
of William of Auxerre (Altissiodorensis), 107, 108, 131, 163, 233, 351

Inhabitation; *see* Indwelling

Invisible missions; *see also* Indwelling, Temporal procession
of the Holy Ghost, 26, 38, 48, 50, 52, 68, 74, 84, 85, 114, 115, 116, 117, 118, 121, 122, 125, 147, 183, 184, 197, 246, 259, 261, 267, 274, 280, 282, 294, 298, 315, 324, 325, 347
of the Son, 38, 39, 50, 51, 52, 61, 68, 74, 83, 84, 85, 114, 115, 117, 118, 121, 122, 125, 147, 183, 184, 197, 262, 267, 277, 283, 294, 298, 314, 315, 347

Knowledge
actual, 53, 68, 118, 208, 258, 263, 266
and Love, 112, 119, 121, 122, 137, 158, 162, 192, 196, 197, 198, 199, 200, 201, 202, 205, 207, 208, 211, 263, 267, 283, 310; *see also* Charity, Love
conjectural, 266
gift of, 160, 222
habitual, 53, 68, 208, 262, 263, 265, 342, 343
immediate, 199, 201, 347
natural, 116, 117, 197, 199, 205, 267, 343, 347
of grace, 112, 115, 117, 196, 197, 198, 200, 201, 206, 225, 346, 354
of Persons, 3, 51, 52, 53, 85, 112, 113, 115, 116, 118, 122, 123, 125, 128, 132, 197, 199, 201, 208, 210, 212, 258, 259, 263, 283, 319, 326, 333, 334, 348, 350, 352
of processions, 52, 85, 112, 113, 116, 119, 120, 121
unformed, 255

Latin Fathers, 22, 35, 36, 40, 46-56, 65, 88, 319, 350
Likeness; *see* Similitude
Logic of *Summa Theologiae* of St. Thomas, 293-295, 302, 306
Love (Dilection), 83, 98, 107, 108, 112, 115, 116, 117, 119, 120, 121, 123, 126, 137, 197, 198, 199, 201, 204, 206, 207, 257, 259, 261, 263, 267, 278, 310, 319, 325, 334, 339, 344, 353, 354; *see also* Charity
and fruition, 119, 120, 121, 158, 162
and knowledge; *see* Knowledge
as formal reason of Indwelling, 108, 118, 119, 122, 123, 129-130, 158, 161, 162, 164, 283
divine, 152, 164, 341, 342, 343, 344
gift of, 160, 184, 250, 256
metaphysics of, 162

natural, 116
psychology of, 162
of Persons, 37, 112, 116, 117, 122, 123, 128, 132, 198, 201, 204, 208, 210, 333, 346, 348
union by, 108, 119, 121, 123, 129, 130, 139, 158, 161, 164, 199
Lumen gloriae, 203, 223; *see also* Beatific Vision

Magisterium of the Church, 5, 7, 9, 27, 39
teaching of, 5-8, 36
Manifestation of Persons, 44, 46, 50, 51, 52, 53, 54, 56, 57, 67, 85, 86, 88, 101, 126, 132, 142, 143, 144, 160, 161, 163, 164, 184, 185, 197, 244, 265, 278, 311, 314, 315, 316, 318, 350, 351, 353
Meaning of Tradition, 34
Means of investigation used in this work, 20-22
Medieval theologians; *see* Schoolmen *(for individual theologians consult Index of Names)*
Medium, formal, of knowledge, 199, 200, 205, 354
Metaphysics, 162, 323
Miracles, 152
Mission of Persons, 7, 12, 26, 34, 38, 44, 45, 46, 50, 51, 52, 74, 75, 81, 82, 83, 84, 86, 111, 112, 114, 115, 116, 117, 118, 119, 121, 122, 123, 124, 126, 130, 131, 142, 143, 147, 151, 154, 160, 161, 164, 178, 181, 182, 183, 184, 185, 197, 198, 202, 212, 227, 232, 234, 236, 238, 239, 240, 242, 251, 257, 261, 263, 266, 270, 272, 273, 274, 276, 279, 280, 283, 291, 292, 293, 295, 296, 297, 298, 299, 300, 301, 302, 303, 304, 305, 306, 307, 308, 312, 313, 315, 316, 317, 320, 324, 325, 331, 348, 349, 350, 353, 355; *see also* Indwelling
definitions of, 52, 84, 85
end of, 125, 126, 273
of the Holy Ghost:
invisible, 26, 38, 48, 50, 52, 68, 74, 84, 85, 114, 115, 116, 117, 118, 121, 122, 125, 147, 183, 184, 197, 246, 259, 261, 267, 274, 280, 282, 294, 298, 315, 324, 325, 347
visible, 51, 52, 74, 294, 299, 324
of the Son:
invisible, 38, 39, 50, 51, 52, 61, 68, 74, 83, 84, 85, 114, 115, 117, 118, 121, 122, 125, 147, 183, 184, 197, 262, 267, 277, 283, 294, 298, 314, 315, 347
visible, 51, 52, 74; *see also* Incarnation
Modern theologians, theories of, 16, 17, 18, 32, 33, 58, 59, 146, 171, 192, 193, 199, 207 *(for individual theologians consult the Index of Names)*
Motion of Holy Ghost, 200, 210; *see also* Operation of Holy Ghost, Operating grace
Mystery, 1, 2, 3, 4, 6, 34, 39, 46, 56, 83, 86, 104, 105, 106, 107, 128, 130, 163, 178, 180, 181, 183, 192, 197, 198, 230, 232, 271, 276, 277, 283, 291, 294, 312, 319, 322, 323, 324, 332, 335, 339, 348, 350, 351, 352, 353, 354, 355; *see also* Incarnation, Indwelling

Natural desire, 344; *see also* Beatitude
Natural knowledge, 116, 117, 197, 199, 205, 267, 343, 347
Natural love, 116
Nature
concept of, 189
divine, 189, 191, 346; *see also* Essence, divine
God, Author of, 152, 205, 343
human, 189, 190, 226
image of; *see* Image of creation
of relation, 9, 10

Object
God as, 10, 12, 30, 94, 111, 120, 158, 191, 196, 202, 208, 209, 210, 212, 223, 323, 324, 325, 331, 338, 343, 347, 348; *see also* God as end, God as fruit, God as term

Persons as, 114, 115, 116, 117, 118, 119, 120, 121, 123, 126, 128, 130, 132, 198, 202, 204, 208, 209, 210, 211, 247, 249, 261, 276, 287, 288, 313, 314, 324, 326, 327, 330, 332, 339, 346, 352, 353; *see also* Persons as fruits
Trinity as, 10, 12, 17, 30, 108, 111, 112, 117, 123, 164, 196, 197, 198, 200, 209, 324, 348; *see also* Trinity as end, Trinity as fruit, Trinity as term
Operating grace, 200, 204; *see also* Motion of Holy Ghost, Actual grace
Operation, 17, 122, 175, 187, 190, 191, 192, 195, 196, 197, 205, 209, 210, 211, 212, 323, 325, 326, 330, 331, 339
 of actual grace, 152
 of God, 114, 143, 144, 152, 154, 163, 187, 188, 196, 204, 220, 288; *see also* God as operating
 of grace, 193, 287, 288
 of Holy Ghost, 144, 150, 189, 196, 197, 244, 246, 249, 339
 of Persons, 143, 145, 150, 274, 275, 276, 279, 282, 325
 of Trinity, 145
 principles of, 247, 325, 326, 327

Participation, 43, 63, 151, 153, 192, 193, 194, 268, 344, 346, 355
Perichoresis (Circuminsession, Concomitance), 84, 99, 147, 183, 191
Person, concept of, 189
Personality, 189, 190
Persons of Trinity
 as causes (principles), 114, 195, 196, 206, 225, 246, 247, 250, 251, 252, 262, 272, 274, 277, 279, 282, 296, 299, 304, 316, 331, 332, 346
 as fruits, 111, 115, 119, 126, 128, 132, 139, 182, 185, 211, 249, 250, 251, 254, 255, 257, 276, 279, 282, 288, 303, 312, 315, 326, 351; *see also* Persons of Trinity as objects
 as objects, 114, 115, 116, 117, 118, 119, 120, 121, 123, 126, 128, 130, 132, 198, 202, 204, 208, 209, 210, 211, 247, 249, 261, 276, 287, 288, 313, 314, 324, 326, 327, 330, 332, 339, 346, 352, 353; *see also* Persons of Trinity as fruits
 as principles; *see* Persons of Trinity as causes
 gift (donation) of, 51, 80, 81, 98, 106, 159, 164, 182, 201, 242, 274, 297, 309, 310, 351, 353
 image of, 46, 55, 112, 117, 121, 123, 149, 193, 333, 339, 344, 345, 346, 347, 353
 Indwelling of, 36, 37, 38, 41, 57, 62, 63, 145, 160, 198, 209, 254, 273, 274, 276, 277, 282, 314, 315, 333, 348, 351, 353
 knowledge of, 3, 51, 52, 53, 85, 112, 113, 115, 116, 118, 122, 123, 125, 128, 132, 197, 199, 201, 208, 210, 212, 258, 259, 263, 283, 319, 326, 333, 334, 348, 350, 352
 love of, 37, 112, 116, 117, 122, 123, 128, 132, 198, 201, 204, 208, 210, 333, 346, 348
 manifestation of, 44, 46, 50, 51, 52, 53, 54, 56, 67, 68, 85, 86, 88, 101, 126, 132, 142, 143, 144, 160, 161, 163, 164, 184, 185, 197, 244, 265, 278, 311, 314, 315, 316, 318, 350, 351, 353
 operation of, 143, 145, 150, 274, 275, 276, 279, 282
 possession ("having") of, 81, 96, 97, 106, 107, 111, 112, 117, 121, 122, 125, 126, 128, 129, 130, 131, 132, 249, 250, 255, 273, 274, 276, 277, 279, 296, 299, 308, 312, 313, 315, 319, 351, 353, 354
 presence of, 15, 56, 58, 80, 81, 83, 84, 103, 116, 118, 120, 121, 126, 130, 139, 147, 152, 154, 160, 161, 164, 181, 182, 193, 194, 200, 201, 202, 204, 205, 206, 208, 209, 211, 247, 250, 251, 253, 257, 261, 272, 275, 279, 288, 296, 299, 303, 313, 331, 333, 339, 346, 349, 352, 353, 354

INDEX OF SUBJECTS

processions of:
  eternal, 50, 85, 88, 112, 116, 123, 126, 142, 160, 181, 184, 195, 196, 215, 238, 254, 259, 264, 270, 278, 281, 288, 296, 298, 299, 300, 304, 316, 331, 332, 346, 351
  temporal, 84, 181, 197, 259, 260, 266, 277, 293, 295, 303, 351; *see also* Mission of Holy Ghost, Mission of Son, Donation
properties of, 63, 97, 194, 196, 247, 259, 260, 262, 263, 264, 275, 312, 326, 330, 331, 353, 354
sign of, 12, 112, 116, 117, 145, 146, 147, 257, 264, 324, 325, 326, 333
temple of, 129, 197
union with, 37, 58, 121, 130, 193, 281, 288
use of; *see* Use of Persons
Power of Holy Ghost, 144
Presence
  of God, 36, 37, 38, 42, 48, 49, 53, 66, 129, 131, 143, 144, 152, 153, 154, 156, 157, 158, 159, 163, 164, 167, 182, 183, 187, 188, 189, 190, 191, 193, 196, 199, 200, 201, 202, 205, 206, 210, 220, 223, 226, 253, 258, 267, 272, 298, 303, 304, 310, 312, 320, 329, 343, 345, 347
  of immensity, 7, 8, 36, 37, 49, 81, 82, 111, 131, 143, 144, 146, 147, 152, 182, 188, 190, 192, 202, 203, 204, 205, 206, 207, 208, 211, 226, 227, 228, 242, 243, 244, 245, 276, 297, 312, 323, 343
  of Persons of Trinity, 15, 56, 58, 80, 81, 83, 84, 103, 116, 118, 120, 121, 126, 130, 147, 152, 154, 160, 161, 164, 181, 182, 193, 194, 200, 201, 202, 204, 205, 206, 208, 209, 211, 247, 250, 251, 253, 257, 261, 272, 274, 275, 279, 288, 296, 299, 303, 313, 331, 333, 339, 346, 349, 352, 353, 354
  of Trinity, 2, 7, 8, 9, 10, 11, 15, 16, 17, 18, 19, 34, 35, 36, 37, 38, 44, 45, 48, 49, 59, 80-82, 83, 84, 103, 107, 109, 111, 113, 114, 115, 120, 122, 123, 125, 127, 128, 129, 130, 142, 143, 146, 148, 149, 153, 154, 155, 156, 158, 159, 161, 164, 178, 182, 184, 185, 191, 192, 195, 197, 202, 204, 205, 209, 212, 230, 238, 249, 297, 312, 324, 337, 348, 349

Principle
  God as, 111, 126, 151, 154, 182, 188, 189, 192, 194, 195, 196, 208, 220, 268, 281, 337, 338, 347; *see also* God as cause
  relation to principiated, 195, 331
Principles
  exegetical, 179
  of operation, 247, 325, 326, 327
  Persons as; *see* Persons of Trinity as causes
  theological, 130, 131, 132, 161, 162, 186, 194, 231, 254, 277, 335, 337, 338
  Thomistic, 58, 152, 179, 181, 185-191, 337, 338, 339
Problem of Indwelling, 6, 8-11, 17, 20-23, 34, 59, 86, 87, 88, 103, 104, 107, 123, 128, 131, 141, 142, 154, 161, 164, 175, 183, 185, 186, 187, 191, 202, 207, 208, 230, 232, 248, 251, 257, 320, 348, 350, 351
  in St. Thomas:
    difference (apparent) of doctrine, 12, 13, 14, 15, 16, 17, 18, 73, 293, 295, 297, 299, 300-302, 321
    dissimilarity of statement, 11-15, 20, 21, 23, 72, 180, 230, 232, 262, 292, 295-299, 301, 303, 317, 318, 321, 339
    identity of doctrine, 11-15, 19, 21, 24, 180, 232, 262, 322-337
Processions
  knowledge of, 52, 85, 112, 113, 116, 119, 120, 121
  of Holy Ghost:
    eternal, 50, 51, 84, 85, 113, 115, 116, 121, 144, 239, 268, 332
    temporal, 84, 105, 106, 182, 184, 239, 242, 244, 246, 249, 254,

273, 274, 277, 278; see also Indwelling of Holy Ghost, Missions of Holy Ghost
of Persons:
  eternal, 50, 85, 88, 112, 116, 123, 126, 142, 160, 181, 184, 195, 196, 215, 238, 254, 259, 264, 270, 278, 281, 288, 296, 298, 299, 300, 304, 316, 331, 332, 346, 351
  temporal, 84, 181, 197, 259, 260, 266, 277, 293, 295, 303, 351; see also Indwelling of Trinity
of Son:
  eternal, 50, 51, 85, 112, 113, 115, 121, 268, 314, 333
  temporal, 184, see also Indwelling of Son, Mission of Son
Progress (Evolution) of theology, 86, 104, 141, 162, 163, 164, 345
Properties of Persons, 63, 97, 146, 194, 196, 247, 259, 260, 262, 263, 264, 275, 312, 326, 330, 331, 353, 354
Prophecy, 152
Psychology, 162, 197, 323, 352

Quasi-experimental knowledge, 196, 198, 199, 201, 202, 204, 205, 206, 208, 211, 222, 259, 275, 283, 325, 333, 347

Ratio; see Exemplary idea
Reasoning, 114, 198, 199, 200, 201, 205, 222, 347, 354; see also Abtraction
Re-creation, image of, 122, 345, 347, 348
Relation
  between cause and effect, 145
  fundament of, 9, 107, 108, 112, 130
  nature of, 9, 10
  of creatures to God, 9, 107, 164, 187, 194, 195, 202, 204, 245, 246, 249, 255, 274, 296, 304, 331
  of God to creatures, 9, 44, 146, 187, 195, 202, 244, 245, 271, 272, 296, 304, 331
  of reason, 9, 187, 271, 272, 296
  of principle to principiated, 195, 331

real, 9, 187, 271, 272, 296
term of, 9, 10, 107, 108, 112, 130, 131, 149, 154, 155, 157, 161, 164, 194, 195, 295, 296, 300, 305, 306, 331
Relations
  between St. Thomas and Schoolmen:
    St. Albert, 237-253, 304
    St. Bonaventure, 239, 240, 305-318
    Summa Alex., 235-237, 238, 240, 253-270, 270-284, 302-304
  of Trinity:
    intratrinitarian, 2, 4, 6, 51, 184, 194, 196, 206, 210, 270, 342, 346
    with creatures, 12, 15, 44, 194; see also Relation of God with creatures, Relation of creatures with God
Renaissance, theological, 179
Representation, 112, 113, 114, 115, 116, 117, 121, 131, 132, 160, 259, 263, 264, 265, 275, 277, 315, 326, 327, 330, 334, 343, 348, 353, 354
Revelation, 2, 45, 48, 188, 192; see also Sacred Scripture
  of Indwelling, 2, 3, 5, 35, 48, 80, 88, 163, 181, 192, 271, 273, 319, 349, 352
  of Son, 37

Sacred Scripture, 22, 35, 36, 37-40, 41, 44, 50, 54, 56, 57, 59, 84, 87, 103, 149, 163, 271, 273, 319, 340; see also Revelation
  exegesis of, 35, 57, 327
  facts of Indwelling in, 36, 39, 40, 56, 88, 351, 352
Sanctification, 39, 42, 43, 58, 61, 65, 273, 275, 277, 279, 290
Sanctifying grace, 7, 10, 38, 59, 82, 83, 86, 88, 113, 115, 120, 130, 131, 143, 157, 182, 183, 191, 192, 193, 194, 197, 211, 227, 254, 257, 259, 260, 263, 280, 281, 282, 283, 300, 301, 312, 313, 315, 320, 346, 350, 351; see also *Gratia gratum faciens*, Habitual grace

INDEX OF SUBJECTS 407

Scholastic tradition, 19, 20, 22, 23, 34, 35, 36, 46, 54, 71, 72, 73, 79-88, 103, 104, 108, 125, 140, 152, 163, 178, 181, 185, 187, 230, 319, 328, 336, 350, 351
  principal elements of, 80-87
  sources of, 22, 34-56, 57, 230, 319
    immediate, 35, 46-56, 230
    remote, 35, 36-46, 230
  summary of, 87, 88
Schoolmen (Scholastics, Medieval theologians), 10, 22, 23, 34, 35, 36, 44, 46, 48, 54, 55, 65, 66, 67, 70, 73, 104, 117, 129, 131, 141, 142, 162, 180, 181, 183, 185, 203, 230, 231, 266, 271, 273, 292, 307, 314, 319, 320, 327, 341, 350, 351, 353 (*for individual Schoolmen consult Index of Names*)
  facts of Indwelling for, 73, 80-88
  relations of St. Thomas with:
    St. Albert, 237, 253-304
    St. Bonaventure, 239, 240, 305-318
    Summa Alex., 235-237, 238, 240, 253-270, 270-284, 302-304
  theories of:
    of early Schoolmen, 103-139
      of Alexander of Hales, 124-128, 155, 163, 164, 233, 351
      of Altissiodorensis; see Theory of William of Auxerre
      of Codex Vaticanus latinus 691, 124, 127, 131, 163, 233
      of Eudes Rigaud (Odo Rigaldus), 127, 131, 163, 233
      of Peter Lombard, 105-107, 233, 351
      of Summa Alex., 109-132, 155, 159, 162, 231, 232, 235, 240, 241, 255, 257, 261, 269, 270, 271, 284, 321, 328, 338, 351, 352, 353
    of great Schoolmen, 73, 79, 88, 132, 162, 180, 230, 231, 248, 328, 341
      of St. Albert, 23, 95, 140-156, 163, 164, 242, 247, 251, 252, 253, 261, 269, 317, 321, 328, 337, 338, 351, 353
      of St. Bonaventure, 23, 140-142, 156-162, 163, 231, 232, 235, 318, 338, 353
      of St. Thomas, 2, 5, 10, 11-15, 20, 21, 23, 72, 73, 88, 104, 111, 142, 162, 164, 178-211, 230, 231, 232, 235, 252, 254, 284, 305, 307, 319, 321, 322, 328, 329, 337, 338, 348, 349, 352, 353, 354, 355
        "intentional" theory of, 16, 322, 324, 327, 328, 331, 332, 335, 338, 339, 348
        "ontological" theory of, 16, 18, 268, 269, 328, 338
  tradition of; see Scholastic tradition
Science, 186, 192, 337
Seal of Persons of Trinity, 15, 45, 48, 193, 206, 250, 251, 256, 257, 327
"Sending" of Persons of Trinity; see Missions
Sign of Persons of Trinity, 12, 113, 116, 117, 145, 146, 147, 257, 264, 265, 324, 325, 326, 333
Similitude (Likeness), 5, 11, 12, 15, 43, 45, 55, 148, 184, 196, 199, 200, 205, 212, 250, 251, 263, 264, 265, 267, 268, 277, 287, 298, 299, 312, 314, 315, 316, 323, 324, 325, 326, 327, 329, 330, 331, 332, 333, 334, 335, 339, 342, 343, 344, 346, 353; see also Image, Seal, Sign
Solutions of problem of Indwelling; see Theories of Indwelling
Son of God (Christ, Second Person)
  as image, 44
  as term, 189
  generation of, 184, 196, 197, 279, 339; see also Eternal procession of
  Incarnation of, 3, 38, 51, 98, 152, 171, 189, 190, 195, 226, 322
  Indwelling of, 36-40, 42, 49, 52, 83, 106, 112, 115, 117, 122,

183, 201, 255, 267, 283, 314, 352; *see also* Invisible mission of
mission of:
invisible, 38, 39, 50, 83, 115, 118, 147, 183, 184, 262, 267, 268, 277, 283, 294, 314; *see also* Indwelling of
visible; *see* Incarnation of
procession of:
eternal, 50, 51, 85, 112, 113, 115, 121, 268, 314, 333; *see also* Generation of
temporal, 184; *see also* Indwelling of, Invisible mission of
revelation of, 37
union with, 1, 2, 5, 37, 189
Sons of God, 37, 38, 83, 101
Soul, just, and Indwelling, 37, 41, 42, 43, 50, 51, 56, 80, 81, 85, 88, 98, 99, 126, 130, 181, 182, 184, 185, 188, 191, 197, 201, 204, 205, 207, 209, 211, 230, 322; *see also* Grace, Grace-state
Sources of Scholastic tradition, 22, 34-56, 57, 230, 319
immediate, 35, 46-56, 230
remote, 35, 36-46, 230
Species, intelligible, 203, 342; *see also* Word
—state, Grace, 8, 38, 44, 53, 82, 88, 121, 128, 183, 208, 226, 319, 349; *see also* Soul, just
Subsistence, 189; *see also* Person, Personality
Substance, 63, 83, 151, 152, 154, 167, 187, 188, 193, 196, 199, 205, 220
Summary of Scholastic tradition, 87-88
Synthesis, theological, 186, 320, 350

"Tasting" of God, 198, 199, 201
Temples
of God, 37, 49, 53, 124, 196, 210, 273
of Holy Ghost, 37, 41, 81, 100, 254, 255
of Persons of Trinity, 129, 197
Temporal procession; *see also* Indwelling, Mission
of Holy Ghost, 84, 105, 106, 182, 184, 239, 242, 244, 246, 249, 254, 273, 274, 277, 278

of Persons of Trinity, 84, 181, 197, 259, 260, 266, 277, 293, 295, 303, 351
of Son, 184
Term; *see also* End, Fruit, Object
God as, 94, 188, 190, 191, 195, 196, 208, 212, 324, 338, 347
Holy Ghost as, 108, 112, 116, 120, 248, 281, 282
notion of, 189
of Incarnation, 189
of Indwelling, 10, 107, 108, 112, 130, 131, 154, 155, 157, 161, 164, 324
of relation, 10, 107, 108, 130, 154, 155, 157, 161, 164, 194, 195
Son as, 189
Trinity as, 16, 194, 195, 211, 279, 321, 332
Theologians
medieval; *see* Schoolmen, *and consult Index of Names for individual theologians*
modern; *see* Theories of modern theologians, *and consult Index of Names for individual theologians*
Theological principles, 130, 131, 132, 161, 162, 186, 194, 231, 254, 277, 335, 337, 338
Theological renaissance, 179
Theological synthesis, 186, 320, 350
Theophania, 68, 163
Theories of Indwelling
of early Schoolmen, 103-139
of Alexander of Hales, 124-128
of Altissiodorensis; *see* Theory of William of Auxerre
of Codex Vaticanus latinus 691, 124, 127, 131, 163, 233
of Eudes Rigaud (Odo Rigaldus), 127, 131, 163, 233
of Peter Lombard, 105-107, 233, 351
of *Summa Alex.*, 109-132, 155, 159, 162, 231, 232, 235, 240, 241, 255, 257, 261, 269, 270, 271, 284, 321, 338, 351, 352, 353
of William of Auxerre, 107-108, 131, 163, 233, 351

of Fathers, 35, 40-56, 349, 350 (*for individual Fathers consult Index of Names*)
of great Schoolmen:
  of St. Albert, 23, 95, 140-156, 163, 164, 231, 232, 235, 240, 241, 242, 247, 251, 252, 253, 261, 269, 317, 321, 328, 337, 338, 351, 353
  of St. Bonaventure, 23, 140-142, 156-162, 163, 231, 232, 235, 318, 338, 353
  of St. Thomas, 2, 5, 10, 11-15, 20, 21, 23, 72, 73, 88, 104, 111, 142, 162, 164, 178-211, 230, 231, 232, 235, 252, 284, 305, 307, 319, 321, 322, 328, 329, 337, 338, 348, 349, 352, 353, 354, 355
    "intentional" theory of, 16, 322, 324, 327, 328, 329, 331, 332, 335, 338, 339, 348
    "ontological" theory of, 16, 18, 268, 269, 328, 338
of modern theologians, 16, 17, 18, 32, 33, 58, 59, 146, 171, 192, 193, 199, 207 (*for individual theologians consult Index of Names*)
of St. Augustine, 48-55, 66, 85, 164, 350, 354
Thomistic principles, 58, 152, 179, 181, 185-191, 337, 338, 339; *see also* Theological principles
Tradition (Common teaching), 5, 6, 26, 34, 35, 36, 40, 41, 45, 47, 48, 50, 54, 70, 71, 72, 80, 84, 87, 88, 163, 271
Franciscan, 109, 110, 130, 141, 159
meaning of, 34
of Fathers, 26, 40-56, 65, 87 (*for individual Fathers consult Index of Names*)
of St. Augustine, 130, 140, 141, 336
St. Thomas and, 34, 104, 181-185
Scholastic, 19, 20, 22, 23, 34, 35, 36, 46, 54, 71, 72, 73, 79-88, 103, 104, 108, 125, 140, 142, 163, 178, 181, 185, 187, 230, 319, 328, 336, 350, 351
principal elements of, 80-87

sources of, 22, 34-56, 57, 230
  immediate, 35, 46-56, 230
  remote, 35, 36-46, 230
summary of, 87-88
Trinity (*see also* Persons of Trinity, Father, Holy Ghost, Son)
  as cause, 7, 152, 195, 196, 207
  as end, 129, 159, 324, 327
  as fruit, 183
  as object, 10, 12, 17, 30, 108, 111, 112, 117, 123, 164, 196, 197, 198, 200, 209, 324, 348
  as term, 16, 108, 194, 195, 211, 279, 324, 332
  Indwelling of, 36, 37, 38, 41, 57, 62, 63, 145, 160, 198, 209, 254, 273, 274, 276, 277, 282, 314, 315, 333, 348, 351, 353
  presence of, 2, 7, 8, 9, 10, 11, 15, 16, 17, 18, 22, 44, 45, 48, 59, 103, 109, 113, 122, 123, 125, 127, 128, 129, 130, 142, 153, 154, 155, 156, 158, 161, 164, 178, 182, 184, 185, 191, 192, 195, 197, 202, 204, 205, 209, 212, 230, 238, 249, 312, 324, 337, 348
  relations of:
    intratrinitarian, 2, 4, 6, 51, 184, 194, 196, 206, 210, 270, 342, 346; *see also* Eternal processions
    with creatures, 12, 15, 44, 194; *see also* Relations to
  relations (of creatures) to, 112, 170, 209, 238, 247, 271
  theology of, 43, 71
  union with, 5, 36, 58, 188, 189, 193, 203, 325, 339

Ubiquity of God, 322; *see also* Presence of God
Uncreated Gift, 154, 309; *see also* Holy Ghost, Uncreated Grace
Uncreated Grace, 10, 151, 282; *see also* Holy Ghost, Uncreated Gift
Understanding, Gift of, 118, 256
Unformed Faith, 82, 119, 197, 268, 273
Unformed knowledge, 255
Union
  by love, 108, 119, 121, 123, 129, 130, 139, 159, 161, 164, 199

Hypostatic, 58, 152, 188, 189, 191, 222; *see also* Incarnation
of operation, 212, 339
with divine things, 198, 211, 222
with Father, 37
with God, 57, 104, 106, 118, 119, 120, 122, 144, 189, 190, 197, 199, 206, 212, 231, 250, 251, 256, 258, 278, 280, 281, 309, 319, 323, 324, 327, 344
with Holy Ghost, 63, 98, 99
with Persons of Trinity, 37, 58, 121, 130, 193, 281, 288, 314, 333, 339; *see also* Union with Trinity
with Son, 1, 2, 5, 37, 189
with Trinity, 5, 36, 58, 188, 189, 193, 314, 331, 339; *see also* Union with Persons of Trinity

Use of Persons of Trinity, 97, 98, 157, 161, 248, 251, 299, 308, 309, 346; *see also* Enjoyment (Fruition, Delectation) of Persons, Possession of Persons

Virtue
grace of, and Gifts, 347; *see also* *Gratia gratum faciens*, Sanctifying grace
supernatural, 182; *see also* Faith, Charity
Visible mission
of the Holy Ghost, 26, 51, 52, 74, 294, 299, 324
of the Son, 51, 52, 74; *see also* Incarnation, Hypostatic Union

Wisdom, Gift of, 118, 121, 126, 150, 184, 198, 199, 200, 201, 205, 206, 208, 209, 210, 211, 222, 250, 256, 257, 261, 283, 315, 318, 319, 320, 326, 327, 333, 347, 352; *see also* Knowledge and love, Love as formal medium of knowledge
Word (Concept, Species), 184, 189, 267, 279, 309, 333, 339, 340, 344

INDEX OF NAMES

Abelard, 70, 71
Alarcón, 93
Albert the Great, St., 10, 23, 71, 75, 76, 77, 78, 79, 81, 83, 84, 85, 86, 87, 91, 92, 95, 96, 100, 105, 127, 140, 141, 142, 163, 164, 173, 174, 178, 219, 231, 232, 233, 234, 235, 237, 240, 241, 254, 257, 261, 262, 265, 266, 267, 274, 285, 286, 290, 334, 341, 342, 351, 353
    rejection of theory by St. Thomas in *Scriptum super Sententiis*, 242-253, 269, 277-280, 284, 321, 328, 338
    relation with *Summa Theologiae* of St. Thomas, 292, 304, 316, 321
    theory (solution of problem) of Indwelling, 142-156
        conclusions concerning, 154-156
        criticism of, 148-154
        exposition of, 142-146
        interpretation of, 146-148
    use of, by St. Thomas in *Scriptum super Sententiis*, 237-239, 321
Alexander of Hales, 71, 74, 75, 76, 78, 79, 80, 83, 87, 89, 90, 92, 95, 105, 111, 119, 120, 122, 123, 124, 130, 139, 142, 154, 155, 156, 157, 159, 163, 164, 173, 175, 233, 351
    theory of, 124-128
Alexander IV, Pope, 110
Alonso, J., 32
Altissiodorensis; *see* William of Auxerre
Ambrose, St., 48, 65, 66, 80, 106
Anciaux, F., 169
Angelic Doctor; *see* Thomas, St.
Anonymous:
    Codex Vaticanus latinus 691, 74, 76, 77, 79, 124, 127, 131, 134, 135, 136, 233, 248
    Summa Alex., 231, 232, 233, 234, 238, 239, 240, 241, 242, 248, 285, 286, 312, 314, 315, 316, 317, 334, 335, 342, 353
    analysis of theory of, 111-113
    authorship of, 74-75, 89-90
    choice of theory of, by St. Thomas in *Scriptum super Sententiis*, 253-269, 270-284, 328, 338
    comparison of theory of, with theory of Alexander of Hales, 124-128
    contribution of, 351-352
    criticism of theory of, 128-132
    dating of, 74-76, 91
    relation with *Summa Theologiae* of St. Thomas, 292, 302-304, 321, 328
    theory of, 109-132
    use of, by St. Thomas in *Scriptum super Sententiis*, 235-237, 321
Anselm, St., 70, 219
Aristotle, 140, 141, 186, 287, 288
Arriaga, 93
Athanasius, St., 42
Augustine, St., 4, 14, 22, 35, 39, 44, 46, 48, 49, 50, 51, 52, 53, 54, 55, 65, 66, 67, 68, 69, 80, 84, 85, 86, 87, 101, 112, 131, 147, 152, 163, 164, 183, 185, 229, 237, 249, 273, 286, 342, 350, 352, 353
    teaching on Indwelling, 48-55

Baius; *see* du Bay, Michael
Banez, D., 4, 32, 149, 150, 196, 219, 229
Bardy, G., 57
Basil, St., 42, 43, 47, 62
du Bay, Michael, 27
Bede, St., 66, 70
Bernard, St., 65, 70
Billuart, C., 32
Bissen, J., 169

Bittremieux, J., 60
Bluett, J., 2
Bonaventure, St., 10, 23, 25, 66, 71, 72, 76, 78, 79, 81, 83, 84, 85, 86, 87, 89, 95, 96, 98, 100, 101, 105, 118, 140, 163, 174, 175, 178, 231, 232, 234, 237, 242, 253, 257, 266, 286, 334, 335, 345, 351, 353
  conclusions concerning theory of, 158-162
  criticism of theory of, 162
  exposition of theory of, 156-158
  relations with *Summa Theologiae* of St. Thomas, 292, 305-318, 321-322, 328, 338
  theory (solution of problem) of Indwelling, 156-162
  use of, by St. Thomas in *Scriptum super Sententiis*, 239-240, 321
Bourassa, F., 58

Cajetan, 30, 32, 148, 151-154, 171, 172, 173, 224, 229, 346
Capponi de Porrecta, 32
Capreolus, 29, 30, 32, 148, 149, 170, 171, 227
Cassian, 65, 70
Chambat, L., 32, 212
Chenu, M., 77, 78, 80
Ciappi, L., 17, 179, 223
Clement of Alexandria, St., 41, 62
Codex Vaticanus latinus 691; *see under* Anonymous
Copleston, F., 142, 166
Cuervo, M., 17, 27, 32, 59, 93, 113, 115, 120
Cyril of Alexandria, St., 42, 43, 45, 62, 63

Damasus, Pope St., 64
Delaye, E., 32
Denifle, H., 91, 92
Didacus de Deza, 16
Didymus the Blind, St., 43, 44, 47, 50, 64
Dockx, S., 58, 223
Donnelly, M., 32, 57, 58
Doucet, V., 89
Duns Scotus, 141, 167

Enrico di St. Teresa, 32
Epiphanius, St., 6, 43

Eröss, A., 60
Eudes Rigaud, 74, 75, 76, 77, 78, 79, 89, 91, 92, 108, 131, 134, 137, 156, 163, 233, 248

Ferrariensis, 32
Fitzgerald, T., 11, 16
Friedrichs, J., 173
Fries, A., 90
Froget, B., 57, 94

Gachter, R., 32
Galtier, P., 32, 53, 57, 58, 59, 61, 68, 94, 146, 148, 192, 218, 225, 229
Gardeil, A., 17, 68, 94, 179, 199, 207, 212, 228
Garrigou-Lagrange, R., 17, 57, 94, 179, 227
Geenen, G., 34
de Ghellinck, J., 89
Giles of Rome, 118
Gilson, E., 159, 176
Glorieux, P., 59, 77, 78, 89
Godoy, 93
Gonet, 32
Gorce, M., 173
Grabmann, M., 212
Grabowski, S., 66
Gratien de Paris, 92
Greenstock, D., 169
Gregory the Great, St., 65, 66, 70, 168
Gregory of Nyssa, St., 43, 44, 62, 65, 70
Guerric de St. Quentin, 76, 78, 90
de Guibert, P., 11

Henquinet, F., 90, 92
Hilary, St., 47, 65, 66
Hippolytus, St., 47
Hugh of St. Cher, 76
Hugh of St. Victor, 71, 136

Ignatius of Antioch, St., 41
de la Immaculada, J., 32
Irenaeus, St., 41, 61
Irrefragable Doctor; *see* Alexander of Hales
Isaye, 62

Jean de la Rochelle, 74, 76, 77, 78, 79, 89, 90, 92, 110, 122, 163; *see also* Anonymous: *Summa Alex.*
Jerome, St., 47, 64, 65

INDEX OF NAMES 413

Joannes de Rupella; *see* Jean de la Rochelle
John of St. Thomas, 10, 27, 32, 59, 68, 93, 129, 131, 167, 179, 205, 207, 216, 224, 225, 227, 228
Joret, F., 32

Koenig, H., 174

Landgraf, A., 90
Lebon, P., 59
Lebreton, J., 57, 61, 68
Leo XIII, Pope, 6, 7
de Letter, P., 32, 60
Lottin, O., 75, 77, 91, 155
Lozano, S., 32

Mahé, J., 63
Mandonnet, P., 78, 140, 166, 212
Manoir de Juaye, H., 63
Martinez-Gomez, C., 32
Master of the Sentences; *see* Peter Lombard
Menendez-Reigada, I., 32
Minges, P., 75, 87, 93, 285
Monsegu, B., 63
Morency, R., 170, 179, 212, 222, 223
Mullaney, T., 58, 171

Nazarius, 32
Novatian, 47

Odo Rigaldus; *see* Eudes Rigaud
Origen, 41, 42, 47

Pagus, John, 76
Passaglia, C., 59
Petau; *see* Petavius
Petavius, 62, 63
Peter Damian, St., 70
Peter de Ledesma, 217, 218, 223, 224, 233, 346
Peter Lombard, 54, 65, 66, 68, 71, 72, 73, 76, 79, 80, 81, 82, 83, 84, 85, 86, 87, 89, 96, 98, 99, 100, 105, 119, 123, 124, 136, 152, 156, 168, 173, 233, 234, 293, 351
    theory of, 105-107
Peter of Tarantasia, 118
Petitot, L., 285
Philips, G., 59
Pius V, Pope St., 27

Pius XII, Pope, 2, 7, 27
Porrecta; *see* Capponi de Porrecta
Prat, F., 57, 63
Primeau, J., 120, 130
Pseudo-Dionysius, 141, 236, 237, 238, 243, 254, 285

Rahner, K., 32
de Régnon, T., 57, 58, 62, 64, 65
Retailleau, M., 16, 32, 57, 94, 192, 207, 218, 228, 229
Richard of Middleton, 118, 159, 163, 176
Richard of St. Victor, 71, 352
Rivière, M., 59
von Rudloff, L., 11, 14, 16, 30, 31, 94, 146, 228, 287, 288

Sagüés, J., 16, 32
Salmanticenses, 32
Schauf, H., 59
Scheeben, M., 57, 58, 64
Schrader, C., 59
Scotus; *see* Duns Scotus
Seraphic Doctor; *see* Bonaventure, St.
Socrates, 141
Sparks, T., 148
Suarez, 32, 94, 129, 130, 207
Sullivan, L., 94
Summa Alex.; see under Anonymous
Sylvius, 32

de la Taille, M., 32, 57, 58, 146, 152, 171
Terrien, J., 15
Tertullian, 47
Thomas Aquinas, St., 3, 4, 5, 7, 10, 18, 19, 20, 21, 22, 23, 24, 25, 31, 32, 34, 35, 46, 54, 58, 59, 61, 66, 68, 71, 72, 73, 78, 87, 88, 93, 94, 95, 98, 104, 105, 107, 109, 111, 118, 119, 129, 131, 133, 142, 150, 152, 155, 162, 165, 167, 168, 170, 173, 175, 219, 220, 222, 225, 226, 230, 231, 232, 285, 286, 287, 319, 320
    appropriation, notion of, 334-335
    assimilation, notion of, 329-331, 334, 335, 339
    choice in *Scriptum super Sententiis* of theory of *Summa. Alex.*, 253-269, 270-284, 321, 338

contribution of, 351-355
doctrine of image of God in man, 330, 335, 336, 340-345
and Indwelling, 345-349
exemplarity, notion of, 331-335
facts of theory of Indwelling, 181-185
familiarity with scholastic works, 233-240
identity of doctrine in *Scriptum super Sententiis* and *Summa Theologiae*, 322-337
  conclusions concerning, 335-337
  doctrinal basis for judgment, 322-327
  historical basis for judgment, 328-335
principles of theory of Indwelling, 185-191
problem of Indwelling in, 11-17, 291-302; *see also* Relation between *Scriptum super Sententiis* and *Summa Theologiae*
recapitulation of theory of Indwelling, 211
rejection in *Scriptum super Sententiis* of theory of St. Albert, 242-253, 269, 277-280, 284, 321, 328, 338
relations of *Summa Theologiae*:
  with St. Albert, 292, 304, 316, 317, 321
  with St. Bonaventure, 305-318, 321-322, 328, 338
  with *Scriptum super Sententiis*, 291-302
    conclusions concerning, 301-302, 321, 339-349
    doctrinal differences of two works, 300-301
    logical differences of two works, 293-295
    stylistic differences of two works, 295-299
similitude, notion of, 329-331, 334, 335, 339
textual comparison with scholastic works, 240-270
  conclusions concerning, 269-270
textual-doctrinal comparison of *Scriptum super Sententiis* and *Summa Alex.*, 270-284
use of works of Schoolmen in *Scriptum super Sententiis*, 235-240
Thomassin, 57, 58
Tromp, S., 28
Trütsch, J., 16, 32

Universal Doctor; *see* Albert, St.
Urdánoz, T., 32, 59, 98, 146, 148, 190, 192, 193, 218, 219, 228, 229

Van der Meersch, 98
Van Steenberghen, F., 141, 166
Vasquez, 15, 31, 32, 93, 94, 207, 208, 228
Vollert, C., 58

Waffelaert, G., 57, 58
Walz, A., 285
Weigl, P., 63
William of Auxerre, 71, 73, 78, 80, 81, 82, 89, 105, 106, 107, 108, 131, 163, 233, 237, 248, 351
William of Miltona, 110

Zubiri, X., 32

www.ingramcontent.com/pod-product-compliance
Lightning Source LLC
Chambersburg PA
CBHW070057020526
44112CB00034B/1428